Management Perspectives
in Marketing

Louis E. Boone

The University of Tulsa

Dickenson Publishing Company, Inc.
Encino, California, and Belmont, California

To my mother and father

Library of Congress Catalog Card Number: 79-167904
Printed in the United States of America

1 2 3 4 5 6 7 8 9 10

ISBN: 0-8221-0001-0

Contents

Preface

Management Perspectives in Marketing has been designed for use as a primary source book in advanced undergraduate and graduate marketing courses and as a supplement for the first marketing course. Its purpose is to provide a managerial orientation to marketing from a total systems viewpoint.

The seven sections encompass a total framework for the marketing decision maker. Emphasis is placed on material from the behavioral sciences and from the quantitative areas. The selections represent a blend of timeless classics and recently published articles analyzing the emerging areas in marketing. Selection of articles was made on the bases of fundamental contributions, ability to stimulate reader involvement, and skill in presentation of ideas and concepts. Two sections are devoted to international marketing and to societal and ethical implications for marketing. Other important and timely subjects include the role of models in marketing, marketing information systems, ghetto marketing, and the role of creativity in marketing. Each selection is preceded by a short integrating summary and an index is included to facilitate use of the book.

Part I deals with the Framework for Marketing Management. It illustrates the meaning and role of the marketing concept in determining the effectiveness of the total business operation.

The articles included in Part II, The Consumer, explore the environmental factors which influence marketing strategies and which must be incorporated into marketing decisions.

Part III, Planning the Marketing Effort, discusses the subjects of market planning, sales forecasting, the role of marketing information systems in decision making, and use of the strategies of product differentiation and market segmentation in achieving company objectives.

Part IV, Aids in Marketing Decision Making, analyzes the role of such quantitative techniques as model building and simulation and stresses the need for creativity in effective marketing decisions.

Part V, Implementing the Plan: The Marketing Mix, explores the decision areas of product strategy, marketing channels, promotional strategy, and pricing problems and policies. Emphasis is placed upon the need to integrate these decisions into a cohesive marketing program.

Part VI expands the scope of marketing to the international market and explores the social, economic, political, and cultural factors involved in developing effective marketing strategies in foreign markets.

The final section, Marketing and Society, views the role of the marketing executive in broader terms of social responsibilities, the impact of government on the market system, marketing ethics, and the welfare of consumers. The impact of consumerism upon marketing policies and decisions is explored.

The author would like to express his appreciation to the publishers and authors for permission to reprint their works. He would also like to thank Harold H. Kassarjian for his suggestions and criticisms in reviewing the preliminary selection of articles.

Louis E. Boone

I FRAMEWORK FOR MARKETING MANAGEMENT

In our consumer-oriented economy marketing has attained a dominant role in the management of American business firms. The new marketing concept of keying all decisions to consumer needs is revolutionizing organizational structures and personal and corporate philosophies. The changes are both radical and recent.

The previous view of marketing could be translated roughly as *selling*. The firm was seen as consisting of three functions: production, finance, and marketing. Production generated salable products; finance was responsible for securing and retaining sufficient operating capital; and the marketing personnel sought markets for the firm's output. Essentially, then, marketing was selling.

Even the latest definition from the American Marketing Association gives this narrow, misleading view:

Marketing is the performance of business activities that direct the flow of goods and services from producer to consumer or user.[1]

But selling is only one subset of marketing. As Theodore Levitt states, " ... marketing is as different from selling as chemistry is from alchemy, astronomy from astrology, chess from checkers."[2]

[1] Committee on Definitions, *Marketing Definitions: A Glossary of Marketing Terms* (American Marketing Association, 1960), p. 15.

[2] Theodore Levitt, *Innovations in Marketing* (New York: McGraw-Hill Book Company, 1962), p. 7.

The modern approach views the firm as an organized behavior system designed to generate outputs of value to consumers. Profitability is achieved through creating customer satisfactions. Application of the marketing concept means that marketing activities must begin with new product concepts and designs analyzed and developed to meet specific unfilled consumer needs — not start with finished goods at the end of the loading dock.

This expanded conception of marketing activities permeating all organizational activities is conveyed in the following definition of marketing:

> Marketing is the analyzing, organizing, planning, and controlling of the firm's customer-impinging resources, policies, and activities with a view to satisfying the needs and wants of chosen customer groups at a profit.[3]

Robert J. Keith, chairman of the board of The Pillsbury Company, analyzes the influence of the marketing concept on his company in the first selection, "The Marketing Revolution." Keith views four evolving eras at Pillsbury, beginning with production orientation during the first era of manufacturing, through sales, then marketing orientation, and finally to the present era of marketing control. He believes that Pillsbury has changed from a company which has accepted the marketing concept to a *marketing company,* and that all activities — from finance to production to marketing — should be geared to profitable consumer satisfaction.

"Marketing Myopia" is undoubtedly the most widely read article in marketing. Levitt's classic stresses the fact that, contrary to superficial appearances, there is no such thing as a growth industry. A business or industry will survive only by viewing itself "not as producing goods and services but as buying customers, as doing the things that will make people want to do business with it."

The final selection in Part I introduces a new philosophy of business which the author titles "The Human Concept." According to Dawson, the "human concept" transcends the narrowly defined "marketing concept" by emphasizing the social responsibility of the business firm and requiring a balancing of necessary corporate profits with achievements of a "genuine internal and external social purpose within the ultimate environment by contributing to the identification and fulfillment of the real human needs of our time."

---

[3]Philip Kotler, *Marketing Management* (Englewood Cliffs, N.J.: Prentice-Hall, Inc., 1967), p. 12.

Business today is in the throes of a marketing revolution. This revolution is based on a change of philosophy, and one of its effects will be the emergence of marketing as the dominant function in American business.

The Marketing Revolution

Robert J. Keith

The consumer, not the company, is in the middle.

In today's economy the consumer, the man or woman who buys the product, is at the absolute dead center of the business universe. Companies revolve around the customer, not the other way around.

Growing acceptance of this consumer concept has had, and will have, far-reaching implications for business, achieving a virtual revolution in economic thinking. As the concept gains ever greater acceptance, marketing is emerging as the most important single function in business.

A Revolution in Science

A very apt analogy can be drawn with another revolution, one that goes back to the sixteenth century. At that time astronomers had great difficulty predicting the movements of the heavenly bodies. Their charts and computations and celestial calendars enabled them to estimate the approximate positions of the planets on any given date. But their calculations were never exact — there was always a variance.

Then a Polish scientist named Nicolaus Copernicus proposed a very simple answer to the problem. If, he proposed, we assume that the sun, and not the earth, is at the center of our system, and that the earth moves around the sun instead of the sun moving around the earth, all our calculations will prove correct.

Reprinted by permission of the author and the publisher from the *Journal of Marketing,* published by the American Marketing Association, Vol. 24, No. 3 (January, 1960), pp. 35-38.

The Pole's idea raised a storm of controversy. The earth, everyone knew, was at the center of the universe. But another scientist named Galileo put the theory to test — and it worked. The result was a complete upheaval in scientific and philosophic thought. The effects of Copernicus' revolutionary idea are still being felt today.

A Revolution in Marketing

In much the same way American business in general — and Pillsbury in particular — is undergoing a revolution of its own today: a marketing revolution.

This revolution stems from the same idea stated in the opening sentence of this article. No longer is the company at the center of the business universe. Today the customer is at the center.

Our attention has shifted from problems of production to problems of marketing, from the product we *can* make to the product the consumer *wants* us to make, from the company itself to the market place.

The marketing revolution has only begun. It is reasonable to expect that its implications will grow in the years to come, and that lingering effects will be felt a century, or more than one century, from today.

So far the theory has only been advanced, tested, and generally proved correct. As more and more businessmen grasp the concept, and put it to work, our economy will become more truly marketing oriented.

Pillsbury's Pattern: Four Eras

Here is the way the marketing revolution came about at Pillsbury. The experience of this company has followed a typical pattern. There has been nothing unique, and each step in the evolution of the marketing concept has been taken in a way that is more meaningful because the steps are, in fact, typical.

Today in our company the marketing concept finds expression in the simple statement, "Nothing happens at Pillsbury until a sale is made." This statement represents basic reorientation on the part of our management. For, not too many years ago, the ordering of functions in our business placed finance first, production second, and sales last.

How did we arrive at our present point of view? Pillsbury's progress in the marketing revolution divides neatly into four separate eras — eras which parallel rather closely the classic pattern of development in the marketing revolution.

1st Era — Production Oriented

First came the era of manufacturing. It began with the formation of the company in 1869 and continued into the 1930s. It is significant that the *idea* for the formation of our company came from the *availability* of high-quality wheat and the *proximity* of water power − and not from the availability and proximity of growing major market areas, or the demand for better, less expensive, more convenient flour products.

Of course, these elements were potentially present. But the two major elements which fused in the mind of Charles A. Pillsbury and prompted him to invest his modest capital in a flour mill were, on the one hand, wheat, and, on the other hand, water power. His principal concern was with production, not marketing.

His thought and judgment were typical of the business thinking of his day. And such thinking was adequate and proper for the times.

Our company philosophy in this era might have been stated this way: "We are professional flour millers. Blessed with a supply of the finest North American wheat, plenty of water power, and excellent milling machinery, we produce flour of the highest quality. Our basic function is to mill high-quality flour, and of course (and almost incidentally) we must hire salesmen to sell it, just as we hire accountants to keep our books."

The young company's first new product reveals an interesting example of the thinking of this era. The product was middlings, the bran left over after milling. Millfeed, as the product came to be known, proved a valuable product because it was an excellent nutrient for cattle. But the impetus to launch the new product came not from a consideration of the nutritional needs of cattle or a marketing analysis. It came primarily from the desire to dispose of a by-product! The new product decision was production oriented, not marketing oriented.

2nd Era − Sales Oriented

In the 1930s Pillsbury moved into its second era of development as a marketing company. This was the era of sales. For the first time we began to be highly conscious of the consumer, her wants, and her prejudices, as a key factor in the business equation. We established a commercial research department to provide us with facts about the market.

We also became more aware of the importance of our dealers, the wholesale and retail grocers who provided a vital link in our chain of distribution from the mill to the home. Knowing that consumers and dealers as well were vital to the company's success, we could no longer simply mark them down as unknowns in our figuring. With this realization, we took the first step along the road to becoming a marketing company.

Pillsbury's thinking in this second era could be summed up like this: "We are a flour-milling company, manufacturing a number of products for the consumer market. We must have a first-rate sales organization which can dispose of all the products we can make at a favorable price. We must back up this sales force with consumer advertising and market intelligence. We want our salesmen and our dealers to have all the tools they need for moving the output of our plants to the consumer."

Still not a marketing philosophy, but we were getting closer.

3rd Era — Marketing Oriented

It was at the start of the present decade that Pillsbury entered the marketing era. The amazing growth of our consumer business as the result of introducing baking mixes provided the immediate impetus. But the groundwork had been laid by key men who developed our sales concepts in the middle forties.

With the new cake mixes, products of our research program, ringing up sales on the cash register, and with the realization that research and production could produce literally hundreds of new and different products, we faced for the first time the necessity for selecting the best new products. We needed a set of criteria for selecting the kind of products we would manufacture. We needed an organization to establish and maintain these criteria, and for attaining maximum sale of the products we did select.

We needed, in fact, to build into our company a new management function which would direct and control all the other corporate functions from procurement to production to advertising to sales. This function was marketing. Our solution was to establish the present marketing department.

This department developed the criteria which we would use in determining which products to market. *And these criteria were, and are, nothing more nor less than those of the consumer herself.* We moved the mountain out to find out what Mahomet, and Mrs. Mahomet, wanted. The company's purpose was no longer to mill flour, nor to manufacture a wide variety of products, but to satisfy the needs and desires, both actual and potential, of our customers.

If we were to restate our philosophy during the past decade as simply as possible, it would read: "We make and sell products for consumers."

The business universe, we realized, did not have room at the center for Pillsbury or any other company or groups of companies. It was already occupied by the customers.

This is the concept as the core of the marketing revolution. How did we put it to work for Pillsbury?

The first move was to transform our small advertising department into a marketing department. The move involved far more than changing the name on organizational charts. It required the introduction of a new, and vitally important, organizational concept — the brand-manager concept.

The brand-manager idea is the very backbone of marketing at Pillsbury. The man who bears the title, brand manager, has total accountability for results. He directs the marketing of his product as if it were his own business. Production does its job, and finance keeps the profit figures. Otherwise, the brand manager has total responsibility for marketing his product. This responsibility encompasses pricing, commercial research, competitive activity, home service and publicity coordination, legal details, budgets, advertising plans, sales promotion, and execution of plans. The brand manager must think first, last, and always of his sales target, the consumer.

Marketing permeates the entire organization. Marketing plans and executes the sale — all the way from the inception of the product idea, through its development and distribution, to the customer purchase. Marketing begins and ends with the consumer. New product ideas are conceived after careful study of her wants and needs, her likes and dislikes. Then marketing takes the idea and marshals all the forces of the corporation to translate the idea into product and the product into sales.

In the early days of the company, consumer orientation did not seem so important. The company made flour, and flour was a staple — no one would question the availability of a market. Today we must determine whether the American housewife will buy lemon pudding cake in preference to orange angel food. The variables in the equation have multiplied, just as the number of products on the grocers' shelves have multiplied from a hundred or so into many thousands.

When we first began operating under this new marketing concept, we encountered the problems which always accompany any major reorientation. Our people were young and frankly immature in some areas of business; but they were men possessed of an idea and they fought for it. The idea was almost too powerful. The marketing concept proved its worth in sales, but it upset many of the internal balances of the corporation. Marketing-oriented decisions resulted in peaks and valleys in production, schedules, labor, and inventories. But the system worked. It worked better and better as maverick marketing men became motivated toward tonnage and profit.

4th Era – Marketing Control

Today marketing is coming into its own. Pillsbury stands on the brink of its fourth major era in the marketing revolution.

Basically, the philosophy of this fourth era can be summarized this way: "We are moving from a company which has the marketing concept to a marketing company."

Marketing today sets company operating policy short-term. It will come to influence long-range policy more and more. Where today consumer research, technical research, procurement, production, advertising, and sales swing into action under the broad canopy established by marketing, tomorrow capital and financial planning, ten-year volume and profit goals will also come under the aegis of marketing. More than any other function, marketing must be tied to top management.

Today our marketing people know more about inventories than anyone in top management. Tomorrow's marketing man must know capital financing and the implications of marketing planning on long-range profit forecasting.

Today technical research receives almost all of its guidance and direction from marketing. Tomorrow marketing will assume a more creative function in the advertising area, both in terms of ideas and media selection.

The marketing revolution has only begun. There are still those who resist its basic idea, just as there are always those who will resist change in business, government, or any other form of human institution.

As the marketing revolution gains momentum, there will be more changes.

The concept of the customer at the center will remain valid; but business must adjust to the shifting tastes and likes and desires and needs which have always characterized the American consumer.

For many years the geographical center of the United States lay in a small Kansas town. Then a new state, Alaska, came along, and the center shifted to the north and west. Hawaii was admitted to the Union and the geographical mid-point took another jump to the west. In very much the same way, modern business must anticipate the restless shifting of buying attitudes, as customer preferences move north, south, east, or west from a liquid center. There is nothing static about the marketing revolution, and that is part of its fascination. The old order has changed, yielding place to the new — but the new order will have its quota of changes, too.

At Pillsbury, as our fourth era progresses, marketing will become the basic motivating force for the entire corporation. Soon it will be true that every activity of the corporation — from finance to sales to production — is aimed at satisfying the needs and desires of the consumer. When that stage of development is reached, the marketing revolution will be complete.

Shortsighted managements often fail to recognize that in fact there is no such thing as a growth industry. What is this malady called marketing myopia and how may it be prevented?

Marketing Myopia

Theodore Levitt

Every major industry was once a growth industry. But some that are now riding a wave of growth enthusiasm are very much in the shadow of decline. Others which are thought of as seasoned growth industries have actually stopped growing. In every case the reason growth is threatened, slowed, or stopped is *not* because the market is saturated. It is because there has been a failure of management.

Fateful Purposes

The failure is at the top. The executives responsible for it, in the last analysis, are those who deal with broad aims and policies. Thus:

●The railroads did not stop growing because the need for passenger and freight transportation declined. That grew. The railroads are in trouble today not because the need was filled by others (cars, trucks, airplanes, even telephones), but because it was *not* filled by the railroads themselves. They let others take customers away from them because they assumed themselves to be in the railroad business rather than in the transportation business. The reason they defined their industry wrong was because they were railroad-oriented instead of transportation-oriented; they were product-oriented instead of customer-oriented.

● Hollywood barely escaped being totally ravished by television. Actually, all the established film companies went through drastic reorganizations. Some simply disappeared. All of them got into trouble not because of TV's inroads but

Reprinted by permission of the publishers from Edward C. Bursk and John F. Chapman, eds., *Modern Marketing Strategy*. Cambridge, Mass.: Harvard University Press, Copyright, 1964, by the President and Fellows of Harvard College, pp. 24-48.

because of their own myopia. As with the railroads, Hollywood defined its business incorrectly. It thought it was in the movie business when it was actually in the entertainment business. "Movies" implied a specific, limited product. This produced a fatuous contentment which from the beginning led producers to view TV as a threat. Hollywood scorned and rejected TV when it should have welcomed it as an opportunity – an opportunity to expand the entertainment business.

Today TV is a bigger business than the old narrowly defined movie business ever was. Had Hollywood been customer-oriented (providing entertainment), rather than product-oriented (making movies), would it have gone through the fiscal purgatory that it did? I doubt it. What ultimately saved Hollywood and accounted for its recent resurgence was the wave of new young writers, producers, and directors whose previous successes in television had decimated the old movie companies and toppled the big movie moguls.

There are other less obvious examples of industries that have been and are now endangering their futures by improperly defining their purposes. I shall discuss some in detail later and analyze the kind of policies that lead to trouble. Right now it may help to show what a thoroughly customer-oriented management *can* do to keep a growth industry growing, even after the obvious opportunities have been exhausted; and here there are two examples that have been around for a long time. They are nylon and glass – specifically, E. I. duPont de Nemours & Company and Corning Glass Works:

Both companies have great technical competence. Their product orientation is unquestioned. But this alone does not explain their success. After all, who was more pridefully product-oriented and product-conscious than the erstwhile New England textile companies that have been so thoroughly massacred? The DuPonts and the Cornings have succeeded not primarily because of their product or research orientation but because they have been thoroughly customer-oriented also. It is constant watchfulness for opportunities to apply their technical know-how to the creation of customer-satisfying uses which accounts for their prodigious output of successful new products. Without a very sophisticated eye on the customer, most of their new products might have been wrong, their sales methods useless.

Aluminum has also continued to be a growth industry, thanks to the efforts of two wartime-created companies which deliberately set about creating new customer-satisfying uses. Without Kaiser Aluminum & Chemical Corporation and Reynolds Metals Company, the total demand for aluminum today would be vastly less than it is.

Some may argue that it is foolish to set the railroads off against aluminum or the movies off against glass. Are not aluminum and glass naturally so versatile that the industries are bound to have more growth opportunities than the railroads and movies? This view commits precisely the error I have been talking about. It defines an industry, or a product, or a cluster of know-how so narrowly as to guarantee its premature senescence. When we mention "railroads," we should make sure we mean "transportation." As transporters, the railroads still have a good chance for very considerable growth. They are not limited to the railroad business as such (though in my opinion rail transportation is potentially a much stronger transportation medium than is generally believed).

What the railroads lack is not opportunity, but some of the same managerial imaginativeness and audacity that made them great. Even an amateur like Jacques Barzun can see what is lacking when he says:

I grieve to see the most advanced physical and social organization of the last century go down in shabby disgrace for lack of the same comprehensive imagination that built it up. [What is lacking is] the will of the companies to survive and to satisfy the public by inventiveness and skill. [1]

Shadow of Obsolescence

It is impossible to mention a single major industry that did not at one time qualify for the magic appellation of "growth industry." In each case its assumed strength lay in the apparently unchallenged superiority of its product. There appeared to be no effective substitute for it. It was itself a runaway substitute for the product it so triumphantly replaced. Yet one after another of these celebrated industries has come under a shadow. Let us look briefly at a few more of them, this time taking examples that have so far received a little less attention:

● *Dry cleaning* — This was once a growth industry with lavish prospects. In an age of wool garments, imagine being finally able to get them safely and easily clean. The boom was on.

Yet here we are 30 years after the boom started and the industry is in trouble. Where has the competition come from? From a better way of cleaning? No. It has come from synthetic fibers and chemical additives that have cut the need for dry cleaning. But this is only the beginning. Lurking in the wings and ready to make chemical dry cleaning totally obsolescent is that powerful magician, ultrasonics.

● *Electric utilities* — This is another one of those supposedly "no-substitute" products that has been enthroned on a pedestal of invincible growth. When the incandescent lamp came along, kerosene lights were finished. Later the water wheel and the steam engine were cut to ribbons by the flexibility, reliability, simplicity and just plain easy availability of electric motors. The prosperity of electric utilities continues to wax extravagant as the home is converted into a museum of electric gadgetry.

How can anybody miss by investing in utilities, with no competition, nothing but growth ahead?

But a second look is not quite so comforting. A score of nonutility companies are well advanced toward developing a powerful chemical fuel cell which could sit in some hidden closet of every home silently ticking off electric power. The electric lines that vulgarize so many neighborhoods will be eliminated. So will the endless demolition of streets and service interruptions during storms. Also on the horizon is solar energy, again pioneered by nonutility companies.

[1] Jacques Barzun, "Trains and the Mind of Man," *Holiday,* February 1960, p. 21.

Who says that the utilities have no competition? They may be natural monopolies now, but tomorrow they may be natural deaths. To avoid this prospect, they too will have to develop fuel cells, solar energy, and other power sources. To survive, they themselves will have to plot the obsolescence of what now produces their livelihood.

● *Grocery stores* — Many people find it hard to realize that there ever was a thriving establishment known as the "corner grocery store." The supermarket has taken over with a powerful effectiveness. Yet the big food chains of the 1930's narrowly escaped being completely wiped out by the aggressive expansion of independent supermarkets. The first genuine supermarket was opened in 1930, in Jamaica, Long Island. By 1933 supermarkets were thriving in California, Ohio, Pennsylvania, and elsewhere. Yet the established chains pompously ignored them. When they chose to notice them, it was with such derisive descriptions as "cheapy," "horse-and-buggy," "cracker-barrel storekeeping," and "unethical opportunists."

The executive of one big chain announced at the time that he found it "hard to believe that people will drive for miles to shop for foods and sacrifice the personal service chains have perfected and to which Mrs. Consumer is accustomed." [2] As late as 1936, the National Wholesale Grocers convention and the New Jersey Retail Grocers Association said there was nothing to fear. They said that the supers' narrow appeal to the price buyer limited the size of their market. They had to draw from miles around. When imitators came, there would be wholesale liquidations as volume fell. The current high sales of the supers was said to be partly due to their novelty. Basically people wanted convenient neighborhood grocers. If the neighborhood stores "cooperate with their suppliers, pay attention to their costs, and improve their service," they would be able to weather the competition until it blew over. [3]

It never blew over. The chains discovered that survival required going into the supermarket business. This meant the wholesale destruction of their huge investments in corner store sites and in established distribution and merchandising methods. The companies with "the courage of their convictions" resolutely stuck to the corner store philosophy. They kept their pride but lost their shirts.

But memories are short. For example, it is hard for people who today confidently hail the twin messiahs of electronics and chemicals to see how things could possibly go wrong with these galloping industries. They probably also cannot see how a reasonably sensible businessman could have been as myopic as the famous Boston millionaire who 50 years ago unintentionally sentenced his heirs to poverty by stipulating that his entire estate be forever invested exclusively in electric streetcar securities. His posthumous declaration, "There will always be a big demand for efficient urban transportation," is no

[2] For more details see M. M. Zimmerman, *The Super Market: A Revolution in Distribution* (New York, McGraw-Hill Book Company, Inc., 1955), p. 48.
[3] Ibid., pp. 45-47.

consolation to his heirs who sustain life by pumping gasoline at automobile filling stations.

Yet, in a casual survey I recently took among a group of intelligent business executives, nearly half agreed that it would be hard to hurt their heirs by tying their estates forever to the electronics industry. When I then confronted them with the Boston streetcar example, they chorused unanimously, "That's different!" But is it? Is not the basic situation identical?

In truth, *there is no such thing* as a growth industry, I believe. There are only companies organized and operated to create and capitalize on growth opportunities. Industries that assume themselves to be riding some automatic growth escalator invariably descend into stagnation. The history of every dead and dying "growth" industry shows a self-deceiving cycle of bountiful expansion and undetected decay. There are four conditions which usually guarantee this cycle:

1. The belief that growth is assured by an expanding and more affluent population.
2. The belief that there is no competitive substitute for the industry's major product.
3. Too much faith in mass production and in the advantages of rapidly declining unit costs as output rises.
4. Preoccupation with a product that lends itself to carefully controlled scientific experimentation, improvement, and manufacturing cost reduction.

I should like now to begin examining each of these conditions in some detail. To build my case as boldly as possible, I shall illustrate the points with reference to three industries — petroleum, automobiles, and electronics — particularly petroleum, because it spans more years and more vicissitudes. Not only do these three have excellent reputations with the general public and also enjoy the confidence of sophisticated investors, but their managements have become known for progressive thinking in areas like financial control, product research, and management training. If obsolescence can cripple even these industries, it can happen anywhere.

Population Myth

The belief that profits are assured by an expanding and more affluent population is dear to the heart of every industry. It takes the edge off the apprehensions everybody understandably feels about the future. If consumers are multiplying and also buying more of your product or service, you can face the future with considerably more comfort than if the market is shrinking. An expanding market keeps the manufacturer from having to think very hard or imaginatively. If thinking is an intellectual response to a problem, then the absence of a problem leads to the absence of thinking. If your product has an automatically expanding market, then you will not give much thought to how to expand it.

One of the most interesting examples of this is provided by the petroleum industry. Probably our oldest growth industry, it has an enviable record. While there are some current apprehensions about its growth rate, the industry itself tends to be optimistic. But I believe it can be demonstrated that it is undergoing a fundamental yet typical change. It is not only ceasing to be a growth industry, but may actually be a declining one, relative to other business. Although there is widespread unawareness of it, I believe that within 25 years the oil industry may find itself in much the same position of retrospective glory that the railroads are now in. Despite its pioneering work in developing and applying the present-value method of investment evaluation, in employee relations, and in working with backward countries, the petroleum business is a distressing example of how complacency and wrongheadedness can stubbornly convert opportunity into near disaster.

One of the characteristics of this and other industries that have believed very strongly in the beneficial consequences of an expanding population, while at the same time being industries with a generic product for which there has appeared to be no competitive substitute, is that the individual companies have sought to outdo their competitors by improving on what they are already doing. This makes sense, of course, if one assumes that sales are tied to the country's population strings, because the customer can compare products only on a feature-by-feature basis. I believe it is significant, for example, that not since John D. Rockefeller sent free kerosene lamps to China has the oil industry done anything really outstanding to create a demand for its product. Not even in product improvement has it showered itself with eminence. The greatest single improvement, namely, the development of tetraethyl lead, came from outside the industry, specifically from General Motors and DuPont. The big contributions made by the industry itself are confined to the technology of oil exploration, production, and refining.

Asking for Trouble

In other words, the industry's efforts have focused on improving the *efficiency* of getting and making its product, not really on improving the generic product or its marketing. Moreover, its chief product has continuously been defined in the narrowest possible terms, namely, gasoline, not energy, fuel, or transportation. This attitude has helped assure that:

● Major improvements in gasoline quality tend not to originate in the oil industry. Also, the development of superior alternative fuels comes from outside the oil industry, as will be shown later.

● Major innovations in automobile fuel marketing are originated by small new oil companies that are not primarily preoccupied with production or refining. These are the companies that have been responsible for the rapidly expanding multipump gasoline stations, with their successful emphasis on large and clean layouts, rapid and efficient driveway service, and quality gasoline at low prices.

Thus, the oil industry is asking for trouble from outsiders. Sooner or later, in this land of hungry inventors and entrepreneurs, a threat is sure to come. The possibilities of this will become more apparent when we turn to the next dangerous belief of many managements. For the sake of continuity, because this second belief is tied closely to the first, I shall continue with the same example.

Idea of Indispensability

The petroleum industry is pretty much persuaded that there is no competitive substitute for its major product, gasoline — or if there is, that it will continue to be a derivative of crude oil, such as diesel fuel or kerosene jet fuel.

There is a lot of automatic wishful thinking in this assumption. The trouble is that most refining companies own huge amounts of crude oil reserves. These have value only if there is a market for products into which oil can be converted — hence the tenacious belief in the continuing competitive superiority of automobile fuels made from crude oil.

This idea persists despite all historic evidence against it. The evidence not only shows that oil has never been a superior product for any purpose for very long, but it also shows that the oil industry has never really been a growth industry. It has been a succession of different businesses that have gone through the usual historic cycles of growth, maturity, and decay. Its over-all survival is owed to a series of miraculous escapes from total obsolescence, of last-minute and unexpected reprieves from total disaster reminiscent of the Perils of Pauline.

Perils of Petroleum

I shall sketch in only the main episodes:

• First, crude oil was largely a patent medicine. But even before that fad ran out, demand was greatly expanded by the use of oil in kerosene lamps. The prospect of lighting the world s lamps gave rise to an extravagant promise of growth. The prospects were similar to those the industry now holds for gasoline in other parts of the world. It can hardly wait for the underdeveloped nations to get a car in every garage.

In the days of the kerosene lamp, the oil companies competed with each other and against gaslight by trying to improve the illuminating characteristics of kerosene. Then suddenly the impossible happened. Edison invented a light which was totally nondependent on crude oil. Had it not been for the growing use of kerosene in space heaters, the incandescent lamp would have completely finished oil as a growth industry at that time. Oil would have been good for little else than axle grease.

• Then disaster and reprieve struck again. Two great innovations occurred, neither originating in the oil industry. The successful development of coal-burning domestic central-heating systems made the space heater obsolescent. While the industry reeled, along came its most magnificent boost yet — the internal combustion engine, also invented by outsiders. Then when the prodigious expansion for gasoline finally began to level off in the 1920's, along came the miraculous escape of a central oil heater. Once again, the escape was provided by an outsider's invention and development. And when that market weakened, wartime demand for aviation fuel came to the rescue. After the war the expansion of civilian aviation, the dieselization of railroads, and the explosive demand for cars and trucks kept the industry's growth in high gear.

• Meanwhile centralized oil heating — whose boom potential had only recently been proclaimed — ran into severe competition from natural gas. While the oil companies themselves owned the gas that now competed with their oil, the industry did not originate the natural gas revolution, nor has it to this day greatly profited from its gas ownership. The gas revolution was made by newly formed transmission companies that marketed the product with an aggressive ardor. They started a magnificent new industry, first against the advice and then against the resistance of the oil companies.

By all the logic of the situation, the oil companies themselves should have made the gas revolution. They not only owned the gas; they also were the only people experienced in handling, scrubbing, and using it, the only people experienced in pipeline technology and transmission, and they understood heating problems. But, partly because they knew that natural gas would compete with their own sale of heating oil, the oil companies pooh-poohed the potentials of gas.

The revolution was finally started by oil pipeline executives who, unable to persuade their own companies to go into gas, quit and organized the spectacularly successful gas transmission companies. Even after their success became painfully evident to the oil companies, the latter did not go into gas transmission. The multibillion dollar business which should have been theirs went to others. As in the past, the industry was blinded by its narrow preoccupation with a specific product and the value of its reserves. It paid little or no attention to its customers' basic needs and preferences.

● The postwar years have not witnessed any change. Immediately after World War II the oil industry was greatly encouraged about its future by the rapid expansion of demand for its traditional line of products. In 1950 most companies projected annual rates of domestic expansion of around 6% through at least 1975. Though the ratio of crude oil reserves to demand in the Free World was about 20 to 1, with 10 to 1 being usually considered a reasonable working ratio in the United States, booming demand sent oil men searching for more without sufficient regard to what the future really promised. In 1952 they "hit" in the Middle East; the ratio skyrocketed to 42 to 1. If gross additions to reserves continue at the average rate of the past five years (37 billion barrels annually), then by 1970 the reserve ratio will be up to 45 to 1. This abundance of oil has weakened crude and product prices all over the world.

Uncertain Future

Management cannot find much consolation today in the rapidly expanding petrochemical industry, another oil-using idea that did not originate in the leading firms. The total United States production of petrochemicals is equivalent to about 2% (by volume) of the demand for all petroleum products. Although the petrochemical industry is now expected to grow by about 10% per year, this will not offset other drains on the growth of crude oil consumption. Furthermore, while petrochemical products are many and growing, it is well to remember that there are nonpetroleum sources of the basic raw material, such as coal. Besides, a lot of plastics can be produced with relatively little oil. A 50,000-barrel-per-day oil refinery is now considered the absolute minimum size for efficiency. But a 5,000-barrel-per-day chemical plant is a giant operation.

Oil has never been a continuously strong growth industry. It has grown by fits and starts, always miraculously saved by innovations and developments not of its own making. The reason it has not grown in a smooth progression is that each time it thought it had a superior product safe from the possibility of competitive substitutes, the product turned out to be inferior and notoriously subject to obsolescence. Until now, gasoline (for motor fuel, anyhow) has escaped this fate. But, as we shall see later, it too may be on its last legs.

The point of all this is that there is no guarantee against product obsolescence. If a company's own research does not make it obsolete, another's will. Unless an industry is especially lucky, as oil has been until now, it can easily go down in a sea of red figures — just as the railroads have, as the buggy whip manufacturers have, as the corner grocery chains have, as most of the big movie companies have, and indeed as many other industries have.

The best way for a firm to be lucky is to make its own luck. That requires knowing what makes a business successful. One of the greatest enemies of this knowledge is mass production.

Production Pressures

Mass-production industries are impelled by a great drive to produce all they can. The prospect of steeply declining unit costs as output rises is more than most companies can usually resist. The profit possibilities look spectacular. All effort focuses on production. The result is that marketing gets neglected.

John Kenneth Galbraith contends that just the opposite occurs. [4] Output is so prodigious that all effort concentrates on trying to get rid of it. He says this accounts for singing commercials, desecration of the countryside with advertising signs, and other wasteful and vulgar practices. Galbraith has a finger on something real, but he misses the strategic point. Mass production does indeed generate great pressure to "move" the product. But what usually gets emphasized is selling, not marketing. Marketing, being a more sophisticated and complex process, gets ignored.

The difference between marketing and selling is more than semantic. Selling focuses on the needs of the seller, marketing on the needs of the buyer. Selling is preoccupied with the seller's need to convert his product into cash; marketing with the idea of satisfying the needs of the customer by means of the product and the whole cluster of things associated with creating, delivering, and finally consuming it.

In some industries the enticements of full mass production have been so powerful that for many years top management in effect has told the sales departments, "You get rid of it; we'll worry about profits." By contrast, a truly marketing-minded firm tries to create value-satisfying goods and services that consumers will want to buy. What it offers for sale includes not only the generic product or service, but also how it is made available to the customer, in what form, when, under what conditions, and at what terms of trade. Most important, what it offers for sale is determined not by the seller but by the buyer. The seller

[4] *The Affluent Society* (Boston, Houghton Mifflin Company, 1958), pp. 152-160.

takes his cues from the buyer in such a way that the product becomes a consequence of the marketing effort, not vice versa.

Lag in Detroit

This may sound like an elementary rule of business, but that does not keep it from being violated wholesale. It is certainly more violated than honored. Take the automobile industry:

Here mass production is most famous, most honored, and has the greatest impact on the entire society. The industry has hitched its fortune to the relentless requirements of the annual model change, a policy that makes customer orientation an especially urgent necessity. Consequently the auto companies annually spend millions of dollars on consumer research. But the fact that the new compact cars are selling so well in their first year indicates that Detroit's vast researchers have for a long time failed to reveal what the customer really wanted. Detroit was not persuaded that he wanted anything different from what he had been getting until it lost millions of customers to other small car manufacturers.

How could this unbelievable lag behind consumer wants have been perpetuated so long? Why did not research reveal consumer preferences before consumers' buying decisions themselves revealed the facts? Is that not what consumer research is for — to find out before the fact what is going to happen? The answer is that Detroit never really researched the customer's wants. It only researched his preferences between the kinds of things which it had already decided to offer him. For Detroit is mainly product-oriented, not customer-oriented. To the extent that the customer is recognized as having needs that the manufacturer should try to satisfy, Detroit usually acts as if the job can be done entirely by product changes. Occasionally attention gets paid to financing, too, but that is done more in order to sell than to enable the customer to buy.

As for taking care of other customer needs, there is not enough being done to write about. The areas of the greatest unsatisfied needs are ignored, or at best get stepchild attention. These are at the point of sale and on the matter of automotive repair and maintenance. Detroit views these problem areas as being of secondary importance. That is underscored by the fact that the retailing and servicing ends of this industry are neither owned and operated nor controlled by the manufacturers. Once the car is produced, things are pretty much in the dealer's inadequate hands. Illustrative of Detroit's arm's-length attitude is the fact that, while servicing holds enormous sales-stimulating, profit-building opportunities, only 57 of Chevrolet's 7,000 dealers provide night maintenance service.

Motorists repeatedly express their dissatisfaction with servicing and their apprehensions about buying cars under the present selling setup. The anxieties and problems they encounter during the auto buying and maintenance processes are probably more intense and widespread today than 30 years ago. Yet the automobile companies do not *seem* to listen to or take their cues from the anguished consumer. If they do listen, it must be through the filter of their own preoccupation with production. The marketing effort is still viewed as a necessary consequence of the product, not vice versa, as it should be. That is the legacy of mass production, with its parochial view that profit resides essentially in low-cost full production.

What Ford Put First

The profit lure of mass production obviously has a place in the plans and stragety of business management, but it must always *follow* hard thinking about the customer. This is one of the most important lessons that we can learn from the contradictory behavior of Henry Ford. In a sense Ford was both the most brilliant and the most senseless marketer in American history. He was senseless because he refused to give the customer anything but a black car. He was brilliant because he fashioned a production system designed to fit market needs. We habitually celebrate him for the wrong reason, his production genius. His real genius was marketing. We think he was able to cut his selling price and therefore sell millions of $500 cars because his invention of the assembly line had reduced the costs. Actually he invented the assembly line because he had concluded that at $500 he could sell millions of cars. Mass production was the *result* not the cause of his low prices.

Ford repeatedly emphasized this point, but a nation of production-oriented business managers refuses to hear the great lesson he taught. Here is his operating philosophy as he expressed it succinctly:

Our policy is to reduce the price, extend the operations, and improve the article. You will notice that the reduction of price comes first. We have never considered any costs as fixed. Therefore we first reduce the price to the point where we believe more sales will result. Then we go ahead and try to make the prices. We do not bother about the costs. The new price forces the costs down. The more usual way is to take the costs and then determine the price, and although that method may be scientific in the narrow sense; it is not scientific in the broad sense, because what earthly use is it to know the cost if it tells you that you cannot manufacture at a price at which the article can be sold? But more to the point is the fact that, although one may calculate what a cost is, and of course all of our costs are carefully calculated, no one knows what a cost ought to be. One of the ways of discovering . . . is to name a price so low as to force everybody in the place to the highest point of efficiency. The low price makes everybody dig for profits. We make more discoveries concerning manufacturing and selling under this forced method than by any method of leisurely investigation.[5]

Product Provincialism

The tantalizing profit possibilities of low unit production costs may be the most seriously self deceiving attitude that can afflict a company, particularly a "growth" company where an apparently assured expansion of demand already tends to undermine a proper concern for the importance of marketing and the customer.

[5] Henry Ford, *My Life and Work* (New York, Doubleday, Page & Company, 1923), pp. 146-147.

The usual result of this narrow preoccupation with so-called concrete matters is that instead of growing, the industry declines. It usually means that the product fails to adapt to the constantly changing patterns of consumer needs and tastes, to new and modified marketing institutions and practices, or to product developments in competing or complementary industries. The industry has its eyes so firmly on its own specific product that it does not see how it is being made obsolete.

The classical example of this is the buggy whip industry. No amount of product improvement could stave off its death sentence. But had the industry defined itself as being in the transportation business rather than the buggy whip business, it might have survived. It would have done what survival always entails, that is, changing. Even if it had only defined its business as providing a stimulant or catalyst to an energy source, it might have survived by becoming a manufacturer of, say, fanbelts or air cleaners.

What may some day be a still more classical example is, again, the oil industry. Having let others steal marvelous opportunities from it (e.g., natural gas, as already mentioned, missile fuels, and jet engine lubricants), one would expect it to have taken steps never to let that happen again. But this is not the case. We are now getting extraordinary new developments in fuel systems specifically designed to power automobiles. Not only are these developments concentrated in firms outside the petroleum industry, but petroleum is almost systematically ignoring them, securely content in its wedded bliss to oil. It is the story of the kerosene lamp versus the incandescent lamp all over again. Oil is trying to improve hydrocarbon fuels rather than to develop *any* fuels best suited to the needs of their users, whether or not made in different ways and with different raw materials from oil.

Here are some of the things which nonpetroleum companies are working on:

● Over a dozen such firms now have advanced working models of energy systems which, when perfected, will replace the internal combustion engine and eliminate the demand for gasoline. The superior merit of each of these systems is their elimination of frequent, time-consuming, and irritating refueling stops. Most of these systems are fuel cells designed to create electrical energy directly from chemicals without combustion. Most of them use chemicals that are not derived from oil, generally hydrogen and oxygen.

● Several other companies have advanced models of electric storage batteries designed to power automobiles. One of these is an aircraft producer that is working jointly with several electric utility companies. The latter hope to use off-peak generating capacity to supply overnight plug-in battery regeneration. Another company, also using the battery approach, is a medium-size electronics firm with extensive small-battery experience that it developed in connection with its work on hearing aids. It is collaborating with an automobile manufacturer. Recent improvements arising from the need for high-powered miniature power storage plants in rockets have put us within reach of a relatively small battery capable of withstanding great overloads or surges of power. Germanium diode applications and batteries using sintered-plate and nickel-cadmium techniques promise to make a revolution in our energy sources.

● Solar energy conversion systems are also getting increasing attention. One usually cautious Detroit auto executive recently ventured that solar-powered cars might be common by 1980.

As for the oil companies, they are more or less "watching developments," as one research director put it to me. A few are doing a bit of research on fuel cells, but almost always confined to developing cells powered by hydrocarbon chemicals. None of them are enthusiastically researching fuel cells, batteries, or solar power plants. None of them are spending a fraction as much on research in these profoundly important areas as they are on the usual run-of-the-mill things like reducing combustion chamber deposit in gasoline engines. One major integrated petroleum company recently took a tentative look at the fuel cell and concluded that although "the companies actively working on it indicate a belief in ultimate success . . . the timing and magnitude of its impact are too remote to warrant recognition in our forecasts."

One might, of course, ask: Why should the oil companies do anything different? Would not chemical fuel cells, batteries, or solar energy kill the present product lines? The answer is that they would indeed, and that is precisely the reason for the oil firms having to develop these power units before their competitors, so they will not be companies without an industry.

Management might be more likely to do what is needed for its own preservation if it thought of itself as being in the energy business. But even that would not be enough if it persists in imprisoning itself in the narrow grip of its tight product orientation. It has to think of itself as taking care of customer needs, not finding, refining, or even selling oil. Once it genuinely thinks of its business as taking care of people's transportation needs, nothing can stop it from creating its own extravagantly profitable growth.

"Creative Destruction"

Since words are cheap and deeds are dear, it may be appropriate to indicate what this kind of thinking involves and leads to. Let us start at the beginning — the customer. It can be shown that motorists strongly dislike the bother, delay, and experience of buying gasoline. People actually do not buy gasoline. They cannot see it, taste it, feel it, appreciate it, or really test it. What they buy is the right to continue driving their cars. The gas station is like a tax collector to whom people are compelled to pay a periodic toll as the price of using their cars. This makes the gas station a basically unpopular institution. It can never be made popular or pleasant, only less unpopular, less unpleasant.

To reduce its unpopularity completely means eliminating it. Nobody likes a tax collector, not even a pleasantly cheerful one. Nobody likes to interrupt a trip to buy a phantom product, not even from a handsome Adonis or a seductive Venus. Hence, companies that are working on exotic fuel substitutes which will eliminate the need for frequent refueling are heading directly into the outstretched arms of the irritated motorist. They are riding a wave of inevitability, not because they are creating something which is technologically superior or more sophisticated, but because they are satisfying a powerful customer need. They are also eliminating noxious odors and air pollution.

Once the petroleum companies recognize the customer-satisfying logic of what another power system can do, they will see that they have no more choice about working on an efficient, long-lasting fuel (or some way of delivering present fuels without bothering the motorist) than the big food chains had a choice about going into the supermarket business, or the vacuum tube companies had a choice about making semiconductors. For their own good the oil firms will have to destroy their own highly profitable assets. No amount of wishful thinking can save them from the necessity of engaging in this form of "creative destruction."

I phrase the need as strongly as this because I think management must make quite an effort to break itself loose from conventional ways. It is all too easy in this day and age for a company or industry to let its sense of purpose become dominated by the economies of full production and to develop a dangerously lopsided product orientation. In short, if management lets itself drift, it invariably drifts in the direction of thinking of itself as producing goods and services, not customer satisfactions. While it probably will not descend to the depths of telling its salesmen, "You get rid of it; we'll worry about profits," it can, without knowing it, be practicing precisely that formula for withering decay. The historic fate of one growth industry after another has been its suicidal product provincialism.

Dangers of R & D

Another big danger to a firm's continued growth arises when top management is wholly transfixed by the profit possibilities of technical research and development. To illustrate I shall turn first to a new industry — electronics — and then return once more to the oil companies. By comparing a fresh example with a familiar one, I hope to emphasize the prevalence and insidiousness of a hazardous way of thinking.

Marketing Shortchanged

In the case of electronics, the greatest danger which faces the glamorous new companies in this field is not that they do not pay enough attention to research and development, but that they pay *too much* attention to it. And the fact that the fastest growing electronics firms owe their eminence to their heavy emphasis on technical research is completely beside the point. They have vaulted to affluence on a sudden crest of unusually strong general receptiveness to new technical ideas. Also, their success has been shaped in the virtually guaranteed market of military subsidies and by military orders that in many cases actually preceded the existence of facilities to make the products. Their expansion has, in other words, been almost totally devoid of marketing effort.

Thus, they are growing up under conditions that come dangerously close to creating the illusion that a superior product will sell itself. Having created a successful company by making a superior product, it is not surprising that management continues to be oriented toward the product rather than the people who consume it. It develops the philosophy that continued growth is a matter of continued product innovation and improvement.

A number of other factors tend to strengthen and sustain this belief:

1. Because electronic products are highly complex and sophisticated, managements become top-heavy with engineers and scientists. This creates a selective bias in favor of research and production at the expense of marketing. The organization tends to view itself as making things rather than satisfying customer needs. Marketing gets treated as a residual activity, "something else" that must be done once the vital job of product creation and production is completed.

2. To this bias in favor of product research, development, and production is added the bias in favor of dealing with controllable variables. Engineers and scientists are at home in the world of concrete things like machines, test tubes, production lines, and even balance sheets. The abstractions to which they feel kindly are those which are testable or manipulatable in the laboratory, or, if not testable, then functional, such as Euclid's axioms. In short, the managements of the new glamour-growth companies tend to favor those business activities which lend themselves to careful study, experimentation, and control — the hard, practical, realities of the lab, the shop, the books.

What gets shortchanged are the realities of the *market*. Consumers are unpredictable, varied, fickle, stupid, shortsighted, stubborn, and generally bothersome. This is not what the engineer-managers say, but deep down in their consciousness it is what they believe. And this accounts for their concentrating on what they know and what they can control, namely, product research, engineering, and production. The emphasis on production becomes particularly attractive when the product can be made at declining unit costs. There is no more inviting way of making money than by running the plant full blast.

Today the top-heavy science-engineering-production orientation of so many electronics companies works reasonably well because they are pushing into new frontiers in which the armed services have pioneered virtually assured markets. The companies are in the felicitous position of having to fill, not find markets; of not having to discover what the customer needs and wants, but of having the customer voluntarily come forward with specific new product demands. If a team of consultants had been assigned specifically to design a business situation calculated to prevent the emergence and development of a customer-oriented marketing viewpoint, it could not have produced anything better than the conditions just described.

Stepchild Treatment

The oil industry is a stunning example of how science, technology, and mass production can divert an entire group of companies from their main task. To the extent the consumer is studied at all (which is not much), the focus is forever on getting information which is designed to help the oil companies improve what they are now doing. They try to discover more convincing advertising themes, more effective sales promotional drives, what the market shares of the various companies are, what people like or dislike about service station dealers and oil companies, and so forth. Nobody seems as interested in probing deeply into the basic human needs that the industry might be trying to satisfy as in probing into the basic properties of the raw material that the companies work with in trying to deliver customer satisfactions.

Basic questions about customers and markets seldom get asked. The latter occupy a stepchild status. They are recognized as existing, as having to be taken care of, but not worth very much real thought or dedicated attention. Nobody gets as excited about the customers in his own backyard as about the oil in the Sahara Desert. Nothing illustrates better the neglect of marketing than its treatment in the industry press:

The centennial issue of the *American Petroleum Institute Quarterly,* published in 1959 to celebrate the discovery of oil in Titusville, Pennsylvania, contained 21 feature articles proclaiming the industry's greatness. Only one of these talked about its achievements in marketing, and that was only a pictorial record of how service station architecture has changed. The issue also contained a special section on "New Horizons," which was devoted to showing the magnificent role oil would play in America's future. Every reference was ebulliently optimistic, never implying once that oil might have some hard competition. Even the reference to atomic energy was a cheerful catalogue of how oil would help make atomic energy a success. There was not a single apprehension that the oil industry's affluence might be threatened or a suggestion that one "new horizon" might include new and better ways of serving oil's present customers.

But the most revealing example of the stepchild treatment that marketing gets was still another special series of short articles on "The Revolutionary Potential of Electronics." Under that heading this list of articles appeared in the table of contents:

● "In the Search for Oil"
● "In Production Operations"
● "In Refinery Processes"
● "In Pipeline Operations"

Significantly, every one of the industry's major functional areas is listed, *except* marketing. Why? Either it is believed that electronics holds no revolutionary potential for petroleum marketing (which is palpably wrong), or the editors forgot to discuss marketing (which is more likely, and illustrates its stepchild status).

The order in which the four functional areas are listed also betrays the alienation of the oil industry from the consumer. The industry is implicitly defined as beginning with the search for oil and ending with its distribution from the refinery. But the truth is, it seems to me, that the industry begins with the needs of the customer for its products. From that primal position its definition moves steadily backstream to areas of progressively lesser importance, until it finally comes to rest at the "search for oil."

Beginning & End

The view that an industry is a customer-satisfying process, not a goods-producing process, is vital for all businessmen to understand. An industry begins with the customer and his needs, not with a patent, a raw material, or a selling skill. Given the customer's needs, the industry develops backwards, first concerning itself with the physical *delivery* of customer satisfactions. Then it moves back further to *creating* the things by which these satisfactions are in part achieved. How these materials are created is a matter of indifference to the customer, hence the particular form of manufacturing, processing, or what-have-you cannot be considered as a vital aspect of the industry. Finally, the industry moves back still further to *finding* the raw materials necessary for making its products.

The irony of some industries oriented toward technical research and development is that the scientists who occupy the high executive positions are totally unscientific when it comes to defining their companies' over-all needs and purposes. They violate the first two rules of the scientific method — being aware of and defining their companies' problems, and then developing testable hypotheses about solving them. They are scientific only about the convenient things, such as laboratory and product experiments. The reason that the customer (and the satisfaction of his deepest needs) is not considered as being "the problem" is not because there is any certain belief that no such problem exists, but because an organizational lifetime has conditioned management to look in the opposite direction. Marketing is a stepchild.

I do not mean that selling is ignored. Far from it. But selling, again, is not marketing. As already pointed out, selling concerns itself with the tricks and techniques of getting people to exchange their cash for your product. It is not concerned with the values that the exchange is all about. And it does not, as marketing invariably does, view the entire business process as consisting of a tightly integrated effort to discover, create, arouse, and satisfy customer needs. The customer is somebody "out there" who, with proper cunning, can be separated from his loose change.

Actually, not even selling gets much attention in some technologically minded firms. Because there is a virtually guaranteed market for the abundant flow of their new products, they do not actually know what a real market is. It is as if they lived in a planned economy, moving their products routinely from factory to retail outlet. Their successful concentration on products tends to convince them of the soundness of what they have been doing, and they fail to see the gathering clouds over the market.

Conclusion

Less than 75 years ago American railroads enjoyed a fierce loyalty among astute Wall Streeters. European monarchs invested in them heavily. Eternal wealth was thought to be the benediction for anybody who could scrape a few thousand dollars together to put into rail stocks. No other form of transportation could compete with the railroads in speed, flexibility, durability, economy, and growth potentials. As Jacques Barzun put it, "By the turn of the century it was an institution, an image of man, a tradition, a code of honor, a source of poetry, a nursery of boyhood desires, a sublimest of toys, and the most solemn machine — next to the funeral hearse — that marks the epochs in man's life." [6]

Even after the advent of automobiles, trucks, and airplanes, the railroad tycoons remained imperturbably self-confident. If you had told them 60 years ago that in 30 years they would be flat on their backs, broke, and pleading for government subsidies, they would have thought you totally demented. Such a future was simply not considered possible. It was not even a discussable subject, or an askable question, or a matter which any sane person would consider worth speculating about. The very thought was insane. Yet a lot of insane notions now have matter-of-fact acceptance — for example, the idea of 100-ton tubes of metal moving smoothly through the air 20,000 feet above the earth, loaded with 100 sane and solid citizens casually drinking martinis — and they have dealt cruel blows to the railroads.

What specifically must other companies do to avoid this fate? What does customer orientation involve? These questions have in part been answered by the preceding examples and analysis. It would take another article to show in detail what is required for specific industries. In any case, it should be obvious that building an effective customer-oriented company involves far more than good intentions or promotional tricks; it involves profound matters of human organization and leadership. For the present, let me merely suggest what appear to be some general requirements.

Obviously the company has to do what survival demands. It has to adapt to the requirements of the market, and it has to do it sooner rather than later. But mere survival is a so-so aspiration. Anybody can survive in some way or other, even the skid-row bum. The trick is to survive gallantly, to feel the surging impulse of commercial mastery; not just to experience the sweet smell of success, but to have the visceral feel of entrepreneurial greatness.

No organization can achieve greatness without a vigorous leader who is driven onward by his own pulsating *will to succeed.* He has to have a vision of grandeur, a vision that can produce eager followers in vast numbers. In business, the followers are the customers. To produce these customers, the entire corporation must be viewed as a customer-creating and customer-satisfying organism. Management must think of itself not as producing products but as providing customer-creating value satisfactions. It must push this idea (and everything it means and requires) into every nook and cranny of the organization. It has to do this continuously and with the kind of flair that excites and stimulates the people in it. Otherwise, the company will be merely a series of pigeonholed parts, with no consolidating sense of purpose or direction.

In short, the organization must learn to think of itself not as producing goods or services but as *buying customers,* as doing the things that will make people *want* to do business with it. And the chief executive himself has the inescapable responsibility for creating this environment, this viewpoint, this attitude, this aspiration. He himself must set the company's style, its direction, and its goals. This means he has to know precisely where he himself wants to go, and to make

[6] Op. cit., p. 20.

sure the whole organization is enthusiastically aware of where that is. This is a first requisite of leadership, for *unless he knows where he is going, any road will take him there.*

If any road is okay, the chief executive might as well pack his attache case and go fishing. If an organization does not know or care where it is going, it does not need to advertise that fact with a ceremonial figurehead. Everybody will notice it soon enough.

The marketing concept has served business well in the postwar years as a basic corporate philosophy. However, indications abound that business is entering a new era in which unprecedented human and social demands will be made upon it. The perspectives of the marketing concept are too limited to cope with such pressures, and indeed it appears that a new and broader philosophy has gradually evolved in a number of progressive business enterprises. The author describes this as the "human concept," and argues that its general acceptance by the business community could have tremendous significance for human progress as well as for the future of business.

The Human Concept: New Philosophy for Business

Leslie M. Dawson

One of the more intriguing examples of graffiti reported in recent years is the scrawl on a New York City sidewalk, "Marvin Can't Relate to His Environment." While it is unlikely that Marvin was a business executive at the time of his immortalization in cement, a growing number of businessmen nonetheless share his problem. Certainly the business professional, in common with everyone else, has a vital need for *some* orientation to a world that daily grows more complex, convulsive, and confounding. To lack such a sense of relationship is to be "disoriented" or, according to *Webster's*, "to lose an appreciation of place and time or of one's own identity." Much of the literature of business since the end of World War II has harped on the idea that we live in a "marketing era" and that firms ought to adopt a marketing orientation or a marketing concept as the cornerstone of their corporate philosophy. A crucial question to be asked today,

Reprinted by permission of the author and the publisher from *Business Horizons*, Vol. 12, No. 6 (December, 1969), pp. 29-38.

however, is whether a marketing orientation remains the correct orientation for the business executive.

Irwin Miller, chairman of Cummins Engine, observed recently that we are living in a remarkable and perplexing time; despite the long list of accomplishments of American business and the unprecedented prosperity of the nation, the businessman feels insecure and under attack from many groups: workers, customers, government, children, education, and even the church. [1] While the marketing concept may indeed have been ideally attuned to a marketing era, the evidence builds that we are well on the way into an era that must be described in some other way. The eminent sociologist, Pitirim A. Sorokin, has identified the decay of the sensate culture, with its emphasis upon materialism, and a movement toward an ideational, spiritually based form of culture as one of the basic trends of our time.

In the past several years, a number of institutions and foundations have undertaken serious research projects involving speculation as to the future. The Ford Foundation, the Rand Corporation, and the Hudson Institute have sponsored such studies, and the American Academy of Arts and Sciences has created the Committee on the Year 2000. A general theme of agreement in their published reports is that a strong accentuation of human values is likely to dominate the last third of this century. The committee makes this statement:

> Let it be added tnat in this 'super-affluent' society of year 2000, it is not likely that efficiency (defined by the criteria of maximizing profit or income) will still be primary, though it will doubtless remain important . . . We could think of this phenomenon as a shift to humanistic rather than vocational or advancement-oriented values, and conjecture that this tendency will increase over the next 33 years.[2]

This article suggests that, *first*, we are no longer living in a marketing era and are witnessing the start of what may ultimately be termed the human era; *second*, today's executive must cope with a variety of issues, many vaguely or directly threatening, which extend far beyond mere market considerations; *third*, a marketing concept is of little help in coping with such problems; and *fourth*, the actions of many leading corporations today do in fact testify to the gradual replacement of the marketing concept with a more embracing philosophy which, for want of a better term, may be called the human concept.

Historical-Ecological Perspective

At least one business scholar has suggested that cultural ecology, the study of the adaptation of a social system to its environment, provides a more meaningful perspective from which to study business activity than economics or any other social science. [3] Cultural ecology focuses upon the capacity of an organized

---

[1] Irwin Miller, "Business Has a War to Win," *Harvard Business Review*, XLVII (March-April, 1969), p. 4.

[2] Herman Kahn and Anthony J. Weiner, *The Year 2000: A Framework for Speculation on the Next Thirty-Three Years* (New York: The Macmillan Co., 1967), pp. 214-15.

[3] Wroe Alderson, *Dynamic Marketing Behavior* (Homewood, Ill.: Richard D. Irwin, Inc., 1965), Ch. 13.

behavior system to sustain itself by drawing upon the resources of its environment, in terms analogous to the capacity of a living creature to utilize life-sustaining resources. Survival and equilibrium are critical concepts in cultural ecology. Survival is the ultimate goal of the organized behavior system, but the system can exist only by adapting to environmental change and maintaining a dynamic ecological equilibrium.

It can be argued that the main thrust of business thought and action has always tended to reflect the basic orientation that top management believes to be most compatible with perceived contemporary environmental conditions. For example, three distinct phases of managerial orientation in twentieth century American business have been observed: [4]

Production orientation (1900-30) — An emphasis upon production volume and plant efficiency, in response to newly developed technology for mass production and expanded markets combined with a steady rise in consumer affluence and spending.

Sales orientation (1930-50) — An emphasis upon aggressive sales and distributive practices in response to mounting production saturation combined with new caution and moderation in consumer spending and business investment.

Marketing orientation (1950-?) — An emphasis upon consumer satisfaction, crystallized in the marketing concept, in response to new competitive interfaces among products and industries, an unprecedented level of consumer affluence, and a volatile mixture of other new postwar pressures.

Wroe Alderson has called attention to two crucial environmental levels in the cultural ecology of business: first, the proximate environment, the external domain with which a system is in direct and continuous contact (for a marketing firm, the markets in which it buys and sells and competes) and, second, the more embracing ultimate environment, composed of the technological, ideological, moral, and social dimensions of the culture. The figure illustrates this environmental perspective. In the long run the business enterprise must maintain dynamic ecological equilibrium with *both* environments. A system that fails to do so may fall into an "extinction mode."

None of the basic orientations described has been especially attuned to the relationship of the firm to its ultimate environment. Even the ubiquitous marketing concept, relevant and valuable as it has been in an era of marketing emphasis, has serious weaknesses as a management guide in an era reflecting deepened human concern. A fuller consideration of the marketing concept and the environmental conditions that spawned it may be helpful as a prelude to discussing these weaknesses.

The Marketing Concept — Yesterday and Today

In the post-World War II years, the nation's economy not only recovered

[4] Robert J. Keith, "The Marketing Revolution," *Journal of Marketing*, XXIV (January, 1960), pp. 35-38.

from the effects of the Depression, but swiftly advanced well beyond the highest prewar levels. Postwar prosperity ushered in the age of the affluent society in the United States. The postwar consumer not only was economically better off, better educated, and more sophisticated, but before long more saturated with goods as well. The notion of a limit to the "capacity to consume" became more than a mere theoretical concern, and the survival of the business enterprise depended largely upon its skill in determining, and flexibility in adjusting to, shifts in consumer tastes. An all-out commitment to market considerations — expressed as the "marketing concept" — became vital. A typical definition of this concept is the following:

A managerial philosophy concerned with the mobilization, utilization, and control of total corporate effort for the purpose of helping consumers solve selected problems, in ways compatible with planned enhancement of the profit position of the firm. [5]

The implementation of a marketing concept often necessitates major organizational and operational changes for the firm. At the very least a new accentuation is placed upon interdepartmental consultation and synchronization (the "systems approach"). Reversal of the "normal" planning sequence is emphasized, so that plans and strategies are formulated first with a view to the marketplace and then translated "backwards" into the development of a profitable market offering. But in its essence the marketing concept represents a basic corporate philosophy, a rationale for the existence of the enterprise. The rationale is not the production of a particular product or service, but the fulfillment of a selected consumer need category, and thus the attention of management is redirected from precedent to potential.

The marketing concept has been one of the most plausible and useful concepts to emerge from business literature, and it has gained virtually universal acceptance in principle. In the context of the figure, the marketing concept represents an outward extension of environmental awareness and sensitivity in contrast to the more inward-looking production and sales orientations. Yet the perspective of the marketing concept remains essentially confined to the proximate environment. Preoccupied as it is with consumers and competitors, the concept is not especially attentive to the healthfulness of a firm's relationship to the various dimensions of the ultimate environment.

New Pressures on Business

It seems clear that the environmental forces which resulted in a greater focus on the marketplace will endure and intensify. Rapid technological progress, increased production efficiency, growing consumer affluence, a broader range of competitive interfaces among industries, the profit squeeze — these and similar pressures, which evoked the marketing orientation, are not likely to let up.

At the same time, the tumultuous events ushering in the last third of this century suggest that powerful new currents of change have begun to flow

---

[5] Robert L. King, "The Marketing Concept," in George Schwartz, ed., *Science in Marketing* (New York: John Wiley & Sons, 1965), pp. 70-97.

through the ultimate environment — currents that will profoundly affect the future of business in America. Consistent with the prediction of Sorokin and others, a great share of the pressures emanating from this environmental realm, ideological, moral, and social in nature, revolve around a deepening concern over the "human condition." The demand has been made for a far deeper commitment by business interests to the solution of the social problems which plague America, and for that matter, the entire world. Pressures are being brought upon business to exercise its vast power in such missions as the elimination of poverty, the cleansing of the atmosphere and waterways, and the eradication of social injustice in all its manifestations. Demands are made upon business to provide more genuine opportunities for individual development within the industrial organization. Business leaders are mandated to adopt roles of leadership in the advancement of our society to new levels of moral conduct.

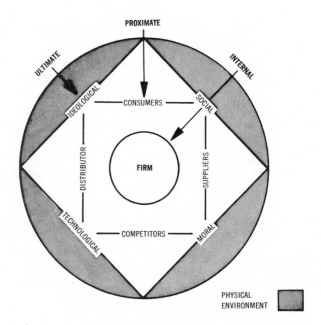

It is significant that these pressures and demands are prominently associated with the brightest and best of the nation's youth. The business image among college students has ramifications for the future which extend far beyond the special (and worsening) problem of attracting a sufficient number of college graduates to business careers. The available evidence leaves room for disagreement as to the depth and breadth of student disenchantment with business, but it does show that the criticism of business is not limited to a vocal minority of young radicals whose value orientation is out of the mainstream of American life. *Fortune's* recent report on the present college generation indicates that fully 40 percent of the nation's college students can be included in a group characterized by a notable "lack of concern for making money" and "an extraordinary rejection of traditional American values." [6] Significantly, *Fortune* refers to this group as the "forerunners," believing that as our society grows more affluent their percentage of the total college population will increase.

The Harris poll of the attitudes of the general public toward business, undertaken for *Newsweek* in 1966, covered 2,000 Americans in all age and income brackets. [7] The results led *Newsweek* to conclude that business faces a "clear and cogent mandate" to adopt a new and broader set of social goals.

The Marketing Concept Falters

In an environment that exerts upon the business enterprise a new milieu of pressures, predominantly oriented to humanistic values, the marketing concept appears unsuitable for providing the executive with a meaningful and viable sense of identity and direction. Several of its weaknesses become clear when thought is given to some new developments that are, or should be, of concern to several major industries.

1. The marketing concept stresses a *consumer* orientation. In one definition, the consumer is said to become "the absolute dead center of the universe" for the business firm. A consumer orientation directs the attention of the firm only to some fraction of the population of the society which supports it. Moreover, insofar as present or potential consumers are concerned, the consumer orientation generates concern only with the individual's role as a buyer or consumer of a particular product or service. Thus, the consumer orientation is limited in scope and one-dimensional in nature.

The tobacco industry has certainly been consumer oriented in postwar years. Playing a fine tune of market segmentation and product differentiation, the industry has adapted skillfully to changing consumer preferences as the major prewar brands have yielded to a proliferation of new shapes and styles. Industry sales and per capita cigarette consumption have gained steadily. Do we conclude that a consumer orientation is enabling this industry to adapt with perfect harmony to environmental change? Hardly. A powerful and growing array of forces are united in an effort to erase the industry altogether. These forces emanate from state and federal government, the medical profession, and concerned citizens at large. They are generated by persons whose most likely common bond is that they are *not* consumers of the product. These individuals have managed to create a steady stream of woe for the tobacco industry over the past five years.

It is irrelevant to speculate as to whether these forces will succeed (though it is worth noting that per capita cigarette consumption showed declines both in

---

[6] Daniel Seligman, "A Special Kind of Rebellion," *Fortune*, LXXIX (January, 1969), p. 67.

[7] "Speak Now . . . a Newsweek Report," *Newsweek* (1966).

1967 and 1968). The important point is that a consumer orientation can help not at all in eliminating what is unquestionably the major threat to the survival of this industry, because the threat specifically emanates from nonsmoking sectors of society. What has made the future of this industry in the coming decades a question-mark is not its failure to provide consumers with a pleasant, satisfying product, but rather the product's vulnerability to society's deepening concern over human well-being.

Small firearms are another example of this vulnerability. Obviously, manufacturers are satisfying consumers with their product array of pistols, high-powered rifles, and shotguns; in fact, few industries can count upon a similar degree of consumer loyalty and dedication. The gun lobby, spearheaded by the National Rifle Association, has successfully fought off Presidents, senators, judges, public safety officials, and the FBI in their efforts to curb the sale and possession of guns. The cultural and constitutional aspects of gun ownership in a country with a revolutionary and pioneering heritage are complicated and fraught with emotion. But surely such vestiges of the frontier spirit are being wiped out by the slaughter of political leaders and by rising crime rates. The *Wall Street Journal* recently editorialized as follows:

> It seems predictable that in an urbanized and crowded America the gun lobby will in the end, for good or ill, find itself overwhelmed — much as the equally competent doctors' lobby eventually was in its fight against Medicare. Like civil rights legislation, domestic disarmament is likely to be voted in successive and increasing doses. [8]

Should the environmental clouds swirling about this industry continue to darken, a consumer orientation would be of little help to a member firm in clearing the way to a healthy long-run ecological balance.

2. The marketing concept emphasizes research and long-range planning, but with an almost exclusive stress on technological trends and product improvement. To be sure, a consumer orientation seeks to alert management to possible long-run shifts in tastes and preferences. But neither the technological nor the consumer perspective calls attention to a much broader form of "cultural obsolescence" which may occur in a world of rapidly changing values and priorities.

However naive and futile the peace demonstrator may appear amidst the violence and tensions which mark the international scene, industries that depend heavily upon military and defense contracts might do well to ponder their long-term prospects. From the M-1 rifle to the multimegaton neutron bomb the applied science of death and destruction represents a high degree of technological perfection. Yet throughout the world the clamor for arms control and ultimate disarmament grows louder. An expenditure in the billions is proposed in this nation for a thin antiballistic missile system, and yet the experts admit that it may be be obsolete before it is completed. Nations which cannot afford to feed their people adequately pour a steady stream of their national incomes into armaments.

[8] "Domestic Disarmament," *Wall Street Journal,* July 3, 1968.

Well-founded mistrust and caution certainly make genuine disarmament a long-range prospect at best. What is important here, however, is that the marketing concept is not very effective in alerting management of a firm heavily involved in armament production to the fact that the habitability of the environment may ultimately be in question, and that, indeed, society is trying to make the environment unsuitable for the continuation of such production.

The clamor against war and violence has even spilled over into the children's toy industry. In recent years the New York City toy fair has been picketed by mothers and children protesting the manufacture and sale of war-like toys. In a recent address to European toy manufacturers, Pope Paul VI added his voice to the outcry against toys that encourage anti-social behavior. This industry may find its future influenced far more by cultural acceptance than by mere consumer preferences or technical product improvements.

In fact, all manufacturers of consumer durable goods would be well-advised to raise their long-range planning sights above the levels of technology and taste to the more fundamental changes in life styles that may accompany the maturation of the next generation of young Americans. *Fortune* raises a crucial question in commenting upon the current "youthquake" in our culture:

> In its visible and audible impact on styles and tastes, the youthquake has been mostly fun so far . . . Still, there is something a bit spooky, from a business point of view, about some implications that can be found in youth's widespread rejection of middle-class life styles ('Cheap is in'). Like so much else among the young that rejection may prove to be transient, but if it persists and becomes a dominant orientation, will these children of affluence grow up to be consumers on quite the economy-moving scale of their parents? [9]

3. Perhaps the most fundamental weakness of the marketing concept is that it satisfies selfish interest, thereby becoming incompatible with an age in which society demands a higher degree of selfless sacrifice on the part of its institutions and constituents. A marketing concept inevitably casts the industrial organization in the role of one of society's more predatory creatures, a giant corporation stealthily and eagerly stalking the marketplace, always at the ready to leap upon a new market opportunity or to devour a competitor. We can dust the cobwebs off models of pure competition and insist that the persistent search for commercial self-gain somehow, sometimes leads to ultimate good for all.

But indications mount that insofar as social and human progress is concerned, our society is becoming impatient and intolerant — unwilling to settle for the accidental by-products generated by business' self-centered pursuit of greater market opportunities and profit. Because of the market focus, the involvement of major corporations in social reform projects is more often than not met with skepticism and cynicism by the public. The young, in particular, are inclined to dismiss such activities as conniving public relations gestures, financed by otherwise-taxable profits, and all aimed ultimately toward enhancing market

[9] Sheldon Zaleznick, "The Youthquake in Pop Culture," *Fortune*, LXXIX (January, 1969), p. 134.

position. Indeed, the marketing concept certainly does imply that the justification for social pursuits by business must ultimately rest upon market considerations.

Certainly it can be argued that it is a matter of self-interest, if not selfish interest, for business to lead in the fight against the grave weaknesses which beset our society, and thus such actions are not inconsistent with a marketing concept. But semantic confusion, if nothing else, renders the marketing concept less useful in a contemporary environmental context, simply because market considerations alone, even long run, can no longer determine what is good or bad, right or wrong, prudent or imprudent, urgent or nonurgent in the business community.

The Human Concept

We have only to look at the actions of major business firms in recent years to recognize that many progressive organizations already are operating under some concept far more broad and meaningful for today's conditions than the marketing concept. These news stories have appeared during the last few years:

Detroit's Big Three automakers take on tens of thousands of hard-core unemployables in massive retraining effort.

Lockheed Space and Missile inaugurates new vocation improvement program with hiring limited to dropouts, welfare recipients, exconvicts, and others with entirely unsatisfactory work records.

Control Data opens new plants in black slums of Washington, D.C. and Minneapolis; AVCO opens new plant in Boston ghetto.

SK & F Laboratories establishes information center to advise its black neighbors in Philadelphia ghetto on wide variety of employment, housing, health, education problems; Quaker Oats has similar program in Chicago slum area.

U.S. Gypsum turns tenements into pleasant living units in pioneer private industry slum rehabilitation projects in New York, Cleveland, and Chicago ghetto areas.

Life insurance industry pledges $1 billion investment in housing and industry in massive effort to reclaim slum areas.

Such actions are hardly more understandable under a marketing concept than under the economists' anarchronism of profit maximization; therefore, the author suggests that they are manifestations of the gradual evolution of a new concept influencing the thoughts and actions of progressive business leaders. Far more responsive to human needs and values in their totality than the marketing concept, this is perhaps best described as the "human concept." An appraisal of the current range of concerns and activities of prominent business corporations indicates that a business enterprise, operating under a human concept, directs its attention, resources, and energies toward the fulfillment of human needs at three levels.

The *first* level is internal in nature, and pertains to the role of the enterprise as a developer of human resources within the organization. The benefits and security commonly provided for all levels of employees today testify to the gradual assumption by American business of a responsibility for employee welfare that transcends short-run profit goals. As indicated in the preceding examples, a number of corporations have now taken on the tremendous challenge of transforming the hard-core unemployables of our society into productive members of the work force.

This may be the beginning of an all-out commitment by private industry to a massive program of reclaiming the lost human resources of our society. But the interest of progressive management in human welfare has not been limited to the disadvantaged. All managerial levels are more interested in creating work opportunities that allow individuals to develop their full potentials and that genuinely meet the need of workers for occupational self-fulfillment. Private industry has become increasingly aware of the importance of recognition, esteem, and perceived contribution as complements to material rewards in producing a job satisfaction.

Dr. Edwin H. Land, president of Polaroid, has said that the function of industry is the development of people. When Charles H. Percy headed Bell and Howell, he stated that "our basic objective is the development of individuals." [10] The fulfillment of such objectives thrusts upon management a vastly enlarged responsibility in the design and redesign of jobs and job relationships, refinements in selection and placement techniques, and advances in the provision of necessary education and training.

The *second* level of the human concept concerns the relationship of the enterprise to its consumers, competitors, suppliers, and distributors, that is, the proximate environment. It is primarily at this level where profit, the life-blood of the enterprise, is generated. The human concept implies no lessening in the need for the business organization to remain in dynamic ecological equilibrium with its proximate environment. The consumer orientation and need fulfillment imperatives, so well expounded and thoroughly developed under the doctrine of the marketing concept, remain vital to the firm under the human concept.

The *third* level concerns the relationship of the enterprise to society in general, that is, the ultimate environment. At this level the human concept commits the firm to involvement in a "market" far more significant and vast than the markets for toothpaste, television sets, or cars. This is the market for human fulfillment.

J. Wilson Newman, chairman of Dun & Bradstreet, argues that the purpose of business has always been to answer human wants, and that the American market is now undergoing a transformation wherein the predominant wants are not material but psychological and social. [11] He foresees a total market averaging as much as $100 billion a year over the rest of the century to lift the smog, clean the rivers, rebuild the cities, unsnarl the traffic, and educate and reeducate the young and old. Marketing expert William Lazer has stated that "one of the next marketing frontiers may well be related to markets that extend beyond mere

[10] Quoted by Henry G. Pearson, A New Co-Aim for Business," *MSU Business Topics,* XVI (Spring, 1968), pp. 51-56.

[11] J. Wilson Newman, "Does Business Have a Future?" *MSU Business Topics,* XV (Autumn, 1967), pp. 16-20.

profit considerations to intrinsic values — to markets based on social concern, markets of the mind, and markets concerned with the development of people to the fullest extent of their capabilities." [12]

At the third level the human concept establishes an external social purpose for the business enterprise by linking its energies to the efforts of mankind to achieve a way of life that fulfills the human yearning not only for material comforts, but for security, dignity, and spiritual solace. Clearly the capacity of every business enterprise to contribute to this effort must be evaluated individually. By virtue of size, product category, or other unique attributes, some organizations have a far greater potential for such contributions than others. But the most important attributes undoubtedly are will and vision. A number of the corporate projects mentioned above are partially funded by public agencies. In some instances, modest profits have even been realized, though naturally less than could have been earned in alternative capital expenditures. The smaller enterprise should be able to participate too, whether on its own or in cooperation with state and local agencies and foundations.

The following is offered as a tentative attempt to summarize the meaning and scope of the human concept in definitional form:

A managerial philosophy centered upon the continuous search for and evaluation of opportunities for the mobilization, utilization, and control of total corporate effort in: (1) achieving a genuine internal social purpose in the development of organization members to their fullest potential; (2) generating the necessary profit input within the proximate environment by devising solutions to selected consumer problems; (3) achieving a genuine external social purpose within the ultimate environment by contributing to the identification and fulfillment of the real human needs of our time.

Implementation of a human concept may involve organizational role and structure change, particularly in larger organizations, at least as fundamental as those called for under a marketing concept. For instance, the sales management position may have to be redefined to accentuate responsibility for the total development of the members of the selling force, constituting an important share of the firm's human resources. Whereas this objective has traditionally been secondary to volume, or more recently profit, it is doubtful that such should be the case for an enterprise committed to a human concept. In a number of progressive firms the old-line public relations department has been supplanted, or at least supplemented, by such new departments as "community relations" and "college relations." These are surely reflections of increased awareness by business of the need for more links to the ultimate environment.

The Concept, Profits, the Future

Change in the ultimate environment is likely to assume special significance to

[12] William Lazer, "Marketing's Changing Social Relationships," *Journal of Marketing,* XXXIII (January, 1969), p. 4.

the firm's destiny in the last third of the century. A marketing concept is not adequate to help business retain healthy ecological balance with an environment characterized by an increasing shift from sensate values to human, social, and moral values. A broader human concept can provide management with a sense of direction in an era of increased concern over the human condition by committing the business organization to the service of an internal and an external social purpose concurrent with the service of profit.

It is not suggested that the human concept offers, at last, an easy solution to the classic management conundrum of profit maximization versus social responsibility. At the one extreme, the private corporation clearly cannot be expected to become a philanthropic institution so long as its survival is in large measure determined in a competitive marketplace. At the other extreme, over several generations the will of the nation has been expressed, legally and otherwise, to restrain unbridled competition for maximum profits on the part of big business. Countless efforts have been made to apply a semantic crowbar to force a convergence of the two goals. For example, if profit is defined in sufficiently long-run and indirect terms, it can justifiably be argued that slum clearance maximizes profits by forestalling destructive riots, or that purification of the atmosphere maximizes profits by preventing customers (and everyone else) from being poisoned. What emerges from such arguments is a compromise goal of "enlightened profit maximization," wherein recognition is given to some socially determined limit on what the maximum can be.

The point is, simply, that the firm concerned only with profit performance may find its lack of other internal or external social purpose to be a growing threat to its survival in an increasingly humanistic world. To borrow from the lexicon of economics, profit may become the necessary, but not sufficient, condition for the survival of the firm. There is no need to remind the business executive of the sanctions imposed within the proximate environment for profit failure. But there *is* need to point out that the ultimate environment can impose very real sanctions too for a failure in social purpose. One of the more familiar of these is restrictive legislation. But such sanctions may take other forms as well: the drying up of the wellspring of new business recruits from the colleges; turmoil for the corporate headquarters not unlike contemporary campus disorders (Dow Chemical has already suffered through some relatively minor experiences); or work-interfering demonstrations such as those recently conducted by blacks against the construction unions and steel producers in Pittsburgh.

The contribution of the human concept lies in focus and commitment; it can extend the vision of management into those areas of corporate involvement where social purpose beyond profit can be found. Every business organization, regardless of size, can find genuine social purpose in its attitudes and actions concerning employees. Most firms, in alliance with local, state, and federal agencies and institutions, can find genuine external social purpose.

The human concept is not an easy cure for the managerial schizophrenia that may result from the attempt to reconcile profit with social responsibility. The human concept can no more supply the kind of executive judgment, sensitivity, creativity, and courage required for its successful implementation than could the marketing concept. It is for this very reason that business has an answer to the bright young people who turn away from a business career because they believe it offers no challenge and serves no lasting purpose. Challenge of the highest order is implicit in the human concept, and so is purpose of the utmost significance to human progress.

In considering the real value of the human concept as a basic corporate philosophy, one is reminded of the classic anecdote of the two bricklayers at a construction site. Each was asked what he was doing. The first replied, "I am laying bricks." The second answered, "I am building a cathedral." Business can answer its critics, revitalize its ranks, and provide itself with an unlimited future through acceptance of the spirit of the human concept. Such acceptance could be one of history's momentous turning points.

II   THE CONSUMER

Successful implementation of the marketing concept requires an understanding of consumer behavior. Marketing investigators have long recognized that understanding consumer behavior requires a knowledge of *human behavior* and have been ardent students of the behavioral sciences in the search for insights into the mental processes involved in consumer decision making.

Consumer behavior is determined through an interaction of such *individual* predispositions as needs, attitudes, perceptions, and personality and also by the influence of *others*. The environmental influences include cultural factors, reference groups, social class, and family influences. The decision to purchase certain brands or product classes or to patronize a particular store results from the interaction of these individual and group influences.

In the first selection Kotler develops five models of buyer behavior from the theories of Marshall, Pavlov, Freud, Veblen, and Hobbes and applies each to marketing.

Businessmen attempt to satisfy our change-oriented society through a steady stream of new products. The vast majority of new products fail, resulting in company losses and a total cost to society through the misallocation of resources. Research in anthropology and sociology has pointed to the existence of individuals who are first-adopters of new products and services and who could possibly supply advanced information regarding the likelihood of product success or failure. In the second selection Louis E. Boone reviews the research conducted by marketing's sister disciplines in identifying first-adopters and reports the results of marketing research studies designed to identify the consumer innovator.

Kim Rotzoll analyzes "The Effect of Social Stratification on Market Behavior" in the third selection. He discusses the concept of social class and examines its role in influencing consumption patterns.

The low-income consumer has been the subject of concentrated research in recent years in an attempt to maximize the purchasing power of his limited income. In the final selection in Part II, Boone and Bonno describe characteristics of the ghetto food shopper and argue that his behavior, like other individual market segments, is logical in terms of his specific need structure (even though society may lament the result).

*What happens in the buyer's mind between
the acts of receiving impressions about
products and making his purchasing
decisions? Several theories exist, but there is
no generally accepted comprehensive theory.
Here the author contrasts buyer behavioral
models based on five major theories, and
shows how each has unique marketing
applications.*

Behavioral Models for Analyzing Buyers

Philip Kotler

In times past, management could arrive at a fair understanding of its buyers through the daily experience of selling to them. But the growth in the size of firms and markets has removed many decision-makers from direct contact with buyers. Increasingly, decision-makers have had to turn to summary statistics and to behavioral theory, and are spending more money today than ever before to try to understand their buyers.

Who buys? How do they buy? And why? The first two questions relate to relatively overt aspects of buyer behavior, and can be learned about through direct observation and interviewing.

But uncovering *why* people buy is an extremely difficult task. The answer will tend to vary with the investigator's behavioral frame of reference.

The buyer is subject to many influences which trace a complex course through his psyche and lead eventually to overt purchasing responses. This conception of the buying process is illustrated in Figure 1. Various influences and their modes of transmission are shown at the left. At the right are the buyer's responses in choice of product, brand, dealer, quantities, and frequency. In the center stands the buyer and his mysterious psychological processes. The

Reprinted by permission of the author and the publisher from the *Journal of Marketing,* published by the American Marketing Association, Vol. 29, No. 4 (October, 1965), pp. 37-45.

buyer's psyche is a "black box" whose workings can be only partially deduced. The marketing strategist's challenge to the behavioral scientist is to construct a more specific model of the mechanism in the black box.

Unfortunately no generally accepted model of the mechanism exists. The human mind, the only entity in nature with deep powers of understanding, still remains the least understood. Scientists can explain planetary motion, genetic determination, and molecular behavior. Yet they have only partial, and often partisan, models of *human* behavior.

Nevertheless, the marketing strategist should recognize the potential interpretative contributions of different partial models for explaining buyer behavior. Depending upon the product, different variables and behavioral mechanisms may assume particular importance. A psychoanalytic behavioral model might throw much light on the factors operating in cigarette demand, while an economic behavioral model might be useful in explaining machine-tool purchasing. Sometimes alternative models may shed light on different demand aspects of the same product.

What are the most useful behavioral models for interpreting the transformation of buying influences into purchasing responses? Five different models of the buyer's "black box" are presented in the present article, along with their respective marketing applications: (1) the Marshallian model, stressing economic motivations; (2) the Pavlovian model, learning; (3) the Freudian model, psychoanalytic motivations; (4) the Veblenian model, social-psychological factors; and (5) the Hobbesian model, organizational factors. These models represent radically different conceptions of the mainsprings of human behavior.

The Marshallian Economic Model

Economists were the first professional group to construct a specific theory of buyer behavior. The theory holds that purchasing decisions are the result of largely "rational" and conscious economic calculations. The individual buyer seeks to spend his income on those goods that will deliver the most utility (satisfaction) according to his tastes and relative prices.

The antecedents for this view trace back to the writings of Adam Smith and Jeremy Bentham. Smith set the tone by developing a doctrine of economic growth based on the principle that man is motivated by self-interest in all his actions.[1] Bentham refined this view and saw man as finely calculating and weighing the expected pleasures and pains of every contemplated action.[2]

Bentham's "felicific calculus" was not applied to consumer behavior (as opposed to entrepreneurial behavior) until the late 19th century. Then, the "marginal-utility" theory of value was formulated independently and almost

[1] Adam Smith, *An Inquiry into the Nature and Causes of the Wealth of Nations*, 1776 (New York: The Modern Library, 1937).

[2] Jeremy Bentham, *An Introduction to the Principles of Morals and Legislation*, 1780 (Oxford, England: Clarendon Press, 1907).

simultaneously by Jevons[3] and Marshall[4] in England, Menger[5] in Austria, and Walras[6] in Switzerland.

Alfred Marshall was the great consolidator of the classical and neoclassical tradition in economics; and his synthesis in the form of demand-supply analysis constitutes the main source of modern micro-economic thought in the English-speaking world. His theoretical work aimed at realism, but his method was to start with simplifying assumptions and to examine the effect of a change in a single variable (say, price) when all other variables were held constant.

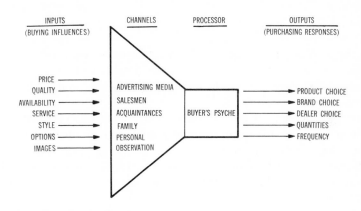

Figure 1   The buying process conceived as a system of inputs and outputs

He would "reason out" the consequences of the provisional assumptions and in subsequent steps modify his assumptions in the direction of more realism. He employed the "measuring rod of money" as an indicator of the intensity of human psychological desires. Over the years his methods and assumptions have been refined into what is now known as *modern utility theory*: economic man is bent on maximizing his utility, and does this by carefully calculating the "felicific" consequences of any purchase.

As an example, suppose on a particular evening that John is considering whether to prepare his own dinner or dine out. He estimates that a restaurant meal would cost $2.00 and a home-cooked meal 50 cents. According to the Marshallian model, if John expects less than four times as much satisfaction from the restaurant meal as the home-cooked meal, he will eat at home. The economist typically is not concerned with how these relative preferences are formed by John, or how they may be psychologically modified by new stimuli.

[3] William S. Jevons, *The Theory of Political Economy* (New York: The Macmillan Company, 1871).

[4] Alfred Marshall, *Principles of Economics,* 1890 (London: The Macmillan Company, 1927).

[5] Karl Menger, *Principles of Economics,* 1871 (Glencoe, Illinois: Free Press, 1950).

[6] Leon Walras, *Elements of Pure Economics,* 1874 (Homewood, Illinois: Richard D. Irwin, Inc., 1954).

Yet John will not always cook at home. The principle of diminishing marginal utility operates. Within a given time interval — say, a week — the utility of each additional home-cooked meal diminishes. John gets tired of home meals and other products become relatively more attractive.

John's *efficiency* in maximizing his utility depends on the adequacy of his information and his freedom of choice. If he is not perfectly aware of costs, if he misestimates the relative delectability of the two meals, or if he is barred from entering the restaurant, he will not maximize his potential utility. His choice processes are rational, but the results are inefficient.

Marketing Applications of Marshallian Model

Marketers usually have dismissed the Marshallian model as an absurd figment of ivory-tower imagination. Certainly the behavioral essence of the situation is omitted, in viewing man as calculating the marginal utility of a restaurant meal over a home-cooked meal.

Eva Mueller has reported a study where only one-fourth of the consumers in her sample bought with any substantial degree of deliberation.[7] Yet there are a number of ways to view the model.

From one point of view the Marshallian model is tautological and therefore neither true nor false. The model holds that the buyer acts in the light of his best "interest." But this is not very informative.

A second view is that this is a *normative* rather than a *descriptive* model of behavior. The model provides logical norms for buyers who want to be "rational." Although the consumer is not likely to employ economic analysis to decide between a box of Kleenex and Scotties, he may apply economic analysis in deciding whether to buy a new car. Industrial buyers even more clearly would want an economic calculus for making good decisions.

A third view is that economic factors operate to a greater or lesser extent in all markets, and, therefore, must be included in any comprehensive description of buyer behavior.

Furthermore, the model suggests useful behavioral hypotheses such as: (a) The lower the price of the product, the higher the sales. (b) The lower the price of substitute products, the lower the sales of this product; and the lower the price of complementary products, the higher the sales of this product. (c) The higher the real income, the higher the sales of this product, provided that it is not an "inferior" good. (d) The higher the promotional expenditures, the higher the sales.

The validity of these hypotheses does not rest on whether *all* individuals act as economic calculating machines in making their purchasing decisions. For example, some individuals may buy *less* of a product when its price is reduced. They may think that the quality has gone down, or that ownership has less

---

[7] Eva Mueller, "A Study of Purchase Decisions," Part 2, *Consumer Behavior, The Dynamics of Consumer Reaction,* edited by Lincoln H. Clark (New York: New York University Press, 1954), pp. 36-87.

status value. If a majority of buyers view price reductions negatively, then sales may fall, contrary to the first hypothesis.

But for most goods a price reduction increases the relative value of the goods in many buyers' minds and leads to increased sales. This and the other hypotheses are intended to describe average effects.

The impact of economic factors in actual buying situations is studied through experimental design or statistical analyses of past data. Demand equations have been fitted to a wide variety of products — including beer, refrigerators, and chemical fertilizers. [8] More recently, the impact of economic variables on the fortunes of different brands has been pursued with significant results, particularly in the case of coffee, frozen orange juice, and margarine. [9]

But economic factors alone cannot explain all the variations in sales. The Marshallian model ignores the fundamental question of how product and brand preferences are formed. It represents a useful frame of reference for analyzing only one small corner of the "black box."

The Pavlovian Learning Model

The designation of a Pavlovian learning model has its origin in the experiments of the Russian psychologist Pavlov, who rang a bell each time before feeding a dog. Soon he was able to induce the dog to salivate by ringing the bell whether or not food was supplied. Pavlov concluded that learning was largely an associative process and that a large component of behavior was conditioned in this way.

Experimental psychologists have continued this mode of research with rats and other animals, including people. Laboratory experiments have been designed to explore such phenomena as learning, forgetting, and the ability to discriminate. The results have been integrated into a stimulus-response model of human behavior, or as someone has "wisecracked," the substitution of a rat psychology for a rational psychology.

The model has been refined over the years, and today is based on four central concepts — those of *drive, cue, response,* and *reinforcement.* [10]

Drive. Also called needs or motives, drive refers to strong stimuli internal to the individual which impels action. Psychologists draw a distinction between primary physiological drives — such as hunger, thirst, cold, pain, and sex — and learned drives which are derived socially — such as cooperation, fear, and acquisitiveness.

Cue. A drive is very general and impels a particular response only in relation

[8] See Erwin Nemmers, *Managerial Economics* (New York: John Wiley & Sons, Inc., 1962), Part II.

[9] See Lester G. Telser, "The Demand for Branded Goods as Estimated from Consumer Panel Data," *Review of Economics and Statistics,* Vol. 44 (August, 1962), pp. 300-324; and William F. Massy and Ronald E. Frank, "Short Term Price and Dealing Effects in Selected Market Segments," *Journal of Marketing Research,* Vol. 2 (May, 1965), pp. 171-185.

[10] See John Dollard and Neal E. Miller, *Personality and Psychotherapy* (New York: McGraw-Hill Book Company, Inc., 1950), Chapter III.

to a particular configuration of cues. Cues are weaker stimuli in the environment and/or in the individual which determine when, where, and how the subject responds. Thus, a coffee advertisement can serve as a cue which stimulates the thirst drive in a housewife. Her response will depend upon this cue and other cues, such as the time of day, the availability of other thirst-quenchers, and the cue's intensity. Often a relative change in a cue's intensity can be more impelling than its absolute level. The housewife may be more motivated by a 2-cents-off sale on a brand of coffee than the fact that this brand's price was low in the first place.

Response. The response is the organism's reaction to the configuration of cues. Yet the same configuration of cues will not necessarily produce the same response in the individual. This depends on the degree to which the experience was rewarding, that is, drive-reducing.

Reinforcement. If the experience is rewarding, a particular response is reinforced; that is, it is strengthened and there is a tendency for it to be repeated when the same configuration of cues appears again. The housewife, for example, will tend to purchase the same brand of coffee each time she goes to her supermarket so long as it is rewarding and the cue configuration does not change. But if a learned response or habit is not reinforced, the strength of the habit diminishes and may be extinguished eventually. Thus, a housewife's preference for a certain coffee may become extinct if she finds the brand out of stock for a number of weeks.

Forgetting, in contrast to extinction, is the tendency for learned associations to weaken, not because of the lack of reinforcement but because of nonuse.

Cue configurations are constantly changing. The housewife sees a new brand of coffee next to her habitual brand, or notes a special price deal on a rival brand. Experimental psychologists have found that the same learned response will be elicited by similar patterns of cues; that is, learned responses are *generalized.* The housewife shifts to a similar brand when her favorite brand is out of stock. This tendency toward generalization over less similar cue configurations is increased in proportion to the strength of the drive. A housewife may buy an inferior coffee if it is the only brand left and if her drive is sufficiently strong.

A counter-tendency to generalization is *discrimination.* When a housewife tries two similar brands and finds one more rewarding, her ability to discriminate between similar cue configurations improves. Discrimination increases the specificity of the cue-response connection, while generalization decreases the specificity.

Marketing Applications of Pavlovian Model

The modern version of the Pavlovian model makes no claim to provide a complete theory of behavior — indeed, such important phenomena as perception, the subconscious, and interpersonal influence are inadequately treated. Yet the model does offer a substantial number of insights about some aspects of behavior of considerable interest to marketers. [11]

An example would be in the problem of introducing a new brand into a highly competitive market. The company's goal is to extinguish existing brand habits and form new habits among consumers for its brand. But the company must first get customers to try its brand; and it has to decide between using weak and strong cues.

Light introductory advertising is a weak cue compared with distributing free samples. Strong cues, although costing more, may be necessary in markets characterized by strong brand loyalties. For example, Folger went into the coffee market by distributing over a million pounds of free coffee.

To build a brand habit, it helps to provide for an extended period of introductory dealing. Furthermore, sufficient quality must be built into the brand so that the experience is reinforcing. Since buyers are more likely to transfer allegiance to similar brands than dissimilar brands (generalization), the company should also investigate what cues in the leading brands have been most effective. Although outright imitation would not necessarily effect the most transference, the question of providing enough similarity should be considered.

The Pavlovian model also provides guide lines in the area of advertising strategy. The American behaviorist, John B. Watson, was a great exponent of repetitive stimuli; in his writings man is viewed as a creature who can be conditioned through repetition and reinforcement to respond in particular ways. [12] The Pavlovian model emphasizes the desirability of repetition in advertising. A single exposure is likely to be a very weak cue, hardly able to penetrate the individual's consciousness sufficiently to excite his drives above the threshold level.

Repetition in advertising has two desirable effects. It "fights" forgetting, the tendency for learned responses to weaken in the absence of practice. It provides reinforcement, because after the purchase the consumer becomes selectively exposed to advertisements of the product.

The model also provides guide lines for copy strategy. To be effective as a cue, an advertisement must arouse strong drives in the person. The strongest product-related drives must be identified. For candy bars, it may be hunger; for safety belts, fear; for hair tonics, sex; for automobiles, status. The advertising practitioner must dip into his cue box — words, colors, pictures — and select that configuration of cues that provides the strongest stimulus to these drives.

The Freudian Psychoanalytic Model

The Freudian model of man is well known, so profound has been its impact

---

[11] The most consistent application of learning-theory concepts to marketing situations is found in John A. Howard, *Marketing Management: Analysis and Planning* (Homewood, Illinois: Richard D. Irwin, Inc., revised edition, 1963).

[12] John B. Watson, *Behaviorism (New York: The People's Institute Publishing Company, 1925)*.

on 20th century thought. It is the latest of a series of philosophical "blows" to which man has been exposed in the last 500 years. Copernicus destroyed the idea that man stood at the center of the universe; Darwin tried to refute the idea that man was a special creation; and Freud attacked the idea that man even reigned over his own psyche.

According to Freud, the child enters the world driven by instinctual needs which he cannot gratify by himself. Very quickly and painfully he realizes his separateness from the rest of the world and yet his dependence on it.

He tries to get others to gratify his needs through a variety of blatant means, including intimidation and supplication. Continual frustration leads him to perfect more subtle mechanisms for gratifying his instincts.

As he grows, his psyche becomes increasingly complex. A part of his psyche — the id — remains the reservoir of his strong drives and urges. Another part — the ego — becomes his conscious planning center for finding outlets for his drives. And a third part — his super-ego — channels his instinctive drives into socially approved outlets to avoid the pain of guilt or shame.

The guilt or shame which man feels toward some of his urges — especially his sexual urges — causes him to repress them from his consciousness. Through such defense mechanisms as rationalization and sublimation, these urges are denied or become transmuted into socially approved expressions. Yet these urges are never eliminated or under perfect control; and they emerge, sometimes with a vengeance, in dreams, in slips-of-the-tongue, in neurotic and obsessional behavior, or ultimately in mental breakdown where the ego can no longer maintain the delicate balance between the impulsive power of the id and the oppressive power of the super-ego.

The individual's behavior, therefore, is never simple. His motivational wellsprings are not obvious to a casual observer nor deeply understood by the individual himself. If he is asked why he purchased an expensive foreign sports-car, he may reply that he likes its maneuverability and its looks. At a deeper level he may have purchased the car to impress others, or to feel young again. At a still deeper level, he may be purchasing the sports-car to achieve substitute gratification for unsatisfied sexual strivings.

Many refinements and changes in emphasis have occurred in this model since the time of Freud. The instinct concept has been replaced by a more careful delineation of basic drives; the three parts of the psyche are regarded now as theoretical concepts rather than actual entities; and the behavioral perspective has been extended to include cultural as well as biological mechanisms.

Instead of the role of the sexual urge in psychic development — Freud's discussion of oral, anal, and genital stages and possible fixations and traumas — Adler [13] emphasized the urge for power and how its thwarting manifests itself in superiority and inferiority complexes; Horney [14] emphasized cultural mechanisms; and Fromm [15] and Erickson [16] emphasized the role of existential

[13] Alfred Adler, *The Science of Living* (New York: Greenberg, 1929).

[14] Karen Horney, *The Neurotic Personality of Our Time* (New York: W. W. Norton & Co., 1937).

[15] Erich Fromm, *Man For Himself* (New York: Holt, Rinehart & Winston, Inc., 1947).

[16] Erik Erikson, *Childhood and Society* (New York: W. W. Norton & Co., 1949).

crises in personality development. These philosophical divergencies, rather than debilitating the model, have enriched and extended its interpretative value to a wider range of behavioral phenomena.

Marketing Applications of Freudian Model

Perhaps the most important marketing implication of this model is that buyers are motivated by *symbolic* as well as *economic-functional* product concerns. The change of a bar of soap from a square to a round shape may be more important in its sexual than its functional connotations. A cake mix that is advertised as involving practically no labor may alienate housewives because the easy life may evoke a sense of guilt.

Motivational research has produced some interesting and occasionally some bizarre hypotheses about what may be in the buyer's mind regarding certain purchases. Thus, it has been suggested at one time or another that

- Many a businessman doesn't fly because of a fear of posthumous guilt — if he crashed, his wife would think of him as stupid for not taking a train.
- Men want their cigars to be odoriferous, in order to prove that they (the men) are masculine.
- A woman is very serious when she bakes a cake because unconsciously she is going through the symbolic act of giving birth.
- A man buys a convertible as a substitute "mistress."
- Consumers prefer vegetable shortening because animal fats stimulate a sense of sin.
- Men who wear suspenders are reacting to an unresolved castration complex.

There are admitted difficulties of proving these assertions. Two prominent motivational researchers, Ernest Dichter and James Vicary, were employed independently by two separate groups in the prune industry to determine why so many people dislike prunes. Dichter found, among other things, that the prune aroused feelings of old age and insecurity in people, whereas Vicary's main finding was that Americans had an emotional block about prunes' laxative qualities. [17] Which is the more valid interpretation? Or if they are both operative, which motive is found with greater statistical frequency in the population?

Unfortunately the usual survey techniques — direct observation and interviewing — can be used to establish the representativeness of more superficial characteristics — age and family size, for example — but are not feasible for establishing the frequency of mental states which are presumed to be deeply "buried" within each individual.

Motivational researchers have to employ time-consuming projective techniques in the hope of throwing individual "egos" off guard. When carefully administered and interpreted, techniques such as word association, sentence completion, picture interpretation, and role-playing can provide some insights

[17] L. Edward Scriven, "Rationality and Irrationality in Motivation Research," in Robert Ferber and Hugh G. Wales, editors, *Motivation and Marketing Behavior* (Homewood, Illinois: Richard D. Irwin, Inc., 1958), pp. 69-70.

into the minds of the small group of examined individuals; but a "leap of faith" is sometimes necessary to generalize these findings to the population.

Nevertheless, motivation research can lead to useful insights and provide inspiration to creative men in the advertising and packaging world. Appeals aimed at the buyer's private world of hopes, dreams, and fears can often be as effective in stimulating purchase as more rationally-directed appeals.

The Veblenian Social-Psychological Model

While most economists have been content to interpret buyer behavior in Marshallian terms, Thorstein Veblen struck out in different directions.

Veblen was trained as an orthodox economist, but evolved into a social thinker greatly influenced by the new science of social anthropology. He saw man as primarily a *social animal* — conforming to the general forms and norms of his larger culture and to the more specific standards of the subcultures and face-to-face groupings to which his life is bound. His wants and behavior are largely molded by his present group-memberships and his aspired group-memberships.

Veblen's best-known example of this is in his description of the leisure class. [18] His hypothesis is that much of economic consumption is motivated not by intrinsic needs or satisfaction so much as by prestige-seeking. He emphasized the strong emulative factors operating in the choice of conspicuous goods like clothes, cars, and houses.

Some of his points, however, seem overstated by today's perspective. The leisure class does not serve as everyone's reference group; many persons aspire to the social patterns of the class immediately above it. And important segments of the affluent class practice conspicuous underconsumption rather than overconsumption. There are many people in all classes who are more anxious to "fit in" than to "stand out." As an example, William H. Whyte found that many families avoided buying air conditioners and other appliances before their neighbors did.

Veblen was not the first nor the only investigator to comment on social influences in behavior; but the incisive quality of his observations did much to stimulate further investigations. Another stimulus came from Karl Marx, who held that each man's world-view was determined largely by his relationship to the "means of production." The early field-work in primitive societies by social anthropologists like Boas and Malinowski and the later field-work in urban societies by men like Park and Thomas contributed much to understanding the influence of society and culture. The research of early Gestalt psychologists — men like Wertheimer, Kohler, and Koffka — into the mechanisms of perception led eventually to investigations of small-group influence of perception.

[18] Thorstein Veblen, *The Theory of the Leisure Class* (New York: The Macmillan Company, 1899).

Marketing Applications of Veblenian Model

The various streams of thought crystallized into the modern social sciences of sociology, cultural anthropology, and social psychology. Basic to them is the view that man's attitudes and behavior are influenced by several levels of society — culture, subcultures, social classes, reference groups, and face-to-face groups. The challenge to the marketer is to determine which of these social levels are the most important in influencing the demand for his product.

Culture

The most enduring influences are from culture. Man tends to assimilate his culture's mores and folkways, and to believe in their absolute rightness until deviants appear within his culture or until he confronts members of another culture.

Subcultures

A culture tends to lose its homogeneity as its population increases. When people no longer are able to maintain face-to-face relationships with more than a small proportion of other members of a culture, smaller units or subcultures develop, which help to satisfy the individual's needs for more specific identity.

The subcultures are often regional entities, because the people of a region, as a result of more frequent interactions, tend to think and act alike. But subcultures also take the form of religions, nationalities, fraternal orders, and other institutional complexes which provide a broad identification for people who may otherwise be strangers. The subcultures of a person play a large role in his attitude formation and become another important predictor of certain values he is likely to hold.

Social Class

People become differentiated not only horizontally but also vertically through a division of labor. The society becomes stratified socially on the basis of wealth, skill, and power. Sometimes castes develop in which the members are reared for certain roles, or social classes develop in which the members feel empathy with others sharing similar values and economic circumstances.

Because social class involves different attitudinal configurations, it becomes a useful independent variable for segmenting markets and predicting reactions. Significant differences have been found among different social classes with respect to magazine readership, leisure activities, food imagery, fashion interests, and acceptance of innovations. A sampling of attitudinal differences in class is the following:

Members of the *upper-middle* class place an emphasis on professional competence; indulge in expensive status symbols; and more often than not show a taste, real or otherwise, for theater and the arts. They want their children to show high achievement and precocity and develop into physicists, vice-presidents, and judges. This class likes to deal in ideas and symbols.

Members of the *lower-middle* class cherish respectability, savings, a college education, and good housekeeping. They want their children to show self-control and prepare for careers as accountants, lawyers, and engineers.

Members of the *upper-lower* class try to keep up with the times, if not with the Joneses. They stay in older neighborhoods but buy new kitchen appliances. They spend proportionately less than the middle class on major clothing articles, buying a new suit mainly for an important ceremonial occasion. They also spend proportionately less on services, preferring to do their own plumbing and other work around the house. They tend to raise large families and their children generally enter manual occupations. This class also supplies many local businessmen, politicians, sports stars, and labor-union leaders.

Reference Groups

There are groups in which the individual has no membership but with which he identifies and may aspire to — reference groups. Many young boys identify with big-league baseball players or astronauts, and many young girls identify with Hollywood stars. The activities of these popular heroes are carefully watched and frequently imitated. These reference figures become important transmitters of influence, although more along lines of taste and hobby than basic attitudes.

Face-to-Face Groups

Groups that have the most immediate influence on a person's tastes and opinions are face-to-face groups. This includes all the small "societies" with which he comes into frequent contact: his family, close friends, neighbors, fellow workers, fraternal associates, and so forth. His informal group memberships are influenced largely by his occupation, residence, and stage in the life cycle.

The powerful influence of small groups on individual attitudes has been demonstrated in a number of social psychological experiments.[19] There is also evidence that this influence may be growing. David Riesman and his coauthors have pointed to signs which indicate a growing amount of *other-direction*, that is, a tendency for individuals to be increasingly influenced by their peers in the definition of their values rather than by their parents and elders.[20]

For the marketer, this means that brand choice may increasingly be influenced by one's peers. For such products as cigarettes and automobiles, the influence of peers is unmistakable.

The role of face-to-face groups has been recognized in recent industry campaigns attempting to change basic product attitudes. For years the milk

[19] See, for example, Solomon E. Asch, "Effects of Group Pressure Upon the Modification & Distortion of Judgments," in Dorwin Cartwright and Alvin Zander, *Group Dynamics* (Evanston, Illinois: Row, Peterson & Co., 1953), pp. 151-162; and Kurt Lewin, "Group Decision and Social Change," in Theodore M. Newcomb and Eugene L. Hartley, editors, *Readings in Social Psychology* (New York: Henry Holt Co., 1952).

[20] David Riesman, Reuel Denney, and Nathan Glazer, *The Lonely Crowd* (New Haven, Connecticut: Yale University Press, 1950).

industry has been trying to overcome the image of milk as a "sissified" drink by portraying its use in social and active situations. The men's-wear industry is trying to increase male interest in clothes by advertisements indicating that business associates judge a man by how well he dresses.

Of all face-to-face groups, the person's family undoubtedly plays the largest and most enduring role in basic attitude formation. From them he acquires a mental set not only toward religion and politics, but also toward thrift, chastity, food, human relations, and so forth. Although he often rebels against parental values in his teens, he often accepts these values eventually. Their formative influence on his eventual attitudes is undeniably great.

Family members differ in the types of product messages they carry to other family members. Most of what parents know about cereals, candy, and toys comes from their children. The wife stimulates family consideration of household appliances, furniture, and vacations. The husband tends to stimulate the fewest purchase ideas, with the exception of the automobile and perhaps the home.

The marketer must be alert to what attitudinal configurations dominate in different types of families, and also to how these change over time. For example, the parent's conception of the child's rights and privileges has undergone a radical shift in the last 30 years. The child has become the center of attention and orientation in a great number of households, leading some writers to label the modern family a "filiarchy." This has important implications not only for how to market to today's family, but also on how to market to tomorrow's family when the indulged child of today becomes the parent.

The Person

Social influences determine much but not all of the behavioral variations in people. Two individuals subject to the same influences are, not likely to have identical attitudes, although these attitudes will probably converge at more points than those of two strangers selected at random. Attitudes are really the product of social forces interacting with the individual's unique temperament and abilities.

Furthermore, attitudes do not automatically guarantee certain types of behavior. Attitudes are predispositions felt by buyers before they enter the buying process. The buying process itself is a learning experience and can lead to a change in attitudes.

Alfred Politz noted at one time that women stated a clear preference for G.E. refrigerators over Frigidaire, but that Frigidaire continued to outsell G.E.[21] The answer to this paradox was that preference was only one factor entering into behavior. When the consumer preferring G.E. actually undertook to purchase a new refrigerator, her curiosity led her to examine the other brands. Her perception was sensitized to refrigerator advertisements, sales arguments, and different product features. This led to learning and a change in attitudes.

[21] Alfred Politz, "Motivation Research – Opportunity or Dilemma?", in Ferber and Wales, same reference as footnote 17, at pp. 57-58.

The Hobbesian Organizational-Factors Model

The foregoing models throw light mainly on the behavior of family buyers.

But what of the large number of people who are organizational buyers? They are engaged in the purchase of goods not for the sake of consumption, but for further production or distribution. Their common denominator is the fact that they (1) are paid to make purchases for others and (2) operate within an organizational environment.

How do organizational buyers make their decisions? There seem to be two competing views. Many marketing writers have emphasized the predominance of rational motives in organizational buying.[22] Organizational buyers are represented as being most impressed by cost, quality, dependability, and service factors. They are portrayed as dedicated servants of the organization, seeking to secure the best terms. This view has led to an emphasis on performance and use characteristics in much industrial advertising.

Other writers have emphasized personal motives in organizational buyer behavior. The purchasing agent's interest to do the best for his company is tempered by his interest to do the best for himself. He may be tempted to choose among salesmen according to the extent they entertain or offer gifts. He may choose a particular vendor because this will ingratiate him with certain company officers. He may shortcut his study of alternative supplies to make his work day easier.

In truth, the buyer is guided by both personal and group goals; and this is the essential point. The political model of Thomas Hobbes comes closest of any model to suggesting the relationship between the two goals.[23] Hobbes held that man is "instinctively" oriented toward preserving and enhancing his own well-being. But this would produce a "war of every man against every man." This fear leads men to unite with others in a corporate body. The corporate man tries to steer a careful course between satisfying his own needs and those of the organization.

Marketing Applications of Hobbesian Model

The import of the Hobbesian Model is that organizational buyers can be appealed to on both personal and organizational grounds. The buyer has his private aims, and yet he tries to do a satisfactory job for his corporation. He will respond to persuasive salesmen and he will respond to rational product arguments. However, the best "mix" of the two is not a fixed quantity; it varies with the nature of the product, the type of organization, and the relative strength of the two drives in the particular buyer.

Where there is substantial similarity in what suppliers offer in the way of products, price, and service, the purchasing agent has less basis for rational

[22] See Melvin T. Copeland, *Principles of Merchandising* (New York: McGraw-Hill Book Co., Inc., 1924).

[23] Thomas Hobbes, *Leviathan,* 1651 (London: G. Routledge and Sons, 1887).

choice. Since he can satisfy his organizational obligations with any one of a number of suppliers, he can be swayed by personal motives. On the other hand, where there are pronounced differences among the competing vendors' products, the purchasing agent is held more accountable for his choice and probably pays more attention to rational factors. Short-run personal gain becomes less motivating than the long-run gain which comes from serving the organization with distinction.

The marketing strategist must appreciate these goal conflicts of the organizational buyer. Behind all the ferment of purchasing agents to develop standards and employ value analysis lies their desire to avoid being thought of as order-clerks, and to develop better skills in reconciling personal and organizational objectives.[24]

Summary

Think back over the five different behavioral models of how the buyer translates buying influences into purchasing responses.

Marshallian man is concerned chiefly with economic cues — prices and income — and makes a fresh utility calculation before each purchase.

Pavlovian man behaves in a largely habitual rather than thoughtful way; certain configurations of cues will set off the same behavior because of rewarded learning in the past.

Freudian man's choices are influenced strongly by motives and fantasies which take place deep within his private world.

Veblenian man acts in a way which is shaped largely by past and present social groups.

And finally, Hobbesian man seeks to reconcile individual gain with organizational gain.

Thus, it turns out that the "black box" of the buyer is not so black after all. Light is thrown in various corners by these models. Yet no one has succeeded in putting all these pieces of truth together into one coherent instrument for behavioral analysis. This, of course, is the goal of behavioral science.

---

[24] For an insightful account, see George Strauss "Tactics of Lateral Relationship: The Purchasing Agent," *Administrative Science Quarterly*, Vol. 7 (September, 1962), pp. 161-186.

The author summarizes diffusion research conducted by anthropologists, sociologists, rural sociologists, and marketing investigators and reports the results of a study designed to isolate socioeconomic characteristics and personality traits of the first-adopters of a new consumer service.

The Search for the Consumer Innovator

Louis E. Boone

The acceptance of newness by the members of a particular society or culture is a subject of major interest to anthropologists, sociologists, and businessmen. How are new ideas, practices, and products diffused from one individual or group to another? Are there some groups or individuals who are more receptive to newness than others?

Successful innovation is the key to business success. Yet new-product failure rates are estimated as high as 95 percent.[1] New-product introductions appear to be not only the most important undertaking in marketing but also the most difficult.

Within the past ten years businessmen have discovered that for a number of years the related disciplines of anthropology and sociology have been conducting significant research relating to the diffusion of innovations. Their findings appear to be applicable to the marketing problems involved in introducing new products.

Reprinted by permission of the author and the publisher from *The Journal of Business*, Vol. 43, No. 2 (April 1970), pp. 135-140.

[1] S. J. Shaw, "Behavioral Science Offers Fresh Insights of New Product Acceptance," *Journal of Marketing* (January 1965), p. 9.

Related Research

Anthropological Studies

Since the nineteenth century anthropologists have been studying the spread of ideas and practices among widely separated cultures. Although some anthropologists have discussed the speed of diffusion,[2] they have generally been more interested in the spreading of ideas and practices between societies than within a particular society. An important exception is H. G. Barnett, who has theorized that certain members of a society are predisposed to accept new ideas or practices and that these individuals possess identifiable biographical (socioeconomic) characteristics.[3]

Sociology

Sociologists have been writing on the subject of diffusion for over sixty years. Tarde was the first to point out that the process of diffusion takes the shape of the normal curve.[4] A few innovators adopt the practice first; then the majority of the community follow the lead of the innovators and adopt; finally, the remaining members accept the innovation. Tarde was also the first to note the presence of cosmopolitism (intersocietal orientation) in the innovators.

The classic drug study[5] isolated a number of characteristics of the physician-innovator: younger age, larger number of medical journal subscriptions, greater attachment to medical institutions outside the community. It was also discovered that doctors who were mentioned by a number of other physicians as sources of advice and information used the new drug earlier than those doctors mentioned by few or none of their colleagues, indicating a definite relationship between opinion leadership and innovativeness.

Rural Sociology

The largest number of diffusion studies has been conducted by the rural sociologists. Their research studies, frequently financed by funds from the U.S. Department of Agriculture, number over 1,000.[6] Studies such as the investigation of the diffusion of hybrid seed corn[7] have isolated the following characteristics of the farmer innovator: (1) higher income, (2) larger farm, (3) higher educational levels, (4) younger age, (5) community prestige, (6) frequent trips to the nearest metropolitan center (cosmopolitism), and (7) use of farm information sources.

[2] C. Wissler, *Man and Culture* (New York: Thomas Crowell Co., 1923), pp. 115-16.

[3] H. G. Barnett, *Innovation: The Basis of Cultural Change* (New York: McGraw-Hill Book Co., 1953), pp.329-410.

[4] G. Tarde, *The Laws of Imitation* (New York: Henry Holt & Co., 1903), pp. 87-88.

[5] J. Coleman, E. Katz, and H. Menzel, "The Diffusion of an Innovation among Physicians," *Sociometry* (December 1957), pp. 253-70.

[6] See E. M. Rogers, *Bibliography on the Diffusion of Innovations* (East Lansing: Department of Communications, Michigan State University, 1967).

[7] B. Ryan and N. Gross, "The Diffusion of Hybrid Seed Corn in Two Iowa Communities," *Rural Sociology* (March 1943), pp. 15-24.

Two sociologists, Rogers and Straus, have mentioned the possibility of relating personality traits and innovativeness.[8] Rogers feels that mental rigidity and change orientation (dogmatism) may be significantly related to farm-practice adoption. Straus hypothesizes that such traits as ascendancy and sociability are likely to be related to innovativeness.

Marketing Studies

Of the more than 900 research studies on file in the Diffusion Documents Center at Michigan State University, less than 5 percent can be classified as marketing studies.

The first diffusion research in marketing was conducted in 1959 by Opinion Research Corporation (ORC).[9] After interviewing 105 household heads regarding their first use of a number of consumer products, ORC concluded that approximately 27 percent of the population could be classified as "high mobiles" — and that these individuals constituted the leadership elite in the United States. They characterized this group by occupational mobility, continued education, higher incomes, gregariousness, and more frequent travel than the remainder of the population.

A second marketing study revealed that first purchasers of color television and stereophonic equipment had high family income, were highly educated, and were concentrated in the professions and in managerial occupations.[10]

Gorman appears to have been the first to apply the model of the rural sociologists to the diffusion of a consumer good.[11] His conclusions regarding the first purchasers of color television receivers were identical with those of Bell.

A recent attempt to related personality traits to innovativeness was unsuccessful. The investigators were unable to distinguish between purchasers and nonpurchasers of consumer goods on the basis of respondents' scores on a personality inventory.[12]

The CATV Study

Although several marketing investigations had verified the possibility of identifying first adopters of consumer goods on the basis of income, education, and occupation, no empirical research had obtained more probing behavioral characteristics from all adopters over a period of years following the

[8] E. M. Rogers, "Personality Correlates of the Adoption of Technological Practices," *Rural Sociology* (September 1957), pp. 267-68; M.A. Straus, "Personality Testing the Farm Population, *Rural Sociology* (June 1956), pp. 293-94.

[9] *America's Tastemakers* (Princeton, N.J.: Opinion Research Corp., 1959).

[10] W. E. Bell, "Consumer Innovators: A Market for Newness," in *Toward Scientific Marketing,* ed. S. A. Greyser (Chicago: American Marketing Association, 1964).

[11] W. P. Gorman, "Market Acceptance of a Consumer Durable Good Innovation: A Socioeconomic Analysis of First and Second Buying Households of Color Television Receivers in Tuscaloosa, Alabama" (Ph.D.diss., University of Alabama, 1966).

[12] T. R. Robertson and J. G. Myers, "Personality Correlates of Opinion Leadership and Innovative Buying Behavior," *Journal of Marketing Research* (May 1969), pp. 164-68.

introduction of the innovation. Also, many of the studies have relied entirely upon subject recall of date of first adoption. The authors of the drug study discovered that people would consistently state that they had adopted the drug much earlier than they actually had.

Finally, only one investigation has been conducted to search for common personality characteristics among early adopters of new producer or consumer goods.[13] This study also suffered from the previously mentioned limitation and compared only housewives identifying themselves as innovators and others considered as nonadopters.

The Innovation

The five-year-old community antenna television system (CATV) in a small southern city was selected as the innovation subject. The city's viewers received strong signals from the local station and weak signals from a second station in a nearby city with the aid of an outside antenna. The cable provided clear reception from stations in five additional cities and broadcast continuous local weather reports and FM music to subscribers at a cost of $5.00 per month. To facilitate the diffusion of the innovation and to reduce the perceived risk of potential adopters, the franchisee made an initial offer of free installation of the service and has periodically repeated the offer of free installation.

Methodology

Identification of all adopters and adoption dates were available from the files of the local franchise. Since the franchisee provided the only CATV service in the city, the problem of determining relative dates of adoption was avoided.

A 10 percent systematic sample was selected containing fifty-two Consumer Innovators (persons who subscribed within three months following the initial offering) and fifty-five Consumer Followers (persons first subscribing at least six months following the first offering). Personal interviews were conducted, and relevant socioeconomic characteristics were recorded.

The California Psychological Inventory (CPI) was then administered to the fifty Consumer Innovators and forty-eight Consumer Followers who agreed to participate. The CPI, unlike many other personality inventories, is designed primarily for "normal" subjects. Its eighteen scales provide a comprehensive portrait of the individual.[14]

Findings

Socioeconomic Characteristics

More than 92 percent of the Consumer Innovators were married, as

[13] *Ibid.*

[14] H. G. Gough, *Manual for the California Psychological Inventory* (Palo Alto, Calif.: Consulting Psychologists Press, 1964).

compared with 81 percent of the Consumer Followers. The differences were significant at the .05 level. Both groups showed a much larger percentage of married households than the 66.8 percent reported for the city by the 1960 Census Bureau reports.

Findings regarding income, occupation, and educational levels of the Consumer Innovators coincided with those of Bell and Gorman. Fifty-five percent of the Consumer Innovators were employed in professional, managerial, or proprietorial occupations, as compared with 41 percent of the later adopters and 22 percent of all household heads in the city.

Employment in nonsalaried occupations would possibly expose the Innovator to more risk than those household heads in other occupational categories. All consumer behavior involves risk in that the consumer's actions will produce uncertain, and possibly unpleasant, consequences. Therefore consumers tend to develop decision strategies so that they can act with relative confidence when faced with risk-filled situations.[15] It is possible that certain risk-filled occupations provide the individual with additional experience and additional confidence when making decisions where considerable risk is involved.

Median household income for the first adopters was $12,000, as compared with $7,900 for the Consumer Followers. Twenty-five percent of the Consumer Innovators earned $20,000 or more, while only 3.6 percent of the later adopters reported incomes as high as this.

Since the Innovator is first to adopt, he must take risks that can be avoided by later adopters. Some of these new untried products are likely to prove unsatisfactory. Thus the Innovator must be willing to absorb the loss from the occasional failures. And the wealthy individual risks proportionately less than does the less affluent individual in making the first purchase of the innovation.

Occupational mobility of the household head was significantly greater for the Consumer Innovators than for the later adopters. Nearly 25 percent of the first adopters had changed jobs at least once between 1964 and 1968, as compared with 16 percent of the Consumer Followers. In this respect the Consumer Innovators appear to resemble the "high mobiles" of the Opinion Research Corporation study. Occupational mobility proved an important means of distinguishing the "high mobiles" in the ORC study.

The first adopters also differed significantly from the Consumer Followers in the number of memberships in social and civic clubs, professional associations, and organized church groups. Consumer Innovators averaged 4.7 club memberships — almost twice as many as the 2.4 average for Consumer Followers. Over 10 percent of the Consumer Innovators belonged to eleven or more organizations.

The Innovators also held an average of 1.4 offices in local and area clubs and organizations — 2.5 times as many as the Consumer Followers, who averaged 0.6 offices per household. More than 15 percent of the first adopters held four or

---

[15] See R. A. Bauer, "Consumer Behavior as Risk Taking," in *Proceedings of the 43rd National Conference of the American Marketing Association,* ed. R. S. Hancock (Chicago: American Marketing Association, 1960), pp. 389-98.

more offices, while only 3.6 percent of the Consumer Follower households held four offices or more.

The sizable difference in the number of offices held by the two innovator categories strongly suggests the presence of opinion leadership among Consumer Innovator households. Over fifteen studies by rural sociologists have shown that farmer innovators have more opinion leadership than do later adopters.[16]

Neither age nor number of visits with friends, neighbors, and relatives was statistically significant. Although the differences were not statistically significant, the first adopters did subscribe to an average of 4.5 magazines, as compared with 3.4 for the Consumer Followers. They also averaged 3.4 distant trips per month, compared with 2.5 for the later adopters, suggesting a slightly larger number of impersonal sources of information and slightly greater cosmopolitism.

Personality Traits of CATV Adopters

The Consumer Innovators scored significantly higher than the later adopters on ten of the eighteen scales of the California Psychological Inventory: Dominance, Capacity for Status, Sociability, Social Presence, Self-Acceptance, Sense of Well-Being, Tolerance, Achievement via Conformance, Achievement via Independence, and Intellectual Efficiency.

Table 1
Mean Scores of Low Income Innovators, Consumer Innovators, and Consumer Followers on the California Psychological Inventory

Scale	Low Income Consumer Innovators (N = 10)	Consumer Innovators (N = 50)	Consumer Followers (N = 48)
Dominance	30.10	29.72	24.64
Capacity for Status	19.10	18.97	15.73
Sociability	27.10	24.97	20.16
Social Presence	32.90	31.82	26.76
Self-Acceptance	22.30	21.46	18.78
Sense of Well-Being	41.00	38.15	34.69
Tolerance	24.00	22.13	18.62
Achievement via Conformance	28.90	28.18	25.33
Achievement via Independence	19.20	18.74	16.78
Intellectual Efficiency	38.80	37.28	32.84

The Dominance scale measures leadership ability and initiative. The high scores by the Consumer Innovators on this scale appear to reflect an important aspect of their personality. They are also consistent with the leadership ability displayed by the disproportionately larger number of offices held in the organized groups and clubs.

[16] See E. M. Rogers, *Diffusion of Innovations* (New York: Free Press, 1962), p. 184.

The Capacity for Status scale indicates persons who are ambitious, active, and forceful; who are ascendant and self-seeking; who are effective in communication; and who possess a breadth of interests.

High scorers on the Sociability scale tend to be opinion leaders; low scorers are likely to be submissive and overly influenced by the opinions of others. These findings add further validity to the association of opinion leadership and innovativeness.

The Social Presence scale assessed factors of poise and self-confidence in personal and social interaction. Low scorers tend to be more deliberate and uncertain in their decisions, less original in their thinking, than are higher scorers.

Persons with higher scores on the Self-Acceptance scale are usually aggressive and possess more self-confidence and self-assurance than others. Cognitive dissonance is typically present at the purchase of some new untried product or service, and confidence in one's ability to make wise decisions would likely be present more often in the Consumer Innovator.

Consumer Innovators scored an average of 10 percent higher than did the adopters on the Sense of Well-Being scale, indicating persons with the necessary ambition and self-confidence to make innovative purchases without having to rely upon the experience of others.

The Tolerance scale identifies individuals with accepting, nonjudgmental attitudes. High scorers tend to be more open-minded about differing beliefs and values and commonly possess broad and varied interests themselves. The presence of a tolerant personality appears to be an important prerequisite for innovative behavior.

The Consumer Innovators scored significantly higher than the later adopters on all three measures of achievement potential and intellectual efficiency. Likely explanations are the higher educational levels, predominance of household heads employed in the professions or as managers or proprietors, and the larger number of magazine subscriptions possessed by households in this adopter category.

Some writers have pointed out that many of the characteristics commonly associated with early adopters, such as value of house and lot and number of pieces of entertainment equipment, can be related to household income and that income might be the common denominator in identifying potential innovators.[17] But several of the Consumer Innovators in the CATV study earned smaller annual incomes than did some of the later adopters. An examination of the personality traits of the first adopters with the lowest reported annual incomes revealed that they had scored higher than the remaining Consumer Innovators on all of the personality scales. Their scores on the Tolerance scale, for example were almost 10 percent higher than those of the remainder of the first adopters. Apparently several combinations of affluence and personality are possible in determining innovativeness. Higher scores on particular personality

[17] See, for example, P. E. Rockwood, "Comments on the Diffusion of Color Television Sets into a Metropolitan Fringe Area Market," *Southern Journal of Business* (July 1968), pp. 58-64.

traits may be sufficient in overcoming income deficiencies which otherwise would have prevented individual innovativeness.

Discussion

The CATV study has shown that the Consumer Innovator possesses most of the same distinguishing socioeconomic characteristics as his counterpart who first adopts producer goods and services. He is more highly educated, earns a larger annual income, and is more likely to be employed in the professional, managerial, and proprietorial occupations than others in the community. He is more likely to be married, change jobs more often, and belong to, and hold offices in, social and civic clubs, professional associations, and organized church groups than are later adopters of the innovation.

The Consumer Innovator also possesses different personality traits which may distinguish him from the later adopter. He exhibits more leadership ability, is more ascendant, and possesses more self-confidence, a greater acceptance of newness, and higher achievement levels than does the later adopter. He welcomes and initiates change.

The author applies the Warner social-class structure as a frame of reference and draws conclusions about the relationship of social stratification to purchasing, shopping, and spending and saving behavior.

The Effect of Social Stratification on Market Behavior

Kim B. Rotzoll

Today as never before advertising research is awash in the social sciences.[1] Psychologists, sociologists, and anthropologists are increasingly asked to offer insights into the complexities of market behavior.

The effect of social stratification on the activities of consumers has received appropriate attention ranging from traditional community studies, through the academic literature of sociology, and into business-sponsored research studies. As findings are extremely diverse, a synthesis of some of the more significant material will result in a broader assessment of the potential impact of social stratification on "consumerism" than has been possible to date.

Developmental Perspective

There seems to be general agreement among sociologists that class-inspired market behavior is closely related to the breakdown of the high degree of inter-personal communication that typified the early American community. Indeed, as Veblen has suggested, in lieu of the "subtle means of appraisal" typical of the small town, there is a tendency as a community grows "for its citizens to put relatively more of their possessions 'on their backs,' into cars and other seeable goods."

The Middletown (1937) and Yankee City (1941) studies offered empirical evidence of the influence of social factors on market decisions that had long

Reprinted by permission of the author and the publisher from the *Journal of Advertising Research* (March, 1967), pp. 60-69, © 1967, Advertising Research Foundation.

[1] The author would like to acknowledge the consultation afforded by Dr. David L. Westby, Assistant Professor of Sociology at the Pennsylvania State University.

been considered purely economic phenomena. Glock and Nicosia (1963) discussed later important studies in this area such as the paradigms of Lazarsfeld and Katona, the extensive activities of Martineau's *Chicago Tribune* staff, as well as the studies of the Foundation for Research in Human Behavior and the Bureau of Applied Social Research.

Several other significant contributions include: Caplovitz's *The Poor Pay More* (1963), Rainwater, Coleman, and Handel's *Workingman's Wife* (1959), as well as Ryan's work with the Simmons data (1964), and Vidich and Bensman's *Small Town in Mass Society* (1958).

A Frame of Reference

In order effectively to synthesize this often heterogeneous material, it seems practical to utilize the Warner class structure as a frame of reference. This is undertaken with full knowledge of the relativity of the structure as well as some of the conceptual problems that plague it. It is, however, still widely used as a standard both inside and outside the field of sociology.

I have attempted to synthesize material on the four lower classes of the six-class framework. It is generally conceded that these classes include more than 90 per cent of the American population and they have been extensively investigated.

All investigations are cursed with working definitions of one form or another. Mine are these:

Lower-lower class — the unskilled labor group.
Upper-lower class — the wage earner, skilled worker group.
Lower-middle class — the white collar, salaried group.
Upper-middle class — mostly the professionals and successful businessmen.

Three facets of market behavior will be considered for each class: (1) consumption patterns, (2) shopping patterns, (3) spending and saving patterns.

Lower-Lower Class

Consumption Patterns

There is considerable evidence to suggest that social factors affect the purchasing behavior of low-income families. Caplovitz (1963), in his study of consumer practices in three Manhattan public housing developments, makes early reference to the fact that low-income families are consumers of many major durables, predominately new, and often the more expensive models. It was also observed that the scarcely utilitarian symbol of modern living — the color telephone — was present in 23 per cent of the apartments with telephones.

He suggests that this behavior can best be described as "compensatory consumption" (a term he attributes to Robert K. Merton, 1950). With this view, a relative lack of occupational mobility may lead to an emphasis on the non-restricted sphere of consumption where the family can attempt to emulate what passes for "the American way of life." Kahl (1959) suggests a similar pattern with his distinction between "standards" of living (attitudes and values) and "levels" of living (current possessions and expenditures patterns).

It is interesting to speculate about how consumption "standards" for the lower income groups are set. Television may be a major factor here, given the oft-observed inverse relationship between television viewing and income level (e.g. Simmons – 1963).

Vidich and Bensman (1960) add a significant dimension to the study of the consumption patterns of this group by observing the rejection of the traditionally middle class "deferred gratification" ethic. They observe that Springdale's "Shack People" tend to reject middle class standards in such areas as housing and prefer instead to spend their money on immediate needs and fancies such as sporting equipment. Martineau (1960) tends to support this observation:

The Lower-Lower Class individual is far less interested in his castle, and is more likely to spend his income for flashy clothes or an automobile.

Shopping Patterns

It seems apparent that if the lower income groups are increasingly trying to bridge the gap between their levels and standards of living, that some form of credit must serve as the span. Yet these families by their low-income status are often the poorest of credit risks. Caplovitz observes that this paradox is solved with the personalized services offered by local merchants. By avoiding the more bureaucratic credit contacts, the merchant (and the flourishing door-to-door peddler) is often able to offer credit by applying social rather than legal pressure to assure payment. This, of course, literally forces the consumption-oriented family to deal with local merchants who offer this financing service tailormade for low-income areas. Martineau (1958) offers similar observations concerning the provinciality of the shopping patterns of lower-income families.

Spending and Saving Patterns

The precarious nature of saving activity in low-income families is summarized by this finding from the Martineau Chicago study:

The aspirations of the Lower-Status person are just as often for spending as they are for saving. The saving is usually a non-investment saving where there is almost no risk, funds can be quickly converted to spendable cash, and returns are small. When the Lower-Status person does invest his savings, he will be specific about the mode of investment, and is very likely to prefer something tangible and concrete – something he can point at and readily display.

Upper-Lower Class

Consumption Patterns

Technological mobility has clearly been an important influence on this wage earner/skilled labor group. Rainwater, Coleman, and Handel's (1959) major study of working class wives suggests that one of the strongest motivations operating within this group is a desire to put "distance" between themselves and those in lower socio-economic positions; that is, to acquire "respectability." There is, thus, far more emphasis on the home than is found in the lower stratum. Indeed, Martineau observes:

The Upper-Lower Class man sees his home as his castle, his anchor to the world, and loads it down with hardware — solid heavy appliances — as his symbols of security.

The evidence suggests that the aspirations of this group seem focused first on the desire to achieve a "decency level" of housing and then on a drive toward the oft-sought "level of the Common Man" in the consumption sphere. The results of a hypothetical income advance in the *Workingman's Wife* study suggest the operating value system of the sample families:

Even at the fantasy level of $7,000 a year, they do not express an above average desire for the ephemeral appearance of glamour and well-being granted by expensive clothing. It is the more solid symbols of modernity and well-being such as appliances, furniture, and an automobile, which exercise the greatest attraction upon working class women.

Thus, purchases tend, as Martineau has observed, to be more "artifact-oriented" than "experience-oriented."

It is interesting to note evidence of a certain degree of class loyalty regardless of economic condition. Martineau, in the *Tribune's* study of the class structure of Chicago, notes the emergence of the upper-lower "Stars" or Light-blue Collar Workers described as "high-income individuals who have the income for more ostentatious living than the average factory worker but who lack the personal skills or desire for high status by social mobility."

Kahl states:

Some observers believe that despite the entry of so many blue-collar workers into the middle-income group, there is still an important distinction between their value standards and those of white-collar workers. According to this view, those at the top of the blue collar hierarchy feel they have arrived as far as they can go, or as far as a man should desire; they are satisfied and do not spend their money for conspicuous symbols of display that would raise their prestige in the eyes of the community, such as "good address." Indeed, they would consider it snobbish to behave that way.

Kahl warns against generalizations in this area, although several of the *Tribune* studies offer strong support for the existence of an informally accepted "ceiling" for consumption activities along this stratum.

Shopping Patterns

There is general agreement between studies in this area that Upper-Lower families are somewhat less provincial in their shopping habits than Lower-Lower, but are still relatively limited compared to middle class standards.

Martineau suggests that this can be partially explained by familiar social "clues" offered by the local stores being more harmonious with the values shared by the class members, than those of the more "impersonal" establishments of the downtown areas and, less so, the suburban shopping centers.

Spending and Saving Patterns

Rainwater *et al.* (1959) observed a strong cash orientation among this group, perhaps attributable to the vivid memories of economic instability in the not-too-distant past.

It may not be going too far to imagine that they conceive of time payments as an almost immoral self-indulgence. They perhaps feel that an object which cannot be purchased outright is an unsafe, uncertain source of pleasure which might in the long run be denied them by someone else's whim.

The authors add, however, that these values are often compromised by overriding wants resulting in ". . . plunging into the installment-planned existence without ever feeling comfortably at ease in the debt pool." This differs markedly from the attitudes toward credit in the lower income groups studied by Caplovitz.

Lower-Middle Class

Consumption Patterns

Lipset and Bendix (1953) have observed that ". . . the split between manual and nonmanual work is basic in American society." This evidently crucial separation has led to conflicting observations of the motives of the class members. Kahl summarizes the view that holds that these lower echelon white collar workers and small businessmen are at the bottom of the white collar status ladder while their manual counterparts are at or near the top of theirs. He adds, however, that many members of this class are children of immigrants and feel their status is highly cherished by comparison.

The *Tribune's* study of suburban Chicago's "Park Forest" states:

In Park Forest, social acceptability is the keynote for marketing. In this tightly knit community, with considerable community activity, there is a potential for marketing goods as the "keys to social acceptance," rather than as either luxuries or as highly functional utilitarian items.

Lobel and Barber (1953) offer evidence to support this conclusion in their study of women's fashions.

These studies, then, suggest an essentially horizontal orientation rather than an emphasis on "anticipatory socialization" that might appear characteristic of a class at the "bottom of the white collar status ladder."

The promise of upward social mobility is, however, an important thread in studies of this class. The *Tribune* study states, "Many Park Foresters regard their community as a temporary stopping off place on the way to bigger things." It is also in this class that we find increased emphasis on purchases for their symbolic worth. Ryan's "Market III" families, for example, have these noted consumption patterns:

. . . to own stocks and purchase goods and services with select appeal — such as air travel, pianos, automatic dishwashers, combination washer-dryers, large face value life insurance policies, 35 mm cameras, 33 1/3 rpm records, hard cover books, and men's suits.

It is possible, then, to suggest that these are manifestations of the education factor on social class consumption patterns. Indeed, a reshaping of the relative *values* that families place on purchases seems to be present throughout a great deal of the literature concerning blue and white collar consumption patterns.

Shopping Patterns

The social consciousness evidenced in the foregoing examination of Lower-Middle consumption patterns is generally reflected in shopping habits. An illuminating sidelight on the emphasis of what is "socially acceptable" is offered by this excerpt from the *Tribune* study of Park Forest.

Middle-Class people had no hesitancy in buying refrigerators and other appliances in discount houses and bargain stores because they felt they could not "go wrong" with the nationally advertised names. But taste in furniture is much more elusive and subtle because the brand names are not known; and therefore, one's taste is on trial. Rather than commit a glaring error in taste which would exhibit an ignorance of the correct status symbols, the same individual who buys appliances in the discount house generally retreats to a status store for buying furniture. She needs the support of the store's taste.

The Lower-Middle class woman's shopping sphere thus appears considerably greater than her working class counterpart. The symbolic nature of her purchases apparently forces a certain degree on shopping flexibility.

Spending and Saving Patterns

The desire for social "correctness" implies a certain willingness to "play the game" and a corresponding emphasis on high family expenditures. This stands in reasonably sharp contrast to the Upper-Lower "dilemma" of cash-orientation and the desire for purchases that can be made with credit. There is little evidence that Lower-Middle families experience the same conflict.

This stratum's attitudes toward savings again reflect certain symbolic implications. Martineau observes:

Middle-Class people usually have a place in their aspirations for some form of savings. This saving is more often in the form of investment, where there is risk, long-term involvement, and the possibility of higher return. Saving, investment saving, and intangible investment saving — successively each of these become for them increasingly symbols of their higher status

Upper-Middle Class

Consumption Patterns

The Upper-Middle class is composed of family units headed by individuals who have achieved success in their respective endeavors. With high education levels and the assurance of occupational competence, there seems a marked lack of adherence to group norms of consumption above a certain accepted level. Indeed, some of the more prominent consumption patterns seem to reflect the emulation of higher strata. There seems, in short, apparently somewhat more of a reliance on one's *own* taste than has been found at any of the previous levels. These factors combine to thwart any attempt to comfortably pigeon hole consumption patterns associated with this stratum. There are, however, some emerging patterns.

Warner's *Jonesville* (1949), for example, paints a disturbing picture of an upper-middle class that is "desperately" trying to separate itself from what Martineau has called, "the middle majority." Bergel (1962) adds support to this observation.

The most ambitious people are in the upper-middle and lower-upper classes. In these groups, talents, achievement, and success are concentrated. Yet in many respects these are also marginal groups, always in danger of losing status, of being overtaken by others with more talent and more impressive achievements. Here are not only the "status seekers" but also the "status clingers." If their prestige is high, they will lose it unless they can keep their performance on a high level. If their income is substantial, their expenditures are even more so if they hold positions requiring "conspicuous consumption."

The effect of education on consumption patterns becomes even more pronounced at this level. This increasingly manifests itself in what Martineau refers to as "experience centered" expenditures. This is spending where one is left typically with only a memory. It would include hobbies, recreation, self-education and travel. Further general indication of the consumption values of this class can be gleaned from an examination of the buying habits of Ryan's Market I families comprising . . .

. . . only 7.7 per cent of all U.S. households. Yet it includes a full 46.7 per cent of all college graduates, 40.8 per cent of all households owning

two or more cars bought new, and almost one-third of all adults who
have traveled outside of the U.S. in the past five years.

Shopping Patterns

There is, predictably, an apparent emphasis on the environment of the selling
situation as revealed in the *Tribune* studies. The store must be clean, orderly,
reflect good taste, and be staffed with clerks who are not only well versed in
their particular merchandise line, but also appropriately aware of the status of
the customer. This clearly favors the specialty stores both in the suburbs and the
urban areas with a corresponding distrust of the more general outlets.

Spending and Saving Patterns

Warner and Lunt have observed:

. . . the budget of an individual or family is a symbol system, or a set of
collective representations that expresses the social values of a person's
membership in group life.

It is, as we have seen, difficult to determine precisely what is meant by
"group life" in terms of this stratum. The budget, however, clearly reflects the
necessity for expenditures in terms of their symbolic as well as their functional
value. In addition, however, class members seem strongly oriented toward
financial sacrifice for "good" schooling for their children.

It has already been observed that increased income enhances the opportunity
for increased savings. It is simply not clear on the basis of the sources studied
whether this pattern holds true for this stratum. Their allocation of resources
covers a considerable breadth of endeavors. We can, however, assume with some
certainty that the oft-observed credo of "spending money to make money"
results in more of a strain on the spending:saving ratio than would prevail at a
somewhat more secure social plateau.

Some Conclusions

On the basis of this limited investigation, it is possible to draw some general
conclusions about the relationship of social stratification to purchasing,
shopping, and spending and saving behavior.

Consumption standards of the four American social classes studied appear to
rest at two loci. The first, the so-called "level of the Common Man," seems
essentially the consumption standard of the Lower-Middle class. As such, it
becomes the goal of those classes below it and a norm for the Lower-Middle. It
is, however, essential to remember that the interpretation of this "American
standard" is formed through class value systems which are, in turn, related to the
stratum's "world view." Thus, distinctive interpretations of essentially identical
consumption goals will persist. These deviations commonly form the differences
in life styles that characterize the various strata.

The second locus apparently lies in the Upper class and serves as a consumption reference to the Upper-Middle class of our investigation. Distinctively horizontal reference thus seems to diminish with this stratum of predominately achieved status and resultant self-esteem.

This initial effort will hopefully serve as a reference point from which to deepen the investigation of this area where the pivotal interplay between the social sciences and commercial interests begins to result in a respectable body of knowledge.

References

Advertising Age. New Simmons Reports Pits Magazines vs. TV. *Advertising Age,* August 5, 1963, p. 1 ff.

Bergel, Egon Ernest. *Social Stratification.* New York: McGraw-Hill, 1962.

Caplovitz, David. *The Poor Pay More.* New York: The Free Press of Glencoe, 1963.

Chicago Tribune Research Division: *The New Consumer; A Study of Consumer Attitudes on Beer and Beer Advertising; Cigarettes – Their Role and Function;* and *Automobiles – What They Mean to Americans.*

Fortune (Eds.) *The Changing American Market.* Garden City, N.Y.: Hanover House, 1953.

Foundation for Research on Consumer Behavior. *Trends in Consumer Behavior: The Next Ten Years* (a seminar). Ann Arbor, Mich.: 1957.

Gans, Herbert G. *The Urban Villagers.* New York: The Free Press of Glencoe, 1962.

Glock, Charles Y. and Francesco M. Nicosia. Sociology and the Study of Consumers. *Journal of Advertising Research,* Vol. 3, No. 3, September, 1963, pp. 21-27.

Kahl, Joseph A. *The American Class Structure.* New York: Rinehart & Company, Inc., 1959.

Kemm, Thomas. Defining Markets: Who Belongs to Which Social Class and What are His Wants? *Printers' Ink,* August 29, 1958, p. 60

Lipset, Seymour Martin and John Gordon. Mobility and Trade Union Membership, in Reinhard Bendix and Seymour Martin Lipset, *Class, Status and Power.* Glencoe, Ill.: The Free Press, 1953, pp. 491-501.

Lipset, Seymour Martin and Reinhard Bendix. *Social Mobility and Occupational Career Patterns II. Social Mobility.* As above, pp. 454-465.

Lobel, S. Lyle and Bernard Barber. *'Fashion' in Women's Clothes and the American Social System.* As above, pp. 323-332.

Lynd, Robert S. and Helen Merrell Lynd. *Middletown in Transition.* New York: Harcourt, Brace and Company, 1937.

Maneloveg, Herbert D. Another Way to Look at Audience and Marketing Figures. *Advertising Age,* April 13, 1964, pp. 94-96.

Martineau, Pierre. Social Classes and Spending Behavior. *Journal of Marketing,* Vol. 23, No. 2, October, 1958, pp. 121-130.

Martineau, Pierre. Social Class and Its Very Close Relationship to the Individual's Buying Behavior, in John S. Wright and Daniel S. Warner, *Speaking of Advertising.* New York: McGraw-Hill, 1963, pp. 147-153.

Merton, R. K. and A. Kitt. Contributions to the Theory of Reference Group Behavior, in R. K. Merton and P. F. Lazarsfeld, *Continuities in Social Research.* Glencoe, Ill.: The Free Press, 1950, p. 87.

Packard, Vance. The Pursuit of Status, in Steven J. Shaw and Joseph W. Thompson, *Salesmanship: Modern Viewpoints on Personal Communication.* New York: Henry Holt and Company, Inc., 1960, pp. 92-101.

Printers' Ink. The Working Man: Do Marketing Men Know Him? *Printers' Ink,* December 1, 1961, pp. 48-49.

Rainwater, Lee, Richard P. Coleman, and Gerald Handel. *Workingman's Wife.* New York: Oceana Publications, Inc., 1959.

Tucker, W. T. *The Social Context of Economic Behavior.* New York: Holt, Rinehart and Winston, Inc., 1964.

Vidich, Arthur J. and Joseph Bensman. *Small Town in Mass Society.* New York: Anchor Books, 1960.

Warner, W. Lloyd. *Democracy in Jonesville.* New York: Harper & Brothers, 1949.

Warner, W. Lloyd and Paul S. Lunt. *The Social Life of a Modern Community* (Yankee City Series, Vol. 1). New Haven, Conn.: Yale University Press, 1941.

Weal, W. Bruce. Are We Good Enough for Your Product? *The American Salesman,* July, 1957, p. 12.

Although the poverty-stricken family needs to patronize establishments whose merchandise is economically priced, food shoppers in the poverty group tend to patronize higher priced food stores. This article probes the reasons for choosing the higher priced outlets and offers some controversial conclusions.

Food Buying Habits of the Urban Poor

Louis E. Boone
John A. Bonno

Several research studies have shown that food prices are higher in the small neighborhood stores scattered throughout ghetto areas than in major supermarkets in the same cities.[1] A common suggestion for aiding the poverty-stricken food shopper in expanding his meager purchasing power is to urge him to venture outside his immediate neighborhood to shop at the larger, more efficiently operated stores. Yet these suggestions require that the low-income food shoppers become "super" consumers, to break away from their present life styles, and perhaps to sacrifice many intangible returns not measured by the price of the food basket they buy. This article describes the results of a research study designed to identify the poor food shopper and to compare his shopping habits with those of more affluent shoppers.

By permission of the authors and the New York University Institute of Retail Management, to be published in the *Journal of Retailing.*

[1] David Caplovitz, *The Poor Pay more.* New York: The Free Press, 1963. Charles S. Goodman, "Do the Poor Pay More?" *Journal of Marketing,* Vol. 32 (January 1968), pp. 18-24. Louis E. Boone and John A. Bonno, "The Plight of the Poor: Low Income Families Do Pay More!" *Business Studies,* Vol. 8 (Spring, 1969), pp. 40-45. Donald F. Dixon and Daniel J. McLaughlin, "Do the Inner City Poor Pay More for Food?" *The Economic and Business Bulletin,* Vol. 20 (Spring, 1968), pp. 6-12.

Research Methodology

A section of a small southern city, containing 550 households and 128 blocks, was identified by the local agency of the Office of Economic Opportunity as a chronic poverty area. Each block represented one sampling unit and a total of 119 food shoppers were interviewed.[2]

Each respondent was first asked to identify his primary food store. A total of thirteen stores were mentioned by at least three persons. The stores ranged from major supermarkets to small neighborhood stores lacking refrigeration facilities for meat or produce. Each store was then shopped for a market basket composed of 71 items listed by the U.S. Department of Agriculture as a minimum nutritional menu for a family of four. When a store did not carry a particular item, a price was calculated for the missing item based upon the ratio of the price index of the base store to the store in question. The resulting indices ranged from 96.4 for one of the chain supermarkets to 108.2 for one of the small neighborhood independents.

Table 1
Computed Price Indices for Food Stores
of Low-Income Shoppers

Store	Price Index
Supermarkets	
Delchamps	96.4
A&P	97.9
McCaffrey's	99.8
*Jitney Jungle No. 27	100.0
Jitney Jungle No. 22	101.2
Winn-Dixie	102.1
Better Living	102.4
Major Independents	
Steelman's Grocery	97.4
Self Service Food Store	100.1
Small Neighborhood Independents	
MacDonalds	101.7
Morris Grocery	105.9
Parker's Grocery	107.3
Rebecca Avenue Grocery	108.2

*median store

Who Are the Poor?

Seventy-two of the 119 shoppers interviewed earned less than $3000 last year. The median income was $2428 and 22 percent of the shoppers reported household incomes of less than $1000 per year.

The area was racially mixed with white families living around the fringe of the poverty area and Negro families residing in the core area. Negroes comprised

[2] Nine of the 128 blocks were either entirely commercial or were vacant.

51.3 percent of the respondents, while the remaining 48.7 percent were white.

The most extreme poverty cases were almost exclusively Negro. Nearly 90 percent of the families earning less than $1000 per year were Negroes. In contrast, 68 percent of the white families in the area earned $3000 or more last year.

Table 2
Number of Households in Each Income
Category by Race

		Income	
Race	Less than $1000	*Less than $3000	$3000 or More
White	3	26	32
Negro	23	46	15
Total	26	72	47

*The first two columns are cumulative.

The usual correlations between income and age and level of formal education of the household head were found. Nearly half of the low income families were headed by a wage earner 55 years of age or older. In contrast, 86 percent of the households earning $3000 or more were headed by persons in the peak earning years between the ages of 18 and 54.

Table 3
Age of Household Head and Household Income

Age of Household Head	Income	
	Less than $3000	$3000 or More
15 – 24	6%	15%
25 – 34	10	19
35 – 44	19	23
45 – 54	19	29
55 – 64	18	8
65 and older	28	6
Total	100%	100%

Over 80 percent of the household heads in the low income category failed to complete high school. More than one-fourth of them never finished the sixth grade. In the $3000 and above category, one-third of the household heads were high school graduates and more than 12 percent had attended college.

Table 4
Education of Household Head and Household Income

Education	Income Less than $3000	$3000 or More
Sixth Grade or Less	27.8%	10.6%
Seventh – Twelfth	54.2	51.1
High School Graduate	12.5	25.5
Attended College	5.5	12.8
Total	100.0%	100.0%

Shopping Habits of the Poor

Twenty-two of the 72 respondents earning less than $3000 per year shopped at the higher priced neighborhood food stores. The overwhelming majority of these patrons were Negroes (only 2 of the 22 low-income respondents who shopped at the neighborhood stores were white). Most of the low income white shoppers made their purchases at the supermarkets.

As Figure 1 indicates, Negro food shoppers with incomes in excess of $3000 do not patronize the neighborhood stores. Instead, they chose to shop at the competitively-priced major independents and at the supermarkets. Only two of the relatively more affluent Negro food shoppers made regular purchases at the neighborhood stores.

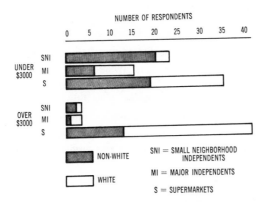

Figure 1   Store classes patronized by area shoppers by income and race. Source: Louis E. Boone and John A. Bonno, "The Plight of the Poor: Low Income Families Do Pay More!" Business Studies, Vol. 8 (Spring, 1969), p. 43.

By shopping at the major independent food stores and at the supermarkets the low income families could increase the real purchasing power of their incomes. But the families living in extreme poverty — those families who most needed to maximize their meager incomes — were the most frequent patrons of the more expensive stores. Their reasons proved quite revealing.

Patronage Motives of the Poor Food Shopper

Three major reasons were forwarded by the poor in choosing their primary store: convenience, friendship, and availability of credit. Many of the lowest income families possessed no means of transportation other than the city bus to shop for food and made use of the delivery service provided by the small stores. In contrast, less than 5 percent of the families with incomes exceeding $3000 used food delivery service.

Over one-fourth of the poor food purchasers mentioned a desire to trade among people of their own race, to keep business in the neighborhood, and to maintain a loyalty to the store owners who enjoyed a long-term friendship with most of the shoppers in the area. These motives proved powerful ties to the small stores. The low-income food shopper was aware of the higher prices she paid at the small neighborhood stores. Two-thirds of the Negro shoppers stated that significant price differences existed among competing food stores, while only one-third of the white shoppers were aware of any large price difference.

The third major reason for shopping at the smaller, higher-priced stores was the availability of credit. The large independent stores and supermarkets did not offer credit for their customers. In many instances this restricted the low-income families to the neighborhood stores which offered credit service.

Conclusions

Low-income families do pay more for food purchases when they stop at the small neighborhood stores. But they are aware of the consequences of their actions and they balance higher prices against the benefits of convenience, personal friendships, and credit service. When these additional intangible benefits are considered, their actions reflect not those of uneducated consumers some writers describe but rather those of purchasers who have deliberately chosen to patronize stores providing them with products and services they desire.

III PLANNING THE MARKETING EFFORT

Planning is a major responsibility of all managers and the marketing executive is no exception. He, too, must face this difficult task. All planning must be preceded by organizational objectives. Objectives serve as guidelines for the decision-maker in developing the marketing plan. Once the objectives are known, alternative plans may be evaluated in the light of whether the implementation of a particular alternative will allow the firm to move closer to the accomplishment of the firm's goals. Company objectives must invariably serve as the bases for planning, implementing, and controlling the marketing program.

As Leon Winer points out in the first selection, "The central idea of marketing planning is to develop marketing objectives that will lead to attainment of the objectives of the firm, and then to devise programs and controls that will help to achieve these marketing objectives." Winer feels that although many firms have developed marketing plans, these plans often do not represent any real *planning* due to emphasis on the *form* rather than the *substance* of the plan.

The first step in planning marketing activities, the sales forecast, is the subject of the second selection by William Lazer. The article investigates the relationship between sales forecasting and integrated management by considering three factors: (1) sales forecasting as a component of the marketing planning process; (2) sales forecasting as a focus for integrative planning; and (3) procedures involved in establishing a comprehensive sales forecasting program.

The development of successful plans requires iniormation. Information allows the decision-maker to evaluate alternative courses of action and make more reasoned choices. Collection of information has been historically the function of the firm's marketing research department. In the last few years, however, many firms have realized that their marketing research departments are inadequate in gathering and disseminating information, and several large firms have implemented planned marketing information systems to encompass the traditional marketing research activities and to systematically collect and disseminate decision-oriented information. The third selection deals with the development of marketing information systems as systematic means of information management. Brien and Stafford describe the benefits derived from establishment of such systems in providing pertinent information flows on a regular basis for improving marketing planning and decision making.

According to Wendell R. Smith, author of the fourth selection, "success in planning marketing activities requires precise utilization of both product differentiation and market segmentation as components of marketing strategy." Smith views product differentiation as an attempt to influence demand through development and promotion of different products, while conceiving of market segmentation as the division of heterogeneous markets into several smaller homogeneous markets with similar product and service preferences.

In the final selection in Part III, Bieda and Kassarjian conclude that previous attempts at market segmentation have been largely unsuccessful. They suggest the use of multivariate techniques in determining demographic, objective, and psychological factors which are related to purchase behavior and in deciding whether these characteristics may be used in identifying consumer segments.

What is wrong with the marketing planning methods many companies use? Can something useful be learned by examining the procedures of leading companies and reviewing the literature of planning? What should a company do **now** *to improve its marketing planning?*

Are You Really Planning Your Marketing?

Leon Winer

The biggest problem in marketing is the *planning*. Many companies have a marketing "plan," yet few of these plans represent any real planning. To demonstrate this point, five steps will describe practices encountered frequently. These practices were observed through intensive interviews with manufacturing firms and their advertising agencies, and have been reported by executives at meetings and seminars attended by the author.

Step 1: Set the market share objective of your brand by adding to its present market share, depending on how ambitious you are.

Step 2: Project total sales volume, for *all* brands of the product, in dollars, for the following year.

Step 3: Multiply the result of Step 1 by the result of Step 2. (Market share objective X projected total dollar market.) This gives the dollar sales objective for the brand.

Step 4: Subtract from the dollar sales objective: (a) total factory cost, (b) an allocated portion of the company's fixed marketing costs, and (c) desired profit. What is left, if anything, is "planned" marketing expenditure.

Step 5: Compose a "marketing mix" of advertising, marketing research, personal selling, price concessions, public relations, package design, point of sales materials, dealer aids, and so on, that will (a) just use up all the marketing funds and (b) yield exactly the forecasted sales volume.

Reprinted by permission of the author and the publisher from the *Journal of Marketing,* published by the American Marketing Association, Vol. 29, No. 1 (January, 1965), pp. 1-8.

These five steps represent the procedures of many companies, yet they are thoroughly unsound, for three reasons:

First, this procedure assumes that an increase in market share is profitable or, for that matter, possible. By definition, not *all* brands of a product can increase their market shares.

Second, this method of marketing planning reverses the cause-and-effect relationship between marketing effort and sales volume. Clearly, the sales volume forecast should depend on the amount of effort expended on marketing, not the other way around.

Third, this method requires the manager to select the "right" marketing mix from among the hundreds, or thousands, of possible marketing mixes. In other words, the manager is given a sales volume objective and a fixed amount of money for marketing, and he is expected to devise the combination of advertising, price reductions, personal selling, marketing research, public relations, point of sale materials, and so on, that will just use up the available money and will attain the sales objective. No human being has the knowledge or the calculating ability to do this, even if it were *theoretically* possible.

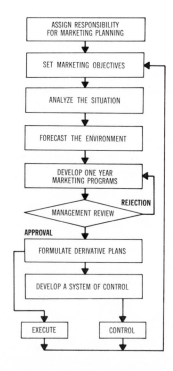

Figure 1   Flow model of a marketing
planning procedure

If the argument presented above is correct, and widely-followed practice is inadequate, what alternatives are available?

To answer this question, a study was made of the marketing planning practices of companies recognized as leaders in this area, and of planning books and articles. The conclusion was that while a certain amount of adaptation is required in each case, a general procedure exists that is applicable to marketing planning. This procedure is presented as a flow model in Figure 1. The discussion of the steps in the model will follow the sequence shown, except that "assigning responsibility for planning" will be discussed last instead of first.

Setting Marketing Objectives

In setting marketing objectives, planners should keep in mind three properties of objectives: (1) multiplicity, the fact that organizations have many objectives; (2) time, objectives need to be set for varying lengths of time; and (3) level, the firm should have many levels of objectives, or a hierarchy of objectives.

Multiplicity

Generally speaking, marketers tend to focus on maximizing next year's profits as being the only proper objective for their efforts. Actually a company may be equally interested in stabilizing profits, or in seeking opportunities for investments for the longer term. Therefore, before doing any marketing planning, it is necessary to explore thoroughly with the company's management what *it* views the company's objectives to be and to derive marketing objectives from those of the company.

Objectives and Time

Given the company's objectives, it does not necessarily follow that these can be realized directly. A firm may not be able to capture a larger share of the market, economically, unless it has an improved product. Therefore, in order to attain a more distant objective of increasing its market share, it will set an intermediate objective of developing an improved product.

Since the firm possesses only limited management and financial resources, in setting the objectives described above, it will very probably have to forsake such alternative objectives as entering a foreign market or acquiring a potentially profitable competitor.

Therefore, in setting long-range objectives, and the intermediate objectives that will lead to their attainment, the firm must consider the alternatives it is forsaking, and select those most suitable to its circumstances.

Hierarchy of Objectives

Even though a firm sets long-term objectives and determines the appropriate intermediate objectives, that may not be enough. It does not do much good to tell the advertising department that the objective of the company is to increase its rate of return on investment unless this objective is translated into specific strategies. Therefore, it is necessary to develop a hierarchy of objectives.

Development of such a hierarchy of objectives is not a simple task. Careful study is required to make sure that sufficient alternatives are considered at each level and that suitable criteria are discovered for deciding which alternatives are to be selected, or emphasized.

An example, showing how a hierarchy of objectives may be derived through flow-modeling, is shown in Figure 2. This is the case of the business market (offices, factories, stores, hospitals, and so on) of the Interstate Telephone Company (a fictitious name for a real company). At the top of the chart is one of the Company's permanent objectives, that of increasing return on invested capital. A rate of return of 7½% is believed to be attainable. Two possible objectives were derived from this one: (1) increase return, or net profit, and (2) reduce the investment base on which return is computed. The second possibility was not believed to be attainable because of (1) population growth, (2) rapidly growing communication needs, and (3) trend toward mechanization and automation. Therefore, attention was focused on the first.

To increase profits, two objectives may be set, following the reasoning of the Interstate Company: (1) increase billings, or (2) reduce costs. Again, the second objective is unlikely to be attained because one of the important sources of the return on investment problem is the rising cost of labor and materials. (One exception should be noted, however. Costs may be reduced by reducing the rate of disconnections due to customer dissatisfaction, since the cost of installing complex equipment often exceeds installation charges.) This leaves the alternative of increasing billings.

To increase billings, the Interstate Company may (1) try to raise rates and risk reduction in usage, (2) persuade customers to increase usage of existing equipment, or (3) sell additional equipment and services in order to increase equipment rentals and, to some extent, usage. However, a public service commission will not grant a rate increase unless return on investment is *below* a certain minimum, say 5½%. Then a commission is not likely to grant a raise that will increase return by as much as two percentage points. The next alternative objective, persuading customers to increase usage, has been used as an objective for promotional efforts of the Company. The third objective, that of selling additional equipment and services, has been selected for particular emphasis. In particular, because of the saturation of the business market with respect to basic equipment, the marketing effort has focused on the sale of auxiliary services and equipment, such as "Call Directors," teletype units, modern switchboards, and interior dialing.

To achieve the objective of selling more auxiliary services and equipment, and reducing disconnections due to customer dissatisfaction, the Company needs to match equipment and services to the *needs* of the customers, by making recommendations based on careful study of these needs. To do this, it seeks to persuade customers, through advertising, to invite "Communications Consultants" to survey their communications problems. In this way, by deriving a hierarchy of objectives, Interstate identifies the specific marketing strategies that will lead to attainment of the Company's highest objectives.

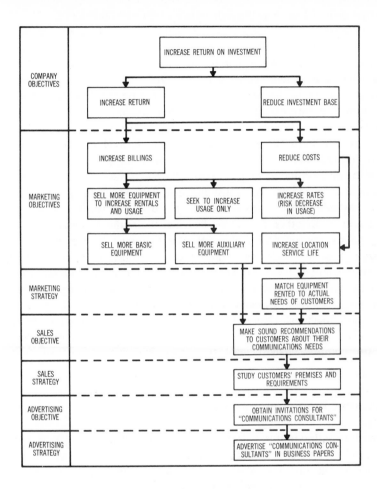

Figure 2   Hierarchy of objectives for the Interstate Telephone Company

Analyzing the Situation

Once the planner has a well-developed set of objectives, the next step is to begin discovering ways of attaining them. To do this, he has to form some ideas about what *actions* of the firm, under what *environmental conditions,* have brought about the *present* situation. He will then be able to identify courses of action that may be used in the future.

Logan[1] has suggested a four-step procedure for conducting the situation analysis:

---

[1] James P. Logan, "Economic Forecasts, Decision Processes, and Types of Plans" (unpublished doctoral dissertation, Columbia University, 1960), pp. 14-19, 76.

Investigation – A wide range of data that may be relevant should be sought, with care being taken to distinguish between facts and opinions.

Classification – The planner sorts the data collected during the investigation.

Generalization – Classes of data are studied to discover relationships. Statistical techniques such as correlation analysis are used to determine whether dependable associations exist between types of events. For example, a distributor may find that leased outlets are more profitable than owned outlets to a degree that prevents attributing the differences to chance.

Estimate of the Situation – Causes are sought for the associations discovered in the previous step. The planner now has some ideas about what actions under past conditions have resulted in the present situation. In this way he has learned several courses of action that he may follow to achieve his objectives. In the example cited previously, the distributor may find, on searching further, that the higher profitability of leased outlets is caused by the superior location of the leased outlets. In other words, the fact that the outlet was leased was *not* the cause of the higher profitability. Rather *both* the leasing *and* the higher profitability were caused by a third factor – superior location. (Owners of well-located outlets were not willing to sell them and therefore the distributor had been forced to lease.) Consequently, the appropriate strategy for the future would not be to prefer leasing to owning, but to seek good locations and leasing, if necessary. Inadequate search for causes might have led to very poor results.

Ideally, the situation analysis should cover other firms in the industry, so that the company may benefit from their experiences, both successes and failures.

Forecasting the Future Environment

The forecasting problem, from the viewpoint of the planner, is to determine *what* conditions he should forecast and *how* to do it. In this article we will limit ourselves to the first part of the problem because the literature of forecasting techniques is too vast to be reviewed adequately here.

Frey[2] has listed five factors that may affect purchases of a product:
1. Population changes.
2. Improvements in, and new-use discoveries for competing types of products.
3. Improvements in, and new-use discoveries for the company's own type of product.
4. Changed consumer attitudes and habits.
5. Changes in general business and conditions.

Howard[3] suggests four criteria for identifying *key* factors:
1. Variability. If a factor is stable over time, there is no need to make a forecast of it.

---

[2] Albert W. Frey, *The Effective Marketing Mix: Programming for Optimum Results*

[3] John Howard, *Marketing Management* (Homewood, Illinois: R. D. Irwin, Inc., 1957), Chapter VI.

2. Co-variation. There must be a relationship between changes in the factor and changes in demand.
3. Measurability.
4. Independence. The factor must not be closely related to another factor already considered.

Essentially, this means that the planner has to find out *which* uncontrollable factors, such as personal income, occupation of consumers, educational level, attitudes, affect sales of his brand, and then he has to forecast the future of these factors. Here, as in situation analysis, statistical methods must be used with care, to avoid erroneous conclusions.

Developing One-Year Marketing Programs

Development of marketing programs requires three steps: (a) formulating alternative courses of action, (b) examining these alternatives, (c) comparing alternatives and selecting the ones to be recommended.

Formulating Alternatives

The first step in conceiving alternative courses of action was described in an earlier section on situation analysis. We reviewed a four-step process for discovering factors that had brought about the present situation, and presumably could be manipulated to achieve future objectives.

However, in addition to the cause-and-effect relationships discovered in situation analysis, there is usually room for innovation, or the development of new courses of action.

The importance of the creative process cannot be under-estimated, because a plan can only be as good as the best of the alternatives considered. Therefore, it is highly rewarding to spend time evolving alternatives. Unfortunately, there is a strong human tendency to stop the search for alternatives as soon as an apparently acceptable course of action is discovered. This is a tendency that planners must guard against.

Examining Alternatives

This step consists of projecting all the outcomes of each alternative course of action evolved above. The outcomes considered should include (1) desirable and undesirable; (2) immediate and long range; (3) tangible and intangible; and (4) certain and only possible.[4]

Clearly, one of the outcomes that must be projected in every case is sales volume and/or profit. In making this projection, errors in both directions are possible. Eldridge[5] discusses the probable consequences of these errors and suggests a solution to the problem.

---

[4] William H. Newman and Charles E. Summer, Jr., *The Process of Management* (Englewood Cliffs, New Jersey: Prentice Hall, Inc., 1961), p. 302.

[5] Clarence E. Eldridge, "Marketing Plans," in E. R. French (editor), *The Copywriter's Guide* (New York: Harper & Bros., 1958), pp. 3-28, on pp. 24-25.

If (the marketing manager) overestimates his sales volume and gross profit, and bases his marketing expenditures on that overestimate . . . he is likely to find . . . that profits are running well below the forecast . . .

If he underestimates his volume and gross profit, he runs the risk of spending less than the product needs—and thereby . . . makes certain that the results are less than hoped for.

Nevertheless, it is probably preferable for the marketing manager, when weaving his way perilously between the devil and the deep sea, to err on the side of conservatism in budgeting sales, his marketing expenditures, and his profits . . .

For himself, his associates, the advertising agency, and the field sales department, it is wholly desirable that objectives should be set on the high side, in order that the attainment of those objectives shall require "reaching . . ."

In other words, Eldridge suggests "keeping two sets of books." The implications of this suggestion will be discussed subsequently.

Comparing and Selecting Alternatives

In this step the planner compares the projected outcomes of the various alternative courses of action. The purpose is to rank the alternatives on the basis of the extent to which they achieve objectives and avoid undesirable results. Then the most desirable alternatives are recommended to management.

This point, after programs are prepared, and before they are reviewed by top management, is suitable for writing down the plans.

On the basis of the argument presented here, the written plan should discuss the following topics, if it is to enable management to evaluate it:

1. Specific objective(s) of the plan.
2. Relationship between the specific objective(s) and the objectives of the firm, or an explanation of the extent to which this plan will advance the higher-level and longer-term objectives of the firm. Quantitative measures should be included, if possible.
3. Other specific objectives considered, and the planner's opinion of the relative values of these specific objectives. This evaluation should also include quantitative measures, if possible.
4. Costs of executing the plan.
5. Forecasts of the firm's environment.
6. Course of action recommended: first, briefly, then in detail.
7. Alternative courses of action and reasons why they were considered inferior to the action recommended.
8. Projected results of the plan, if it is executed.
9. Listing of control standards and procedures to be used for controlling execution of the plan.

Before leaving this discussion of preparation of programs, an important point should be emphasized:

Marketing planning should not be done function by function, as has been the tradition for a long time and still is the practice in many firms. (By "functions" we mean the activities normally performed by a marketing department, such as advertising, personal selling, pricing, marketing research, and product and package development. *Within* these functions are many sub-functions. For example, within personal selling is recruitment, selection, and training of salesmen; assignment of territories; design of compensation systems; sales analysis, and so on. At least 50 functions and sub-functions could easily be listed.)

Marketing planning should be oriented to achieving objectives. Of course, if objectives may be fulfilled entirely within one function, the objective-directed plan will also be "functional." But the approach, even then, will still be from objectives to means rather than from means to objectives.

Management Review

Criteria of reviewing executives may be grouped conveniently as follows: (1) economic, or financial; and (2) subjective.

Economic or financial criteria, such as return on investment, present discounted value of future income, alternative uses of funds, and cut-off rates, are sufficiently well kown that they do not require comment here.

Subjective criteria, on the other hand, may require some discussion. Smith[6] has commented on the role of management as follows: "Management may simply accept the goals indicated ... More frequently ... management's reaction will be one expressed by such comment as: 'Surely we can do better than that ...'"

In the case of the National Paper Company (a fictitious name for a real firm), during one year, management reduced the recommended marketing expenditures by 23%, *without* reducing the sales volume objective. Other, similar, reviewing actions could be cited. Therefore, it appears that management, in reviewing marketing plans, asks itself: "How much 'fat' does this plan contain?" and answers the question somehow, probably subjectively.

Are such reviewing actions justified? In other words, is it fair to the planner to suspect him of "padding" his plan? We have noted earlier the view that: "... when it comes to budgeting (setting sales, profit and marketing expenditure goals), the situation is different (from setting objectives for the advertising agency, the sales force, and the like). The forecasts for financial budgeting should be sufficiently conservative that ... they are certain to be made ..."[7] This commentator appears to be suggesting that the planner should overstate consistently the expenditure needed to achieve the goals of the plan. This appears to recognize that a conflict may exist between the objectives of the planner and those of the firm.

The management literature has emphasized repeatedly that differences exist between the objectives of the employee and those of the employing

---

[6] Wendell R. Smith, "A Rational Approach to Marketing Management," in Eugene J. Kelley and William Lazer (editors), *Managerial Marketing* (Homewood, Illinois: R. D. Irwin & Co., 1958), p. 154.

[7] Eldridge, same reference as footnote 5, p. 25.

organization. Therefore, it seems fair to conclude that the planner, in trying to achieve his personal goals of continued employment and approval of his superiors, may undermine organizational objectives such as maximum return on marketing expenditures. Following this, the problem of the reviewing manager would then appear to be not to decide *whether* there is "fat" in the plan, but rather to estimate the percentage.

Formulating Derivative Plans

Ultimately, at the lowest level in the hierarchy, the result of planning has to be a list of actions, or a program, to be carried out.

For drawing up this program, Newman and Summer[8] suggest six steps:

1. Divide into steps the activities necessary to achieve the objective.
2. Note relations between each of the steps, especially necessary sequences.
3. Decide who is to be responsible for each step.
4. Determine the resources needed for each step.
5. Estimate the time required for each step.
6. Assign definite dates for each part.

In formulating its derivative plans, the Finchley (a fictitious name for a real company) Drug Company, uses the individual plans prepared for each of 50 products. The pertinent information is pulled out of each product plan and reassembled in three derivative plans: (a) detailing (personal selling) schedule, (b) advertising program, and (c) financial summary. These derivative plans are described below:

Detailing Schedule—The Detailing Schedule is structured very much like a calendar. For each month, three products are listed in the order in which they are to be presented to physicians. The schedule serves as a working document for the sales force. As the year passes, 500 copies of each page are made and distributed to Finchley's detail men to be carried out.

Advertising Program—The Advertising Program describes several thousand items of direct mail and journal advertising to be prepared during the course of the year. The items are arranged by month and by day of the month when they are to appear, or to be mailed. As the year progresses, this information is used by technicians and artists in the Advertising Department and the Company's agency to prepare advertisements, buy space and materials, and so on.

Financial Summary—The Financial Summary, unlike the other two documents, is not used by any functional department as a basis for action. Instead, it is essentially a communication and control device. Probably the best way to describe the contents of this document is to list the information presented for *each* actively promoted product:

1. Total market ($).
2. Company's share (%).
3. Company's sales ($).
4. Advertising expenditure ($).

[8] Newman and Summer, same reference as footnote 4, pp. 415-416.

5. Allocated detailing cost ($).
6. Total marketing cost ($).
7. Marketing cost as a % of sales.
8. Gross profit ($).
9. Gross profit as a % of sales.

This information is presented both for the current year and the following year.

As plans are executed, the Financial Summary is used for comparing actual results with plans, or controlling the execution of the plan. The point is that advertising, sales, and financial plans are derived from objective-directed product marketing plans and *not* prepared independently by the separate functions: Advertising, Sales, and Finance.

Developing a System of Control

A system of control should (1) establish standards, (2) measure activities and results (3) compare these measurements to standards, and (4) report variances between measurements and standards.

Control is relevant to planning because control standards have a greater effect in determining actual results than the objectives of the plan. Therefore, it is necessary that the standards which *are* set, reflect very closely the objectives of the plan.

In addition, a system of control informs the planner of the results obtained from execution of his plans. This is helpful because it becomes possible to change plans if they are found to be ineffective either because (1) the cause and effect premise on which they were based turns out to be faulty, or (2) the actual environment is sufficiently different from the forecast environment.

In the first instance, the objectives are still valid, but the method of attaining them needs to be changed. In the second instance, the objective may no longer be appropriate. Therefore, new objectives and strategies may be required, and with them, new courses of action.

Assigning Responsibility for Marketing Planning

In practice, the management decision of assigning responsibility for marketing planning is the first step performed. In this paper, we have postponed discussion of this topic until the end, because organization of the planning function may depend on the kind of planning to be done. Therefore, it was necessary to describe first the steps in marketing planning.

Writers on the subject of marketing planning organization have described several alternatives:

1. Delegation of planning to functional executives, such as managers of the advertising, sales, pricing, sales promotion, marketing research divisions of the marketing department.
2. Planning done by a planning staff group.
3. Planning done by everyone who has a part to play in marketing the brand, including outside organizations.

4. Planning done by brand, or product managers.

However, criteria are lacking in the literature for selecting the appropriate planning organization.

Leading firms often rely on product, or brand managers for planning, although the practice is not universal, and where such managers are used, their responsibilities are not always the same.

To illustrate this point:

1. At the drug company discussed earlier, product managers plan advertising of two kinds, and personal selling.
2. At the household paper products company, brand managers plan consumer advertising and temporary reductions in price charged to retailers and consumers.
3. The telephone company, on the other hand, does not employ product managers. Instead, planning is assigned to sales and advertising executives, for their individual functions.

Possibly these differences in planning organization can be attributed to differences in the means used for communicating with the market. The telephone company needs to communicate with business market customers (that is, business firms, government agencies, and so on) on an individual basis. The reason is that no two customers (other than the very smallest) are likely to need exactly the same combination of products and services. Therefore, a centrally-conceived, uniform approach, used alone, would not be suitable. The household paper products company and the drug company deal with mass markets where the potential profit made from individual customers is small. This rules out the possibility of tailoring a specialized approach to each customer. In addition, the needs and desires of large numbers of potential and actual customers are relatively similar. Therefore, grouping large numbers of customers into a market for a brand is an economical way of approaching the planning problem.

It follows that the "brand" manager is really a *market* manager, the market being the totality of actual and potential consumers of the brand. We may conclude, therefore, that a brand or product manager has a role to play whenever there is an opportunity to use standardized appeals in communicating with numerous customers.

Nevertheless, not all firms require brand managers, even though they may use mass communication media. For example, the Interstate Telephone Company permits all the advertising planning to be done in its advertising department, and delegates the major part of its sales planning to sales executives. The question arises then: what are the key differences that cause such marked differences in planning organization?

The answer that suggests itself is that there are important differences in the marketing objectives of these firms. Two illustrations can be given.

1. At the paper company, two of the important objectives are increase in market share, and product distribution in certain areas. Programming for these objectives requires crossing of functional lines. Therefore there appears to be a need for a special planning executive.

2. At the telephone company the important marketing objectives are: (1) to increase auxiliary equipment and service billings; and (2) to increase location service life of auxiliary equipment. These objectives are interpreted to require that "communications consultants" survey the operations and premises of business market customers. To achieve this, the company tries to persuade customers to avail themselves of the free services of these consultants. Thus, we have three levels of objectives: (a) persuade the customer to invite the communications consultant, in order to (b) have the communications consultant advise the customer, in order to (c) increase billings and service life.

Achieving objectives (a) and (b), the objectives that can be achieved by direct action—(c) obviously cannot—does not require any coordination among functions. Objective (b) is achieved by the Sales Department, and objective (a), by the Advertising Department.

The conclusion is that the planning organization should mirror the hierarchy of objectives: a planning manager is needed wherever there is an objective whose achievement requires coordination of, or selection from among, several functions. In practice, the existing organization may satisfy this requirement, in which case, no new responsibilities need be assigned. However, if existing planning responsibilities do not allow for this type of selection, or coordination, new ones need to be created.

Implications for Marketing Managers

When a new idea or concept is presented to the business world, its *form* often receives more attention that its *substance*. While attempts are made to adopt the new concept, old habits of thought, and procedures, are continued even though they may not be consistent with the new idea.

The central idea of marketing planning is to develop marketing objectives that will lead to attainment of the objectives of the firm, and then to devise programs and controls that will help to achieve these marketing objectives. In deciding to plan its marketing activities, a business firm has to stand ready to scrap its traditional budgeting and functional planning procedures and to re-think and reorganize its marketing. Only those methods and procedures should be retained that fit logically with the pattern of starting with the highest objectives of the firm and refining successive steps of instrumental objectives until courses of action are specified. Any other approach, or procedure, will give inferior results.

Admittedly, it is much easier to go through the five steps outlined in the first few paragraphs, and say that marketing is being planned, than to follow the procedure described in the body of this paper. However, in this instance, as in most, there are no easy short-cuts to the development of good, effective, and profitable plans. Also, there really is no escape from the need to plan conscientiously. Leading companies *are* planning in this way, with obvious financial success. Those who wish to attain similar success will have to apply themselves equally. Successful procedures will not be developed overnight, or even in one year. Most likely, it will take from three to five cycles of planning to establish an effective, smoothly-working procedure. However, nothing will be accomplished if a sincere beginning is not made.

Three aspects of sales forecasting are investigated: sales forecasting as a component of the marketing planning process; sales forecasting as a focus for integrative planning; and the basic components and procedures of a comprehensive sales forecasting program.

Sales Forecasting: Key to Integrated Management

William Lazer

Business organizations are increasingly adopting the marketing management concept. This philosophy of business operation places greater emphasis on marketing planning and forces business executives to design marketing strategies and program marketing effort to achieve realistic and predetermined objectives.

Sales forecasting can aid management greatly in implementing the marketing management approach. It is a basis for developing co-ordinated and goal-directed systems of marketing action. The sales forecast is one of the vital tools of marketing planning since adequate planning and the effective deployment of marketing resources are based on sales forecasting data.

Sales forecasting promotes and facilitates the proper functioning of the many segments of a firm's total spectrum of business and marketing activities. It influences almost every other prediction of business operations. It is used in establishing budgets and marketing controls. Sales forecasts help determine various limiting conditions for management decisions and programs and are useful tools for co-ordinating the integral aspects of business operations. They provide bases for evaluating the functioning and productivity of various segments of business activity. They can guide marketing and other business action toward the achievement of implicit and explicit objectives.

This article investigates three aspects of sales forecasting as a key to integrated management action: (1) sales forecasting as a component of the

Reprinted by permission of the author and the publisher from *Business Horizons,* Vol. 2, No. 3 (Fall, 1959), pp. 61-67.

marketing planning process, (2) sales forecasting as a focus for integrative planning, and (3) the basic components and procedures of a comprehensive sales forecasting program.

In Marketing Planning

Figure 1 illustrates the strategic role of sales forecasting in gathering information for marketing planning. Effective planning of marketing activities can be achieved only if adequate marketing-related information is available. Marketing planning is concerned with the application of analysis and judgment to available information and the prediction of likely occurrences and trends during some future period.

Marketing-related information can refer to either the past or the future. Information about past activities is often referred to as factual information. Information about the future is anything but factual, and might be characterized as assumptive. Past information is available to every business if it has an adequate record-keeping process. It is also available from other secondary data sources, such as information reported by governmental bureaus, university research bureaus, and trade associations. Past information may also be assembled through the use of various primary data-gathering research tools, such as surveys and experiments.

Future information requires the utilization of forecasting techniques and processes. Nevertheless, it is based on past data and is usually the result of the application of predictive tools to available past information.

Whenever a business gathers future data, varying degrees of error are bound to exist. Regardless of the forecasting techniques used and the degree of sophistication achieved, future conditions will always deviate to some degree from the predictions of the forecasters. Thus, management must expect future information to contain some error.

For effective marketing planning, both types of information must be available for executive use. From a planning and decision-making point of view, future, or nonfactual, information may be more significant than information about the past. This becomes clear if one considers that plans and decisions made today are actually based on executive expectations of what will happen during some future period.

If we consider sales forecasting from the point of view of furnishing marketing-related information, we can state that management gathers information as a result of two complementary processes: feedback and sales forecasting. Feedback consists of relating information about past events and relationships back to management. Through the use of such factual data, management can adjust existing operations and plans and thereby improve the effectiveness of all business action.

Sales forecasting furnishes management with information about what market conditions will probably be like during a future period. Management can then use this information as a basis for planning broad company goals and the

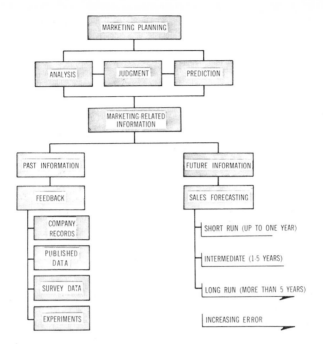

Figure 1

strategies to achieve them. Sales forecasting data are used in establishing various types of potential volume and profit targets that become the bases for guiding and controlling operations.

Past and future information, however, are constantly blending. A sales forecast, although it furnishes future information, eventually takes the form of feedback information. Once this happens, a comparison may be made between actual and forecast sales for a specific period. Through such an audit, deviations may be noted and explanations sought for them. This information can, in turn, help refine the assumptions about future sales forecasts and increase the total effectiveness of the forecasting procedure.

The various predictions made may take the form of short-run sales forecasts of less than a year, intermediate forecasts of from one to five years, and long-run forecasts for periods of more than five years. Generally, the longer range the predictions, the greater the forecasting error.

In Integrative Planning

Another facet of sales forecasting and its role in marketing planning is its position in the integrative planning process. A sales forecast is a useful tool for integrating the external business environment with the internal forces of the company. It reduces to workable management dimensions the external business environment over which management has relatively little control. It delimits those constraints that establish the boundaries within which a company must make decisions and operate and translates them into company programs.

Figure 2 portrays sales forecasting as an aid to integrative planning. It indicates the controllable, partially controllable, and noncontrollable factors that management should integrate and take into account in making effective sales forecasts.

The noncontrollable forces determine the broad environmental limits within which the company will operate. These factors include cultural forces, the economic environment, demographic forces, political factors, ethical and social forces, and various international conditions. They cannot be influenced to any degree by company action; at best, they may be recognized and appraised in an intelligent manner.

On Figure 2, broken lines separate the competitive environment and technological factors from other noncontrollable factors. This is to indicate that management action may have some influence over at least these two external forces, which are considered partially controllable factors. However, even though company action can affect competition and technology, the forces *beyond* company control generally have a more significant impact.

As forecasts become longer run in nature, the necessity of recording the existing external climate becomes more imperative since, in the future, it will be these noncontrollable factors that set the over-all constraints and boundaries within which companies survive and grow or fail. Through an evaluation and projection of external forces, management attempts to make realistic assumptions about the future environment. These assumptions about noncontrollable and partially controllable factors are the foundations of sales forecasts, and intelligent sales predictions can be made only by implicitly or explicitly assuming relationships about these factors.

As an example of the importance of external forces, consider the development of a controlled shopping center. Several years may elapse from the initiation of the original idea and the first inquiry concerning site location until the actual opening of the center. Choices must be made from among alternative sites, and considerable negotiations may follow to obtain the property and construct and finance the center. Then there are a host of operating details to attend to, including the actual leasing of stores.

The profitability of the total investment and the sales realized by retail stores in the shopping center will be affected by external forces. Existing and potential competition, for example, can have great influence on future sales. Demographic and economic forces in the form of population shifts and income trends will shape the retail sales potential of the center. Existing and potential industrial development of the surrounding territory will influence employment and income and will be reflected in marketing opportunity.

Municipal, state, and federal regulations will have an impact on future pricing tactics, on the use of various promotional devices including trading stamps, on store hours, and even on the types of merchandise that may be sold in particular kinds of stores.

Other examples could be presented concerning such industries as wood products, chemicals, mining, petroleum, transportation, the power industry, and communications.

After determining the external business climate for a future period, the sales forecaster must estimate the impact that internal business factors will make on potential markets. This involves an evaluation of those factors over which the company has direct control. They can be adjusted over the longer run by the company itself.

For an effective forecast, the company's know-how, its financial position, the plant capacity, the material resources and personnel available, and the company's reputation, image, and position in the market place must all be evaluated. The market position that a company eventually earns and the sales that it achieves will depend on the impact made by the internal business factors as they are combined into planned management programs carried out within the external business system. A consideration of both climates, external and internal, will give management some guides by which to judge the potential sales opportunity for a company. Through the use of various analyses and by the application of sound judgment, management may map out a company's future sales position.

Thus, sales forecasting helps integrate the management-controllable and management-noncontrollable factors, or the given elements of a total business system within which the company operates and the internal factors of the business itself.

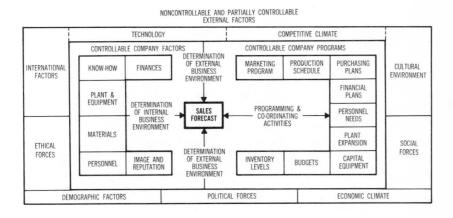

Figure 2   Sales forecasting: a focus for integrative planning

The sales forecast is also a device by means of which management may integrate its objectives, its operating programs, and its targets with potential market opportunity. This can be done by translating the sales forecast into specific profit and sales-volume goals to be realized in a given future period of time. The sales forecast thus becomes a basis for marketing programs, purchasing plans, financial budgets, personnel needs, production schedules, plant and equipment requirements, expansion programs, and perhaps most other aspects of management programming.

The right half of Figure 2 presents sales forecasting as a vehicle for translating the noncontrollable, partially controllable, and internal business environments into specific controllable management programs. The figure also emphasizes the interrelationships between sales forecasts and company programs.

Forecasting Program

Figure 3 outlines the elements of a total sales forecasting program. Four major stages of forecasting, the specific procedures to be followed, and their sequence are presented. These stages are: assembling the forecasting information; evaluating and projecting the data; applying the sales forecast operationally; and auditing the forecast. These four steps are broken down further, and some of the techniques that may be utilized at each stage and the results achieved are described. Figure 3 starts with the noncontrollable business environment and internal business climate and works down through the various predictions about controllable business plans, programs, and objectives.

The first step in a comprehensive sales forecasting program is assembling forecasting information. This involves the recognition of noncontrollable and partially controllable environments through observation and listing of significant external factors. The result is the identification of pertinent social, cultural, ethical, economic, political, demographic, international, technological, and competitive forces that will influence the projections.

Next, information can be assembled about these noncontrollable factors and an investigation made of such outside sources of information as governments, industries, and universities.

The third step in assembling forecasting information is that of gathering information about the controllable company environment, which involves research into company records. This should result in the selection of relevant company forecasting information.

After forecasting information has been assembled, the data must be evaluated and projected. This activity has two components: analyzing the data and making the actual forecast. To analyze the data, such analytical tools as time series analysis, least squares methods of fitting a straight line, fitting curves, simple and multiple correlation, the use of input-output tables, and breakeven charts may be used. This leads to the determination of patterns and relationships through lead and lag indicators, cycles, seasonal indexes, trend lines, and measures of covariation.

The actual sales projections may be made through extrapolation, a straight percentage increase in sales, executive opinion polls, end-use analysis, historical analogy, a panel of experts, the grass-roots approach, samples and surveys, models, experiments, hunches, judgments, and the oft-used crystal ball. After these projections have been made, the prediction and definition of future dollar and unit sales, and maximum and minimum sales ranges is possible.

Figure 3
A Total Sales Forecasting Program

Stages of Process	Techniques	Results
Assembling Information		
Recognize noncontrollable and partially controllable business environment.	Observe and list significant external factors.	Identification of pertinent cultural, social, economic, political, demographic, competitive, ethical, international, technological forces.
Gather information about noncontrollable and partially controllable forces.	Investigate outside sources of information.	Selection and gathering of data from government, industry, university research, Federal Reserve Board, company records.
Gather information about controllable forces.	Investigate company records.	Selection of relevant company forecasting information.
Evaluating and Projecting Data		
Analyze data.	Apply analytical tools: time series analysis, least squares, simple correlation, multiple correlation, input-output tables, breakeven charts.	Determination of patterns and relationships: lead and lag indicators, cycles, seasonal indexes, trend lines, covariation.
Forecast future sales.	Employ extrapolation, constant percentage of increase, end-use analysis, executive opinion, historical analogy, panel of experts, grassroots techniques, surveys, models, experiments, samples, hunches, judgment, and crystal ball.	Prediction and definition of future dollar sales, unit sales, maximum and minimum ranges.
Operationally Applying Forecast		
Refine sales forecast.	Break sales down by volume and profit control units: product lines, territories, customers, salesmen.	Establishment of specific sales targets.
Translate specific targets into operational programs.	Establish and co-ordinate plans: marketing program, production schedules, purchasing plans, financial requirements, personnel needs, plant expansion, capital equipment budgets, inventory levels.	Identification of controllable business environment.
Auditing the Forecast		
Review forecast.	Compare actual and forecast sales regularly and analyze discrepancies.	Determination of reasons for deviations.
Modify forecast and forecasting procedures.	Re-evaluate projections and adjust forecasting techniques.	More accurate sales forecasting.

Then the forecast must be applied operationally, which involves refining the sales forecast. This is done by breaking it down on the basis of volume and profit control units by product lines, salesmen, customers territories, and other managerial units. Specific sales targets can thus be established, and sales forecasting data become the basis for programming marketing, production, purchasing, finance, plant expansion, capital equipment acquisition, personnel, and inventory needs. Controllable business programs have now been really determined.

The last step in a comprehensive sales forecasting program is that of auditing the forecast. This involves reviewing the forecast by comparing actual and forecast sales and analyzing any deviations or discrepancies. The purpose here is to determine the reasons for the deviations. Then future forecasts and even the forecasting techniques can be modified. The end result is more accurate sales forecasts.

The total sales forecasting process is one of refinement. It starts with the more general factors—the external noncontrollable environment and the internal business environment—quantifies them, and finally establishes specific operational goals and targets.

Marketing planning often suffers because management does not develop an effective sales forecasting program. One of the great inducements to ignore or neglect sales forecasting is the difficulty of making predictions. It is a trying task for anyone to try to determine future relationships and their implications for potential sales. It is much more comfortable to turn to the consideration of current operating problems, which are more concrete, are somewhat easier to grasp, and for which some corrective action may be initiated almost immediately.

However, professional marketing management cannot afford to neglect the sales forecasting process. It must become concerned with the development of well co-ordinated, planned, and forceful systems of business action. It must plan the use of company resources so that a firm can establish itself in the market place and grow.

The future marketing climate is likely to be one of keener competition, an exhilarating pace of market change, heavier fixed costs, and an increasing emphasis on innovation. Adequate marketing planning will become the foundation for integrated marketing action. Since one of the basic components of effective marketing planning is sales forecasting, it seems obvious that in the future an increasing amount of time and resources will be spent by companies in developing more adequate sales forecasts.

The application of the systems approach to marketing management promises to breathe new life into marketing research. In this article the authors present their views of the relationship between decision-information flows and the management process in marketing, and state the case for expanding traditional marketing research into "marketing information systems."

Marketing Information Systems: A New Dimension for Marketing Research

Richard H. Brien

James E. Stafford

Business enterprise in the United States is caught in an ironic dilemma: our economic system generates a massive volume of data daily, and the rate of information generation appears to be increasing exponentially; yet most managers continue to complain that they have insufficient, inappropriate, or untimely information on which to base operating decisions.

In 1958, Adrian McDonough observed: "Half the cost of running our economy is the cost of information. No other field offers such concentrated room for improvement as does information analysis."[1] Today, a decade later, the need for efficient information management is even greater, perhaps especially for marketing management since its job is to match the firm's products with dynamic markets. Marketing is inextricably caught up in the "Communications Revolution." The new era, "The Age of Information," will

Reprinted by permission of the authors and the publisher from the *Journal of Marketing*, published by the American Marketing Association, Vol. 32, No. 3 (July, 1968), pp. 19-23.

[1] "Today's Office—Room for Improvement," *Dun's Review and Modern Industry*, Vol. 73 (September, 1958), p. 50.

emphasize the information gathering and processing structure of the organization.

It is the contention of this article that the problem of securing adequate decision information for marketing must, and now can, be seen from a broader perspective than previously has been the case. In seeking to establish a new outlook on a matter it is often helpful to cast the problem in new terms. The new perspective from which this inquiry will be launched is that of "managerial systems." The process of developing timely, pertinent decision data for marketing management can now be characterized more meaningfully, even if somewhat prematurely, as the functioning of a "marketing information system" rather than simply as "marketing research."

The Role of Marketing Research

Where does research fit into the marketing management process? If the marketing concept—with its emphasis on integrated decision-making—were widely accepted and implemented, the answer would be fairly clear. Research would be used to analyze specified relationships in the various functional areas of marketing, but the emphasis would be on its use in a coordinated, systematic fashion in order to make the total marketing strategy of the firm more efficient. (See Figure 1.)

Research findings would serve at the outset as a basis for establishing objectives and formulating an apparently optimal plan. At this stage the role of research essentially would be *to predict* the results of alternative business decisions (for example, a "penetration" price versus a "skimming" price, or information dissemination through salesmen rather than through advertising). (See the "A" feedbacks in Figure 1.)

If the research effort were extended full cycle, periodic post hoc studies would be conducted *to evaluate* the execution of specific aspects or phases of the marketing program. ("B" feedbacks in Figure 1.) In this role, research would provide the basis for control, modification, or redirection of the overall program.

Control and modification (or redirection), in sum, represent *reformulation,* and the "B" feedbacks (evaluative) in fact would become "A" feedbacks (formulative), for the succeeding stage of the marketing program. This condition simply underscores the fact that marketing management is an ongoing process, or—in the newer terminology—a dynamic system.

Formulative and evaluative information can also come *from inside the firm,* notably from the accounting department. This information flow typically is not considered part of "marketing research." It is definitely an integral part, however, of a marketing information system.

Under the marketing concept, research should also help to anticipate new profit opportunities for the firm in the form of new products or services. ("C" feedback in Figure 1.) In many U.S. industries—especially consumer goods industries—the rate of product innovation, the rate of new product failure, are all extremely high and still rising. To survive in such dynamic markets the firm

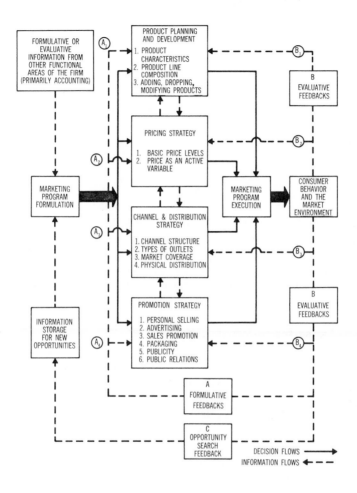

Figure 1   The marketing management process and information flow

must try to develop a sensitivity to changes in consumer behavior and in the conditions that influence behavior, both of which create opportunities for successful new products.

It is meaningless to talk of a new product without considering at the same time the related marketing decisions (the rest of that product's marketing mix) that will have to be made. This consideration would bring the cycle back to the formulative role of research (the "A" feedbacks), suggesting again that marketing research really *should be a coordinating agent.* Each marketing decision should be thought of as an input in the dynamic system, and research should be used as an agent to assist in phasing the inputs. The common goal of the decision inputs is the profitable satisfaction of consumer needs or wants; this brings the matter back to the marketing concept, and the package seems reasonably complete. In fact, if marketing research and the marketing concept had this kind of relationship in widespread practice, the case for marketing information systems would be considerably weakened.

Research by Fits and Starts

A recent survey revealed that unfortunately there is still considerable confusion and wide divergence of opinion regarding the definition and managerial implications of the marketing concept.[2] Especially disappointing was the failure of many companies to cite customer-orientation and integrated decision-making as important aspects of the concept. One of the consequences of this narrow view has been the evolution of marketing research somewhat "by fits and starts."

A widely used definition of marketing research is "the systematic gathering, recording, and analyzing of data about problems relating to the marketing of goods and services."[3] Unfortunately, the research procedure has tended to be unsystematic, to emphasize data collection per se instead of the development of decision-pertinent information, and to concern itself with isolated problems almost on an ad hoc basis. "There is a widespread failure to visualize marketing research as a continuing process of inquiry in which executives are helped to think more effectively."[4]

Toward Marketing Information Systems

The systems approach to marketing management is breathing new life into marketing research. The emphasis that systems theory places on interaction and integration in the decision-making process makes it clear that the particularistic, "brush-fire" approach that has characterized traditional marketing research is rapidly becoming obsolete. What is needed is *"a marketing intelligence* system tailored to the needs of each marketer. Such a system would serve as the ever-alert nerve center of the marketing operation."[5]

The "nerve center" concept is the theme used by Philip Kotler who has drafted a blueprint for a new organizational unit within the firm, the Marketing Information and Analysis Center (MIAC).[6] MIAC represents a complete overhaul and expansion of the marketing research department into a comprehensive executive marketing information service.

---

[2] Martin L. Bell, *Marketing: Concepts and Strategy* (Boston: Houghton Mifflin Company, 1966), p. 10.

[3] Committee on Definitions of the American Marketing Association, Ralph S. Alexander, Chairman, *Marketing Definitions: A Glossary of Marketing Terms* (Chicago: American Marketing Association, 1962), p. 16-17.

[4] Joseph W. Newman, "Put Research Into Marketing Decisions," *Harvard Business Review,* Vol. 40 (March-April, 1962), p. 106.

[5] Lee Adler, "Systems Approach to Marketing," *Harvard Business Review,* Vol. 45 (May-June, 1967), p. 110.

[6] Philip Kotler, "A Design for the Firm's Marketing Nerve Center," *Business Horizons,* Vol. 9 (Fall, 1966), p. 70.

Definition of MIS

Despite minor variations in terminology, it is clear that many of the critics of the narrow view of the role of marketing research are advocating a common concept—"the concept of careful search to generate a flow of ideas and information which will help executives make better decisions."[7]

The notion of a sustained flow of decision-information leads to the term, "marketing information system," defined as follows:

A structured, interacting complex of persons, machines and procedures designed to generate an orderly flow of pertinent information collected from both intra- and extra-firm sources, for use as the bases for decision-making in specified responsibility areas of marketing management.

It will be helpful to take a closer look at the essential components of the definition: first, a *structured, interacting complex.* The important notion here is that the marketing information system is a carefully developed master plan for information flow, with explicit objectives and a home in the formal organization. Successful information systems will not evolve spontaneously within the organization, nor will they result if their creation is left exclusively to information technicians. Donald Cox and Robert Good point out that a characteristic common to each of the companies that so far has had success with its marketing information system is the *support of top management.*[8]

A marketing information system is a structured, interacting complex of *persons, machines, and procedures,* requiring the coordinated efforts of many departments and individuals, including:
- Top management
- Marketing management, brand management
- Sales management
- New product groups
- Market research personnel
- Control and finance departments
- Systems analysts and designers
- Operations researchers, statisticians, and model builders
- Programmers
- Computer equipment experts and suppliers.[9]

It is clear that in traditional management terms both line and staff personnel inevitably will be involved in any marketing information system. Decision-makers will have to be a great deal more precise in specifying their information needs, and a complete crew of information specialists will be called upon to satisfy them.

What is not clear is the determination of the most effective organization

---

[7] Same reference as footnote 4.

[8] Donald F. Cox and Robert E. Good, "How to Build a Marketing Information System," *Harvard Business Review,* No. 3, Vol. 45 (May-June, 1967), p. 149.

[9] Same reference as footnote 8.

pattern for implementing and administering the system. In fact, the organization problem is probably the greatest deterrent to the more rapid and widespread diffusion of the information systems concept. The question, like many others in the area of organization structure, is not generically answerable; each firm's system will have to be tailor-made.

One of the major factors that makes it meaningful to talk of information systems is the tremendous improvement since World War II in information handling *technology and machinery.* The building of the first primitive computer, only slightly more than two decades ago, has been designated the beginning of a revolution in the information sciences.

There has been some confusion, however, about the relationship between computers and information systems. They are not synonymous; nor is either the sine qua non of the other. The system is the structure and procedure of the entire organization's communicative process; the computer is a processing device that may or may not be included in the information system.

The consideration of the use of computers has, however, forced many organizations to pay explicit attention to their information systems. "The flexibility and power of the new tool, as well as its great cost, has caused many managers to think for the first time of formally planning their information flows and processing functions."[10]

Business information systems include many machines other than the computer and some of them promise to have an impact on future systems that will rival the computer's influence. In particular, data copying, storage, and retrieval machines have greatly expanded management's information processing capability.

It is estimated that in 1966 some half a million duplicating machines spewed out 400 billion copies.[11] At the same time, a new document storage system was developed permitting the storage of up to 500,000 single-page documents on a single 7,200 foot reel of videotape. This means that roughly 20,000 articles or chapters from books could be stored on one reel with a retrieval time measured in seconds.

But the physical capacity to generate and process fantastic volumes of data at very high speed is an asset only if the types of data to be gathered and the sources from which they are to be elicited are carefully prescribed. The definition of a marketing information system alleged that it is *designed to generate an orderly flow of pertinent information, collected from both intra- and extra-firm sources.*

Computer-Based Reporting Systems

Internal information includes fundamental records of costs, shipments, and sales and any analyses of these that can be made to measure the firm's

[10] Frederick G. Withington, *The Use of Computers in Business Organizations* (Reading, Mass.: Addison-Wesley, 1966), p.3.

[11] E. B. Weiss, "The Communications Revolution and How It Will Affect All Business and All Marketing," a special issue reprinted from *Advertising Age* (Chicago: Advertising Publications, Inc., 1966), p. 22.

performance (distribution cost analysis, market shares by product and region, and the like). The computer and more progressive accounting departments that see their role as the provision of management information rather than as simply "scorekeeping" have been two of the most important contributors to the integration of such data, on a regular basis, into the marketing information flow.

Many companies are experimenting with "computerized marketing information" in an attempt to shorten the delay between the performance of their products in the market and the receipt of performance reports. In doing so, they stand to sharpen their strategy by gaining valuable lead-time over their competitors.

One producer and nation-wide marketer of consumer goods gets monthly reports on 3,000 key accounts 20 days earlier than before, thanks to computer-based reporting systems. Each account is compared with its performance at the same point in time during the previous year and with the company's current total volume in the particular market zone. Also provided are gross daily tabulations for each package size of each brand by geographic district.

When the doors open each morning at another company, a major grocery products manufacturer, marketing management has a complete sales analysis and inventory position as of closing time the previous day. The data are fed by teletypewriter from the company's sales offices and warehouses to a central computer which analyzes the day's orders. In addition, each salesman is required to "mark sense" his daily call reports and send them in to headquarters each evening for computer analysis. Once accumulated, these reports on the in-store impact of frontings, shelf positions, and point-of-sale materials provide marketing management with an up-to-date retail product-movement picture.[12]

Integrating Research into the MIS

The most important notion in these examples is that a timely, basic data flow has been established to chart the firm's progress and raise warning signals when there is a marketing malfunction. Such a framework will make additional data needs much clearer, allowing special supplementary information to be collected, *as needed,* from external sources through surveys, panels or experiments. At this point, then, the proper order will have been established: *the need for conducting "marketing research" and the technique to be used will be determined in the context of specific managerial information requirements.*

Such an approach will help assure that any data gathered are *pertinent,* another important aspect of the definition of a marketing information system. It is perhaps a more grievous sin to collect unnecessary or redundant information than it is to fail to collect any data at all about a particular matter. Superfluous information costs money to develop and wastes decision-makers' time; it represents a serious misallocation of managerial resources. It must be remembered, the definition asserts, that the data generated are to be used as *the*

[12] Same reference as footnote 11.

bases for decision-making in specified responsibility areas of marketing management.

Thus, the questions of the types of data the information system is to generate and the sources from which it is to elicit the data really can be answered only in the framework of a careful designation of the organizational decision-structure and the specification of the information requirements for the decision process. In fact, according to many organizational theorists, information processing and decision-making are inseparable in practice. A decision occurs only on "the receipt of some kind of communication, it consists of a complicated process of combining communication from various sources and it results in the transmission of further communications."[13]

Mr. Paul Funk, executive vice-president of McCann/ITSM, contends that marketing information management *is* the basic business of business:

Only by putting together an over-all construction of the total marketing process; only by identifying—and in most instances by visualizing—interrelationships, information flows, concurrent and sequential work patterns and critical decision points can one truly grasp control of the bewildering and complex range of activities engaged in by the present-day major corporation.[14]

The pursuit of marketing information systems, then, really involves much more than expanding and automating the data gathering process. It is an inextricable part of the larger pursuit of more efficient forms and methods of organization for marketing management.

We Are Running Late

There is ample evidence that marketing decision-making is becoming more complex, making the need for a systematic approach to information management all the greater. First, there is a growing complexity of the areas that have to be managed, largely a function of the tendency toward larger scale enterprise. Second, as expanded marketing effort takes the firm across existing environmental frontiers, whether geographic, economic or social (or, more likely, all three), the information needs of the enterprise are substantially compounded. It is highly likely that the most crucial constraint currently imposed on the growth of international marketing, for example, is the dearth of pertinent decision-information.

But perhaps the most compelling argument for marketing information systems is the "Information Explosion" itself. The world's store of knowledge has allegedly doubled during the past decade and is expected at least to double again in the next decade.

---

[13] John T. Dorsey, Jr., "A Communication Model for Administration," *Administrative Science Quarterly,* Vol. 2 (December, 1957), p. 309.

[14] "Why Industrial Marketers Aren't Using Computers," *Industrial Marketing,* Vol. 51 (November, 1966), pp. 88-89.

Information, including management information, is growing by the microsecond and even nanosecond. We cannot turn off the flow. We had therefore better learn to control it—and we are already running late.[15]

[15] Howell M. Estes, "Will Managers Be Overwhelmed by the Information Explosion?," *Armed Forces Management,* Vol. 13 (December, 1966), p. 84.

Success in planning marketing strategies requires the utilization of both product differentiation and market segmentation as components of strategy. Despite the emphasis on the differences between the two concepts, both are closely related in the setting of an imperfectly competitive market.

Product Differentiation and Market Segmentation as Alternative Marketing Strategies

Wendell R. Smith

During the decade of the 1930's, the work of Robinson and Chamberlin resulted in a revitalization of economic theory. While classical and neoclassical theory provided a useful framework for economic analysis, the theories of perfect competition and pure monopoly had become inadequate as explanations of the contemporary business scene. The theory of perfect competition assumes homogeneity among the components of both the demand and supply sides of the market, but diversity or heterogeneity had come to be the rule rather than the exception. This analysis reviews major marketing strategy alternatives that are available to planners and merchandisers of products in an environment characterized by imperfect competition.

Diversity in Supply

That there is a lack of homogeneity or close similarity among the items offered to the market by individual manufacturers of various products is obvious in any variety store, department store, or shopping center. In many cases the

Reprinted by permission of the author and the publisher from the *Journal of Marketing*, published by the American Marketing Association, Vol. 21, No. 1 (July, 1956), pp. 3-8.

impact of this diversity is amplified by advertising and promotional activities. Today's advertising and promotion tends to emphasize appeals to *selective* rather than *primary* buying motives and to point out the distinctive or differentiating features of the advertiser's product or service offer.

The presence of differences in the sales offers made by competing suppliers produces a diversity in supply that is inconsistent with the assumptions of earlier theory. The reasons for the presence of diversity in specific markets are many and include the following:

1. Variations in the production equipment and methods or processes used by different manufacturers of products designed for the same or similar uses.
2. Specialized or superior resources enjoyed by favorably situated manufacturers.
3. Unequal progress among competitors in design, development, and improvement of products.
4. The inability of manufacturers in some industries to eliminate product variations even through the application of quality control techniques.
5. Variations in producers' estimates of the nature of market demand with reference to such matters as price sensitivity, color, material, or package size.

Because of these other factors, both planned and uncontrollable differences exist in the products of an industry. As a result, sellers make different appeals in support of their marketing efforts.

Diversity of Variations in Consumer Demand

Under present-day conditions of imperfect competition, marketing managers are generally responsible for selecting the over-all marketing strategy or combination of strategies best suited to a firm's requirements at any particular point in time. The strategy selected may consist of a program designed to bring about the *convergence* of individual market demands for a variety of products upon a single or limited offering to the market. This is often accomplished by the achievement of product differentiation through advertising and promotion. In this way, variations in the demands of individual consumers are minimized or brought into line by means of effective use of appealing product claims designed to make a satisfactory volume of demand *converge* upon the product or product line being promoted. This strategy was once believed to be essential as the marketing counterpart to standardization and mass production in manufacturing because of the rigidities imposed by production cost considerations.

In some cases, however, the marketer may determine that it is better to accept *divergent* demand as a market characteristic and to adjust product lines and marketing strategy accordingly. This implies ability to merchandise to a heterogeneous market by emphasizing the precision with which a firm's products can satisfy the requirements of one or more distinguishable market segments. The strategy of product differentiation here gives way to marketing programs based upon measurement and definition of market differences.

Lack of homogeneity on the demand side may be based upon different customs, desire for variety, or desire for exclusiveness or may arise from basic differences in user needs. Some divergence in demand is the result of shopping errors in the market. Not all consumers have the desire or the ability to shop in a sufficiently efficient or rational manner as to bring about selection of the most needed or most wanted goods or services.

Diversity on the demand side of the market is nothing new to sales management. It has always been accepted as a fact to be dealt with in industrial markets where production to order rather than for the market is common. Here, however, the loss of precision in the satisfying of customer requirements that would be necessitated by attempts to bring about convergence of demand is often impractical and, in some cases, impossible. However, even in industrial marketing, the strategy of product differentiation should be considered in cases where products are applicable to several industries and may have horizontal markets of substantial size.

Long-Term Implications

While contemporary economic theory deals with the nature of product differentiation and its effects upon the operation of the total economy, the alternative strategies of product differentiation and market segmentation have received less attention. Empirical analysis of contemporary marketing activity supports the hypothesis that, while product differentiation and market segmentation are closely related (perhaps even inseparable) concepts, attempts to distinguish between these approaches may be productive of clarity in theory as well as greater precision in the planning of marketing operations. Not only do strategies of differentiation and segmentation call for differing systems of action at any point in time, but the dynamics of markets and marketing underscore the importance of varying degrees of diversity *through time* and suggest that the rational selection of marketing strategies is a requirement for the achievement of maximum functional effectiveness in the economy as a whole.

If a rational selection of strategies is to be made, an integrated approach to the minimizing of total costs must take precedence over separate approaches to minimization of production costs on the one hand and marketing costs on the other. Strategy determination must be regarded as an over-all management decision which will influence and require facilitating policies affecting both production and marketing activities.

Differences Between Strategies of Differentiation and Segmentation

Product differentiation and market segmentation are both consistent with the framework of imperfect competition.[1] In its simplest terms, *product*

---

[1] Imperfect competition assumes lack of uniformity in the size and influence of the firms or individuals that comprise the demand or supply sides of a market.

differentiation is concerned with the bending of demand to the will of supply. It is an attempt to shift or to change the slope of the demand curve for the market offering of an individual supplier. This strategy may also be employed by a group of suppliers such as a farm cooperative, the members of which have agreed to act together. It results from the desire to establish a kind of equilibrium in the market by bringing about adjustment of market demand to supply conditions favorable to the seller.

Segmentation is based upon developments on the demand side of the market and represents a rational and more precise adjustment of product and marketing effort to consumer or user requirements. In the language of the economist, segmentation is *disaggregative* in its effects and tends to bring about recognition of several demand schedules where only one was recognized before.

Attention has been drawn to this area of analysis by the increasing number of cases in which business problems have become soluble by doing something about marketing programs and product policies that overgeneralize both markets and marketing effort. These are situations where intensive promotion designed to differentiate the company's products was not accomplishing its objective—cases where failure to recognize the reality of market segments was resulting in loss of market position.

While successful product differentiation will result in giving the marketer a horizontal share of a broad and generalized market, equally successful application of the strategy of market segmentation tends to produce depth of market position in the segments that are effectively defined and penetrated. The differentiator seeks to secure a layer of the market cake, whereas one who employs market segmentation strives to secure one or more wedge-shaped pieces.

Many examples of market segmentation can be cited; the cigarette and automobile industries are well-known illustrations. Similar developments exist in greater or lesser degree in almost all product areas. Recent introduction of a refrigerator with no storage compartment for frozen foods was in response to the distinguishable preferences of the segment of the refrigerator market made up of home freezer owners whose frozen food storage needs had already been met.

Strategies of segmentation and differentiation may be employed simultaneously, but more commonly they are applied in sequence in response to changing market conditions. In one sense, segmentation is a momentary or short-term phenomenon in that effective use of this strategy may lead to more formal recognition of the reality of market segments through redefinition of the segments as individual markets. Redefinition may result in a swing back to differentiation.

The literature of both economics and marketing abounds in formal definitions of product differentiation. *From a strategy viewpoint,* product differentiation is securing a measure of control over the demand for a product by advertising or promoting differences between a product and the products of competing sellers. It is basically the result of sellers' desires to establish firm market positions and/or to insulate their businesses against price competition. Differentiation tends to be characterized by heavy use of advertising and promotion and to result in prices that are somewhat above the equilibrium levels associated with perfectly competitive market conditions. It may be classified as a *promotional* strategy or approach to marketing.

Market segmentation, on the other hand, consists of viewing a heterogeneous market (one characterized by divergent demand) as a number of smaller homogeneous markets in response to differing product preferences among important market segments. It is attributable to the desires of consumers or users for more precise satisfaction of their varying wants. Like differentiation, segmentation often involves substantial use of advertising and promotion. This is to inform market segments of the availability of goods or services produced for or presented as meeting their needs with precision. Under these circumstances, prices tend to be somewhat closer to perfectly competitive equilibrium. Market segmentation is essentially a *merchandising* strategy, merchandising being used here in its technical sense as representing the adjustment of market offerings to consumer or user requirements.

The Emergence of the Segmentation Strategy

To a certain extent, market segmentation may be regarded as a force in the market that will not be denied. It may result from trial and error in the sense that generalized programs of product differentiation may turn out to be effective in some segments of the market and ineffective in others. Recognition of, and intelligent response to, such a situation necessarily involves a shift in emphasis. On the other hand, it may develop that products involved in marketing programs designed for particular market segments may achieve a broader acceptance than originally planned, thus revealing a basis for convergence of demand and a more generalized marketing approach. The challenge to planning arises from the importance of determining, preferably in advance, the level or degree of segmentation that can be exploited with profit.

There appear to be many reasons why formal recognition of market segmentation as a strategy is beginning to emerge. One of the most important of these is decrease in the size of the minimum efficient producing or manufacturing unit required in some product areas. American industry has also established the technical base for product diversity by gaining release from some of the rigidities imposed by earlier approaches to mass production. Hence, there is less need today for generalization of markets in response to the necessity for long production runs of identical items.

Present emphasis upon the minimizing of marketing costs through self-service and similar developments tends to impose a requirement for better adjustment of products to consumer demand. The retailing structure, in its efforts to achieve improved efficiency, is providing less and less sales push at point of sale. This increases the premium placed by retailers upon products that are presold by their producers and are readily recognized by consumers as meeting their requirements as measured by satisfactory rates of stock turnover.

It has been suggested that the present level of discretionary buying power is productive of sharper shopping comparisons, particularly for items that are above the need level. General prosperity also creates increased willingness "to pay a little more" to get "just what I wanted."

Attention to market segmentation has also been enhanced by the recent ascendancy of product competition to a position of great economic importance. An expanded array of goods and services is competing for the consumer's dollar. More specifically, advancing technology is creating competition between new and traditional materials with reference to metals, construction materials, textile products, and in many other areas. While such competition is confusing and difficult to analyze in its early stages, it tends to achieve a kind of balance as various competing materials find their markets of maximum potential as a result of recognition of differences in the requirements of market segments.

Many companies are reaching the stage in their development where attention to market segmentation may be regarded as a condition or cost of growth. Their *core* markets have already been developed on a generalized basis to the point where additional advertising and selling expenditures are yielding diminishing returns. Attention to smaller or *fringe* market segments, which may have small potentials individually but are of crucial importance in the aggregate, may be indicated.

Finally, some business firms are beginning to regard an increasing share of their total costs of operation as being fixed in character. The higher costs of maintaining market position in the channels of distribution illustrate this change. Total reliance upon a strategy of product differentiation under such circumstances is undesirable, since market share available as a result of such a promotion-oriented approach tends to be variable over time. Much may hinge, for example, upon week-to-week audience ratings of the television shows of competitors who seek to outdifferentiate each other. Exploitation of market segments, which provides for greater maximization of consumer or user satisfactions, tends to build a more secure market position and to lead to greater over-all stability. While traditionally, high fixed costs (regarded primarily from the production viewpoint) have created pressures for expanded sale of standardized items through differentiation, the possible shifting of certain marketing costs into the fixed area of the total cost structure tends to minimize this pressure.

Conclusion

Success in planning marketing activities requires precise utilization of both product differentiation and market segmentation as components of marketing strategy. It is fortunate that available techniques of marketing research make unplanned market exploration largely unnecessary. It is the obligation of those responsible for sales and marketing administration to keep the strategy mix in adjustment with market structure at any point in time and to produce in marketing strategy at least as much dynamism as is present in the market. The ability of business to plan in this way is dependent upon the maintenance of a flow of market information that can be provided by marketing research as well as the full utilization of available techniques of cost accounting and cost analysis.

Cost information is critical because the upper limit to which market segmentation can be carried is largely defined by production cost considerations. There is a limit to which diversity in market offerings can be carried without driving production costs beyond practical limits. Similarly, the employment of product differentiation as a strategy tends to be restricted by the achievement of levels of marketing cost that are untenable. These cost factors tend to define the limits of the zone within which the employment of marketing strategies or a strategy mix dictated by the nature of the market is permissive.

It should be emphasized that while we have here been concerned with the differences between product differentiation and market segmentation as marketing strategies, they are closely related concepts in the setting of an imperfectly competitive market. The differences have been highlighted in the interest of enhancing clarity in theory and precision in practice. The emergence of market segmentation as a strategy once again provides evidence of the consumer's preeminence in the contemporary American economy and the richness of the rewards that can result from the application of science to marketing problems.

Although the concept of market segmentation has captured the imagination of marketers, the results of studies to date have not been very encouraging. This paper reviews some of the findings and implies that the very recent multidimensional approaches to marketing research show much greater potential than previous univariate techniques.

An Overview
of Market Segmentation

John C. Bieda
Harold H. Kassarjian

Not unlike the fad of Motivation Research in the post World War II period, the concept of market segmentation has produced a phenomenal proliferation of articles, studies and papers in the past decade. The concept, itself, was first clearly articulated by Wendell Smith in a 1956 *Journal of Marketing* article,[1] a paper that by now has become a classic. And perhaps this should be so, for market segmentation has permeated the thinking of theorists, researchers and managers perhaps more than any of the other fashions and fads that marketing has passed through. Until very recently the controversial nature of the issue has been not whether or not segmentation leads to meaningful analysis as much as on what basis to segment.

To the earlier marketing manager, the natural segments of population were related to the socio-economic and demographic variables found in U.S. Census of Population. From these variables one could distill out *social class*, the ultimate

Reprinted by permission of the authors and the publisher from *Marketing in a Changing World*, edited by Bernard A. Morin (Chicago: American Marketing Association, 1969), pp. 249-253.
[1] Wendell Smith. "Product Differentiation and Market Segmentation as Alternative Marketing Strategies," *Journal of Marketing*, Vol. 21 (July 1956), 3-8.

conglomerate in the determination of consumer behavior in the view of many. But the field was not to be left to the census analysts alone; for soon after, personality variables such as gregariousness, authoritarianism, inferiority, risk taking and self esteem were to make their impact; and finally such concepts as usage rate, brand loyalty, channel loyalty, advertising susceptibility and even price sensitivity were to make their debut.

The usefulness of any given technique for segmentation, of course, is the ultimate one of applicability. "In other words, a crucial criterion for determining the desirability of segmenting a market along any particular dimension is whether the different sub-markets have different elasticities . . ."[2] The determination of this criterion, according to Kotler, [3] depends upon several conditions.

The first of these is measurability, ". . . the degree to which information exists or is obtainable on various buyers' characteristics. Unfortunately many suggestive characteristics are not susceptible to easy measurement." The size of each segment that purchases toothpaste because of health fears, dislike of dentists, sex appeal, or because of habitual patterns inculcated by parents is difficult to measure.

A second condition is that of *accessibility,* the degree to which any given segment can be differentially reached. Unfortunately those starved for self-esteem, the hypochondrical types, or heavy users of toothpaste do not cooperate by differentially exposing themselves to specific media, purchasing from different outlets or necessarily willing to pay different prices.

Kotler's final condition is that of *substantiality,* the degree to which the segments are large enough to be worth sub-dividing for separate marketing activity.

Two Approaches to Segmentation

As one reviews the literature on marketing segmentation, two approaches seem to emerge. On the one hand, the researcher starts with an existing product. The function of the researcher is to study the customers of that generic product to determine if there are differences between buyers of different brands. In this case the particular segment of the market that the brands are aimed at is determined empirically. Once such information is gleaned, better marketing decisions presumably are made, and perhaps further product differentiation is possible.

A great deal of the commercial research is undoubtedly of this sort answering such questions as, "Who is our market? and how can we better reach them?"

Evans's now often quoted study on the psychological and objective factors related to Ford and Chevrolet owners is an example of this type of approach. Starting with owners of Fords and Chevrolets he collected demographic and

---

[2] Ronald E. Frank, "Market Segmentation Research: Findings and Implications," in Frank M. Bass, Charles W. King, and Edgar A. Pessemier (eds.), *Application of the Sciences in Marketing Management,* New York: John Wiley & Sons, 1968.

[3] Philip Kotler, *Marketing Management,* Englewood Cliffs, N.J.: Prentice-Hall, 1967.

personality data and by the use of discriminant analysis attempted to predict the buyers of each make of automobile. His results parenthetically indicated that demographic variables did a better job of predicting brand choice than did the personality variables.[4]

The second type of segmentation research approaches the problem from the opposite direction. The researcher starts with pre-conceived notions of what the critical segmentation variables are—social class, personality, cultural variables, age and sex. Members of each group or segment are one way or another isolated, and product usage, brand and channel loyalty, or media exposure data, are then collected and analyzed. The question the researcher asks is of the sort, "How do young marrieds differ from older persons?" or "What products do southerners use as compared with northerners?" Rainwater's study on the Workingman's Wife is an example of this approach. He collected masses of data on the behavior of working class and middle class housewives relating to their purchasing activities, attitudes, and so on, and made a number of significant comparisons.[5]

Another example of the pre-categorized approach to segmentation is Joel Cohen's study relating purchasing behavior to personality characteristics. Based on Karen Horney's tripartite conceptions of compliant, detached and aggressive styles of life, Cohen developed a questionnaire and attempted to divide his sample into these three groups of persons. Next he searched for and found some differences between groups on brand preference, usage rates and media exposure.[6]

The following overview of the literature in market segmentation includes further examples of both approaches.

An Overview of Research Findings

Demographic Characteristics

That demographic variables are a useful method of segmentation has become almost axiomatic in marketing, and yet the research evidence is not at all clear. Evans, in his study on Ford and Chevrolet owners concludes, "The linear discriminant function of demographic variables is not a sufficiently powerful predictor to be of much practical use. ... (They) ... point more to the similarity of Ford and Chevrolet owners than to any means of discrimination between them. Analysis of several other objective factors also leads to the same conclusion."[7]

On grocery store products, the Advertising Research Foundation study in 1964 compared toilet tissue purchasing behavior with 15 socio-economic

---

[4] Franklin B. Evans, "Psychological and Objective Factors in the Prediction of Brand Choice," *Journal of Business*, Vol. 32 (Oct. 1959), 340-369.

[5] Lee Rainwater, Richard P. Coleman and Gerald Handel, *Workingman's Wife*, New York: Oceana Publications, 1959.

[6] Joel B. Cohen, "An Interpersonal Orientation to the Study of Consumer Behavior," *Journal of Marketing Research*, Vol. 4. (August 1967), 270-278.

[7] Same reference as Footnote 4.

characteristics. The predictive efficiency of the characteristics was virtually nil.[8] Koponen, using the same J. Walter Thompson panel data but on beer, coffee and tea, found very similar results,[9] while Frank, Massy and Boyd using the Chicago Tribune panel data compared 57 product categories ranging from food to household products with demographic characteristics. The results were again similar with a very small portion of the variance being accounted for in the regression analyses.[10] Unfortunately, study after study throws doubt upon the direct usefulness of demographic characteristics as a predictor for product purchase.

Of course, this is not to deny that sanitary napkins are primarily purchased by women, razor blades by men, the influence of the purchase of sugar coated breakfast cereals by children, and canned boiled peanuts in brine primarily by Southerners. But nevertheless, other than very specific products aimed directly at a specific group, the empirical evidence seems to indicate that demographic measures, outside of education, are not an accurate predictor of consumer behavior.[11]

Social Class

Perhaps some of the most extensive work on market segmentation has been done in the area of social class.[12] Some differences do seem to emerge in spending patterns, product preferences and shopping habits. Martineau for example found some clear preferences between the lower and middle classes for types of retail stores.[13] Glick and Levy found preference differences in television programs with the middle classes preferring current events, drama and audience participation shows while the lower classes preferred soap operas, westerns and quiz shows. However the degree of overlap is so great that a statistical prediction would be most difficult.[14]

Further, many of the social class studies are now several years old. By the 1970's what we will mean by lower class is perhaps not an income-occupation-education type of differentiation but more specifically Negroes, Indians and Mexican-Americans. Whether there is such a thing as a Negro market that is in fact different from the white market is still a controversial and not sufficiently researched issue. However, our expectation is

[8] Ingrid Hildegaard and Lester Krueger, "Are There Customer Types?" as quoted in same reference as Footnote 2.

[9] Arthur Koponen. "Personality Characteristics of Purchasers," *Journal of Advertising Research,* Vol. 1 (Sept. 1960) 6-12.

[10] As quoted in same reference as footnote 2.

[11] Education taken as a uni-variate measure does seem to hold up as a segmentation variable as indicated in several studies and cannot as easily be brushed aside as most other demographic measures.

[12] E.g., James M. Carman, *The Application of Social Class in Market Segmentation.* Berkeley: Research Program in Marketing, Graduate School of Business Administration, 1965.

[13] Pierre D. Martineau, "Social Classes and Spending Behavior," *Journal of Marketing,* Vol. 23 (October 1958) 121-130.

[14] Ira O. Glick and Sidney Levy, *Living with Television,* New York: Aldine Publishing Co., 1962.

that no such market exists. In any case, because of more exposure to the mass media consumption behavior differences between classes probably are disappearing.

Personality

Personality studies have been similarly disappointing. Westfall was able to find differences between convertible owners and sedans but the relationships were weak.[15] Kamen found no evidence to ascertain the consistency of food preferences among personality groups.[16] Koponen in the study mentioned above using J. Walter Thompson data found some minimal differences between smokers and non-smokers on such variables as sex, aggression, achievement, dominance and compliance. However the percentage of variance accounted for both by personality variables and demographic variables combined was less than 12%.[17] Brody and Cunningham on reanalysis of the same data indicated that the personality variables measured by the Edwards Personality Preference Scale on both men and women heads of households accounted for a mere 15% of the variance.[18] Tucker and Painter, similarly found significant but very weak relationships between measures such as responsibility, emotional stability, sociability and ascendency and product preference. Among the products studied personality variables only differentiated between users of deodorants and cigarettes.[19]

Gruen found no relationship between product preference and inner- and other-direction[20] and Kassarjian could not find differences in media exposure between inner- and other-directed subjects.[21]

To sum up the literature, personality as a variable has not been a useful mode of market segmentation. Perhaps it is too much to expect the forces of personality to be powerful enough to differentially produce the purchase of Colgate Toothpaste over Crest or Gilette razor blades over Personna. Also it is possible that marketing has not yet found the right variables to measure, having no personality instruments of its own.

Buyer Characteristics

Finally turning to buyer characteristics such as brand loyalty and usage rate, the findings are not dissimilar. For example, Frank and Massy found no

[15] Ralph Westfall. "Psychological Factors in Predicting Product Choice," *Journal of Marketing,* Vol. 26 (April 1962) 34-40.

[16] Joseph M. Kamen, "Personality and Food Preferences," *Journal of Advertising Research,* Vol. 4 (Sept. 1964), 29-32.

[17] Same reference as footnote 10.

[18] Robert P. Brody & Scott M. Cunningham, "Personality Variables and the Consumer Decision Process," *Journal of Marketing Research,* Vol. 5 (Feb. 1968) 50-57.

[19] William T. Tucker and John J. Painter, "Personality and Product Use," *Journal of Applied Psychology,* Vol. 45 (1961) 325-329.

[20] W. Gruen, "Preference for New Products and Its Relationship to Different Measures of Conformity," *Journal of Applied Psychology,* Vol. 44 (1960) 361-366.

[21] Harold H. Kassarjian, "Social Character and Differential Preference for Mass Communication," *Journal of Marketing Research,* Vol. 2 (May 1965) 146-153.

significant difference in elasticity between brand loyal and non-brand loyal buyers.[22] Although Twedt did find that heavy and light users can be moderately well distinguished on the basis of their different demographic characteristics, his findings, at best, indicated that the relationships are relatively modest.[23] Again using the J. Walter Thompson panel data, Massy, Frank and Lodahl indicated that heavy and light buying households had virtually identical demographic and psychological characteristics.[24] To continue, Farley could not segment the brand loyal customer,[25] and Frank and Boyd could not differentiate between the private label and manufacturer brand customers.[26] And finally Cunningham found little relationship between rate of purchase and brand loyalty.[27] However Brody and Cunningham found in a two brand discriminant analysis they were able to correctly identify 80% of brand choices.[28]

In general, the consistency of the results tends to indicate that the research to date in market segmentation has either been unsuccessful or if a relationship is shown, quite weak.

Turning back to Kotler's criterion for market segmentation, measurability, accessibility, and substantiality, it is clear that at least some of these conditions have not been met to date. In those cases where segmentation variables are measurable they do not seem to be related to purchasing characteristics. Or, even if the relationship is verified, too often the second condition, *accessibility,* is not a simple matter. Unfortunately media exposure, channel loyalty and purchase rate are not differentiated along the same variables as purchase behavior. To the everlasting frustration of the segmentation specialist readers of *Argosy Magazine* and *True Experience* too often buy Cadillacs, while upper income professionals and businessmen too often shop at Macy's or Gimbel's in New York.

Perhaps then, the usual modes of segmentation are not sufficient. For example, Yankelovich argues that the analysis of various product markets should be made on the basis of several modes: patterns of usage, values derived from usage, preferences, aesthetics, and buying attitudes and motivations.[29] This view is enticing. Perhaps there are sufficiently substantial groupings of people who on a multi-variate set of dimensions can be considered a market segment. Unfortunately, Yankelovich does not present us with a method for such an analysis.

[22] Ronald E. Frank and William Massy, "Market Segmentation and the Effectiveness of a Brand's Price and Dealing Policies," *Journal of Business* (April 1965) 188-200.

[23] Dik W. Twedt, "How Important to Marketing Strategy is the Heavy User," *Journal of Marketing,* (January, 1964) 71-72.

[24] As quoted in same reference as Footnote 2.

[25] John Farley, "Brand Loyalty and the Economics of Information." *Journal of Business,* Vol. 37, (October, 1964) 370-381.

[26] Ronald Frank and Harper Boyd, Jr., "Are Private-Brand Prone Food Customers Really Different," *Journal of Advertising Research,* Vol. 5 (December 1965) 27-35.

[27] Ross M. Cunningham, "Brand Loyalty-What, Where, How Much?" *Harvard Business Review,* Vol. 34 (Jan.-Feb., 1956) 127-137.

[28] Brody and Cunningham, *op. cit.*

[29] The conclusion is stated by Norman L. Barnett, "Beyond Market Segmentation," *Harvard Business Review.* Vol. 47 (Jan.-Feb., 1969).

Prospects

Although the results, to date, from studies on market segmentation have not been very encouraging, we might speculate on why so much of the research has been negative when the theory seems so logical and sound on a priori basis. Perhaps the major problem of past research is that in an effort to segment markets we have lost sight of the basic premise of the theory: that different people have different needs and at different times these needs may change. Hence, a company's marketing program will have different elasticities when directed to groups of people where the needs in each group are relatively homogeneous and when the needs between groups are relatively heterogeneous.

Consider for a moment the methodological logic of the past research. First, the researcher has arbitrarily selected a group of products or brands that *he* thinks are serving the same market. Then data on purchase behavior is collected for analysis. The analysis consists of using demographic, socio-economic, and psychological variables as independent variables in either a regression or discriminant analysis. The objective is to find out if buyers of different brands are related in any way to the independent variables. If a strong relationship is found a circular argument is used to establish cause and effect, i.e., because the person jointly had the characteristic and bought the product and because the person would not have bought the product unless he needed it, therefore, the characteristic must be the cause of the need for the product. But we never bother to extrastatistically establish the cause and effect relationship. We might ask at this point 1) what kinds of assumptions are made when this type of analysis is carried out and 2) are the assumptions realistic or are other assumptions more plausible?

First, it is assumed that because people have bought the same brand, they have bought it for the same reason, i.e., the same need, desire, tension. The alternative assumption that people buy the same product for different reasons seems more realistic. For example, one family might buy one brand of potato chips because the kids like ridges in them. Another family might buy the same brand because ridged potato chips do not break quite as easily as straight potato chips when served with a dip.

Second, it is assumed that all people perceive the same set of brands to be alternatives from which to choose. Some recent evidence would tend to indicate that this assumption may not be justified. Green, Carmone, and Fox[30] have shown that television programs were clustered differently, on the basis of similarity, by three groups of people. This would tend to support an alternative hypothesis that all consumers do not perceive the same set of products as competing with one another.

Third, it is assumed that each person has the same set of alternatives (brands) available from which to choose to satisfy his needs. But it is common knowledge

[30] Green, Paul E., Frank J. Carmone, and Leo B. Fox, "Television Programme Similarities: An Application of Subjective Clustering," *Journal of the Market Research Society*, Vol. 22 (January 1969) 70-90.

to every housewife that all stores do not carry the same brands, therefore this assumption does not seem to be justified.

Fourth, it is assumed that people with the same set of characteristics, the same values of the independent variables, have the same needs, wants, and desires. This assumption may be reasonable; however there has been little, if any, systematic research to justify making this assumption on a priori basis.

One final problem with past studies centers on the complete lack of integration into the segmentation analysis of information on the marketing mixes of the products and brands under study. This omission may have contributed to past negative findings if one or both of the following situations occurred.

Situation 1. Suppose that two brands, A and B, were essentially appealing to one set of needs and two other brands, C and D, were essentially appealing to another set of needs. If information on the marketing strategies of the four brands were not incorporated prior to using regression or discriminant analysis then the buyers of each of the brands would be considered a separate group, e.g., we would have a four way discriminant analysis. This being the case, the regression or discriminant function would not be able to distinguish between the buyers of brands A and B nor between the buyers of brands C and D. In this situation we would probably conclude that the results were negative because we could not predict which brand consumers would buy based on the independent variables.

Situation 2. Suppose that one brand was appealing to several segments using different marketing mixes for each segment. If this were the case then we would expect to find the brand satisfying a unique set of needs for buyers in each of the segments. When one or more companies follow this practice a discriminant or regression analysis would not be able to identify purchasers for the different brands because the buyers for each brand are aggregated even though they may belong in different market segments.

A next logical question is: What might we do to obtain more meaningful results on the subject? We would suggest attacking the problem as follows:

1. Determine what products or brands appeal to which set of needs, wants, and desires by the following two-stage procedures. First, apply multivariate analytical techniques to similarity data, i.e., that data obtained by asking the consumers what products or brands they consider similar; then determine homogeneous groups (=clusters) of consumers that perceive the market in a similar manner, i.e., that see the same set of products as being similar. Second, for each of the homogeneous groups again use multivariate techniques to cluster products that are perceived to be similar. Then find out what basic set of needs are being met by each cluster or products. The works of Barnette and Stefflre,[31] Green, Carmone, and Robinson,[32] and Green, Carmone, and Fox[33] are significant contributions in this direction.

---

[31] Norman L. Barnett and Volney J. Stefflre, "An Empirical Approach to the Development of New Products," Unpublished manuscript, 1967.

2. At this point it is proposed that preference data from the consumers be incorporated into the analysis, i.e., the data obtained by asking the consumer which product(s) he prefers. The preference data, in conjunction with the similarity data provides a method of determining an ideal point for *each* individual in the homogeneous group obtained in the previous analysis. The ideal point for an individual would represent a product whose characteristics would be most preferred by the individual.[34] The ideal point for an individual would also serve an additional function as a reference point for determining how closely other sets of needs, represented by the clusters of products, match the needs of the individual. The degree to which the individual's needs and the needs being served by any cluster of products coincide should be an inverse function of the distance of the cluster to the ideal point, i.e., the more similar the two sets of needs the shorter the distance between that cluster and the individuals ideal point. Finally we should cluster the ideal points within each of the homogeneous groups. It would then be appropriate to determine if certain characteristics could meaningfully describe the consumers in each of these groups. This information would, of course, be used in determining future strategy for marketing to these segments.

It should be noted that the current approach takes into account differences in individuals' needs whereas previous work in this area has aggregated individuals over the entire market making it impossible to identify how different products or even the same product is related to individuals' differing needs.

The advantage of this approach is two-fold: first, we can study the basic needs of the consumers as they are currently being served by the market and, in doing so, we make no restrictions on the number or interdependence of the needs each brand can service; second, we can incorporate information on the marketing programs of the brands under study to determine the differential elasticities for each brand in each of the sub-markets.

Summary

In summary, although the concept of market segmentation has captured the imagination of marketers, the results of studies to date have not been very encouraging. Univariate studies on demographic, objective and psychological factors related to consumer behavior have on the whole leaned towards indicating that product choice cannot be predicted from these types of variables.

However, in recent months a series of multivariate studies have emerged that indicate a real potential for a better understanding of the concept of market segmentation.

[32] Green, Paul E., Frank J. Carmone, and Patrick J. Robinson, *Analysis of Marketing Behavior Using Nonmetric Scaling and Related Techniques,* Technical Monograph (Interim), Marketing Science Institute, March 1968.

[33] Same reference as Footnote 30.

[34] Same reference as Footnote 30.

IV AIDS IN MARKETING DECISION MAKING

The primary function of the business executive is decision making. The increased complexities of the marketing task have resulted in making marketing decisions extremely difficult. As discussed in Part III, many firms have established planned marketing information systems to provide for regular flows of decision-oriented information designed to facilitate decision making. The availability of computers has allowed the development of complex models and simulations of market activity. And the role of creativity is increasingly emphasized in the generation and evaluation of problem solving alternatives.

Stanley F. Stasch believes that marketing has been much slower than the other business areas in applying quantitative techniques and the computer to problem solving. He lists three factors as causes: the difficulty of quantifying the behavioral aspects of marketing; the lack of a data collection tradition in marketing; and poor communications between marketers and computer specialists. Stasch stresses the total systems approach as a necessary condition for applying quantitative techniques to marketing.

The second selection is titled "The Use of Mathematical Models in Marketing." The author shows how the basic mathematical tools of matrix algebra, calculus, probability theory, and simulation are used in developing and solving models to aid the marketing executive in making decisions. These models are applied to such marketing decision areas as media selection, new product development, and determination of optimum size of company sales forces.

The third selection analyzes "The Promise of Simulation in Marketing." The article describes how simulation is currently being applied to marketing; its strengths and weaknesses; the different forms, structure, and purposes of simulation models; and its promise as a technique for future marketing analysis.

In the final selection M. O. Edwards provides a thorough discussion of various methods for improving individual and group creativity. Edwards suggests the use of the creative techniques in combination with traditional problem solving methods.

This article points out some reasons for marketing's lag in the use of computers and quantitative techniques. The systems approach is suggested as one which can minimize or eliminate the causes of this lag. The systems approach outlined by the author uses marketing theory to guide the firm's efforts in establishing performance criteria, organizing an information collection activity, and developing analytic models.

Systems Analysis for Controlling and Improving Marketing Performance

Stanley F. Stasch

The executive of a very large packaged goods firm was recently quoted: "I don't know of a single case where the computer or operations research has contributed substantially to the solution of any marketing problem."[1] A recent headline read: "Computer's marketing use is in primitive stage, especially in industrial field."[2] In a recent article, Adler comments on the shortcomings of model building in marketing.

There is no better evidence of this than the gulf between the elegant and sophisticated models with which recent marketing literature abounds and the actual number of situations in which those models really work. For the truth of the matter is that we are still in the foothills of this development, despite the advances of a few leaders.[3]

Reprinted by permission of the author and the publisher from the *Journal of Marketing,* published by the American Marketing Association, Vol. 33, No. 2 (April, 1969), pp. 12-19.

[1] John J. Cardwell, "Marketing and the Management Sciences," a paper presented to the Chicago Chapter of TIMS (May 24, 1967), p. 1.

[2] "Computer Forces User to Answer Basic Operating Question; More Data Needed," *Marketing Insights,* Vol. 1, (April 10-14, 1967), pp. 10-11.

[3] Lee Adler, "Systems Approach to Marketing," *Harvard Business Review,* Vol. 45, (May-June, 1967), p. 115.

This paper will (1) briefly explore some of the causes of marketing's poor record of computer applications and (2) propose that the systems approach to marketing can greatly facilitate a substantial increase in marketing's use of the computer and appropriate quantitative techniques.

Why the Lag in Marketing?

Why has marketing fallen behind the other business areas in applying quantitative techniques and the computer to problem solving? This lag can be attributed to three factors:

1. Behavioral phenomena are difficult to quantify and hence difficult to computerize. It is to be expected that marketing problems with strong behavioral aspects will not be computerized until they have been quantified, and this development must await further behavioral research.

2. Of the large quantities of marketing data available, only small amounts have been collected, and not all of that in an organized manner. Any second or third generation computer can store millions of memory "bits." But what is overlooked by most industrial marketers—and by many of their bosses—is that those "bits" do not come pre-packed in the computer. They have to be gathered painstakingly by the computer user, and this is where most users fall short.[4]

3. Marketing people have not taken the initiative in closing the communications gap between themselves and computer personnel.[5] If the computer—and appropriate quantitative techniques—are to be applied to decision areas in marketing, the nature and structure of those problem areas must be explained *in detail* to the computer specialists. The marketing decision maker must be able to communicate the following to the computer specialists and quantitative analysts:

    (a) The details of the specific problem.
    (b) The theoretical structure of the marketing phenomenon, at least as the marketing manager understands it.[6]
    (c) The alternative decision choices associated with the problem.
    (d) The specific information, and its form, *required by the decision maker.*
    (e) The source, form, and frequency of availability of raw data to be used in the decision-making process.

---

[4] Same reference as footnote 2.

[5] Donald F. Cox and Robert E. Good, "How to Build a Marketing Information system," *Harvard Business Review,* Vol. 45, (May-June, 1967), p. 149; C. W. Plattes, "The Requirements for Problem Solving and Quantitative Aids to Decision-Making in Marketing Consumer Products," remarks made at the panel session on Using OR *Effectively in Advertising and Marketing—Why and How,* at the Thirty-First Annual Meeting of the Operations Research Society of America, New York City, (May 31, 1967), pp. 2-3; John J. Cardwell, "Marketing and the Management Sciences," a paper presented at the Chicago Chapter of TIMS (May 24, 1967), pp. 30-31.

[6] Peter F. Drucker, "The Manager and the Moron," *The McKinsey Quarterly,* Vol. III, (Spring, 1967), pp. 48-49.

Only when the quantitative analysts and computer specialists have been given all of this information will it be possible for them to apply *their skills* to the problem.

Role of the Systems Approach

Guided by a list of *management's problems* and the *information needed by management* for solving those problems, data collection can be organized within the framework of an information system.[7] The task of identifying the specific information needed by the decision maker can be facilitated if managers will first organize their thinking according to the five points mentioned above. In so doing, they will have thought through thoroughly all facets of their problems, they will understand their information needs, and they will then be in a position to communicate effectively with non-marketing computer specialists.

Of the three reasons given earlier for marketing's poor record of computer usage, only the first represents a situation which cannot be influenced by management; and a systems approach can be very helpful in dealing with the remaining two. If managers could adequately describe their problems and the information requirements associated with those problems, they would be in a position both to organize their data collection activity and to communicate with non-marketing computer specialists. These simple steps would rectify the second and third causes of marketing's poor record of successful computer applications.

What Is a Marketing System?

A marketing system is comprised of a number of separate sub-systems, each concerned with only one of the marketing activities performed by the firm. The primary purpose of each sub-system is the measurement and evaluation of current performance and, if a marketing activity is not being performed as economically as possible, the evaluation of proposed alternative courses of action to determine which will lead to more economical performance. These goals are attained by bringing together the components shown in Figure 1.

1. An Actual Operating System Based on Past Decisions

There must be actual or real system currently in use; that is, the firm's marketing functions are currently being performed, and someone or something must be performing them. The firm has warehouses where products are inventoried, transport facilities of some kind are used to ship their products, salesmen are calling on certain customers in certain territories, advertising of a given type is being used in certain media, and still other marketing activities are being performed. These items constitute the actual operating systems of the firm, and each represents a *past decision* made by management.

[7] Donald F. Cox and Robert E. Good, "How to Build a Marketing Information System," *Harvard Business Review,* Vol. 45, (May-June, 1967).

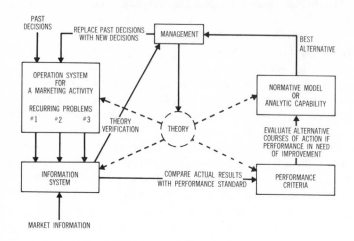

Figure 1   A marketing sub-system

2. An Information System Guided by Recurring Problems

Parallel to an operating system is an information system which records data from a number of sources. Two major sources provide the required information. Data concerning operations and performance of the firm's various marketing activities are obtained directly from those activities. Data describing the firm's markets are obtained from internal sources and external secondary sources. This information-collecting activity is guided by a *specific list of frequently occurring problems or decision areas*. The list of recurring problems is required for the identification of the information managers need when making decisions in each of these problem areas.

3. A Theoretical Structure Required for Each Recurring Problem

The decisions made in the past by management were based upon, or guided by, some marketing theories and concepts which decision-making managers considered applicable to their particular problem areas. This theoretical foundation is necessary if computer specialists are to develop a computerized information system for decision making. These specialists must be informed of the kinds of input data provided for them and how these data should be processed in order to transform them into output information which management can use when making decisions.

In effect, the computer specialist must understand how management conceptualizes the problem phenomenon before he can develop a computer program capable of generating information useful in decision making. Consequently, decision makers should take it upon themselves to provide the computer specialists with (a) the number and kind of variables (data) that constitute the theory on which decision processes are based and (b) a structural relationship of all variables, how they fit together, and how they are interrelated.[8]

This aspect of systems analysis serves two additional purposes. First, it forces the manager to think through his decision-making processes in great detail, probably in greater detail than he has ever done before. Second, it requires that the manager be capable of communicating, or that he develop the ability to communicate, with those who do not have his marketing knowledge or experience.

4. Theory Verification Through Organized Data Collection

Before decisions based on theoretical concepts can be made operationally effective, the theoretical concepts used must first be measured and verified. For example, a marketing manager may well believe that his firm would experience a diminishing returns effect if sales effort were increased indefinitely. He may even be absolutely certain that this is the case. However, he must know at least one of two things in order to make an intelligent decision concerning the amount of sales effort to be authorized. He must know either the sales volume at which diminishing returns are such that increased effort will no longer be profitable, or he must know the level of sales effort at which this diminishing returns effect will be experienced. If he knows either of these things, he can increase his effort until the critical sales volume is reached, or until the critical level of sales effort is reached. If he knows neither of these things, he can make a decision based only on experience and intuition.

Consequently, management should require that certain data collection procedures designed to verify appropriate theories and concepts be included in each marketing sub-system. Such data should be transformed into information which will permit the quantification of the relationships associated with those theories and concepts.

5. Develop Criteria for Evaluating Performance

Since the purpose of a marketing sub-system is to improve performance, it is necessary to compare the effects of current performance with criteria reflecting a level of performance considered good, or at least acceptable. Such criteria might be the desired number of sales calls or advertising exposures, actual sales compared with market potential, sales compared with profits, or any one of a large number of other possible criteria. Clearly, these criteria reflect certain marketing theories and concepts embraced by management. In order to make them operational, management must communicate the essence of these criteria to the computer specialist.

The results should be a better measure of both the distance (the separation)

[8] For an illustration, see William F. Massy and Jim D. Savvas, "Logical Flow Models for Marketing Analysis," *Journal of Marketing,* Vol. 28 (January, 1964).

between actual and desired performance and the direction in which actual performance should move to attain the desired level of performance.

6. Construct a Normative Model
Using Analytic Techniques

As a result of the foregoing five steps, a manager will know the direction in which to move and how far, but he is told nothing about how this should be done. He may even have a number of alternatives available, each of which might achieve the desired objective. Before he can choose between them, he must evaluate these alternatives and, hopefully, select the best one. However, in this case, he gets no help from the performance criteria suggested above.

This difficulty will be eliminated if the sub-system includes a normative model capable of evaluating the effects of various alternatives without actually operationalizing each alternative. If it is not possible to construct a normative model, some other analytic capability should be devised. Although not as desirable as a normative model, such a capability is likely to be an improvement over the use of a performance criterion based only on theoretical concepts. However, regardless of which is used, the end product should be the joint effort of the manager's knowledge of marketing theory and the computer specialist's knowledge of quantitative techniques.

If such a model were constructed, management could use it to evaluate all alternatives and then select the one alternative which will result in each marketing activity being performed as economically as possible. This information should then be used to improve the performance of the actual operating system. In so doing, management must discard some of the *past decisions* (see number one above), and replace them with the new decisions suggested by the analysis utilizing the normative model. It is only through such analyses that management can be confident that its marketing activities are being performed as inexpensively as possible.

It should be noted that the sub-system illustrated in Figure 1 represents a dynamic process occurring over time. Decisions made in the past influence the system's current performance, and the system's current performance is compared to some standard. Even though performance may have been up to standard last period, the firm is not guaranteed that this period's performance is also up to standard. Changes beyond the firm's control—a change or shift in the number of customers, the emergence of new technology such as railroad piggy-backing, a reduction in air freight rates, or an increase in space rates in a media vehicle, to mention a few—may cause a reduction in current performance. When such developments occur, alternatives should be reevaluated utilizing the normative model in the appropriate sub-system. When such developments result in current performance not being up to standard, past decisions must be replaced with new ones, the current operating system must be modified in some way, and the modified system will then influence future performance. Future performance will, in turn, be compared against a standard, and the procedure described above will be repeated. In effect, this transforms the procedure into a

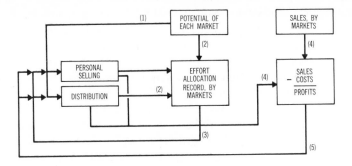

Figure 2   Evolution of a total
marketing system

process occurring again and again over time. The result should be a regular and continuous improvement in the performance of the actual operating system.

Evolution of a Marketing System

How is the systems approach applied to marketing? It appears that the evolution of a marketing system is at least a two-stage process. As an illustration of this process, consider the case of a firm manufacturing products for a large number of geographically dispersed industrial users. The firm sells directly to their customers, and because customers request fast delivery the firm maintains its own distribution facilities. In other words, although personal selling is the primary demand stimulant, fast delivery is an important element in the firm's marketing mix. The marketing system of such a firm might consist primarily of three sub-systems: market potential, personal selling, and distribution.[9]

The first stage in the development of such a marketing system would find the firm concentrating its efforts on the individual sub-systems. When these sub-systems have been developed, management will have an accurate measure of the potential in each of its markets and the capability of (1) measuring the performance of each of its marketing activities—requires an organized data collection effort—and (2) analyzing and improving the performance of those activities not being performed efficiently—requires both the availability of data and the use of appropriate analytic techniques. Once this level of analysis and sophistication has been achieved, management is ready to move on to the second stage in the development of their marketing system.

The second stage calls for integrating the sub-systems into a larger system which utilizes information taken from all sub-systems. Figure 2 illustrates how

[9] For a more detailed description of these individual sub-systems, see Stanley F. Stasch, "Marketing Systems and Quantitative Analysis," in R.B. Cunningham, editor, *Dynamic Competition in Utility Marketing* (Chicago: American Marketing Association, 1967), pp. 77-94.

this might be done. Although not shown specifically, both the personal selling and distribution sub-systems would consist of those components shown in Figure 1. In addition, the market potential sub-system could be quite complex, possibly using such techniques as regression analysis, econometric models, input-output techniques and still others.[10]

Figure 2 is useful in explaining the evolutionary process by which a marketing system takes shape. In the initial phases of the system's development, the information generated by the system will be somewhat incomplete. Nevertheless, because it is still necessary for the firm to make decisions concerning the allocation of its marketing effort, such decisions can only be based on market potential information at this stage of the system's development. In such a case, the effort expended by each marketing activity can be allocated in proportion to the potential believed to exist in each market. (See (1) and (2) in Figure 2.) At the end of the accounting period, information available from each of the sub-systems should verify if, in fact, effort had been allocated in proportion to potential. If it had not, this information should be fed back to each sub-system and an attempt should be made during the following time period to rectify whatever discrepancies existed. (See (3) in Figure 2.)

Because of competition and still other factors, the profitability of various markets displaying the same potential could differ substantially. This suggests, of course, that potential is a useful criterion when nothing better is available, but that it is not necessarily the most desirable criterion. As the first stage of the marketing system nears completion, the firm will begin to have available, for each marketing activity, cost information which accurately reflects the performance of each of those marketing activities. (The firm will, in effect, be performing each of its marketing activities as economically as possible in each of the markets it serves.) When the firm has this capability, it is ready to complete the second phase of this evolutionary process. The profitability of each market is then a valid criterion for effort allocation *because the costs used in calculating profitability will represent dollars spent in an efficient manner.* Until this is true, that is, until the firm can accurately measure marketing costs and the marketing effort associated with those costs, profits will not accurately reflect each market's response to the firm's efforts. Consequently, market potential should be used initially as the effort allocation criterion. When cost information which accurately reflects performance becomes available, the potential criterion can be replaced with the profit criterion and effort can then be re-allocated to those markets which are more profitable. (See (4) and (5) in Figure 2.)

Because of the second stage—the integration of the individual sub-systems

> Marketing Revenue (units sold times manu-
> facturing gross margin)
> Less: Marketing Costs Accurately Re-
> flecting Effort Expended in That
> Market
> ───────────────────────────────
> Equals: Market Profitability

into a larger system—the firm will be provided with still more information. One result of the first stage is that the firm will know the proportion of each marketing activity allocated to each of the markets it serves. By selecting a market and summing the amount of effort allocated to *each of the marketing activities used in that market,* the firm can develop a record of how its total marketing effort was allocated to its many markets. In addition, the firm will have a record of how the various marketing activities were combined within each market. This is essentially the marketing mix problem. If the firm knows the profitability of each market, it will then be in a position to make better decisions concerning both the allocation of its marketing effort and the composition of its marketing mix.[11]

Additional Advantages

It has been argued that the use of the systems approach by a firm will encourage the collection of data pertinent to its marketing problems, and that such an approach will facilitate communications between marketers and computer personnel. Both of these developments should lead to an increased use of the computer and appropriate quantitative techniques. In addition, management will be in a better position to cope with two significant marketing problems—effort allocation and marketing mix.

There are a number of other advantages which a firm can realize through the use of the systems approach. The literature concerned with quantitative models stresses the fact that a model usually facilitates a "sensitivity analysis"—that is, the ability to ask how much, if at all, the optimum decision would change if certain data were only partially accurate or if certain assumptions were not valid. Another advantage of a quantitative model lies in the fact that it is possible to vary the model's inputs experimentally while observing the changes in the output.

There is wide agreement that model-building and simulation is perhaps the most significant of those things not otherwise possible without a computer. As of now, an electronic digital computer is the only device that can handle variable on top of variable and give management a choice of alternatives while there is still time to make a decision.[12]

Because models and other analytic techniques are an integral part of the

---

[10] For more detailed descriptions of such sub-systems: R.J. Twery, "The Role of EDP in Sales Forecasting," pp.21-25; G.B. Hegeman, "The Role of EDP in Market Forecasting," pp. 26-28; S.T. Pender, "LAMBASTE-Determining Market Potentials Statistically," pp. 33-35, all in *Chemical Marketing and the Computer,* Proceedings of the Chemical Marketing Research Association meetings, November 16 and 17, 1965.

[11] An interesting and appropriate discussion of effort allocation can be found in Richard A. Feder, "How to Measure Marketing Performance," *Harvard Business Review,* Vol. 43 (May-June, 1965), pp. 132-142.

[12] "Computers Begin to Solve the Marketing Puzzle," *Business Week,* No. 1859 (April 17, 1965), p. 133.

individual sub-systems of a marketing system, these same advantages are also realized by the firm utilizing the system's approach. In addition, a firm with a marketing system will enjoy a number of benefits which would be unavailable to them if they did not have such a system. Three of these advantages are discussed below.

1. Frequent or Numerous Decisions

The marketing manager is concerned with a number of situations wherein decisions must be made periodically, that is, at regular intervals in time such as weekly, monthly, quarterly, and so on. He is also concerned with situations which require that essentially the same decision be made over and over at a given point in time. Such high frequency decisions abound in most marketing-oriented firms. They range from determining the profitability of various products and/or markets to determining the distribution system's ability to service customers within certain time and cost limitations. As more and more of these decision areas are systematized, management will find that they have more time to spend on those problem areas less well defined or less susceptible to quantitative analysis at present.

Table 1
Quantitative Sophistication, Data
Requirements and Data Collection Time

Quantitative Sophistication	Data Requirements	Data Collection Time	Illustration of Sales Territory Determination
Little or no quantitative analysis involved.	Readily available from many secondary sources.	Less than one year.	Use managerial judgment in determining the number of salesmen to use. Each sales territory should represent an equal amount (approximately) of sales potential.
Some simple quantitative techniques used.	Uses some data from primary sources. Firm must gather data.	One to three years.	Same as the example above except that historical data are used to determine the amount of sales potential which can be most effectively exploited. This information suggests the appropriate number of salesmen to use. (See reference 1.)
Highly complex quantitative techniques used.	Strong emphasis on primary data collected by the firm.	Three to five years.	The sales effort required to just attain each customer's saturation level is determined and summed over all customers in a territory. This is then compared with the effort available to determine if the territory is too large, too small, or just the right size. (See reference 2.)

References:
[1] Walter J. Semlow, "How Many Salesmen Do You Need?", *Harvard Business Review,* Vol. 37 (May-June, 1959), pp. 126-132.
[2] Arthur A. Brown, Frank T. Hulswit, and John D. Kettelle, "A Study of Sales Operations," *Operations Research,* Vol. 4 (June, 1956), pp. 296-308; Clark Waid, Donald F. Clark, and Russell L. Ackoff, "Allocation of Sales Effort in the Lamp Division of the General Electric Company," *Operations Research,* Vol. 4 (December, 1956), pp. 629-647.

2. Theory Usage and Validation

It seems realistic to assume that all managers base their decisions on certain theories and concepts. Although these are likely to be explicit, in many cases they may be implicit. For example, the sales manager is likely to believe that calling on a customer has some effect on the sales eventually made to that customer. On the other hand, it is unlikely that he will feel that an infinite number of sales calls will lead to an infinite amount of sales. This indicates that the sales manager, either explicitly or implicitly, believes in the diminishing returns of sales effort.

The real issue facing the manager is whether or not the diminishing returns theory is, in fact, valid and, if so, at what level of operation diminishing returns occur. The manager knows that sales will not approach infinity as effort is increased, but he does not know the scale at which to operate in order to avoid those diseconomies associated with diminishing returns. This cannot be determined without a great deal of empirical data which, generally speaking, is not available today. This then is the situation facing management. If management does not know the shape of the diminishing returns response, they will have no way of knowing if their operations fall within the range of diminishing returns *in spite of the fact that they may be completely certain of the presence of the diminishing returns phenomenon.*[13]

This illustrates the second advantage accompanying the use of a marketing system. Many marketing problems cannot be solved or even analyzed today because of the lack of empirical verification of those theories required for their solution. The use of a marketing system, however, gives management the opportunity to provide for the generation and collection *over time* of the information which will tell them if the theory being used is valid. Thus, the use of a marketing system is a necessary prerequisite in those problem areas where theory verification must precede the use of quantitative analysis.

3. Adaptive Considerations

Frequently a given problem can be analyzed in different ways, each of which may utilize a different quantitative technique. Those different techniques usually reflect various levels of quantitative sophistication and input information. The more sophisticated quantitative techniques typically require larger amounts of, and generally less accessible, data. Table 1 lists three different levels of quantitative sophistication, the input data requirements associated with them, and the approximate time span required for the collection of those data. In addition, the column farthest right in the exhibit shows how the problem of determining sales territories might be approached in three different ways.

Many decisions must be made periodically, regardless of how much information has been collected and regardless of what quantitative techniques, if any, are being used to assist in those decision-making processes. One

[13] An interesting case study illustrating this point can be found in Clark Waid, Donald F. Clark, and Russell L. Ackoff, "Allocation of Sales Effort in the Lamp Division of the General Electric Company," *Operations Research,* Vol. 4 (December, 1956), pp. 629-647.

consequence of the unavailability of data is that it may be necessary initially to use the least sophisticated quantitative techniques to aid in the decision-making process. At the same time, however, management should be preparing to utilize increasingly more sophisticated quantitative techniques in later years by setting up the systematic procedures which will collect now the data they will require.

This illustrates the third advantage of a marketing system. Some quantitative techniques may never be used by a firm which does not utilize the systems approach for the simple reason that some quantitative techniques require data normally unavailable except after a long period of collection activity. It may therefore be necessary for a firm to be simultaneously collecting data for two or more quantitative techniques in those problem areas wherein a hierarchy of quantitative techniques can be applied. The least sophisticated techniques will be used initially, with the more sophisticated techniques being employed as the required data are collected. A marketing system is ideally suited for facilitating such an adaptive process and for making possible the use of the more sophisticated quantitative techniques.

Conclusions

This paper has presented the case for utilizing a systems approach in marketing. The main points presented in the foregoing can be briefly summarized.

Marketing has not utilized the computer or quantitative techniques to the same extent as the other functional areas of business. Three factors were seen to account for this lag: the difficulty of quantifying the behavioral aspects of marketing, the lack of a data collection tradition in marketing, and poor communications between marketers and computer specialists. Although the behavioral aspects of marketing may not succumb to the computer for quite some time, other aspects of marketing can be computerized if management structures its marketing problems and decision areas in terms of pertinent marketing theory, and if it then organizes the data collection activity in proper relationship to the structured marketing problems and decision areas. This is the essence of the systems approach, and it will greatly facilitate the application of the computer to marketing.

The collection of pertinent data, and both a more complete description of the marketing problems faced and the underlying theory associated with those problems, will encourage the use of operations research, management science, and other quantitative techniques in marketing. Because these analytic techniques would be an integral part of the individual sub-systems within a marketing system, all of the advantages purported to be associated with quantitative techniques and model building would also accrue to a firm using a marketing system. Thus the systems approach might be viewed as a necessary condition for the successful application of quantitative techniques to marketing.

Marketing executives and mathematicians have joined forces in a search for improved decision models to handle such problems as new product development, media selection, retail inventory control, and size of the sales force. The author of this article explains and illustrates those operations research models which hold greatest promise in the marketing area.

The Use of Mathematical Models in Marketing

Philip Kotler

The modern marketing man has to be multilingual, for he obtains his material from many disciplines.

He must be able to converse with *economists* about marginal analysis, elasticity, and diminishing returns; with *psychologists* about projective techniques, latent needs, and nonrational behavior; with *sociologists* about acculturation, social norms, and subcultures; and with *statisticians* about standard error, least squares, and correlation.

Now another language—that of higher mathematics—is needed in marketing. Many marketing men are uncomfortable about this. They do not look askance at mathematical concepts, but they are a bit anxious because of a "language barrier." Fortunately, however, the language barrier is not insurmountable. Linear programming, waiting-line theory, and the like are simply unfamiliar names for some significant ideas.

The purpose of this article is to reduce some of the "mysticism" of the new

Reprinted by permission of the author and the publisher from the *Journal of Marketing,* published by the American Marketing Association, Vol. 27, No. 4 (October, 1963), pp. 31-41.

mathematics by defining its vocabulary and illustrating its central ideas in the context of marketing.

Decision Making

Quantitative analysis is not alien to the field of marketing. For many decades marketing research departments have conducted consumer surveys, prepared sales forecasts, and analyzed sales reports. A few practitioners have even used higher mathematics for complex problem-solving in marketing. But until recently the mathematical "sophistication" underlying the typical research project could be found between the covers of a textbook in elementary statistics. And much of the research has amounted to routine information gathering.

Today the emphasis is changing. The focus of research is on *decision making,* and not fact gathering for its own sake. The belief is spreading that models can be built which identify and relate the key factors in a problem situation, and which offer explicit directions for decision making.

Today's marketing executive is asked to distinguish carefully between alternative strategies in making a major decision. Each strategy will lead to one of several outcomes, depending in part upon events beyond the firm's control; and the possible outcomes for each strategy must somehow be weighed, to achieve an estimated value for that strategy. The values of the various strategies must be compared, and the executive must then attempt to select the strategy promising the highest value or payoff.[1]

The Tools of Mathematics

The mathematician carries in his attaché case four basic tools, plus a *potpourri* of special models. His basic tools are *matrix algebra, calculus, probability theory,* and *simulation.*

Matrix Algebra

One tool is *matrix algebra,* by which large arrays of numbers in the form of *vectors* and *matrices* can be manipulated by rules similar to those found in ordinary algebra.

As a miniature example, suppose (6,000, 3,200, 5,000) is a *vector* (for our purposes, a single array of numbers) whose component numbers represent sales targets in three geographical markets—(say) East, West, and South respectively. Past records show that on the average it takes ½ hour of sales effort and $1 of advertising expenditure to produce a sale in the first market; ¼ hour of sales effort and $2 of advertising expenditure to produce a sale in the second market;

---

[1] Two excellent articles illustrating this approach are Robert D. Buzzell and Charles C. Slater, "Decision Theory and Marketing Management," *Journal of Marketing,* Vol. 27 (July, 1962), pp. 7-16; and Paul E. Green, "Bayesian Decision Theory in Pricing Strategy," *Journal of Marketing,* Vol. 28 (January, 1963), pp. 5-14.

and 1/5 hour of sales effort and $3 of advertising expenditure to produce a sale in the third market. This information can be summarized in a *matrix* (for our purposes a rectangular array of numbers):

	Sales effort (in hours)	Advertising expenditure (in dollars)
East	1/2	$1
West	1/4	$2
South	1/5	$3

To find the total hours of sales effort and dollars of advertising expenditure required to achieve the geographical sales targets, we multiply the vector by the matrix:

$$(6,000, 3,200, 5,000) \quad \begin{array}{cc} 1/2 & 1 \\ 1/4 & 2 \\ 1/5 & 3 \end{array}$$

For example, we can call the vector A and the matrix B, and we then proceed to find their product, that is, A·B.

There are definite rules for the multiplication of a vector by a matrix (and for that matter, for the multiplication of two vectors or two matrices, etc.). In the example above, the product A·B is (6,000 X 1/2 + 3,200 X 1/4 + 5,000 X 1/5, 6,000 X 1 + 3,200 X 2 + 5,000 X 3) or, collecting terms, (4,800, $27,400). This new vector is the solution; and it means that the company must have enough salesmen to make 4,800 hours of calls, and also an advertising budget of at least $27,400.

Matrix algebra is essentially a symbolic shorthand for the manipulation of large arrays of data. It affords the advantage of economy in quantitative expression.

Calculus

The second tool which the mathematician brings to marketing is *calculus*. Using *differential calculus,* the mathematician can, among other things, determine what combination of inputs will maximize some output.

A marketing mix is a combination of inputs, such as price and advertising. Suppose that it were possible experimentally to vary the price input and the advertising input while controlling other factors. The effect of these variations on sales could then be recorded, and the profit implied by each level of sales estimated.

The task is to find an equation which best describes how profit varies with variations in price and advertising. A form for such an equation as well as a method of estimating the coefficients (usually "least squares" regression) must be decided upon. Suppose the following equation is found to give a good fit to the data:

$$I = 320 - 2P^2 - 3P + 4PA - 7A^2 + 60A$$

On the left side of the equation is profit (represented by I). Profit is treated here as the *dependent variable,* because its value is conceived to depend upon the values taken on by variables listed on the right side of the equation. These *independent variables* are price (P) and advertising (A). The particular numbers in the equation are constants and coefficients, which are estimated by an appropriate statistical method.

If such an equation can be found, what unique mix of price and advertising would maximize profit? The nonmathematician can use trial and error to arrive at the profit-maximizing mix, but this will be frustrating and time consuming. The mathematician can determine this mix in a very short time by using calculus. Although this is not the place to explain the procedure, his calculations will show that the optimum price is $4.95, and the optimum advertising budget is $5.7 (in some appropriate unit).

The chief contribution of differential calculus to marketing is to enable a direct determination of optimal action where differentiable functions are involved. In fact, *marginal analysis* which is applied by economists to all kinds of decision situations—such as determination of the best price, or the number of salesmen—actually is a gross application of differential calculus.

Integral calculus, representing the other branch of calculus, is not used to find the maximum and minimum values of a function, but rather the *area* under a function, among other things. An area can have a meaningful marketing interpretation.

Suppose on a particular billing date that a department store ranks all of its charge accounts by dollar size. These change accounts range from $0 to $198. The frequency distribution of all the accounts by dollar size is shown in Figure 1. The shaded area under the curve between $50 and $150 represents the percentage of all accounts falling in this range. How can this area be measured? It does not have the simplicity of a rectangle, triangle, or circle. This area, or other areas under the curve, can be readily measured through integral calculus, provided that the frequency distribution can be represented by a mathematical equation with certain properties.

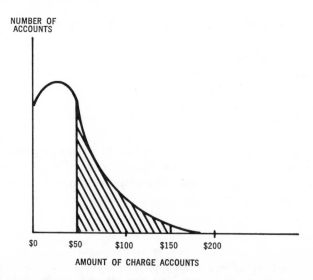

Figure 1   Frequency distribution of charge accounts

Probability Theory

The third important tool of the mathematician for use in marketing is *probability theory.*

How should the marketing man handle the uncertainty that surrounds legislation, consumer intentions, and competitors' acts? He can try to list all the possible consequences of a business move, along with their probabilities. The probabilities can be based on the frequency distribution of past outcomes for similar business moves, or on personal judgment. The assigned probability numbers must satisfy only two requirements:

1. The probability that a particular consequence will occur is given numerically by some number between 0 and 1 inclusive.
2. The sum of the probabilities of all possible consequences is 1.

Probability numbers can serve as "weights" for appraising various money (or utility) outcomes. Suppose a manufacturer has developed a new product and must hire and train a special sales force to sell it. The number of salesmen to hire will depend upon his estimate of market potential, among other things.

Suppose that he is uncertain whether there is a potential of 2,000, 3,000, or 4,000 units, and he is trying to decide whether to hire 60 or 70 salesmen. Too few salesmen will mean that some potential sales are never realized, and too many salesmen will mean that excess selling costs are incurred. It would help to estimate the profits under different assumptions as to market potential and sales-force size. The estimates will depend upon an appropriate set of assumptions concerning product price, production costs, the effect of the number of salesmen on sales, and selling costs. A hypothetical set of profit estimates is shown in Table 1.

If market potential is 2,000 units, the manufacturer will lose $20,000 with 60 salesmen and $40,000 with 70 salesmen. If market potential is 3,000 units, the manufacturer will earn $50,000 with 60 salesmen, and $40,000 with 70 salesmen. Finally, if market potential is 4,000 units, he will earn still larger profits. In this last case, the profit is higher with 70 salesmen because 60 salesmen are inadequate to tap the full potential.

Should the manufacturer hire 60 or 70 salesmen? By hiring 70, he has the opportunity to gain more but also to lose more. His decision will depend upon the personal probabilities he assigns to the three estimates of market potential. Suppose he quantifies his beliefs as follows: there is a .2 probability that the market potential is 2,000 units, a .3 probability that it is 3,000 units, and a .5 probability that it is 4,000 units. If this were a game of chance which the manufacturer could play repeatedly facing the same payoffs and the same probabilities, and if he had adequate funds, it would be easy to define a good decision rule: choose the act which has the highest *expected monetary value* (EMV). EMV is a weighted average of the alternative profit consequences of an act, the weights being the probabilities assigned to the alternatives. For the example we have:

EMV (60) = −$20,000 X .2 + $50,000 X .3 + $60,000 X .5 = $41,000.
EMV (70) = −$40,000 X .2 + $40,000 X .3 + $70,000 X .5 = $39,000.

The results present an interesting paradox. The manufacturer is optimistic about the market potential, and yet EMV is higher with 60 salesmen. His optimism is not quite strong enough.

Table 1
Estimated Profits for Different Combinations
of Market Potential and Sales-Force Size

| | | *Market Potential* | | |
		2,000 units	*3,000 units*	*4,000 units*
Decision?	60	−$20,000	$50,000	$60,000
	70	−$40,000	$40,000	$70,000

The use of EMV as a decision criterion in a once-only decision is generally acceptable, if the best consequence is not too great nor the worst consequence too bad. Were the money stakes unusually high for the decision maker, it would be necessary to employ a utility index instead of a money index. This utility index can be constructed from preferences expressed by the decision maker between given sums of money and certain gambles. Instead of the maximization of EMV, the decision criterion would be the maximization of expected utility.[2]

Simulation

The great majority of marketing problems probably will remain intractable to ordinary mathematical solution. For example, the correct price to charge depends upon such elements as the future sales outlook, the possible reactions of competitors, the time lags of these reactions, the intended level of advertising support, ad infinitum. A complex phenomenon is characterized by feedbacks, distributed lags, uncommon probability distributions, and other features which render exact mathematical solutions difficult or impossible. But mathematicians are undaunted: "When all else fails, *simulate!*"

A simulation is essentially a hypothetical testing, as opposed to a field testing, of the consequences of alternative business decisions. The first step is the construction of a model which spells out how the key variables interact in the situation. The second step is the testing of alternative decisions on the model. Simulations can range from simple paper-and-pencil exercises to full scale computer analyses. The purpose is to speculate on the consequences of changing a price, or dropping small distributors, or introducing a new pattern of trade deals, before risking the irrevocable judgment of the marketplace.

The model used in the simulation may be *exact* or *probabilistic*. In an exact model, the effect of one variable upon another is known with certainty. In a probabilistic model, one of several effects might take place, and we presume to know only their respective probabilities.

---

[2] Robert Schlaifer, *Probability and Statistics for Business Decisions* (New York: McGraw-Hill Book Company, Inc., 1959), Chapter 2.

Retail inventory control can be used to illustrate a probabilistic model. The problem is to adopt purchasing rules which will balance inventory losses against sales losses. Suppose a supermarket wishes to reconsider its present purchasing policy with respect to one product—for example, eggnog. The daily demand for eggnog fluctuates, and each day of the week has its own demand distribution. Suppose that on a sample of past Tuesdays the number of quarts demanded has varied between 0 and 4, according to the probabilities shown in Table 2.

Table 2
Probability Distribution of Demand
for Eggnog on Tuesdays

Number of quarts demanded	Probability	Monte Carlo numbers
0	.07	00-06
1	.20	07-26
2	.22	27-48
3	.33	49-81
4	.18	82-99
	1.00	

The third column of Table 2 consists of an allocation of 100 2-digit numbers (between 00 and 99) to all possible events in proportion to their probabilities. Thus, on 7% of the Tuesdays no eggnog will be demanded; so we assign 7 different 2-digit numbers (00 to 06 inclusive) to this event. Likewise, we assign 20 different 2-digit numbers (07-26 inclusive) to the event of 1 quart being demanded, etc.

We now go to a table of *random* digits. The digits are listed in this table in no apparent pattern. The fact is that each of the digits had the same chance of appearing on each trial. While there is no pattern, we know that all the digits will by approximately *equally* represented in a large sample of such digits.

We draw 2 digits at a time. If the first 2-digit number is 43, this can be looked up in the Monte Carlo column in Table 2 and would be interpreted as 2 quarts. In other words, on this Tuesday the demand at the supermarket is 2 quarts. By repeatedly drawing 2-digit random numbers, we can generate a characteristic picture of demand for a succession of Tuesdays.

We can use a different demand distribution, based on store records, for each day of the week. Then we can make assumptions about supply, such as a delivery period every other day and a decision rule to purchase (say) 3 quarts each time. With this information, we can manually or mechanically generate daily demand-and-supply quantities to learn the likely magnitude and frequency of excess inventories and shortages. We compare the average losses incurred under different purchasing rules and choose the loss-minimizing rule.

The probabilistic feature provides realism and has given rise to the name of *Monte Carlo* simulation. In the more complex simulations, a computer is used to produce the random numbers, interpret the events, make the necessary computations, and summarize the results. Computer simulation has been conducted on such marketing problems as media selection; department-store ordering and pricing; site location for retail outlets; and customer facility planning in retail outlets.

The Major Models

The tools of matrix algebra, calculus, probability theory, and simulation are fundamental in setting up and solving many of the models which have been developed to aid marketing executives in decision making. Some of these models are designed for *normative decision making,* and others for the *analysis of a process.* Most of them originated out of operations research activities.

The following models appear particularly "ripe" for marketing application:

1. Allocation models
2. Competitive strategy models
3. Brand-switching models
4. Waiting-line models
5. Critical-path scheduling models

Some of the examples below may seem too simple, if not contrived. However, the examples are illustrative only. Model building is not just a "fun" exercise for those who like to solve puzzles, but can be a serious attack on decision making in business.

Actually the final model for a real decision problem can be quite elaborate and represent a "hooking together" of several elementary models and techniques.

1. Allocation Models

The economic aspect of business decision making is the "allocation of scarce resources to competing ends." In marketing, the scarce resources may be salesmen who are too few to make all the desirable contacts, or advertising dollars which are too limited to produce adequate exposure, or many other possibilities. Nevertheless, a decision must be made on how to allocate or *program* these limited resources to territories, classes of customers, and product lines.

Take, for example, the development of a media plan. The number of available media vehicles is very great. But when any particular product is considered, there are a number of constraints which severely delimit the range of media choice.

First, the advertising budget is finite. Second, the message must be directed at specific market segments (such as mothers in the case of a baby lotion); and certain media vehicles are more effective than others in reaching these segments. Third, the geographical distribution of the market segments imposes restrictions on the choice of media. Finally, the media vehicles or the advertiser, or both, may impose restrictions.

Nevertheless a large number of different media plans would satisfy all the constraints. Of these, which plan will be the most effective? An *effectiveness criterion* needs to be developed against which every feasible plan can be rated. In media selection, the criterion is the number of expected effective exposures, or some variant of this. *Programming* is one of the mathematical models that can be used for the discovery of an exposure-maximizing media plan.

As an example, a media plan is to be prepared consisting of the purchase of X_1 advertising units of medium 1 and X_2 advertising units of medium 2. Table 3 indicates the relevant characteristics of the two media.

The following constraints are made explicit in a discussion between the media planner and the advertiser:

1. The total advertising budget is \$39,600.
2. At least 1,800,000 exposures are to be achieved in region 1, and 7,280,000 in region 2.
3. No more than 2,400,000 exposures are to take place among single women.
4. At least 2,000,000 exposures are to take place among college educated women.

The problem is to find the number of issues of the two media which would maximize the total number of effective exposures subject to the various constraints. A mathematical statement of the problem is given in Table 4.

Each constraint has been expressed as a mathematical inequality. For example, the budget constraint reads: The number of advertisements purchased in medium 1 (X_1) times their unit cost (\$2,700), plus the number purchased in medium 2 (X_2) times their unit cost (\$900), must be less than or equal to the budget of \$39,600.

The second constraint reads: The number of advertisements placed in medium 1 must not exceed 12. The other inequalities are similarly interpreted.

Table 3
Selected Characteristics of Two Media

	Medium 1	Medium 2
Cost of an advertising unit	\$ 2,700	\$ 900
Maximum number of units	12	40
Minimum number of units	0	9
Total number of effective exposures per unit	720,000	360,000
Number of effective exposures in region 1 per unit	60,000	100,000
Number of effective exposures in region 2 per unit	660,000	260,000
Number of exposures to single women per unit	100,000	80,000
Number of exposures to college educated women per unit	400,000	40,000

Table 4
Mathematical Statement of Media Problem

Maximize		$720,000X_1 +$	$360,000X_2$			
subject to	(1)	$2,700X_1 +$	$900X_2 \leqslant$	39,600	budget constraint
	(2)	X_1		$\leqslant$	12	
	(3)		$X_2 \leqslant$	40	individual medium usage
	(4)	X_1		$\geqslant$	0	constraints
	(5)		$X_2 \geqslant$	9	
	(6)	$60,000X_1 +$	$100,000X_2 \geqslant$	1,800,000	regional constraints
	(7)	$660,000X_1 +$	$260,000X_2 \geqslant$	7,280,000	
	(8)	$100,000X_1 +$	$80,000X_2 \leqslant$	2,400,000	customer characteristics
	(9)	$400,000X_1 +$	$40,000X_2 \geqslant$	2,000,000	constraints

The constraints have the effect of eliminating most combinations of X_1 and X_2 but there are still a large number of remaining combinations which would satisfy all the inequalities. But only one of these (usually) will also maximize the total number of effective exposures. Mathematical programming is the technique for finding the best solution.

In this simple case, the inequalities could be drawn on graph paper; and this would help to delimit the set of media plans (points) which would satisfy all of the constraints. Then there is a procedure for locating the best plan, the details of which are beyond the scope of this article.

The best plan calls for 8 advertisements in medium 1, and 20 advertisements in medium 2. This plan will cost exactly $39,600 and yield 12,960,000 exposures.

There are several types of mathematical programming. *Linear programming* implies that the criterion and the constraints in the problem can be represented by straight-line segments. The essence of a straight line is that the slope is constant, which means that the ratio of a change in one variable to a change in the other is constant. For example, a linear cost function means that the cost of an additional unit is constant; and a linear exposure function means that the effect of an additional advertising exposure is constant. In other words, diminishing or increasing returns are ruled out in strictly linear models.

Since the assumption of constant marginal returns and costs is patently false in many situations, what explains the popularity of *linear programming models?* The answer is largely that the linear assumption is the easiest to work with and solve. As an additional consideration, many important functions are linear or nearly linear over much of their range.

A number of techniques are available for solving a linear programming problem, once it has been expressed mathematically. *Graphical solutions* are possible when the number of variables is not more than three. Alternatively, the *simplex algorithm* is an all-purpose method. The word "simplex" has nothing to do with "simple"; the *simplex* is a well-defined mathematical concept which has a geometric interpretation. An *algorithm* is a systematic method for testing various solutions; it guarantees that each successive solution will represent an improvement until the best solution is reached.

The term *non-linear programming* is reserved for a problem formulation where either some constraint(s) or the effectiveness criterion, or both, are not linear. One example is *quadratic programming,* which uses a second-degree curve for some of the constraints or effectiveness criterion, or both.

Integer programming is a variant so named because the optimal solution is constrained to consist of whole numbers. For example, suppose X_1 represents how many salesmen should be hired. If the answer is *not* constrained to be an integer, it could be a mixed decimal such as 9.4. What does it mean to hire 9.4 salesmen? Should the answer be "rounded" to 9 salesmen or 10 salesmen? The solution is not obvious, and the decision may involve a difference of many thousands of dollars. Integer programming is a way of avoiding the ambiguities of fractional answers.

Dynamic programming, the most complicated of the programming variants, is applied to problems where a series of consecutive *interdependent* decisions have to be made. Purchasing decisions, for example, must be made throughout the year; and today's decision must be made in terms of what it implies for the decision choices in the next period, which in turn will affect the decision choices in the following period, and so on.

In summary, a programming model is applied to problems where there seem to be many different ways to allocate resources. Constraints (usually in the form of mathematical inequalities) are introduced to reduce the number of admissible solutions. Then a search is made for that solution among the feasible set which is optimal in terms of some effectiveness criterion. The programming model holds great promise for aiding in the solution of such important marketing problems as media selection; allocation of sales force; determination of the best product line in terms of a firm's resource base; site location, and selection of channels of distribution.

There are some specialized versions of the programming model which are useful in a marketing context. One of these is the *transportation model,* which defines the existence of several *origins* (such as warehouses) and *destinations* (such as retail stores), and the unit cost of shipping from every origin to every destination. Furthermore, the amount of goods available for shipment from each warehouse and the amount of goods ordered by each retail store are specified. Under the given constraints, the problem is to find which warehouses should ship their supplies to which stores, in order to minimize total transportation costs.

A sample problem is shown in Table 5—try to find the least-cost shipping allocation by trial and error. Mathematical analysis would show that there is a shipment allocation which would cost only $5,800. It is possible to convert this problem into a standard linear programming problem and then solve it by the simplex method. Alternatively, special techniques have been developed to solve the problem directly, using the format in Table 5.

The transportation model has been used for a number of years in some large companies to develop shipping schedules. It has a useful variant, called the *assignment model,* with promising applications to other problems than transportation. In the assignment model, the number of origins *equal* the number of destinations; and each origin is to be associated with *only one* destination.

As an example, suppose 4 salesmen are to be *assigned* to 4 territories. The salesmen have differing skills, and the territories are in different stages of development. The sales manager makes an estimate of the expected annual sales that would result from each man being assigned to each territory. This information is summarized in Table 6.

There are 24 (4x3x2x1) different possible assignments. Because this is a small-scale example it is not difficult to arrive at the total sales maximizing assignment by trial and error—A3; B1; C4; D2; total sales, $325.

In more complex examples, the number of possible solutions increases factorially, and a mathematical analysis is necessary. Incidentally, the model could be used for assignment of salesmen to other than territories, to different company products, or to different types of customers, for example.

Another problem is known as the *"traveling-salesman" problem.* Although not involving allocation, it has certain similarities to an assignment problem. A salesman must make calls in *n* cities. This means that there are *n* factorial possible routes. One of these routes would minimize the total travel *cost;* and another route (possibly the same) would minimize the total travel *time.* The problem is to find the "best" route in terms of whichever is the stated objective. To date, general solutions are lacking, but certain important theorems have been discovered, such as the fact that the best route never involves any crossing of paths; and mathematical solutions are available where special simplifying assumptions are made. A simulation approach also can be used to search for a reasonable solution.

Table 5
Unit Shipping Costs from Various
Warehouses to Various Stores

	Store 1	Store 2	Store 3	Warehouse availabilities
Warehouse				
A	$5	$3	$6	300
B	$2	$9	$4	200
C	$3	$7	$8	600
D	$6	$1	$4	500
Store requirements →	200	1,000	400	1,600

Table 6
Estimated Annual Sales from
the Assignment of Different
Salesmen to Different Territories

Salesman	Territory 1	2	3	4
A	$90,000	$57,000	$82,000	$45,000
B	$73,000	$75,000	$40,000	$51,000
C	$60,000	$30,000	$51,000	$75,000
D	$92,000	$95,000	$75,000	$70,000

2. Competitive Strategy Models

Profit outcomes are not only a function of the decision of a firm, but of this decision in conjunction with the decisions made by competitors. A marketing decision must be based on an estimate of what competitors are likely to do, even though their intentions may not be known in advance.

Game theory is the name given to the systematic investigation of rational decision making in the context of uncertainty concerning the moves of competitors. As an example, suppose Row and Column are the managers of two competing supermarkets. Every week, each of the managers chooses some item to promote as the "Special of the Week." Neither manager knows in advance what the other is going to feature. However, each can estimate the approximate profit that would result from every pair of possible choices. Suppose Row estimates the payoffs shown in Table 7.

The table is interpreted as follows. If Row featured sugar and his competitor featured flour, Row would gain 4 (say in hundreds of dollars); that is, more of the marginal customers will "flow" to his store, and the profit derived from this extra trade is estimated as 4. And Column will lose 4.

Table 7
Payoffs Resulting from Various
Strategy Combinations

		Column	
		Flour	*Coffee*
	Sugar	4	1
Row	Tea	6	−2

If Row featured sugar and his competitor featured coffee, Row would gain only 1 on Column. If Row featured tea and his competitor featured flour, then Row would gain 6. However, if Row featured tea and Column featured coffee, Row would lose 2.

The problem is whether Row should adopt one item and feature it week after week (a *pure strategy*), or choose an item randomly each week according to a constant though not necessarily equal set of probabilities (a *mixed strategy*).

If Row is to use a pure strategy, should it be sugar or tea? According to one doctrine, he should make the move which would minimize his maximum possible loss (the *minimax rule*). Tea would lead both to the largest possible gain and the largest possible loss, whereas sugar at least guarantees to Row a small but steady gain of 1.

Furthermore, Column can minimize his maximum loss by featuring coffee, and he undoubtedly will. This is a stalemated game where, so long as the same payoffs persist, Row will feature sugar and Column will feature coffee; and it would not be to either's advantage to make a surprise change. On the other hand, there are other payoff matrices which possess no such equilibrium solution, and where a mixed random strategy could be employed to advantage.

The Row-and-Column example illustrates one of the simplest types of games: *a 2-person, zero-sum game.* Only two players are involved, and they transfer a fixed sum of money between each other. The term "zero-sum" is used because in each play the sum of one player's gain (positive) and the other player's loss (negative) is zero.

More interesting, but at the same time more mathematically difficult, are the *3-or-more person, non-zero-sum games.* The 3-or-more-person feature allows the formation of coalitions where certain players can gain more by not acting independently. The non-zero-sum feature refers to the fact that competitive actions may expand the size of the market (that is, the total stakes) in addition to shifting market shares.

Game models have been designed for a variety of military and political situations, but some have interesting marketing possibilities. One is a game of timing involving two duelists (competitors) who at a signal are to begin approaching each other at some constant uniform rate. Each has only one available bullet (a new product) and is free to fire it whenever he wishes, with the knowledge that his chance of hitting the opponent improves as the distance narrows. When should the duelist fire?

Another game involves distributing an army over several battlefields, with the knowledge that each battlefield is "won" by the side which has disposed more troops in that battlefield. How should an army distribute its troops (or a company distribute its salesmen) in this situation?

Another game, "gambler's ruin," involves two competitors with different initial endowments of capital. A coin is tossed repeatedly with a probability p that competitor A will win and a probability $1-p$ that competitor B will win. The game ends when the capital of one competitor is exhausted. Given specific data, it is possible to estimate such things as the probability of "ruin" for each gambler, and the likely duration of the game.

Although to date game models do not seem to have much predictive power, they do suggest a useful analytical approach to such competitive problems as pricing, sales-force allocation, and advertising outlays. They may help to clarify the strategic implications of such moves as surprise, threat, and coalition.[3]

Finally, game theory should be distinguished from *operational gaming*. The latter term describes the modeling of a game around a realistic situation, where the participants actually make decisions (often in teams), and where the results of their interacting decisions are reported and become the data inputs for the next round of decisions. A large number of management and marketing games have been developed and used both in formal management-training programs and in research settings.[4]

3. Brand-Switching Models

Marketing executives must watch their *market share* just as much as their profits. Present customers can never be taken for granted.

The attitude of marketing executives toward brand switching is quite simple: the switching-out rate must be slowed down, and the switching-in rate must be increased. The factors affecting brand choice must be analyzed, and this knowledge applied where possible in order to alter existing brand-switching rates.

Switching rates can be estimated from data showing the individual brand choices made over time by a representative panel of consumers. Suppose three brands are involved, A, B, and C. We can ask what proportion of those who bought A in the last period purchased A again, and what proportions switched to B and C. These proportions for each product can be conveniently exhibited in matrix form. Table 8 is a hypothetical example.

[3] R. Duncan Luce and Howard Raiffa, *Games and Decisions* (New York: John Wiley & Sons, 1957); Martin Shubik, *Strategy and Market Structure* (New York: John Wiley & Sons, 1959).

[4] J. F. McRaith and Charles R. Goeldner, "A Survey of Marketing Games," *Journal of Marketing*, Vol. 26 (July, 1962), pp. 69-72.

Table 8
Hypothetical Brand-Switching Matrix

		To		
		A	B	C
From	A	.70	.20	.10
	B	.17	.33	.50
	C	.00	.50	.50

Note that each row adds up to 1.00. The first row reads: Of those who purchased brand A in the last period, 70% bought A again, 20% bought B, and 10% bought C. Thus, A retained 70% of its previous customers and lost 30%, with twice as many of its previous customers going to B as C. This means that B poses a more competitive threat to A than does C. The other two rows are interpreted similarly.

We have seen where A's ex-customers go. Where do new customers come from? This is revealed by column A, rather than row A. Note that A picks up 17% of the customers lost by B, and none lost by C. This is further evidence that A and B are in close competition.

The brand-switching matrix provides information about:

1. The *repeat-purchase rate* for each brand, indicated by the principal diagonal numbers. Under certain assumptions, the repeat purchase rate can be interpreted as a measure of brand loyalty.
2. The *switching-in and switching-out rate* for each brand, represented by the off-diagonal numbers.

But this is not all. If the switching rates are likely to remain constant, at least for the short run, the matrix becomes a useful tool in forecasting both the magnitude and speed of change in future market shares on the basis of the present market shares. Even where the switching rates change, if they change in a predictable way, a forecast of market shares is possible.

In this connection, important research has taken place to determine how switching rates are affected by price and promotion changes. Some of the products which have been studied in terms of brand switching rates are margarine, frozen orange juice concentrate, and instant and regular coffee.[5]

4. Waiting-Line Models

Waiting appears in many marketing situations—customers wait for service, and companies wait for both customers and deliveries. Waiting is of interest because it imposes a cost. The customer who waits in a supermarket line bears a cost in terms of more desirable alternative uses of her time. If she regards the waiting time as excessive, she may leave and buy elsewhere, and the cost of her waiting would be shifted to the supermarket.

While waiting time imposes a cost, so does the effort to reduce waiting time. The supermarket might reduce waiting time by adding more counters or

[5] Lester G. Telser, "The Demand for Branded Goods as Estimated from Consumer Panel Data," *Review of Economics and Statistics,* Vol. 44 (August, 1962), pp. 300-324; Alred A. Kuehn, "A Model for Budgeting Advertising," in reference 2.

personnel, or both. The decision problem is one of balancing the cost of lost sales against the cost of additional facilities. In marginal terms, the supermarket should increase its servicing facilities up to the point where the cost of an additional facility would just overtake the profits lost due to customer impatience.

The decision problem is illustrated graphically in Figure 2. The higher the average waiting time in the system, the greater the cost of lost sales (2), but the lower cost of facilities and personnel (1). The two cost curves are added vertically to derive a combined cost curve (3). The lowest point on this combined cost curve indicates the average waiting time, W_1, which will minimize combined costs. The implied investment in service facilities is F_1. The lowest point on (3) can be found graphically, or through differential calculus if appropriate cost equations can be found.

The cost of additional facilities is not difficult to measure; but it is very difficult to measure the value of lost sales which take place due to customer impatience. People vary considerably in their attitudes toward waiting; and customer impatience is also a function of the difference between anticipated and actual waiting time, and anticipated waiting varies by situations. Also, customers who feel impatient may decide not to "abandon" the store if they think that alternative stores are no better.

Waiting line theory, also called *queuing theory,* is not designed to answer how much waiting time should be built into a system. This is primarily an economic question as shown in Figure 2.

The theory is designed instead to handle two preliminary questions: What amount of waiting time may be expected in a particular system? How can this waiting time be altered?

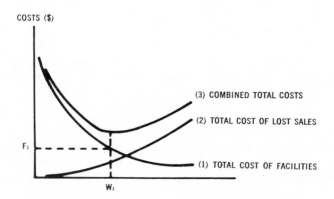

Figure 2   Costs as related to average waiting time

The waiting time depends on four dimensions of the system:
1. *The inter-arrival time.* The time between arrivals into the system has a probability distribution which can be estimated from frequency data. The

mean, standard deviation, and other characteristics of inter-arrival time can then be derived from the probability distribution.

2. *The service time.* The time between the initiating of a service and its completion can also be viewed as having a probability distribution.

3. *The number of service facilities.* The number affects the amount of waiting time.

4. *The service method.* Usually customers are serviced in the order in which they arrive (called first-in, first-out). But other methods are to give service to the most "important" customers first; to service the shortest orders first; and to service at random.

When these four dimensions are specified for a particular system, it is possible to estimate queuing characteristics, such as expected waiting time, expected queue length, and the variability of waiting time and queue length. For certain simple queuing situations, it is possible to derive these answers mathematically; but for more complicated systems, estimates can be derived through *simulation.*

If the system breeds long queues, the decision maker can simulate the effects of different hypothetical changes. In the case of a supermarket with a serious queuing problem on Saturday, four possible attacks are indicated by the dimensions. The supermarket can try to influence its customers to do their shopping on other days—this would have the effect of increasing the time between arrivals on Saturdays. Or the supermarket can decrease the service times, as by employing baggers to aid the cashiers. Or more service channels can be added. Or some of the channels can be specialized to handle smaller orders.

Most of the literature about queuing deals with facility planning for telephone exchanges, highways and toll roads, docks, and airline terminals. Yet retailing institutions such as supermarkets, filling stations, and airline ticket offices also face critical queuing problems; and marketing executives of such organizations can be expected to show increased interest in waiting line models.

5. Critical-Path Scheduling Models

A technique called **PERT** (*Program Evaluation and Review Technique*) deals with the tactical questions of managing a complex project. As an example, consider new-product development.

Suppose that management has just finished reviewing and approving ideas for a new product. Some important tactical questions are: (1) What is the one best way to sequence the various activities which must be performed? (2) With normal departmental resources, how long will it be before the product is ready for sale? (3) What extra resources would be necessary to complete the project x weeks earlier?

Each new product will require the starting and completion of hundreds of different activities. The completion of an *activity* is called an *event.* As a simplified illustration, suppose the following six events must take place:

A. Corporate approval granted

B. Engineering and styling completed

C. Marketing analysis completed

D. Advertising campaign plans completed

E. Manufacturing preparation completed

F. Market testing completed

After these events are identified, a PERT analysis consists of three steps:

1. Preparing a Program Network. In what order should the above events take place? Certain events will be in a *priority* relationship, and others in a *concurrent* relationship.

The best way to see this distinction is to work backward from the terminal event. Before a market test can be started, let alone completed, two prior events must take place. The advertising campaign plans must be completed and the product must be manufactured.

But these two prior events are themselves in a concurrent relationship—the activities leading to the completion of each can be carried on concurrently. The next step would be to examine each of these events separately, to determine what events must precede each. When there are hundreds of events, the task of preparing a "network" for these events is neither easy nor free from ambiguity. But for the six events listed above, the most efficient network is fairly straightforward. By representing the events as circles and the activities as arrows connecting the circles, we would prepare the network shown in Figure 3.

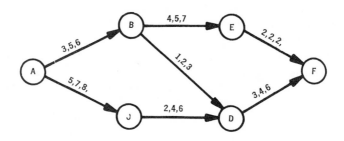

Figure 3   A PERT network

2. Estimating Activity Times. The department responsible for each activity is asked to estimate the *most likely time* to complete that activity, given the department's normal resources. This estimate is supplemented by both an optimistic and pessimistic estimate, again assuming normal departmental resources. For convenience, the three estimates are connected by commas and placed along side the activity arrows. (See Figure 3.) As an example, the department responsible for event B estimates that it will take between 3 and 6 weeks, with the most likely time being 5 weeks.

3. Finding the Critical Path. What is the earliest time the market test could be completed? It is necessary to trace back through all the paths which must be traveled, and the total time each will take.

There are three paths leading to the market test: ABEF, ABDF, and ACDF. On a *most likely time basis* (a different measure is used in practice), path ABEF will take 5 + 5 + 2 = 12 weeks; path ABDF will take 5 + 2 + 4 = 11 weeks; and path ACDF will take 7 + 4 + 4 = 15 weeks. This last path is, therefore, considered the *critical path;* since it must be traversed and it consumes the greatest sum of time, it sets the earliest most likely time for completion.

What is equally interesting is that events along a noncritical path, such as ABEF, can take place later than estimated without necessarily delaying the 15-week estimate for the project as a whole. In other words, activities along noncritical paths have some "slack" in their required completion time.

In actual applications, the network will be extremely complicated, and its characteristics would be very time-consuming to discern through manual calculations. However, a computer can be used to estimate the likely completion date and the slack times associated with the noncritical activities. Every few weeks a new computation is made, to reflect new information affecting the completion date. Alternative decisions about shifting resources can be simulated to see what effect they would have on completion time.[6]

PERT offers a number of benefits. It forces the various participants in the planning process to make careful estimates of activity completion time; it affixes responsibility; it highlights subtle interdependencies in the planning process; it suggests where resources may be shifted to shorten completion times; and it quantifies an estimate of meeting scheduled dates.

PERT will undoubtedly play an increasing role as a scheduling-and-control technique in the development of new products. It will also aid in the planning of other complex marketing projects such as advertising campaigns, special promotions, new-store development, and salesmen-training programs.

Implications

Operations researchers have developed a number of other models to analyze special situations—such as replacement models and sequencing models—but the ones described here have the most relevance for marketers. The major purpose served by these models is to "organize our ignorance."

Yet model-building is only half the task. The other half is to find the necessary data. Sophistication in model building must be matched by further refinement in marketing research procedures.

A more quantitative approach is needed for adequate decision making in marketing. Nonetheless, there are clear limitations. Many of the known variables cannot be handled mathematically, and all the variables are never known. Intuition and experience and judgment can not be transplanted into a machine.

There is the danger also that mathematics might be used by some to lend authority to some essentially ill-conceived decisions.

Marketing men will be subject to further mathematical name-dropping in written reports and at their conventions—cybernetics, information theory, econometrics, distributed lags, Bayesian decision theory, and so forth. Although these terms stand for perfectly good ideas, they should be viewed as part of a larger plan to advance knowledge, and not just represent verbal glibness.

[6] Robert W. Miller, "How to Plan and Control with PERT," *Harvard Business Review,* Vol. 40 (March-April, 1962), pp. 93-104. For an alternative model to PERT, see Borge M. Christensen and J.R. Greene, "Planning, Scheduling, and Controlling the Launching of a New Product Via CPM," in reference 1.

Following is a list of some significant collections of readings and references on model building in marketing:

1. Wroe Alderson and Stanley Shapiro, editors, *Marketing and the Computer* (New York: Prentice-Hall, Inc., 1962).

2. Frank M. Bass and others, editors, *Mathematical Methods and Models in Marketing* (Homewood, Illinois: Richard D. Irwin, Inc., 1961).

3. Robert D. Buzzell, editor, *A Basic Bibliography on Mathematical Methods in Marketing* (Chicago: American Marketing Association, 1962).

4. Ronald Frank and others, editors, *Quantitative Techniques in Marketing* (Homewood, Illinois: Richard D. Irwin, Inc., 1962).

5. David W. Miller and Martin K. Starr, *Executive Decisions and Operations Research* (New York: Prentice-Hall, Inc., 1960), especially Chapter 9.

This article reviews the applications of simulation to marketing. The author evaluates the strengths and weakness of simulation and suggests its growing promise as a technique for future marketing analysis.

The Promise of Simulation in Marketing

Harold Weitz

Simulation, as a technique, is one of the most talked-about methods in the field of management science today in spite of a rather negating definition from Webster's dictionary which states: "Simulation is the art or process of simulating; to assume an appearance which is feigned or not true; to counterfeit; to imitate; the act of willful deception; and misrepresentation." The results of a recent survey[1] show how simulation is being applied to marketing problems; its strengths and weaknesses; the different forms, structure, and purposes of simulation models; and its promise as a technique for future marketing analysts.

Range of Applications

During the past decade, simulation has been increasingly applied to a wide spectrum of marketing problems, both theoretical and practical. The range of applications includes: management information systems design and evaluation, industrial demand analysis, investment analysis, pricing, pre-testing field interviewing plans, staffing of a service organization, physical distribution (including warehouse location), predicting media exposure, evaluating advertising-message effectiveness, marketing-games for training, and models for evaluating alternative market strategies.[2]

Reprinted by permission of the author and the publisher from the *Journal of Marketing,* published by the American Marketing Association, Vol. 31, No. 3 (July, 1967), pp. 28-33.

[1] Harold Weitz, *"Simulation Models in Marketing,"* IBM Technical Report 17-192, IBM Advanced Systems Development Division, Yorktown Heights, N.Y. (1966).

[2] A description of the structure of each of these models, their characteristics, strengths, and weaknesses is included in footnote 1.

In spite of the clear and growing use of simulation in marketing, the full potential of this technique remains largely unexploited, at least insofar as can be ascertained from the applications described in the literature. (Clearly, many applications of simulation are not reported in the literature. Some successful applications may be of a proprietary nature; other unsuccessful applications may remain unpublicized.) The reasons for this are numerous. Market phenomena are complex processes and not clearly understood. Sufficient knowlege of the effects of market-mix variables has not been generally available and such relationships are necessary to the construction of viable and meaningful models.

Another reason lies perhaps in the kinds of skills traditionally brought to bear on marketing problems. Not only is knowledge of management science techniques (including simulation) necessary, but increasingly it is becoming clear that the skills of the behavioral scientist (psychologist, sociologist) and the economist are also needed to attack what is basically a socio-economic problem. Much of the emphasis in early management science was placed upon analytical techniques which yielded optimum solutions. Unfortunately, the solutions offered required a simplification of reality that often made the results grossly inadequate. Because of decreases in the cost of computation and in the cost of obtaining information, the utilization of management and behavioral-science personnel and, because of increasing pressures by management to make more effective utilization of marketing resources, the use of simulation should grow manyfold.

Classifying Simulation Models

The lack of a precise and universally accepted definition of simulation makes difficult any classification of the different kinds of simulation models. No widely accepted terminology is available, but many terms frequently used to describe certain characteristics of simulation models are included in a three-level classification which may be useful as a starting framework for looking at simulation. This classification is by:

1. *Purpose*
   a. Prognostic models
   b. Process or behavioral models
2. *Degree of System Definition*
   a. Tactical models
   b. Strategic models
3. *Structural Characteristics*
   a. Static/dynamic models
   b. Deterministic/stochastic models
   c. Aggregate/disaggregate models

Purpose of Simulation Model

Almost all simulation models constructed have as their ultimate aim a predictive capability. *Prognostic* models are primarily intended to simulate the results of a system, whereas *process* models seek to simulate the dynamics of the system itself as well as future results. The two types might be distinguished by considering the classic "black box." In one case (prognostic) the interest is simply in the outputs of the black box; in the second (process), primary interest lies in exploring the phenomena occurring within the "black box" and in constructing theories to describe that behavior.

Degree of System Definition

In a *tactical* model, one is generally interested in exploring the impact of alternate decision rules or parameter values within well-defined and well-understood structures. Questions raised by such a model may be:
a. What is the impact upon either the waiting time or the size of the queue if the service time is decreased?
b. What is the effect on a production system of alternative priority rules for assigning shop orders?

In both these cases, the mechanisms or elements within the system are well-defined, such as the distribution of time required to service individual customers, or the time required to machine parts. The *strategic* model applies when there is an interest in exploring the behavioral properties of ill-defined problems involving elements and relationships which are largely unknown or which are poorly understood, for example, consumer behavior. A model in which certain behavioral relationships are assumed is constructed and then tested against reality. The emphasis, as with process models, is on understanding the dynamics of a system so that a theory can be constructed. Once the theory has been sufficiently validated, the model can be used to simulate the outcomes of the system under a wide variety of conditions.

Structural Characteristics of Models

A *static* model would seek to describe or predict the total response of a system as if it occurred at a single instant of time; a *dynamic* model would seek to explore the changes occurring within the system over some period of time. A *deterministic* model would contain no probabilistic elements; a *stochastic* model would contain one or more elements, or mechanisms, involving random or probabilistic characteristics. An *aggregate* model is so structured that it can only answer questions of an aggregate nature, for example, the total response to an advertisement; a *disaggregate* model (there are various levels of aggregation or disaggregation) is so constructed as to yield information of a more detailed nature such as the number of men between the ages X and Y, having incomes beyond R and S who respond to an advertisement. Unlike the aggregate model, the disaggregate model can respond not only to a variety of detailed questions, but is by nature a more microscopic representation or model of the phenomena under study. An example of a disaggregate model would be one in which the behavior of each member of a hypothetical data bank of persons is individually simulated. Other terms could be added to further distinguish the structure of simulation models such as discrete or continuous, fixed or variable time intervals. The above characterization will suffice for our purpose.

This classification is intended more to clarify the nature and uses of simulation than it is to serve as a universal classification scheme. It is somewhat arbitrary and the categories are not completely unique; a single model may be classified as: process, strategic, dynamic, stochastic, and disaggregate.

The Advantages and Disadvantages of Simulation

Marketing generally involves a complex environment about which relatively little is known with respect to predicting the *impact* of a marketing decision. Analytical optimization techniques, such as linear programming, frequently employ unrealistic simplifications as with a linear objective function (which is often not linear) that maximizes media exposure (which often is not the central problem). Another tool frequently employed is regression analysis which treats covariance; it does not treat cause and effect nor get at the dynamic characteristics underlying market behavior. Although valuable, Markov and other kinds of probabilistic models which have been proposed for predicting consumer buying behavior (for example, brand loyalty) similarly employ simplifications which detract from their utility.

Frequently in developing an analytical approach, simplifications are made in order to arrive at a feasible and reasonable solution. These simplifications may augment the utility of a model but not if they permit too significant deviation from reality so that the results become of questionable value.

Some important advantages of simulation are:

1. Solutions to complex problems can often be obtained more readily through simulation than by analytical solutions. Simulation overcomes the deficiencies of other methods for dealing with complex, interacting, dynamic processes which marketing generally entails. This technique utilizes a set of mathematical and logical relationships which represent the essential features of the process being studied, however complex these relationships may be. Simplifications and assumptions are not required for simulation to the extent that they are demanded by analytical solutions.

2. Simulation offers an opportunity for relatively inexpensive experimentation, even where precise data is lacking. A simulation permits one to conduct a series of experiments on a computer or by hand computation, using the model developed to describe some process without recourse to actual field studies. It permits the use of data which may be known only imprecisely which after simulation studies is revealed to be relatively insensitive over a wide range of values.

3. Analytical models which can yield optimum solutions can frequently be developed as a result of simulation studies. Without reservation, a model which immediately and directly leads to an optimum solution is preferable to simulation. It is the difficulty which complex processes present that makes analytical solutions arduous and often questionable. Frequently, however, in developing and using a simulation model, insights are gained which, in turn, permit meaningful analytical solutions.

4. Simulation languages are available which offer further stimulation to the use of simulation because of lowered programming costs, and the relative ease of learning and applying simulation models to a wide diversity of problems. Just as FORTRAN is both easy to learn and less costly to program than machine languages, specially designed simulation languages are available which offer similar advantages. (The simulation languages most frequently used in the U.S.A. are: the General Purpose System Simulator (GPSS), and SIMSCRIPT.) Additionally, these languages offer a conceptual view of a system, or process which facilitates the construction and programming of simulation models.

5. The non-technical manager can comprehend simulation easier than a complex mathematical analytical model, and, in fact, less sophistication may be required to develop it. In general, a simulation model is simpler to understand and explain, for it is in essence only a description of the behavior of some processes or phenomena.

Simulation does, however, have basic problems which should be recognized by the marketing analyst. It does not easily produce optimum solutions. Each simulation run is, in effect, a single experiment conducted under a given set of conditions as defined by a set of values for the input variables. To determine an optimum, or close to optimum condition, a number of simulation runs will be required sufficient for a response curve to be established.

Simulation may be time consuming. This follows from the necessity to conduct a number of different types or successive simulation runs as previously described. As the number of input variables increase, the difficulty in finding the optimum values for a set of strategic variables increases manyfold and requires careful design of experimental runs and optimum search methods; otherwise, there may be excessive and needless cost. When the question relates to finding an optimum value for a single input variable, for example, the advertising expenditure for media X, several runs will be required using various values of this variable. As additional input variables (that is, strategies) are examined, the number of possible combinations requiring exploration increase in factorial fashion.

Simulation may become a convenient or easy alternative to applying appropriate effort toward the development of an efficient analytical solution, ideally, required. As the ability to employ simulation increases, there may be a tendency to rely on this technique because of its relative ease of application. Simulation should be used where appropriate; it should not be substituted for the use of analytical techniques which may be more efficient.

The Potential of Simulation

Previously cited were areas of marketing in which simulation has already been applied. More sophisticated, viable, and valid models will continue to be developed in these and other areas. Promising work is currently in progress. Furthermore, other aspects of marketing appear to be appropriate for the application of simulation.

Predicting Consumer Reaction to New Products

One area in which simulation should have significant impact in the future is that relating to the prediction of consumer reaction to new products. The capability of predicting a latent demand for a product not now on the market, without costly surveys, is certainly a desirable one. Such a capability would be based on the planned characteristics of consumers. It would answer questions relating to market potential: who would buy? What is the reaction of potential customers to the color, design, etc.? Knowledge, now unavailable, is required; research, now going on, offers some promise toward satisfying this "latent demand" objective. Volney Stefflre reported on techniques of product development which are based on the notion that "an individual behaves towards a new thing in a manner similar to the way he behaves towards other things he sees the new thing as similar to."[3]

Recently Abelson and Bernstein published a description of a model for the simulation of a referendum on the question of fluoride in the water supply.[4] The referendum simulation suggests techniques for simulating the test marketing of new products, as it would be for simulating an advertising campaign to answer the questions: what message? what media? and what frequency? The referendum model exposes some 500 hypothetical individuals having certain characteristics to a set of communication channels, each of which carries a particular message. The model specifies two processes by which each individual may change his attitudes: (a) by exposure to public assertions appearing in the communication channels, and (b) via conversations with others who have some stand on the issue and who may also make assertions.

Each simulated week an individual is subjected, with varying probabilities of exposure, to several communication channels and to particular assertions made in these channels. Rules determine if an assertion is accepted, depending on the individual's attitudes towards the communication source, previous acquaintance with the assertion, the congeniality of the assertion, and his previous position on the referendum issue. As a result of the model's exposure process, assertions may be accepted, resulting in changes in attitudes towards the communication sources, the probability of exposure to the various channels, and interest in the issue as well as one's position on the issue.

The model's conversational phase considers the level of interest of the individuals in the issue, their compatibility, their respective positions on the issue, their acquaintance with the assertion, and the social network of each. The model is indeed complex, incorporating reasonable hypotheses regarding human behavior. At a recent presentation, Bernstein outlined how this model could be adapted to test marketing.[5] He asserted that for the exposure process, this

---

[3] Volney Stefflre, "Simulation of People's Behavior Towards New Objectives and Events." *The American Behavioral Scientist,* Vol. 8 (May, 1965).

[4] Robert P. Abelson and Alex Bernstein, "A Computer Simulation Model of Community Referendum Controversies." *Public Opinion Quarterly,* Vol. 27 (Spring, 1963).

[5] Alex Bernstein, "An Application of Simulation to Test Marketing." Paper presented at *First Annual Conference on Simulation in Business and Public Health.* American Statistical Association, New York Hilton Hotel, New York (March 2, 1966).

would require knowledge on what assertions people make about a particular class of products. Instead of assertions reflecting peoples' attitudes toward fluorides, for example, concern with the impact of fluorides on health, age, etc., the model would reflect attitudes toward the characteristics of a particular product class, for instance its taste, mildness, or color. Changes would also be required to indicate the locus of stores visited by a particular person, presumably to reflect upon product availability as well as in-store promotion. The effects of competitive efforts would also have to be considered. Although the approach presented was not sufficiently detailed to permit evaluation, it was, nevertheless, intriguing in its possibilities.

Predicting Market Share

Numerous consumer flow models have been designed to predict the expected product market share. These are commonly referred to as brand-shifting, or brand-loyalty models. They basically take the form of Markov, learning, or other kinds of probabilistic models. These models suffer numerous deficiencies, largely because their use requires assumptions which are unrealistic. They further exclude such relevant factors as sales promotion, advertising, and competition. The promise of simulation lies in its capability to consider complex but realistic conditions which minimize the need to make unwarranted simplifying assumptions.

Samuel G. Barton pointed to a conceptual model for short term sales prediction which deserves attention.[6] It encompasses many of the salient variables affecting a sale, such as advertising, pricing, and promotion. Although conceptual, it may offer a basis for a useful operational model for predicting short term sales, appraising the effectiveness of alternative test-market programs, and guiding the allocation of promotional efforts.

Table 1
Inter-Industry Input-Output
for the National Economy

	Industry Sectors	A	B	C	D	•	j
I	A	X_{AA}	X_{AB}	•	•	•	•
N	B	X_{AB}	X_{BB}	X_{BC}	•	•	•
P	C	X_{CA}	•	•	•	•	•
U	D	•	•	•	•	•	•
T	•	•	•	•	•	•	•
	i	•	•	•	•	•	•
	Total Output	A_T	B_T	C_T	D_T	•	•

Where $X_{BC} = \dfrac{\text{input from industry B to industry C}}{\text{total output of industry C, } (C_T)}$

The short term prediction model views a consumer as being influenced at two different times: prior to the point of sale, and at the point of sale. The factors

[6] Samuel G. Barton, "A Marketing Model for Short Term Prediction of Consumer Sales." *Journal of Marketing* (July, 1965), pp. 19-29.

governing these influences are termed consumer momentum, customer intention to change, share of space, and consumer-deal offerings. The weight of these factors, a function of a complex of other factors, varies among the different classes of buyers, that is, new, new repeat, and old customers. To illustrate, the principal factors affecting intention to change include:

1. Share of new product announcements
2. Share of general advertising
3. Share of consumer deal advertising
4. Share of shelf and display stocks

Sufficient data with adequate understanding of market processes to implement such a model probably do not exist, but they may serve as a framework for development.

Competitive Gaming Models

The value of market games, one of the forms which simulation may take, lies in their ability to introduce competitive forces explicitly into consideration. Here lies the potential of games as a vehicle for determining market strategy. Philip Kotler objects to most games because they treat consumers in a superficial way, as an aggregate which responds in some lagged and linear way to market decisions.[7] He outlined a competitive-market simulation which not only has a decision-rich marketing function but also has an environmentally rich market of individuals. His prime interest is in observing whether such a tool could be useful for company predictions.

Typically, the model would have a representative sample of 200 households, differentiated by socio-economic characteristics, through which the computer will cycle each week to determine a buyer's choice as a function of:

1. Socio-economic factors
2. Previous brand choices
3. Interim experience
4. In-store experience

The last two factors are a function of management's decisions; the former are attributes of the consumer. Such a model could be used as a game either with player-managers or without players when an input-decision rule defines a strategy. The latter condition removes the need for player roles.

Input-Output Analysis

Input-Output analysis has until recently been largely regarded as an economic tool. Its power rests on a table of coefficients (see Table 1) which relates the inputs and outputs of 81 industry sectors of the National economy to each other and to final demand. Using this table, one can determine, for example, the direct dollar value of iron and steel required by the automobile and other industries as well as the iron and steel purchased directly by the consumer. The table also shows the intermediate inputs required to make the iron and steel.

[7] Philip Kotler, "The Competitive Marketing Simulator—A New Management Tool." *California Management Review* (Spring, 1965).

From this basic table, a table of inverse coefficients can be derived representing the amounts of input from industry i necessary to produce one unit of final demand (the ultimate demand by consumers) for products of industry j.

Input-Output analysis has been used in a variety of ways to determine the effect on an industry of an increase in the gross national product, the effect upon an industry if sales of some major sector of the economy experiences a significant change, the impact of the Federal highways program upon the U.S. economy, the contribution of the tobacco industry, and the effects of proposed changes to the industrial structure of the Appalachia region. Variations of the input-output model have also been used to forecast total demand for the iron and steel industry.

Some large companies are reported to have individual input-output models (describing the relationships between the various components of the organization) which are coupled to a national input-output model.[8] Such company models are intended to provide greater control and predictive capabilities. Still other applications have been reported; these extend to such areas as evaluating poverty programs for the Office of Economic Opportunity and to evaluating proposed transportation systems.

Efforts by the U.S. Department of Commerce to develop input-output data are currently under way which would be frequently updated for a larger number of industry sectors. With such data the market analyst would have a potentially powerful tool at his fingertips. In addition to those uses mentioned, the following would be permitted.

1. Evaluating more precisely the effects of technological change, for example, as changes occur in the materials used in the manufacture of some product, they would be reflected in the entries to the input-output matrix.
2. Measuring the full impact of a major new government program, such as a major increase in education, a new poverty program, or an economic development project for an economically poor community, and
3. Estimating more precisely the future demand for products and services for each industry.[9]

Several companies offering computer service, including IBM, have announced the use of input-output models to simulate the potential market for a wide range of industries. These services process proprietary data as required, and at the same time, permit referencing it automatically, if desired, to data banks of information gathered and maintained for management use.

The Future

Simulation has already been used in many diverse areas of marketing. It would be difficult to discuss all the areas in which this technique can fruitfully

[8] Wassily W. Lenotief, "The Structure of the U.S. Economy." *Scientific American* (April, 1965).

[9] Typical Brochure: *IBM Industry Information Service,* (Form No. 520-1373) IBM, Data Processing Division, White Plains, New York.

be applied. New applications are being developed continually. Other areas having potential are: strategic long-range planning,[10] the selection of distribution channels, and the location of merchandise and displays in the supermarkets.[11]

The major advantage and stimulant to the use of simulation in marketing lies in its ability to deal with complex, dynamic, and interacting phenomena which are characteristics of marketing. If the processes or phenomena permit adequate description, they can be modeled and experiments can be simulated. Unlike analytical optimization solutions, simulation models, by avoiding over-simplification, tend to be better descriptions of reality.

Simulation will play an increasing role in the future marketing function. Before long, many companies will have a number of market simulators available. These will take diverse forms including that of the strategic, or competitive, gaming simulator. Such models will invariably be complex, representing the channels of distribution, the competition, the environment, the customer, and the firm.

There are those who say that such simulation will form the nucleus of a "war gaming center," typical of that of the Armed Services. Such a capability would readily permit one to investigate new strategies, to rapidly measure the impact of new marketing intelligence, and generally, to improve the operations of the firm. Such a center could be embedded within a larger framework—an Information System for Marketing Managers.

The availability of more powerful and less costly computing systems, larger and more accessible storage devices, and more convenient input-output devices, which can be used with relative ease by the non-programmer, will hasten the development of the "war gaming center" concept. The "conversational" terminal and time-shared systems are further indications of trends narrowing the gap between the computer and the user.

[10] Robert Weinberg, "Simulation Models for Planning Management Strategy." Paper presented at the *First Annual Conference on Simulation in Business and Public Health,* American Statistical Association, New York Hilton Hotel, New York (3/2/66).

[11] Alfred A. Kuehn, "Simulation of Consumer Behavior." Same reference as footnote 10.

When faced with an unusual or different situation, one which cannot be solved through experience, formula, or some other known method, we need stronger medicine. Here are some examples.

Solving Problems Creatively

M. O. Edwards

Do you often find yourself stuck on a problem or feel yourself in a mental rut? If so, would you be interested in knowing about some of the ways which many individuals have found useful to get going again, to generate new ideas, creative approaches to solving their problems? On the following pages this author has attempted to spell out the principal conclusions drawn from the literature in the field of creative problem solving as well as from his own experience in teaching the subject.

Let us first highlight these conclusions and then discuss them in more detail.

1. All persons have some creative potential, with the usual wide individual differences.

2. Most of us do not fully utilize our potential.

3. Most individuals can, through appropriate effort, increase certain creative abilities. These include sensitivity to problems, self-confidence, fluency of ideas, flexibility in thinking, originality of ideas and motivation both to elaborate and to follow through on ideas.

4. There is probably no one single method for nurturing creativity. However, we must be creative in terms of something—hence, the importance of problem-solving.

5. Possibly the single most important factor in creative problem-solving is your attitude. Many of the specific suggestions discussed below bear on this factor either directly or indirectly.

Reprinted by permission of the publisher from *Systems and Procedures Journal*, Vol. 17, No. 1 (January-February, 1966), pp. 16-24.

6. We must learn to recognize the blocks or inhibiting factors to the free use of the imagination and to learn those procedures or techniques which will help us overcome these blocks and facilitate the free flow of ideas.

7. The three-fold *alternation* principle will help to minimize the "inhibitors" and maximize the "facilitators"; i.e., we must learn to *alternate* between: (a) thinking up and judging ideas; (b) individual and team or group effort; and (c) involvement (commitment) and detachment or relaxation (inviting incubation and illumination or insight).

Why the Emphasis on Problems?

We cannot be creative in the abstract; at least we will not be able to demonstrate it to others, and possibly not even to ourselves. We have to be creative in terms of something—not necessarily something tangible or concrete. Hence, the importance of problems and problem solving.

At this point, you might well ask what *is* a problem and what types of problems are we primarily concerned with? John Dewey defined a problem as simply "a felt difficulty"; Von Fange of General Electric as "a perplexing situation"; Arthur Gates, professor of education at Columbia University, defined it as "the condition that exists for an individual when he has a definite goal that he cannot reach by the behavior pattern which he already has available. A problem occurs when there is an obstruction of some sort to the attainment of an objective." (16)

What, then, is creative problem solving? When we can solve our problems through experience or formula or some other known method there may be no need to resort to creative approaches. When, however, we are faced with an unusual or different situation—one in which our knowledge, experience and research present no known ways of going about solving it—we need stronger (or at least different) medicine. Dr. Parnes, director of creative education at the State University of New York at Buffalo, defines creative problem solving as "an effort to solve a problem in a new and better way, without being shown how to do so. To exhibit creativity, your solution must be new to you—not necessarily to someone else. In this respect everyone can be creative." (9)

The late John Arnold of MIT and Stanford University defined creative problem-solving as "that mental process in which you bring to bear all your past experience, distort it perhaps, combine it and recombine it into new patterns, configurations, arrangements, so that the new totality better solves some need of man." (2)

Kinds of Problems

Problems, of course, can be classified in many ways. Dr. Parnes identifies three general types of problems or questions:

1. Fact-finding: e.g., "Do I have the necessary qualifications to join the XYZ organization?"

2. Decision or Judgment: e.g., "Should I take on that new line or territory?"

3. Creative: those calling for ideas or alternatives; e.g., "How might I stimulate my employees to take more interest in their work?" (9)

We are here concerned more with the third type of question or problem for these are the ones which require "divergent" as opposed to "convergent" thinking.[1] These are problems for which there is no one correct answer, although, of course, some responses will certainly be better than others. Obviously, fact-finding and judgment both need to go into the solving of creative problems but by definition these are the types of problems which call for *many* ideas—for unstructured, intuitive thinking and synthesizing as well as for gathering facts, for analysis, reason and logic.

First Exercise

At this point it might be useful if we took a specific example or two. First let's take a problem related to a concrete object. (For convenience, we can further subdivide creative-type problems, as Osborn does, into "people" problems and "thing" problems.) Let us assume that your firm has acquired a whole warehouse full of ordinary paper clips. Take three minutes now to jot down all the good uses you can think of for paper clips besides using them for clipping pieces of paper together. Try to give your imagination some deliberate exercise.[2]

Guilford and other researchers have found that with training—including exercises such as the above and other problems calling for divergent thinking—nearly all of us can increase certain creative abilities—especially sensitivity to problems, self-confidence in ability to solve them, fluency, flexibility in thinking, originality of ideas and motivation both to elaborate and to follow through on ideas. (6)

How did you do on the paper clip exercise? Did you get at least eight items? Did you have difficulty getting started? If you had difficulty, what seemed to impede the free flow of ideas? If you did not, what types of things seemed to facilitate the free flow of ideas?

The Blocks or Inhibitors

Most of us as children exercised our imaginations quite freely, but as we grew up, we became more sophisticated; something happened to impede the free flow of new ideas. Due to the pressures of society to "conform," to the emphasis in our educational system on learning the "right" answers, respect for authority

[1] Dr. Guilford defines convergent thinking as thinking "in different directions, sometimes searching, sometimes seeking variety." (6)

[2] This type of exercise was first suggested by Dr. J.P. Guilford, who until his recent retirement, was director of the Aptitudes Research Project at the University of Southern California. He first suggested as an exercise writing down all of the alternate uses one could think of for a common brick, and one of his widely used creativity tests calls for developing "alternate uses" for such common objects as a newspaper (used for reading); a shoe (used as footwear): a button (used to fasten things): a chair (used for sitting), etc. For a newspaper, for example, you might think of such uses as "to start a fire," "wrap garbage," "swat flies," "stuffing to pack boxes," "line drawers or shelves," "make up a kidnap note," etc.

and just plain lack of use of the imagination, most of us by the time we reach adulthood have acquired a number of more or less artificial "blocks" to the free flow of ideas. By now these blocks have become classified into three broad categories: perceptual, cultural and emotional.

For example, in the paper clip problem, were you bothered by the idea that the problem is a "technical" one and therefore outside the realm of your experience? Did your mind seem "fixed" to thinking about the object in its current form and function, i.e., related to the function of clipping pieces of paper together? These are examples of blocks or inhibitors (partly perceptual, partly habitual or cultural). All of us tend to perceive things in certain ways. Unless we recognize this it may be difficult to "shift" our viewpoint or perspective—to "back off" and look at a situation differently, to allow the mind to range widely, to speculate freely in the search for clues.

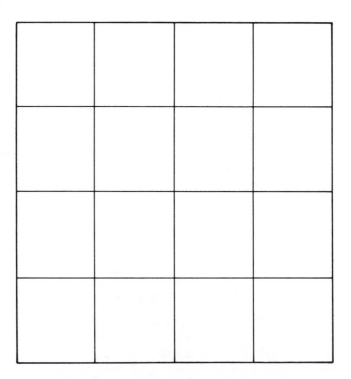

Figure 1   Obviously there are 16 squares in this chart, but if one reflects longer on it, he can readily see many more. Yet many people would be satisfied with finding 16, an example of being hampered by artifical limits or preconceptions.

Take a look at the "squares" chart (Figure 1). How many squares do you see? Obviously, there are 16, but if we pause to reflect that no size limit was placed on the question we can readily see that there is a larger one making 17, and then we see many more (by two's by three's, as well as by four's). Thus, we can easily find 30 squares. But without prompting, many would be satisfied with the first answer. The point is that when you are searching for something new, don't be "hide bound" and see things only one way—as all white or all black. Look at both and possibly all of the "shades of gray" in between. Let your imagination search in all directions, unhampered by any artificial limits or preconceptions.

In your paper clip problem did you have an idea you didn't put down because you thought it impractical, or too costly, or not worthwhile? Judging while trying to think up ideas is a typical example of a detrimental cultural block. Most of us tend to judge or edit our ideas before we put them down—even in the privacy of our own notebooks. This very much inhibits the free association of ideas and therefore the production of new ideas. The German poet-dramatist Friederick Schiller recognized this in 1788 when he advised a friend who had complained to him of his lack of ideas: "Apparently it is not good—and indeed it hinders the creative work of the mind—if the intellect examines too closely the ideas already pouring in, as it were, at the gates." (8)

Osborn Idea Spurring Questions

PUT TO OTHER USES? New ways to use as is? Other uses if modified?

ADAPT? What else is like this? What other ideas does this suggest?

MODIFY? Change meaning, color, motion, sound, odor, taste, form, shape? Other changes?

MAGNIFY? What to add? Greater frequency? Stronger? Larger? Plus ingredient? Multiply?

MINIFY? What to subtract? Eliminate? Smaller? Lighter? Slower? Split up? Less frequent?

SUBSTITUTE? Who else instead? What else instead? Other place? Other time?

REARRANGE? Other layout? Other sequence? Change pace?

REVERSE? Opposites? Turn it backward? Turn it upside down? Turn it inside out?

COMBINE? How about a blend, an assortment? Combine purposes? Combine ideas?

Figure 2   Here are some questions, put forth by Alex F. Osborn, which are designed to act as facilitators for stimulating the flow of ideas.

In the example given, we may have given your mind a "set" or push in this direction by specifying that you put down all the *good* ideas. However, the chances are that even if that word had been omitted, habit would have supplied it unless you have schooled yourself to avoid this pitfall—something anyone can do by constant practice.

Did you have an idea you didn't put down because it seemed silly? You didn't want to appear to advance an apparently "foolish" notion? Fear in one form or another is one of the most pervasive of the emotional blocks. Fear of making a mistake, of making a fool of oneself, of criticism, of failure, etc. It tends to be somewhat more operative in a group situation, but is so powerful that it may (and often does) operate on our minds more or less unconsciously even when we are working alone.

Osborn Rules for Brainstorm Sessions

1. CRITICISM IS RULED OUT:
Judgment is suspended until a later screening or evaluation session. Allowing yourself to be critical at the same time you are being creative is like trying to get hot and cold water from one faucet at the same time. Ideas aren't hot enough; criticism isn't cold enough. Results are tepid.

2. FREE-WHEELING IS WELCOMED:
The wilder the ideas, the better. Even offbeat, impractical suggestions may "trigger" in other panel members practical suggestions which might not otherwise occur to them.

3. QUANTITY IS WANTED:
The greater the number of ideas, the greater likelihood of winners. It is easier to pare down a long list of ideas than puff up a short list.

4. COMBINATION AND IMPROVEMENT ARE SOUGHT:
In addition to contributing ideas of their own, panel members should suggest how suggestions by others can be turned into better ideas, or how two or more ideas could be combined into a still better idea.

Figure 3   The brainstorming rules above are designed to enforce the deferring or suspending of judgment when striving for ideas, which is one way to escape inhibiting blocks to free use of the imagination.

The Facilitators

The above, then, are some of the blocks or inhibitors. What were some of the things which seemed to help or stimulate the flow of ideas? Did you make use of any kind of mental check list (for example, mentally ranging through the house, office, attic, shop, department store, hardware store, etc.)? Did you ask yourself any of the types of questions advocated by Osborn (Figure 2); e.g., Magnify? What to add, etc?) The author recently read about a naval officer who had secured a patent for a new type of office "tab indicator." He had simply added a small piece of plastic to one end of the paper clip on which one could write. Possibly he had asked himself this type of idea-spurring question as well as asking questions of others. Self-questioning of all sorts is a simple but very useful technique.

Take a look at your list of ideas and see how many of them called for using the paper clip in its original form and how many visualized using it in some other form. The latter calls for "flexibility" of thinking as opposed to mere "fluency." One way to get this is to analyze the object by listing its attributes, and then thinking of ways to make use of each one. For example, the paper clip is really a piece of small, malleable steel wire, about 4½ inches long with a certain tensile strength, bent into two overlapping elliptical shapes. If we thought about the "malleability" attribute, for example, we might have come up with uses such as a fish hook, a hanger for Christmas tree ornaments, a "pull" for a blind, an "S" hook for draperies, etc. Next we might have considered its steel "attribute." This technique opens up a wide range of ideas by permitting the exploration of one category at a time and allowing the process of association of ideas to work freely. (This and other techniques are listed in Figure 6.)

Second Exercise

Notice that common to many of the "facilitators" is one general principle—deferring or suspending judgment when striving for ideas. This is one way to get around the inhibiting "blocks" to the free use of the imagination. Why not try another "alternate uses" problem? This time, try to free yourself of all fear of any possible criticism of others to your ideas, and also determine not to judge or edit your own ideas. List all of the ideas which occur to you without judging them in any way. For the moment, forget all about the utility of the ideas. As you go along, you may combine or modify any of the ideas which you already have listed in order to produce additional ideas. Remember that quantity and freedom of expressing without evaluating are called for. With that in mind, take about three minutes to list all of the ideas you can think of for an ordinary wire coat hanger, besides using it to hang clothes.

A Comparison of Exercises

Now go back and compare your two lists. Did you think up more ideas this time than with the paper clip? Did you find your ideas more interesting and potentially more valuable under the "free-wheeling" instruction (on the coat hanger problem) than on the "good ideas only" instruction (on the paper clip problem)?

Dr. Parnes reports that "scientific research at the State University of Buffalo has revealed that students consistently produce substantially more good ideas when they follow the principle of deferred judgment than when they allow their

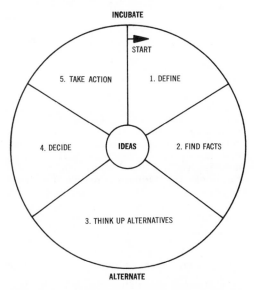

Figure 4   The "systems" approach to problem solving employs the five basic steps shown here. The cycle allows one to start at any point, stop at any point or continue around more than once.

judgment concurrently to interfere with their idea-finding. About twice the number of good ideas per individual was produced as under conventional thinking methodology." (9) If you did better the second time, the increased production of good ideas under the deferred judgment principle was probably the result of freedom from anxiety and some of the other blocks mentioned earlier.

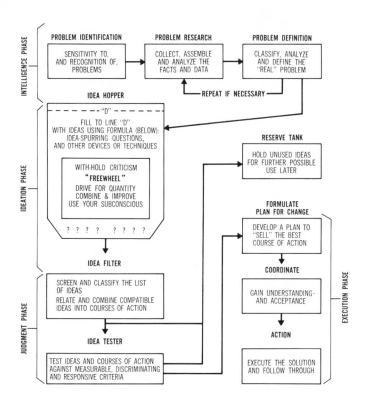

Figure 5   This "how" chart can be useful in helping to think through an involved problem. It is basically similar to the cycle chart in Figure 4, even though it is more elaborate. (U.S. Army Management School, Workbook for Military Creative Problem Solving.)

If we had continued the idea-seeking process for an extended period of time (say, beyond a half hour) we would usually find that many of our better ideas would come later in the period. Parnes found in his studies, for example, that 78 percent more good ideas were produced during the second half of a period of sustained effort than during the first half. So deferment helps here too. We find that we lose nothing by applying this principle. We still get all of the more or less routine ideas we would get anyway, but by "stretching our minds" for ideas, whether alone or with the stimulation of others, we find that many of our memory cells which were long unused are stimulated by associations with current thoughts and impressions. Thus new configurations are developed, hence new ideas, new leads to solutions to our problems. William J. J. Gordon refers to this concept as "foregoing the glittering immediate in favor of shadowy but possibly richer future." Isn't this a small price to pay for a really unique idea? (9)

This does not mean that we forego evaluating our ideas. It simply means that we should think of ourselves as wearing two "hats," first as an "idea man" and then as a "judge." We should alternate between turning on the hot faucet of ideas and the cold faucet of judgment. If we do not, all we will get will be lukewarm ideas.

How About Team or Group Effort?

Much has been written about group thinking, especially about the form of collaboration known as "brainstorming," which was popularized in the 50's. Brainstorming can be quite a help in a number of ways—providing its strengths and limitations are well understood. The brainstorming rules (Figure 3) are designed to enforce the deferment of judgment principle discussed previously. In effect, you were attempting solo brainstorming in the coat hanger exercise above, and you no doubt applied the sense of the four brainstorming rules.

However, for obvious reasons it is even more important in a group to have the rules against criticism strictly enforced. For nearly every original idea, especially in its tentative or initial form, may appear strange or even silly. As Clayton Orcutt of the University of Wisconsin put it, "every jackpot idea was once a crackpot idea." Alfred North Whitehead put it a little more formally: "almost all really new ideas have a certain aspect of foolishness when they are first produced." A new idea is a fragile thing and needs careful nurturing to protect it, at least until we can see whether or not it may lead to something worthwhile. Quite often during the brainstorming session an apparently silly idea will prompt someone to come up with a modification or "hitchhike" idea which may be not only novel but quite useful.

Limits of Brainstorming

Brainstorming is valuable only for the creative-type problems or questions discussed earlier. The technique will not be of use in a fact-type question (unless, for example, it is used in a preliminary way to list all of the factual questions which might be asked about a problem, or to list all of the possible sources or leads where factual answers might be obtained). Likewise it is not of great use in a strictly judgment-type problem (although, again, it may provide alternatives, advantages, disadvantages, etc.), and is no doubt helpful to rendering a well considered decision.

Also, the technique is useful primarily for a problem that is not only well defined but fairly specific in its scope. This caution is particularly applicable in a group situation, when different individuals may be offering leads to quite different aspects of a broad problem and may not really be addressing the same problem. The brainstorming technique may, however, be used in successive "cuts" at a complex or "umbrella" type question: first by breaking it down into its broad sub-problems and then by attacking one or more of these in a similar manner until you get a fairly specific problem.

Used as recommended, group brainstorming can be very helpful in producing a check list of approaches which, if evaluated with an open mind, may in turn lead to new, unique ideas. Also, team or group brainstorming can be very helpful in stimulating individuals to more productive effort on their own. Some persons do better alone than in groups and vice-versa, but generally speaking, most of us are stimulated by group activity, and are actually more productive as a direct result of this stimulation. Thus we can see the value of the second aspect of the alternation principle—alternation between individual and group effort.

Incubation

The third aspect of the value of alternating between a period of involvement in a problem and a period of detachment or incubation. Incubation followed by a sudden burst of insight runs through all of the literature regarding creativity and innovation. Insight may, of course, occur at any time. Courting it is a highly individual proposition if, indeed, it can be done at all. But we do know that insight does occur—sometimes unexpectedly—quite often after one has "immersed" himself in the problem to the point of frustration and then put the problem to one side.

6 Creative Problem-Solving Techniques

Numerals after each give primary reference. All of the above techniques except 2, 13, 14, 15 & 16 are summarized in Jack Taylor's book. (12) Goldner (5) has a one-page "matrix" including many of these techniques.

1. BRAINSTORMING: An intentionally uninhibited, either individual or group approach. The objective is to produce the greatest possible number of alternative ideas for later evaluation and development.[8] (For rules, see Figure 3.)

2. REVERSE BRAINSTORMING: Sometimes useful prior to a brainstorming session. It consists of being critical instead of suspending judgment.
(a) List all the things wrong with the operation, process, system, or product.
(b) Systematically take each flaw uncovered and suggest ways of overcoming it.[13]

3. CATALOG TECHNIQUE: Simply the reference to various and sundry catalogs or other source of printed information as a means of getting ideas that will, in turn, suggest other ideas. May be used in combination with the Forced Relationship Technique.[5]

4. CHECK-LIST TECHNIQUE: A system of getting idea-clues or "leads" by checking the items on a prepared list against the problem or subject under consideration. The objective is to obtain a number of general ideas for further follow-up and development into specific form[8]

5. FREE ASSOCIATION: A method of stimulating the imagination to some constructive purpose.
(a) Jot down a symbol—word, sketch, number, picture—which is related in some key way to some important aspect of the problem or subject under consideration.
(b) Jot down another symbol suggested by the first one.
(c) Continue as in Step 2—AD LIB—until ideas emerge.[12]

The objective is to produce intangible ideas, advertising slogans, designs, names, etc.

6. ATTRIBUTE LISTING: A technique used principally for improving tangible things.
(a) Choose some object to improve.
(b) List the parts of the object.
(c) List the essential, basic qualities, features, or attributes of the object and its parts.
(d) Systematically change or modify the attributes.[3,12]
The objective is to satisfy better the original purpose of the object, or to fulfill a new need with it.

7. FORCED RELATIONSHIP: A method which has essentially the same basic purpose as free association, but which attempts to force association.
(a) Isolate the elements of the problem at hand.
(b) Find the relationships between/among these elements.
(similarities—differences—analogies—cause—and effect)
(c) Record the relationships in organized fashion.
(d) Analyze the record of relationships to find the patterns (or basic ideas) present. Develop new ideas from these patterns.[12,15]

8. MORPHOLOGICAL ANALYSIS: A comprehensive way to list and examine all of the possible combinations that might be useful in solving some given problem.
(a) State your problem as broadly and generally as possible.
(b) Define the independent variables present in the problem—as broadly and completely as possible.
(c) Enter the variables as the axes of a morphological chart—or make a permutational listing.
(d) Select the most promising alternatives and follow them through.
The objective is to find *all* of the possible combinations—for subsequent testing, verification, modification, evaluation, and development.[1,12]

9. INPUT-OUTPUT TECHNIQUE: A method for solving dynamic-system design problems:
(a) Investigate direction (Input, resources, etc.)
(b) Establish measures for testing.
(c) Develop methods.
(d) Optimize a structure.
(e) Accomplish a structure.
(f) Convince others of its value.
The objective is to produce a number of possible solutions which can then be tested, evaluated and developed.[14]

10. SYNECTICS: A structured approach to creative thinking. Operational Mechanisms:
(a) Making - the - strange - familiar (through analysis, generalization, and model-seeking).
(b) Making - the - familiar - strange (through personal analogy, direct analogy, and symbolic analogy).
The objective usually is to produce ONE best idea and to carry it through to testing, verification, development, and production in final form.[4]

11. INSPIRED (BIG DREAM) APPROACH: A "breakthrough" approach which sometimes leads to spectacular advancements.
(a) Think the biggest dream possible—about something to benefit mankind.
(b) Read, study, and think about every subject connected with your big dream—and do so regularly, persistently, continually.
(d) Drop down a dream or so, then engineer your dream into reality.[12]
The objective is to make the greatest possible achievement for human benefit.

12. EDISONIAN METHOD: An approach consisting principally of performing a virtually endless number of trial-and-error experiments. A "last-ditch" approach, to be resorted to only:
(a) When other, more systematic methods have completely failed to produce the desired results; and/or
(b) When one is knowingly and necessarily delving into the unknown into areas of basic research.[12]

13. KEPNER-TRIGOE METHOD: A method particularly calculated to isolating or finding the problem and then deciding what to do about it. A systematic outline is made to describe precisely both the problem and what lies outside the problem but is closely related to it in order to find possible causes of the problem and facilitate decision-making.[11]

14. BIONICS: Ask yourself, "How is this done in nature?" Nature's scheme of things is revealed to those who search. (Note: this technique may come into play in synectics when utilizing analogies.)[5,13]

15. VALUE ANALYSIS (OR ENGINEER-
ING): A specialized application of creative
problem-solving to increase value. It may be
defined as an objective, systematic and formalized method of performing a job to
achieve only necessary functions at minimum cost. Six questions are evoked concerning each part:

(a) What is it?
(b) What must it do?
(c) What does it do?
(d) What did it cost?
(e) What else will do the job?
(f) What will that cost?[7]

16. SCIENTIFIC METHOD. Although
many scientists today say there is no one
"scientific method" the following general
approach is by now regarded as traditional
and is listed here for comparative purposes.

(a) Define the problem.
(b) Analyze the problem.
(c) Gather data to solve the problem.
(d) Analyze the data.
(e) Arrive at solutions.
(f) Test these solutions.[5]

Figure 6   This descriptive list represents a
highly structured approach to problem
solving, but its "operational mechanisms"
emphasize more the non-logical activities of
the mind than do some of the other
methods.

In any event, incubation allows a fresh start at another time. This does not
mean that we do not need to be persistent. We do. But we can operate on an
"alternating" rather than a "direct" current of extended effort.

Organized Approach

This brings us to a discussion of a "systems" approach to deliberate problem
solving. Many steps have been discussed in the past ranging from four steps
(Graham Wallace's "preparation," "incubation," "illumination" and
"verification," or Polya's "understanding the problem," "devise a plan for
solving," "carry out of our plan," "examine solution-check results" to Osborn's
six steps ("problem definition," "preparation," "idea production," "idea
development," "evaluation" and "adoption"). This author prefers Parnes' five
steps, particularly when visualized as a wheel or cycle.[3] (See Figure 4).

Defining the problem may or may not come first. We may sense that
"something is wrong" but need more information about it, so finding facts may
come first in the cycle. Also, the cycle may continue around more than once, or
we may need to cut back to the beginning or to an earlier step at any one point
in the process. We may become frustrated and feel the need to "let up" at any
stage of the process, thus "incubating" on the problem and hopefully inviting
"illumination" or insight.

We may also employ the deferment of judgment principle as well as the
alternation between individual and group, or decide to incubate it at any stage
of the cycle. For example, in Step 4 (Figure 4), deciding or evaluating, we may first
want to suspend judgment and put down all of the criteria or yardsticks we can
think of; then call on our teammate or group for more; then either individually
or collectively evaluate these, and select the most appropriate to use in the
evaluation of our ideas previously developed.

[3] The author is indebted to Joseph G. Mason, advertising executive at Batten, Barton, and
Durstine and Osborn, Inc., of Minneapolis, for this adaptation.

Thus we should school ourselves to consciously alternate both between free wheeling (or "red" light) and critical (or "green" light) thinking and between individual and team or group effort. And at any point we can decide to "sleep on it." Dr. Parnes and others have developed structured workbooks which may be useful in learning to apply these principles; or you may prefer to develop your own.[4]

The creative problem solving "how chart" can also be quite useful in helping to think through a fairly involved problem (Figure 5). Note that here we have four main steps: (1) the intelligence phase consisting of problem identification, problem research, and problem definition; (2) the ideation phase, where we may use any appropriate technique to fill up our "idea hopper" with all the ideas or approaches that we can; (3) the judgment phase, where we first do a preliminary screening and classifying of ideas gathered and then test the more likely one against "measurable, discriminating and responsive criteria"; and (4) the execution phase, wherein we formulate a plan for change, coordinate with others and finally "do something" with the idea or ideas selected.

Note that the "how" (or "hopper") chart is quite similar to the "cycle" chart (Figure 4) varying only in the extent of elaboration of the several steps. Again, however, both are only models useful for discussion and better understanding of some of the ways in which you might go about attacking a problem. In fact, your own approach may be quite different. If your method works for you, by all means stick with it, but if it doesn't, try out one of the organized approaches suggested and/or one or more of the operational techniques (Figure 6).

Operational Techniques: Synectics

These operational methods or techniques are particularly useful for certain types of problems; for each individual or group, one technique might be better than others. Some combination or adaptation might be most useful to you. (For list and brief description, see Figure 6.)

Synectics is a structured approach to creative problem-solving but its operational mechanisms emphasize more the non-logical activities of the mind than do some of the others. As William J. J. Gordon and his associates state,[5] these mechanisms "deliberately copy the subconscious activities we presume are going on when the individual is working at his best. But they compress the work—especially the phase of speculation and incubation—into a much shorter time span. They force new ideas and associations up for conscious consideration rather than waiting for them to arrive fortuitously." (4)

Two basic activities are employed: (a) "making-the-strange-familiar" through analysis, generalization and model-seeking; and (b) "making-the-familiar-strange" through personal analogy (role playing), direct analogy, searching one's

[4]The Creative Education Foundation, 1614 Rand Building, Buffalo, N.Y., publishes a useful catalog of materials, most of which are available at cost, including Dr. Parnes' workbook.

[5]Synectics Inc. was established by Mr. Gordon and others to train individuals and groups in the problem solving process. It also provides trained leaders to assist firms in solving their own tough problems.

experience and knowledge for some phenomenon that is like or has some similar relationships with the subject at hand, and symbolic analogy, a "highly compressed, almost poetic, statement of the implications of a key word having some connection with the problem." (4)

Since the synectics procedure is a highly structured approach to problem solving, individuals leading such seminars require special training. Reading some of the literature on it can be quite helpful to a better understanding of the creative problem solving process itself. We can see, for example, that although principles and procedures are most helpful, the mind does not often proceed in a logical, predictable pattern to the creation of new ideas. Unfortunately, many inventors, writers and other innovators tend to "clean up" their descriptions of the process so that it sounds either quite neat and orderly or highly mystical. In fact, the mind often proceeds in quite a disorderly and non-logical route to new ideas, often proceeding in leaps forward and back, and even around in circles. In thinking about problem solving one needs to understand this. But also one needs to know that aids in the form of principles, procedures and operative mechanisms can be quite useful, and this writer urges you to experiment with those which stimulate your curiousity or interest.

The creative methods or techniques described here are not designed to replace more orthodox methods of problem solving, such as the use of logic and the scientific method, nor are they guaranteed to work in all circumstances; rather they should be considered as additional approaches which should be used in combination with traditional problem solving methods.(15)

Bibliography

1. Allen, Myron S., *Morphological Creativity,* Prentice-Hall, Englewood Cliffs, N.J., 1962.

2. Arnold, John, "Education for Innovation," in *Source Book for Creative Thinking,* ed. by S.J. Parnes & H.F. Harding, Chas. Scribner & Sons, New York, 1962.

3. Crawford, Robert P., *The Techniques of Creative Thinking,* Hawthorne Books, New York. 1959.

4. Gitter, Dean L., W. J. J. Gordon & George M. Prince, *The Operational Mechanism of Synectics,* Syectics, Inc., Cambridge, Mass, 1964.

5. Goldner, Dr. B. B., *The Strategy of Creative Thinking,* Prentice-Hall, Englewood Cliffs, N.J., 1962.

6. Guilford, J. P., "Creativity: Its Measurement and Development" (in *Source Book,* 1962).

7. Miles, L. D., *Techniques of Value Analyses and Engineering,* McGraw-Hill, New York, 1961.

8. Osborn, Alex F., *Applied Imagination,* Chas. Scribner & Sons, New York, 1963.

9. Parnes, Dr. Sidney J., *Instructor's Manual for Semester Courses in Creative Problem-Solving,* The Creative Education Foundation, Buffalo, N.Y., 1963.

10. Parnes, Dr. S. J. & Harding, H. F., *A Source Book for Creative Thinking,* Chas. Scribner & Sons, New York, 1962.

11. Stryker, Perrin, "How to Analyze that Problem," *Harvard Business Review*, May-June and July-August, 1965.
12. Taylor, Jack, *How to Create Ideas*, Prentice-Hall, Englewood Cliffs, N.J., 1961.
13. U.S. Army Management School, *Workbook for Creative Problem-Solving*, Ft. Belvoir, Va., 1964.
14. Von Fange, Eugene K., *Professional Creativity*, Prentice-Hall, Englewood Cliffs, N.J., 1959.
15. Whiting, Chas. S., *Creative Thinking*, Reinhold Publishing Corp., New York, 1958.
16. Williams, Dr. Frank E., *Foundations of Creative Problem-Solving*, Edwards Bros., Inc., Ann Arbor, Michigan, 1960.

V IMPLEMENTING THE PLAN: THE MARKETING MIX

The firm's marketing plan serves as its competitive strategy for profitably satisfying its chosen consumer segments. A marketing strategy consists of the careful blending of four decision variables: product decisions, distribution channel decisions, promotional decisions, and pricing decisions. Part V is divided into these four decision areas and constitutes a major portion of the text.

Products are the *raison d'être* of the firm. Sometimes in all of the discussion and controversy surrounding decisions about such variables as advertising and personal selling, there is the tendency to forget that production and marketing of want-satisfying products are the sole justification for the firm's existence. The most basic product decisions involve (1) development of a product or product line; (2) addition or deletion of products in the product lines; (3) branding and packaging.

Theodore Levitt examines the concept of the product life cycle and demonstrates how this tantalizing concept may be converted into a managerial instrument of competitive power in his article, "Exploit the Product Life Cycle." A necessary counterpart to product introductions is the elimination of "sick" products from the product line. R. S. Alexander proposes a method for dealing with this decision in the next selection. The final selection in the product section is "A Theory of Packaging in the Marketing Mix." Mason bases his theory on the assertion that the major purpose of a package is to influence or control the location of product storage within the marketing channel.

A second crucial decision area is the firm's distribution channels—the functions and institutions involved in moving goods from the point of production to the consumer. Cox and Schutte stress the need to conceive of channels in terms of a total system rather than the activities of a single firm in the first selection. As Bruce Mallen indicates in the second selection, the individual interests of institutions in the channel often conflict, leading to inefficiencies. Although there is disagreement about which channel member should dominate, the channel must act as a unit in order to maximize channel profits and consumer satisfaction.

Louis P. Bucklin uses Copeland's classification scheme of convenience, shopping, and specialty goods to show how retail stores may also be classified. Then, by developing a product-patronage matrix, Bucklin describes circumstances under which consumers purchase certain products from specific types of retailers.

Physical distribution is concerned with integrating the activities of warehousing, transporting, handling, and inventory control into an organized system. In the final selection in the channel section, John F. Magee examines the need for improved physical distribution management and outlines the most promising avenues for improvement.

Edmund D. McGarry introduces the section on promotional strategies with his article, "The Propaganda Function in Marketing." McGarry views the role of advertising as an attempt to influence, persuade, and convince people to purchase goods and services and he suggests that it be evaluated in terms of these objectives. McGarry's article is an interesting contrast with the third selection which stresses "The Informative Role of Advertising." In the second selection George Kirstein gives an amusing and thought-provoking account of how his life was affected "The Day the Ads Stopped."

The promotional mix is composed of three elements: advertising, personal selling, and sales promotion activities. Many economists have attacked advertising as an economic waste resulting in costly misallocation of scarce human and material resources. Jules Backman summarizes the main criticisms leveled against advertising and attempts to answer them based upon a comprehensive survey he conducted under a grant from the Association of National Advertisers. Wendell Smith examines the role of personal selling in the promotional mix in the fourth selection. Carl Rieser, author of the fifth selection, believes that the Willy Loman-type salesman is dead. The old-time, fast-talking, back-slapping salesman is being replaced by a new kind of man doing a new kind of selling job. The new salesman knows more about the marketing concept and how to operate in a market where customer satisfaction is the major objective of the firm. Edward R. Hawkins introduces the section dealing with pricing strategies by relating marketing price policies and practices to the theory of monopolistic competition. The Hawkins article is in sharp contrast with the second selection by Jon G. Udell, "How Important Is Pricing in Competive Strategy?" Udell believes that the traditional approach of economic theory in explaining business behavior in terms of price theory and market structures is misleading. His research findings place more emphasis upon the nature of the product and its market in determining a firm's marketing strategy.

New product pricing is an especially difficult undertaking due to the myriad uncertainties associated with the new product. Stephen J. Welsh presents a seven-step approach to this problem in the final selection.

Built around the concept of the product life cycle should be a product strategy aimed at predicting the likelihood, character, and timing of competitive moves and including a plan for a timed sequence of conditional moves. Management decisions at each stage of the product life cycle must include a consideration of the competitive requirements of the next stage.

Exploit the Product Life Cycle

Theodore Levitt

Most alert and thoughtful senior marketing executives are by now familiar with the concept of the product life cycle. Even a handful of uniquely cosmopolitan and up-to-date corporate presidents have familiarized themselves with this tantalizing concept. Yet a recent survey I took of such executives found none who used the concept in any strategic way whatever, and pitifully few who used it in any kind of tactical way. It has remained—as have so many fascinating theories in economics, physics, and sex—a remarkably durable but almost totally unemployed and seemingly unemployable piece of professional baggage whose presence in the rhetoric of professional discussions adds a much coveted but apparently unattainable legitimacy to the idea that marketing management is somehow a profession. There is, furthermore, a persistent feeling that the life cycle concept adds luster and believability to the insistent claim in certain circles that marketing is close to being some sort of science.[1]

The concept of the product life cycle is today at about the stage that the Copernican view of the universe was 300 years ago: a lot of people knew about it, but hardly anybody seemed to use it in any effective or productive way.

Reprinted by permission of the publisher from *Harvard Business Review,* Vol. 43 (November-December, 1965), pp. 81-94. © 1965 by the President and Fellows of Harvard College; all rights reserved.

[1] For discussions of the scientific claims or potentials of marketing, see George Schwartz, *Development of Marketing Theory* (Cincinnati, Ohio, South-Western Publishing Co., 1963); and Reavis Cox, Wroe Alderson, and Stanley J. Shapiro, editors, *Theory in Marketing* (Homewood, Illinois, Richard D. Irwin, Inc., Second Series, 1964).

Now that so many people know and in some fashion understand the product life cycle, it seems time to put it to work. The object of this article is to suggest some ways of using the concept effectively and of turning the knowledge of its existence into a managerial instrument of competitive power.

Since the concept has been presented somewhat differently by different authors and for different audiences, it is useful to review it briefly here so that every reader has the same background for the discussion which follows later in this article.

Historical Pattern

The life story of most successful products is a history of their passing through certain recognizable stages. These are shown in Exhibit 1 and occur in the following order:

Stage 1. Market Development—This is when a new product is first brought to market, before there is a proved demand for it, and often before it has been fully proved out technically in all respects. Sales are low and creep along slowly.

Stage 2. Market Growth—Demand begins to accelerate and the size of the total market expands rapidly. It might also be called the "Takeoff Stage."

Stage 3. Market Maturity—Demand levels off and grows, for the most part, only at the replacement and new family-formation rate.

Stage 4. Market Decline—The product begins to lose consumer appeal and sales drift downward, such as when buggy whips lost out with the advent of automobiles and when silk lost out to nylon.

Three operating questions will quickly occur to the alert executive:

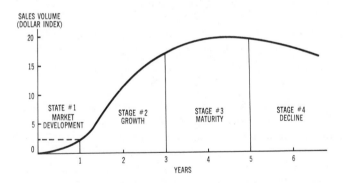

Exhibit 1   Product life cycle—entire industry

- Given a proposed new product or service, how and to what extent can the shape and duration of each stage be predicted?
- Given an existing product, how can one determine what stage it is in?
- Given all this knowledge, how can it be effectively used?

A brief further elaboration of each stage will be useful before dealing with these questions in detail.

Development Stage

Bringing in a new product to market is fraught with unknowns, uncertainties, and frequently unknowable risks. Generally, demand has to be "created" during the product's initial *market development stage*. How long this takes depends on the product's complexity, its degree of newness, its fit into consumer needs, and the presence of competitive substitutes of one form or another. A proved cancer cure would require virtually no market development; it would get immediate massive support. An alleged superior substitute for the lost-wax process of sculpture casting would take lots longer.

While it has been demonstrated time after time that properly customer-oriented new product development is one of the primary conditions of sales and profit growth, what have been demonstrated even more conclusively are the ravaging costs and frequent fatalities associated with launching new products. Nothing seems to take more time, cost more money, involve more pitfalls, cause more anguish, or break more careers than do sincere and well-conceived new product programs. The fact is, most new products don't have any sort of classical life cycle curve at all. They have instead from the very outset an infinitely descending curve. The product not only doesn't get off the ground; it goes quickly under ground—six feet under.

It is little wonder, therefore, that some disillusioned and badly burned companies have recently adopted a more conservative policy—what I call the "used apple policy." Instead of aspiring to be the first company to see and seize an opportunity, they systematically avoid being first. They let others take the first bite of the supposedly juicy apple that tantalized them. They let others do the pioneering. If the idea works, they quickly follow suit. They say, in effect, "The trouble with being a pioneer is that the pioneers get killed by the Indians." Hence, they say (thoroughly mixing their metaphors), "We don't have to get the first bite of the apple. The second one is good enough." They are willing to eat off a used apple, but they try to be alert enough to make sure it is only slightly used—that they at least get the second big bite, not the tenth skimpy one.

Growth Stage

The usual characteristic of a successful new product is a gradual rise in its sales curve during the market development stage. At some point in this rise a marked increase in consumer demand occurs and sales take off. The boom is on. This is the beginning of Stage 2—the *market growth stage*. At this point potential competitors who have been watching developments during Stage 1 jump into the fray. The first ones to get in are generally those with an exceptionally effective "used apply policy." Some enter the market with carbon-copies of the originator's product. Others make functional and design improvements. And at this point product and brand differentiation begin to develop.

The ensuing fight for the consumer's patronage poses to the originating producer an entirely new set of problems. Instead of seeking ways of getting consumers to *try the product,* the originator now faces the more compelling problem of getting them to *prefer his brand*. This generally requires important changes in marketing strategies and methods. But the policies and tactics now adopted will be neither freely the sole choice of the originating producer, nor as experimental as they might have been during Stage 1. The presence of competitors both dictates and limits what can easily be tried—such as, for example, testing what is the best price level or the best channel of distribution.

As the rate of consumer acceptance accelerates, it generally becomes increasingly easy to open new distribution channels and retail outlets. The consequent filling of distribution pipelines generally causes the entire industry's factory sales to rise more rapidly than store sales. This creates an exaggerated impression of profit opportunity which, in turn, attracts more competitors. Some of these will begin to charge lower prices because of later advances in technology, production shortcuts, the need to take lower margins in order to get distribution, and the like. All this in time inescapably moves the industry to the threshold of a new stage of competition.

Maturity Stage

This new stage is the *market maturity stage*. The first sign of its advent is evidence of market saturation. This means that most consumer companies or households that are sales prospects will be owning or using the product. Sales now grow about on a par with population. No more distribution pipelines need be filled. Price competition now becomes intense. Competitive attempts to achieve and hold brand preference now involve making finer and finer differentiations in the product, in customer services, and in the promotional practices and claims made for the product.

Typically, the market maturity stage forces the producer to concentrate on holding his distribution outlets, retaining his shelf space, and, in the end, trying to secure even more intensive distribution. Whereas during the market development stage the originator depended heavily on the positive efforts of his retailers and distributors to help sell his product, retailers and distributors will now frequently have been reduced largely to being merchandise-displayers and order-takers. In the case of branded products in particular, the originator must now, more than ever, communicate directly with the consumer.

The market maturity stage typically calls for a new kind of emphasis on competing more effectively. The originator is increasingly forced to appeal to the consumer on the basis of price, marginal product differences, or both. Depending on the product, services and deals offered in connection with it are often the clearest and most effective forms of differentiation. Beyond these, there will be attempts to create and promote fine product distinctions through packaging and advertising, and to appeal to special market segments. The market maturity stage can be passed through rapidly, as in the case of most women's fashion fads, or it can persist for generations with per capita consumption neither rising nor falling, as in the case of such staples as men's shoes and industrial fasteners. Or maturity can persist, but in a state of gradual but steady per capita decline, as in the case of beer and steel.

Decline Stage

When market maturity tapers off and consequently comes to an end, the product enters Stage 4—*market decline.* In all cases of maturity and decline the industry is transformed. Few companies are able to weather the competitive storm. As demand declines, the overcapacity that was already apparent during the period of maturity now becomes endemic. Some producers see the handwriting implacably on the wall but feel that with proper management and cunning they will be one of the survivors after the industry-wide deluge they so clearly foresee. To hasten their competitors' eclipse directly, or to frighten them into early voluntary withdrawal from the industry, they initiate a variety of aggressively depressive tactics, propose mergers or buy-outs, and generally engage in activities that make life thanklessly burdensome for all firms, and make death the inevitable consequence for most of them. A few companies do indeed weather the storm, sustaining life through the constant descent that now clearly characterized the industry. Production gets concentrated into fewer hands. Prices and margins get depressed. Consumers get bored. The only cases where there is any relief from this boredom and gradual euthanasia are where styling and fashion play some constantly revivifying role.

Preplanning Importance

Knowing that the lives of successful products and services are generally characterized by something like the pattern illustrated in Exhibit 1 can become the basis for important life-giving policies and practices. One of the greatest values of the life cycle is for managers about to launch a new product. The first step for them is to try to foresee the profile of the proposed product's cycle.

As with so many things in business, and perhaps uniquely in marketing, it is almost impossible to make universally useful suggestions regarding how to manage one's affairs. It is certainly particularly difficult to provide widely useful advice on how to foresee or predict the slope and duration of a product's life. Indeed, it is precisely because so little specific day-to-day guidance is possible in anything, and because no checklist has ever by itself been very useful to anybody for very long, that business management will probably never be a science—always an art—and will pay exceptional rewards to managers with rare talent, enormous energy, iron nerve, great capacity for assuming responsibility and bearing accountability.

But this does not mean that useful efforts cannot or should not be made to try to foresee the slope and duration of a new product's life. Time spent in attempting this kind of foresight not only helps assure that a more rational approach is brought to product planning and merchandising; also, as will be shown later, it can help create valuable lead time for important strategic and tactical moves after the product is brought to market. Specifically, it can be a great help in developing an orderly series of competitive moves, in expanding or stretching out the life of a product, in maintaining a clean product line, and in purposely phasing out dying and costly old products.[2]

[2] See Philip Kotler, "Phasing Out Weak Products," HBR March–April 1965, p.107.

Failure Possibilities . . .

As pointed out above, the length and slope of the market development stage depend on the product's complexity, its degree of newness, its fit into customer needs, and the presence of competitive substitutes.

The more unique or distinctive the newness of the product, the longer it generally takes to get it successfully off the ground. The world does not automatically beat a path to the man with the better mousetrap.[3] The world has to be told, coddled, enticed, romanced, and even bribed (as with, for example, coupons, samples, free application aids, and the like). When the product's newness is distinctive and the job it is designed to do is unique, the public will generally be less quick to perceive it as something it clearly needs or wants.

This makes life particularly difficult for the innovator. He will have more than the usual difficulties of identifying those characteristics of his product and those supporting communications themes or devices which imply value to the consumer. As a consequence, the more distinctive the newness, the greater the risk of failure resulting either from insufficient working capital to sustain a long and frustrating period of creating enough solvent customers to make the proposition pay, or from the inability to convince investors and bankers that they should put up more money.

In any particular situation the more people who will be involved in making a single purchasing decision for a new product, the more drawn out Stage 1 will be. Thus in the highly fragmented construction materials industry, for example, success takes an exceptionally long time to catch hold; and having once caught hold, it tends to hold tenaciously for a long time—often too long. On the other hand, fashion items catch on fastest and last shortest. But because fashion is so powerful, recently some companies in what often seem the least fashion-influenced of industries (machine tools, for example) have shortened the market development stage by introducing elements of design and packaging fashion to their products.

What factors tend to prolong the market development stage and therefore raise the risk of failure? The more complex the product, the more distinctive its newness, the less influenced by fashion, the greater the number of persons influencing a single buying decision, the more costly, and the greater the required shift in the customer's usual way of doing things—these are the conditions most likely to slow things up and create problems.

. . . vs. Success Chances

But problems also create opportunities to control the forces arrayed against new product success. For example, the newer the product, the more important it becomes for the customers to have a favorable first experience with it. Newness creates a certain special visibility for the product, with a certain number of people standing on the sidelines to see how the first customers get on with it. If

---

[3] For perhaps the ultimate example of how the world does *not* beat such a path, see the example of the man who actually, and to his painful regret, made a "better" mousetrap, in John B. Matthews, Jr., R.D. Buzzell, Theodore Levitt, and Ronald E. Frank, *Marketing: An Introductory Analysis* (New York, McGraw-Hill Book Company, Inc., 1964), p. 4.

their first experience is unfavorable in some crucial way, this may have repercussions far out of proportion to the actual extent of the underfulfillment of the customers' expectations. But a favorable first experience or application will, for the same reason, get a lot of disproportionately favorable publicity.

The possibility of exaggerated disillusionment with a poor first experience can raise vital questions regarding the appropriate channels of distribution for a new product. On the one hand, getting the product successfully launched may require having—as in the case of, say, the early days of home washing machines—many retailers who can give consumers considerable help in the product's correct utilization and thus help assure a favorable first experience for those buyers. On the other hand, channels that provide this kind of help (such as small neighborhood appliance stores in the case of washing machines) during the market development stage may not be the ones best able to merchandise the product most successfully later when help in creating and personally reassuring customers is less important than wide product distribution. To the extent that channel decisions during this first stage sacrifice some of the requirements of the market development stage to some of the requirements of later stages, the rate of the product's acceptance by consumers at the outset may be delayed.

In entering the market development stage, pricing decisions are often particularly hard for the producer to make. Should he set an initially high price to recoup his investment quickly—i.e., "skim the cream"—or should he set a low price to discourage potential competition—i.e., "exclusion"? The answer depends on the innovator's estimate of the probable length of the product's life cycle, the degree of patent protection the product is likely to enjoy, the amount of capital needed to get the product off the ground, the elasticity of demand during the early life of the product, and many other factors. The decision that is finally made may affect not just the rate at which the product catches on at the beginning, but even the duration of its total life. Thus some products that are priced too low at the outset (particularly fashion goods, such as the chemise, or sack, a few years ago) may catch on so quickly that they become short-lived fads. A slower rate of consumer acceptance might often extend their life cycles and raise the total profits they yield.

The actual slope, or rate of the growth stage, depends on some of the same things as does success or failure in Stage 1. But the extent to which patent exclusiveness can play a critical role is sometimes inexplicably forgotten. More frequently than one might offhand expect, holders of strong patent positions fail to recognize either the market-development virtue of making their patents available to competitors or the market-destroying possiblities of failing to control more effectively their competitors' use of such products.

Generally speaking, the more producers there are of a new product, the more effort goes into developing a market for it. The net result is very likely to be more rapid and steeper growth of the total market. The originator's market share may fall, but his total sales and profits may rise more rapidly. Certainly this has been the case in recent years of color television; RCA's eagerness to make its tubes available to competitors reflects its recognition of the power of numbers over the power of monopoly.

On the other hand, the failure to set and enforce appropriate quality standards in the early days of polystyrene and polyethylene drinking glasses and cups produced such sloppy, inferior goods that it took years to recover the consumers's confidence and revive the growth pattern.

But to try to see in advance what a product's growth pattern might be is not very useful if one fails to distinguish between the industry pattern and the pattern of the single firm—for its particular brand. The industry's cycle will almost certainly be different from the cycle of individual firms. Moreover, the life cycle of a given product may be different for different companies in the same industry at the same point in time, and it certainly affects different companies in the same industry differently.

Originator's Burdens

The company with most at stake is the original producer—the company that launches an entirely new product. This company generally bears most of the costs, the tribulations, and certainly the risks of developing both the product and the market.

Competitive Pressure

Once the innovator demonstrates during the market development stage that a solid demand exists, armies of imitators rush in to capitalize on and help create the boom that becomes the market growth, or takeoff, stage. As a result, while exceedingly rapid growth will now characterize the product's total demand, for the originating company its growth stage paradoxically now becomes truncated. It has to share the boom with new competitors. Hence the potential rate of acceleration of its own takeoff is diminished and, indeed, may actually fail to last as long as the industry's. This occurs not only because there are so many competitors, but, as we noted earlier, also because competitors often come in with product improvements and lower prices. While these developments generally help keep the market expanding, they greatly restrict the originating company's rate of growth and the length of its takeoff stage.

All this can be illustrated by comparing the curve in Exhibit 2 with that in Exhibit 1, which shows the life cycle for a product. During Stage 1 in Exhibit 1 there is generally only one company—the originator—even though the whole exhibit represents the entire industry. In Stage 1 the originator is the entire industry. But by Stage 2 he shares the industry with many competitors. Hence, while Exhibit 1 is an industry curve, its Stage 1 represents only a single company's sales.

Exhibit 2 shows the life cycle of the originator's brand—his own sales curve, not that of the industry. It can be seen that between Year 1 and Year 2 his sales are rising about as rapidly as the industry's. But after Year 2, while industry sales in Exhibit 1 are still in vigorous expansion, the originator's sales curve in Exhibit 2 has begun to slow its ascent. He is now sharing the boom with a great many competitors, some of whom are much better positioned now than he is.

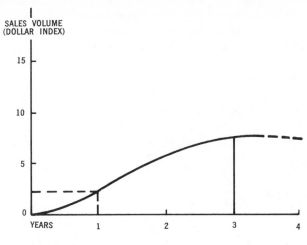

Exhibit 2   Product life cycle—originating company

Profit Squeeze

In the process the originator may begin to encounter a serious squeeze on his profit margins. Exhibit 3, which traces the profits per unit of the originator's sales, illustrates this point. During the market development stage his per-unit profits are negative. Sales volume is too low at existing prices. However, during the market growth stage unit profits boom as output rises and unit production costs fall. Total profits rise enormously. It is the presence of such lush profits that both attracts and ultimately destroys competitors.

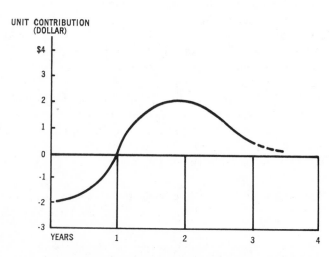

Exhibit 3   Unit profit contribution life cycle—originating company

Consequently, while (1) industry sales may still be rising nicely (as at the Year 3 point in Exhibit 1), and (2) while the originating company's sales may at the same point of time have begun to slow down noticeably (as in Exhibit 2), and (3) while at this point the originator's total profits may still be rising because his volume of sales is huge and on a slight upward trend, his profits per unit will often have taken a drastic downward course. Indeed, they will often have done so long before the sales curve flattened. They will have topped out and begun to decline perhaps around the Year 2 point (as in Exhibit 3). By the time the originator's sales begin to flatten out (as at the Year 3 point in Exhibit 2), unit profits may actually be approaching zero (as in Exhibit 3).

At this point more competitors are in the industry, the rate of industry demand growth has slowed somewhat, and competitors are cutting prices. Some of them do this in order to get business, and others do it because their costs are lower owing to the fact that their equipment is more modern and productive.

The industry's Stage 3—maturity—generally lasts as long as there are no important competitive substitutes (such as, for example, aluminum for steel in "tin" cans), no drastic shifts in influential value systems (such as the end of female modesty in the 1920's and the consequent destruction of the market for veils), no major changes in dominant fashions (such as the hour-glass female form and the end of waist cinchers), no changes in the demand for primary products which use the product in question (such as the effect of the decline of new railroad expansion on the demand for railroad ties), and no changes either in the rate of obsolescence of the product or in the character or introductory rate of product modifications.

Maturity can last for a long time, or it can actually never be attained. Fashion goods and fad items sometimes surge to sudden heights, hesitate momentarily at an uneasy peak, and then quickly drop off into total obscurity.

Stage Recognition

The various characteristics of the stages described above will help one to recognize the stage a particular product occupies at any given time. But hindsight will always be more accurate than current sight. Perhaps the best way of seeing one's current stage is to try to foresee the next stage and work backwards. This approach has several virtues:

•It forces one to look ahead, constantly to try to reforesee his future and competitive environment. This will have its own rewards. As Charles F. Kettering, perhaps the last of Detroit's primitive inventors and probably the greatest of all its inventors, was fond of saying, "We should all be concerned about the future because that's where we'll have to spend the rest of our lives." By looking at the future one can better assess the state of the present.

•Looking ahead gives more perspective to the present than looking at the present alone. Most people know more about the present than is good for them. It is neither healthy nor helpful to know the present too well, for our perception of the present is too often too heavily distorted by the urgent pressures of day-to-day events. To know where the present is in the continuum of competitive time and events, it often makes more sense to try to know what the future will bring, and when it will bring it, than to try to know what the present itself actually contains.

●Finally, the value of knowing what stage a product occupies at any given time resides only in the way that fact is used. But its use is always in the future. Hence a prediction of the future environment in which the information will be used is often more functional for the effective capitalization on knowledge about the present than knowledge about the present itself.

Sequential Actions

The life cycle concept can be effectively employed in the strategy of both existing and new products. For purposes of continuity and clarity, the remainder of this article will describe some of the uses of the concept from the early stages of new product planning through the later stages of keeping the product profitably alive. The chief discussion will focus on what I call a policy of "life extension" or "market stretching." [4]

To the extent that Exhibits 2 and 3 outline the classical patterns of successful new products, one of the constant aims of the originating producer should be to avoid the severe discipline imposed by an early profit squeeze in the market growth stage, and to avoid the wear and waste so typical of the market maturity stage. Hence the following proposition would seem reasonable: when a company develops a new product or service, it should try to plan at the very outset a series of actions to be employed at various subsequent stages in the product's existence so that its sales and profit curves are constantly sustained rather than following their usual declining slope.

In other words, advance planning should be directed at extending, or stretching out, the life of the product. It is this idea of *planning in advance* of the actual launching of a new product to take specific actions later in its life cycle—actions designed to sustain its growth and profitability—which appears to have great potential as an instrument of long-term product strategy.

Nylon's Life

How this might work for a product can be illustrated by looking at the history of nylon. The way in which nylon's booming sales life has been repeatedly and systematically extended and stretched can serve as a model for other products. What has happened in nylon may not have been purposely planned that way at the outset, but the results are quite as if they had been planned.

The first nylon end-uses were primarily military—parachutes, thread, rope. This was followed by nylon's entry into the circular knit market and its consequent domination of the women's hosiery business. Here it developed the kind of steadily rising growth and profit curves that every executive dreams

---

[4] For related ideas on discerning opportunities for product revivification, see Lee Adler, "A New Orientation for Plotting a Marketing Strategy," *Business Horizons,* Winter 1964, p. 37.

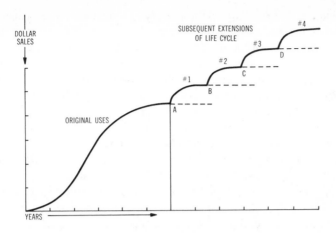

Exhibit 4   Hypothetical life cycle—nylon

about. After some years these curves began to flatten out. But before they flattened very noticeably, Du Pont had already developed measures designed to revitalize sales and profits. It did several things, each of which is demonstrated graphically in Exhibit 4. This exhibit and the explanation which follows take some liberties with the actual facts of the nylon situation in order to highlight the points I wish to make. But they take no liberties with the essential requisites of product strategy.

Point A of Exhibit 4 shows the hypothetical point at which the nylon curve (dominated at this point by hosiery) flattened out. If nothing further had been done, the sales curve would have continued along the flattened pace indicated by the dotted line at Point A. This is also the hypothetical point at which the first systematic effort was made to extend the product's life. Du Point, in effect, took certain "actions" which pushed hosiery sales upward rather than continuing the path implied by the dotted line extension of the curve at Point A. At Point A action #1 pushed an otherwise flat curve upward.

At points B, C, and D still other new sales and profit expansion "actions" #2, #3, #4, and so forth) were taken. What were these actions? Or, more usefully, what was their strategic content? What did they try to do? They involved strategies that tried to expand sales via four different routes:
1. Promoting more frequent usage of the product among current users.
2. Developing more varied usage of the product among current users.
3. Creating new users for the product by expanding the market.
4. Finding new uses for the basic material.

Frequent Usage. Du Pont studies had shown an increasing trend toward "bareleggedness" among women. This was coincident with the trend toward more casual living and a declining perception among teenagers of what might be called the "social necessity" of wearing stockings. In the light of those findings, one approach to propping up the flattening sales curves might have been to reiterate the social necessity of wearing stockings at all times. That would have been a sales-building action, though obviously difficult and exceedingly costly.

But it could clearly have fulfilled the strategy of promoting more frequent usage among current users as a means of extending the product's life.

Varied Usage. For Du Pont, this strategy took the form of an attempt to promote the "fasion smartness" of tinted hose and later of patterned and high textured hosiery. The idea was to raise each woman's inventory of hosiery by obsolescing the perception of hosiery as a fashion staple that came only in a narrow range of browns and pinks. Hosiery was to be converted from a "neutral" accessory to a central ingredient of fashion, with a "suitable" tint and pattern for each outer garment in the lady's wardrobe.

This not only would raise sales by expanding women's hosiery wardrobes and stores' inventories, but would open the door for annual tint and pattern obsolescence much the same as there is an annual color obsolescence in outer garments. Beyond that, the use of color and pattern to focus attention on the leg would help arrest the decline of the leg as an element of sex appeal—a trend which some researchers had discerned and which, they claimed, damaged hosiery sales.

New Users. Creating new users for nylon hosiery might conceivably have taken the form of attempting to legitimize the necessity of wearing hosiery

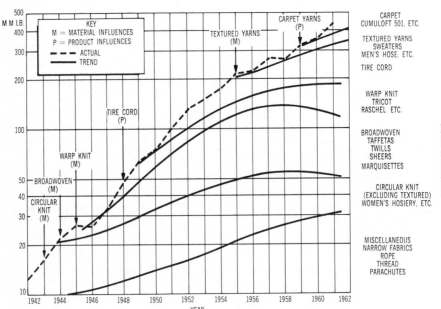

Exhibit 5　Innovation of new products postpones the time of total maturity—nylon industry. Source: *Modern Textiles Magazine,* February 1964, p.33. © 1962 by Jordan P. Yale.

among early teenagers and subteenagers. Advertising, public relations, and merchandising of youthful social and style leaders would have been called for.

New Uses. For nylon, this tactic has had many triumphs—from varied types of hosiery, such as stretch stockings and stretch socks, to new uses, such as rugs, tires, bearings, and so forth. Indeed, if there had been no further product innovations designed to create new uses for nylon after the original military, miscellaneous, and circular knit uses, nylon consumption in 1962 would have reached a saturation level at approximately 50 million pounds annually.

Instead, in 1962 consumption exceeded 500 million pounds. Exhibit 5 demonstrates how the continuous development of new uses for the basic material constantly produced new waves of sales. The exhibit shows that in spite of the growth of the women's stocking market, the cumulative result of the military, circular knit, and miscellaneous grouping would have been a flattened sales curve by 1958. (Nylon's entry into the broadwoven market in 1944 substantially raised sales above what they would have been. Even so, the sales of broadwoven, circular knit, and military and miscellaneous groupings peaked in 1957.)

Had it not been for the addition of new uses for the same basic material—such as warp knits in 1945, tire cord in 1948, textured yards in 1955, carpet yarns in 1959, and so forth—nylon would have had the spectacularly rising consumption curve it has so clearly had. At various stages it would have exhausted its existing markets or been forced into decline by competing materials. The systematic search for new uses for the basic (and improved) material extended and stretched the product's life.

Other Examples

Few companies seem to employ in any systematic or planned way the four product life-stretching steps described above. Yet the successful application of this kind of stretching strategy has characterized the history of such well-known products as General Foods Corporation's "Jell-O" and Minnesota Mining & Manufacturing Co.'s "Scotch" tape.[5]

Jell-O was a pioneer in the easy-to-prepare gelatin dessert field. The soundness of the product concept and the excellence of its early marketing activities gave it beautifully ascending sales and profit curves almost from the start. But after some years these curves predictably began to flatten out. Scotch tape was also a pioneer product in its field. Once perfected, the product gained rapid market acceptance because of a sound product concept and an aggressive sales organization. But, again, in time the sales and profit curves began to flatten out. Before they flattened out very much, however, 3M, like General Foods, had already developed measures to sustain the early pace of sales and profits.

Both of these companies extended their products' lives by, in effect, doing all four of the things Du Pont did with nylon—creating more frequent usage among

[5] I am indebted to my colleague, Dr. Derek A. Newton, for these examples and other helpful suggestions.

current users, more varied usage among current users, new users, and new uses for the basic "materials":

1. The General Foods approach to increasing the frequency of serving Jell-O among current users was, essentially, to increase the number of flavors. From Don Wilson's famous "six delicious flavors," Jell-O moved up to over a dozen. On the other hand, 3M helped raise sales among its current users by developing a variety of handy Scotch tape dispensers which made the product easier to use.

2. Creation of more varied usage of Jell-O among current dessert users involved its promotion as a base for salads and the facilitation of this usage by the development of a variety of vegetable flavored Jell-O's. Similiarly, 3M developed a line of colored, patterened, waterproof, invisible, and write-on Scotch tapes which have enjoyed considerable success as sealing and decorating items for holiday and gift wrapping.

3. Jell-O sought to create new users by pinpointing people who could not accept Jell-O as a popular dessert or salad product. Hence during the Metrecal boom Jell-O employed an advertising theme that successfully affixed to the product a fashion-oriented weight control appeal. Similarly, 3M introduced "Rocket" tape, a product much like Scotch tape but lower in price, and also developed a line of commercial cellophane tapes of various widths, lengths, and strengths. These actions broadened product use in commercial and industrial markets.

4. Both Jell-O and 3M have sought out new uses for the basic material. It is known, for example, that women consumers use powdered gelatin dissolved in liquids as a means of strengthening their fingernails. Both men and women use it in the same way as a bone-building agent. Hence Jell-O introduced a "completely flavorless" Jell-O for just these purposes. 3M has also developed new uses for the basic material—from "doublecoated" tape (adhesive on both sides) which competes with ordinary liquid adhesives, to the reflecting tape which festoons countless automobile bumpers, to marker strips which compete with paint.

Extension Strategies

The existence of the kinds of product life cycles illustrated in Exhibits 1 and 2 and the unit profit cycle in Exhibit 3 suggests that there may be considerable value for people involved in new product work to begin planning for the extension of the lives of their products even before these products are formally launched. To plan for new life-extending infusions of effort (as in Exhibit 4) at this pre-introduction stage can be extremely useful in three profoundly important ways.

1. *It generates an active rather than a reactive product policy.*

It systematically structures a company's long-term marketing and product development efforts in advance, rather than each effort or activity being merely a stop-gap response to the urgent pressures of repeated competitive thrusts and declining profits. The life-extension view of product policy enforces thinking and planning ahead—thinking in some systematic way about the moves likely to be made by potential competitors, about possible changes in consumer reactions to the product, and the required selling activities which best take advantage of these conditional events.

2. *It lays out a long-term plan designed to infuse new life into the product at the right time, with the right degree of care, and with the right amount of effort.*

Many activities designed to raise the sales and profits of existing products or materials are often undertaken without regard to their relationship to each other or to timing—the optimum point of consumer readiness for such activities or the point of optimum competitive effectiveness. Careful advance planning, long before the need for such activity arises, can help assure that the timing, the care, and the efforts are appropriate to the situation.

For example, it appears extremely doubtful that the boom in women's hair coloring and hair tinting products would have been as spectacular if vigorous efforts to sell these products had preceded the boom in hair sprays and chemical hair fixers. The latter helped create a powerful consumer consciousness of hair fashions because they made it relatively easy to create and wear fashionable hair styles. Once it became easy for women to have fashionable hair styles, the resulting fashion consciousness helped open the door for hair colors and tints. It could not have happened the other way around, with colors and tints first creating fashion consciousness and thus raising the sales of sprays and fixers. Because understanding the reason for this precise order of events is essential for appreciating the importance of early pre-introduction life-extension planning, it is useful to go into a bit of detail. Consider:

For women, setting their hair has been a perennial problem for centuries. First, the length and treatment of their hair is one of the most obvious ways in which they distinguish themselves from men. Hence to be attractive in that distinction becomes crucial. Second, hair frames and highlights the face, much like an attractive wooden border frames and highlights a beautiful painting. Thus hair styling is an important element in accentuating the appearance of a woman's facial features. Third, since the hair is long and soft, it is hard to hold in an attractive arrangement. It gets mussed in sleep, wind, damp weather, sporting activities, and so forth.

Therefore, the effective arrangement of a woman's hair is understandably her first priority in hair care. An unkempt brunette would gain nothing from making herself into a blond. Indeed, in a country where blonds are in the minority, the switch from being an unkempt brunette to being an unkempt blond would simply draw attention to her sloppiness. But once the problem of arrangement became easily "solved" by sprays and fixers, colors and tints could become big business, especially among women whose hair was beginning to turn gray.

The same order of priorities applies in industrial products. For example, it seems quite inconceivable that many manufacturing plants would easily have accepted the replacement of the old single-spindle, constantly man-tended screw machine by a computerized tape-tended, multiple-spindle machine. The mechanical tending of the multiple-spindle machine was necessary intermediate step, if for no other reason than that it required a lesser work-flow change, and certainly a lesser conceptual leap for the companies and the machine-tending workers involved.

For Jell-O, it is unlikely that vegetable flavors would have been very successful before the idea of gelatin as a salad base had been pretty well accepted. Similarly, the promotion of colored and patterned Scotch tape as a gift and decorative seal might not have been as successful if department stores had not, as the result of their drive to compete more effectively with mass merchandisers by offering more customer services, previously demonstrated to the consumer what could be done to wrap and decorate gifts.

3. *Perhaps the most important benefit of engaging in advance, pre-introduction planning for sales-extending, market- stretching activities later in the product's life is that this practice forces a company to adopt a wider view of the nature of the product it is dealing with.*

Indeed, it may even force the adoption of a wider view of the company's business. Take the case of Jell-O. What is its product? Over the years Jell-O has become the brand umbrella for a wide range of dessert products, including cornstarch-base puddings, pie fillings, and the new "Whip'n Chill," a light dessert product similar to a Bavarian Creme or French Mousse. On the basis of these products, it might be said that the Jell-O Division of General Foods is in the "dessert technology" business.

In the case of tape, perhaps 3M has gone even further in this technological approach to its business. It has a particular expertise (technology) on which it has built a constantly expanding business. This expertise can be said to be that of bonding things (adhesives in the case of Scotch tape) to other things, particularly to thin materials. Hence we see 3M developing scores of profitable items, including electronic recording tape (bonding electron-sensitive materials to tape), and "Thermo-Fax" duplicating equipment and supplies (bonding heat reactive materials to paper).

Conclusion

For companies interested in continued growth and profits, successful new product strategy should be viewed as a planned totality that looks ahead over some years. For its own good, new product strategy should try to predict in some measure the likelihood, character, and timing of competitive and market events. While prediction is always hazardous and seldom very accurate, it is undoubtedly far better than not trying to predict at all. In fact, every product strategy and every business decision inescapably involves making a prediction about the future, about the market, and about competitors. To be more systematically aware of the predictions one is making so that one acts on them is an offensive rather than a defensive or reactive fashion—this is the real virtue of preplanning for market stretching and product life extension. The result will be a product strategy that includes some sort of *plan for a timed sequence of conditional moves.*

Even before entering the market development stage, the originator should make a judgment regarding the probable length of the product's normal life, taking into account the possibilities of expanding its uses and users. This judgment will also help determine many things—for example, whether to price the product on a skimming or a penetration basis, or what kind of relationship the company should develop with its resellers.

These considerations are important because at each stage in a product's life cycle each management decision must consider the competitive requirements of the next stage. Thus a decision to establish a strong branding policy during the market growth stage might help to insulate the brand against strong price competition later; a decision to establish a policy of "protected" dealers in the market development stage might facilitate point-of-sale promotions during the market growth stage, and so on. In short, having a clear idea of future product development possibilities and market development opportunities should reduce the likelihood of becoming locked into forms of merchandising that might possibly prove undesirable.

This kind of advance thinking about new product strategy helps management avoid other pitfalls. For instance, advertising campaigns that look successful from a short-term view may hurt in the next stage of the life cycle. Thus at the outset Metrecal advertising used a strong medical theme. Sales boomed until imitative competitors successfully emphasized fashionable slimness. Metrecal had projected itself as the dietary for the overweight consumer, an image that proved far less appealing than that of being the dietary for people who were fashion-smart. But Metrecal's original appeal had been so strong and so well made that it was a formidable task later on to change people's impressions about the product. Obviously, with more careful long-range planning at the outset, a product's image can be more carefully positioned and advertising can have more clearly defined objectives.

Recognizing the importance of an orderly series of steps in the introduction of sales-building "actions" for new products should be a central ingredient of long-term product planning. A carefully preplanned program for market expansion, even before a new product is introduced, can have powerful virtues. The establishment of a rational plan for the future can also help to guide the direction and pace of the on-going technical research in support of the product. Although departures from such a plan will surely have to be made to accomodate unexpected events and revised judgments, the plan puts the company in a better position to *make* things happen rather than constantly having to react to things that *are* happening.

It is important that the originator does *not* delay this long-term planning until after the product's introduction. How the product should be introduced and the many uses for which it might be promoted at the outset should be a function of a careful consideration of the optimum sequence of suggested product appeals and product uses. Consideration must focus not just on optimum things to do, but as importantly on their optimum *sequence*—for instance, what the order of use of various appeals should be and what the order of suggested product uses should be. If Jell-O's first suggested use had been as a diet food, its chances of later making a big and easy impact in the gelatin dessert market undoubtedly would have been greatly diminished. Similarly, if nylon hosiery had been promoted at the outset as a functional daytime-wear hosiery, its ability to replace silk as the acceptable high-fashion hosiery would have been greatly diminished.

To illustrate the virtue of pre-introduction planning for a product's later life, suppose a company has developed a nonpatentable new product—say, an ordinary kitchen salt shaker. Suppose that nobody now has any kind of shaker. One might say, before launching it, that (1) it has a potential market of "x" million household, institutional, and commercial consumers, (2) in two years market maturity will set in and (3) in one year profit margins will fall because of the entry of competition. Hence one might lay out the following plan:

1. *End of first year: expand market among current users.* Ideas—new designs, such as sterling shakers for formal use, "masculine" shaker for barbecue use, antique shaker for "Early American" households, miniature shaker for each table place setting, moisture-proof design for beach picnics.

2. *End of second year: expand market to new users.* Ideas—designs for children, quaffer design for beer drinkers in bars, design for sadists to rub salt into open wounds.

3. *End of third year: find new uses.* Ideas—make identical product for use as pepper shaker, as decorative garlic salt shaker, shaker for household scouring powder, shaker to sprinkle silicon dust on parts being machined in machine shops and so forth.

This effort to prethink methods of reactivating a flattening sales curve far in advance of its becoming flat enables product planners to assign priorities to each task, and to plan future production expansion and capital and marketing requirements in a systematic fashion. It prevents one's trying to do too many things at once, results in priorities being determined rationally instead of as accidental consequences of the timing of new ideas, and disciplines both the product development effort that is launched in support of a product's growth and the marketing effort that is required for its continued success.

Products, like men, are mortal. They flourish for a time, then decline and die. While the death of a man is catastrophic in the sense that it occurs at a specific point in time, that of a product tends to be an indefinite process that may continue until its last user forgets that it ever existed and so will no longer try to buy it. The author presents a thoughtful and practical plan for selecting products for elimination; gathering information about them; making decisions about them; and, if necessary, removing the doomed products from the line.

The Death and Burial of "Sick" Products

R. S. Alexander

Euthanasia applied to human beings is criminal; but aging products enjoy or suffer no such legal protection. This is a sad fact of business life.

The word "product" is used here not in its broad economic sense of anything produced—such as wheat, coal, a car, or a chair—but in its narrower meaning of an article made to distinct specifications and intended for sale under a separate brand or catalogue number. In the broader sense of the word, certain products may last as long as industrial civilization endures; in the narrow sense, most of them are playthings of change.

Much has been written about managing the development and marketing of new products, but business literature is largely devoid of material on product deletion.

This is not surprising. New products have glamor. Their management is

Reprinted by permission of the author and the publisher from the *Journal of Marketing,* published by the American Marketing Association, Vol. 28, No. 2 (April, 1964), pp. 1-7.

fraught with great risks. Their successful introduction promises growth in sales and profits that may be fantastic.

But putting products to death—or letting them die—is a drab business, and often engenders much of the sadness of a final parting with old and tried friends. "The portable 6-sided, pretzel polisher was the first product The Company ever made. Our line will no longer be our line without it."

But while deletion is an uninspiring and depressing process, in a changing market it is almost as vital as the addition of new products. The old product that is a "football" of competition or has lost much of its market appeal is likely to generate more than its share of small unprofitable orders; to make necessary short, costly production runs; to demand an exorbitant amount of executive attention; and to tie up capital that could be used more profitably in other ventures.

Just as a crust of barnacles on the hold of a ship retards the vessel's movement, so do a number of worn-out items in a company's product mix affect the company's progress.

Most of the costs that result from the lack of an effective deletion system are hidden and become apparent only after careful analysis. As a result, management often overlooks them. The need for examining the product line to discover outworn members, and for analysis to arrive at intelligent decisions to discard or to keep them, very rarely assumes the urgency of a crisis. Too often, management thinks of this as something that should be done but that can wait until tomorrow.

This is why a definite procedure for deletion of products should be set up, and why the authority and responsibility for the various activities involved should be clearly and definitely assigned. This is especially important because this work usually requires the cooperation of several functional groups within the business firm, including at least marketing, production, finance, and sometimes personnel.

Definite responsibility should be assigned for at least the following activities involved in the process: (1) selecting products which are candidates for elimination; (2) gathering information about them and analyzing the information; (3) making decisions about elimination; and (4) if necessary, removing the doomed products from the line.

Selection of Products for Possible Elimination

As a first step, we are not seeking the factors on which the final decision to delete or to retain turns, but merely those which indicate that the product's continuation in the product mix should be considered carefully with elimination as a possibility. Although removal from the product line may seem to be the prime aim, the result is not inevitably deletion from the line; instead, careful analysis may lead to changes in the product itself or in the methods of making or marketing it.

Sales Trend. If the trend of a product's sales is downward over a time period that is significant in relation to the normal life of others like it, its continuation in the mix deserves careful examination. There may be many reasons for such a decline that in no way point toward deletion; but when decline continues over a period of time the situation needs to be studied.

Price Trend. A downward trend in the price of a new product may be expected if the firm introducing it pursues a skimming-price policy, or if all firms making it realize substantial cost savings as a result of volume production and increased processing know-how. But when the price of an established product whose competitive pattern has been relatively stabilized shows a downward trend over a significant period of time, the future of that product should receive attention.

Profit Trend. A declining profit either in dollars or as a per cent of sales or investment should raise questions about a product's continued place in the product line. Such a trend usually is the result of a price-factory cost squeeze, although it may be the outcome of a loss in market appeal or a change in the method of customer purchase which forces higher marketing expenditures.

Substitute Products. When a substitute article appears on the market, especially if it represents an improvement over an old product, management must face the question of whether to retain or discard the old product. This is true regardless of who introduces the substitute. The problem is especially difficult when the new product serves the same general purpose as the old one but is not an exact substitute for it.

Product Effectiveness. Certain products may lose some of their effectiveness for the purposes they serve. For example, disease germs may develop strains that are resistant to a certain antibiotic. When this happens, the question of whether to keep or delete the drug involves issues not only of the interests of the firm but of the public welfare.

Executive Time. A possible tipoff as to the location of "illness" in a product mix lies in a study of the amount of executive time and attention devoted to each of the items in the product line. Sick products, like sick people, demand a lot of care; but one must be careful to distinguish the "growing pains" of a new product from the more serious disorders of one that has matured and is now declining.

The six indicators mentioned do not of themselves provide evidence justifying deletion. But they can help management to single out from a line of products those upon which it can profitably spend time and money in analyzing them, with elimination from the line as a *possibility*.

Analysis and Decision Making About "Sick" Products

Although the work of analyzing a sick or decrepit product is usually done by other than the management executives who decide what to do about it, the two processes are interdependent. Unless the right factors are chosen for analysis and unless the work is properly done, the decision is not likely to be an intelligent one. Accordingly, these two factors will be discussed together.

What information does a decision-maker need about a product, and what sort of analysis of it should he have in order to render a sound verdict as to its future? The deletion decision should not turn on the sole issue of profitability. Profit is the most important objective of a business; but individual firms often seek to achieve both long-run and short-run objectives other than profit.

So, in any individual case the critical factors and the weights assigned them in making a decision must be chosen in the light of the situation of the firm and the management objectives.

Profits

Profit management in a firm with a multi-product line (the usual situation in our economy) is not the simple operation generally contemplated in economic theory. Such a firm usually has in its product mix (1) items in various stages of introduction and development, some of which may be fantastically profitable and others deep "in the red"; (2) items which are mature but not "superannuated," whose profit rate is likely to be satisfactory; and (3) declining items which may yield a net profit somewhat less than adequate or may show heavy losses.

The task is to manage the whole line or mix so that it will show a satisfactory profit for the company. In this process, two questions are vital; What is a profit? How much profit is satisfactory?

Operating-statement accounting makes it possible to determine with reasonable accuracy the total amount of net profit a company earns on an overall basis. But when the management of a multi-product firm seeks to determine how much of this total is generated by its activities in making and marketing each product in its mix, the process is almost incredibly complex; and the results are almost certain to be conditioned on a tissue of assumptions which are so debatable that no management can feel entirely comfortable in basing decisions on them.

This is because such a large portion of the costs of the average multi-product firm are or behave like overhead or joint expense. Almost inevitably several of the items in the product mix are made of common materials, with the same equipment, and by manpower which is interchangeable. Most of the company's marketing efforts and expenses are devoted to selling and distributing the mix or a line within the mix, rather than individual items.

In general, the more varied the product mix of a firm, the greater is the portion of its total expense that must be classified as joint or overhead. In such a company, many types of cost which ordinarily can be considered direct tend to behave like overhead or joint expenses. This is particularly true of marketing costs such as advertising that does not feature specific items; personal selling; order handling; and delivery.

This means that a large part of a company's costs must be assigned to products on some arbitrary basis and that however logical this basis may be, it is subject to considerable reasonable doubt in specific cases. It also means that if one product is removed from the mix, many of these costs remain to be reassigned to the items that stay in the line. As a result, any attempt to "prune" the product mix entirely on the basis of the profit contribution, or lack of it, of specific items is almost certain to be disappointing and in some cases disastrous.

But if a multi-product firm could allocate costs to individual items in the mix on some basis recognized as sound and thus compute product-profit accurately, what standard of profit should be set up, the failure to meet which would justify deletion?

Probably most managements either formally or unconsciously set overall company profit targets. Such targets may be expressed in terms of dollars, although to be most useful in product management they usually must be translated into percentages on investment, or money used. As an example, a company may have as its profit target 15% on investment before taxes.

Certainly *every* product in the mix should not be required to achieve the target, which really amounts to an average. To do so would be to deny the inevitable variations in profit potential among products.

Probably a practical minimum standard can be worked out, below which a product should be eliminated unless other considerations demand its retention. Such a standard can be derived from a balancing out of the profit rates among products in the mix, so as to arrive at the overall company target as an average. The minimum standard then represents a figure that would tip the balance enough to endanger the overall target.

What role, then, should considerations of product profit play in managerial decisions as to deletion or retention?

1. Management probably will be wise to recognize an overall company target profit in dollars or rate on investment, and to set in relation to it a minimum below which the profit on an individual product should not fall without marking that item for deletion (unless other special considerations demand its retention).

2. Management should cast a "bilious eye" on all arguments that a questionable product be kept in the mix because it helps to defray overhead and joint costs. Down that road, at the end of a series of decisions to retain such products, lies a mix entirely or largely composed of items each busily "sopping up" overhead, but few or none contributing anything to net profit.

3. This does not mean that management should ignore the effect of a product deletion on overhead or joint costs. Decision-makers must be keenly aware of the fact that the total of such costs borne by a sick product must, after it is deleted, be reallocated to other products, and with the result that they may become of doubtful profitability. A detailed examination of the joint or overhead costs charged against an ailing product may indicate that some of them can be eliminated in whole or in part if it is eliminated. Such costs are notoriously "sticky" and difficult to get rid of; but every pretext should be used to try to find ways to reduce them.

4. If a deletion decision involves a product or a group of products responsible for a significant portion of a firm's total sales volume, decision-makers can assess the effects of overhead and joint costs on the problem, by compiling an estimated company operating statement after the deletion and comparing it with the current one. Such a forecasted statement should include expected net income from the use of the capital and facilities released by deletion if an opportunity for their use is ready to hand. Surviving joint and overhead expenses can even be reallocated to the remaining products, in order to arrive at an

estimate of the effect that deletion might have, not only on the total company net income but on the profitability of each of the remaining products as well. Obviously such a cost analysis is likely to be expensive, and so is not justified unless the sales volume stakes are high.

Financial Considerations

Deletion is likely not only to affect the profit performance of a firm but to modify its financial structure as well.

To make and sell a product, a company must invest some of its capital. In considering its deletion, the decision-makers must estimate what will happen to the capital funds presently used in making and marketing it.

When a product is dropped from the mix, most or all of the circulating capital invested in it—such as inventories of materials, goods in process, and finished goods and accounts receivable—should drain back into the cash account; and if carried out in an orderly fashion, deletion will not disturb this part of the capital structure except to increase the ratio of cash to other assets.

This will be true, unless the deletion decision is deferred until product deterioration has gone so far that the decision assumes the aspect of a crisis and its execution that of a catastrophe.

The funds invested in the equipment and other facilities needed to make and market the "sick" product are a different matter. If the equipment is versatile and standard, it may be diverted to other uses. If the firm has no need of it and if the equipment has been properly depreciated, management may find a market for it at a price approaching or even exceeding its book value.

In either case, the capital structure of the company is not disturbed except by a shift from equipment to cash in the case of sale. In such a case management would be wise, before making a deletion decision, to determine how much cash this action promises to release as well as the chances for its reinvestment.

If the equipment is suited for only one purpose, it is highly unlikely that management can either find another use for it or sell it on favorable terms. If it is old and almost completely depreciated, it can probably be scrapped and its remaining value "written off" without serious impairment of the firm's capital structure.

But if it is only partly depreciated, the decision-makers must weigh the relative desirability of two possible courses of action: (1) to delete immediately, hoping that the ensuing improvement in the firm's operating results will more than offset the impairment in capital structure that deletion will cause; or (2) to seek to recapture as much as possible of its value, by continuing to make and market the product as long as its price is enough to cover out-of-pocket costs and leave something over to apply to depreciation.

This choice depends largely on two things: the relation between the amount of fixed and circulating capital that is involved; and the opportunities available to use the funds, executive abilities, manpower, and transferable facilities released by deletion for making profits in other ventures.

This matter of opportunity costs is a factor in every deletion decision. The dropping of a product is almost certain to release some capital, facilities, manpower skills, and executive abilities. If opportunities can be found in which these assets can be invested without undue risk and with promise of attractive profits, it may be good management to absorb considerable immediate loss in deleting a sick product.

If no such opportunities can be found, it is probably wise to retain the product so long as the cash inflow from its sales covers out-of-pocket costs and contributes something to depreciation and other overhead expenses. In such a case, however, it is the part of good management to seek actively for new ventures which promise satisfactory profits, and to be ready to delete promptly when such an opportunity is found.

Employee Relations

The effect which product elimination may have on the employees of a firm is often an important factor in decisions either to drop or to retain products.

This is not likely to be a deciding factor if new product projects are under development to which the people employed in making and marketing the doubtful product can be transferred, unless such transfer would deprive them of the earning power of special skills. But when deletion of a product means discharging or transferring unionized employees, the decision-makers must give careful thought to the effect their action is likely to have on company-union relations.

Even in the absence of union pressure, management usually feels a strong sense of responsibility for the people in its employ. Just how far management can go in conserving specific jobs at the expense of deferring or foregoing necessary deletions before it endangers the livelihood of all the employees of the firm is a nice question of balance.

Marketing Factors

Many multi-product firms retain in their marketing mixes one or more items which, on the basis of profits and the company financial structure, should be deleted. To continue to make and market a losing product is no managerial crime. It is reprehensible only when management does not know the product is a losing one or, knowing the facts, does not have sound reasons for retaining it. Such reasons are very likely to lie in the marketing area.

Deletions of products are often deferred or neglected because of management's desire to carry a "full line," whatever that means. This desire may be grounded on sound reasons of consumer patronage or on a dubious yearning for the "prestige" that a full line is supposed to engender. But there is no magic about a full line or the prestige that is supposed to flow from it. Both should be evaluated on the basis of their effects on the firm's sales volume, profits, and capacity to survive and grow.

Products are often associated in the marketing process. The sale of one is helped by the presence of another in the product mix.

When elimination of a product forces a customer who buys all or a large part of his requirements of a group of profitable items from the firm to turn to another supplier for his needs of the dropped product, he might shift some or all of his other patronage as well. Accordingly, it is sometimes wise for management to retain in its mix a no-profit item, in order to hold sales volume of highly profitable products. But this should not be done blindly without analysis.

Rarely can management tell ahead of time exactly how much other business will be lost by deleting a product, or in what proportions the losses will fall among the remaining items. But in many cases the amount of sales volume can be computed that will be *hazarded* by such action; what other products will be subject to that hazard; and what portion of their volume will be involved. When this marketing interdependence exists in a deletion problem, the decision-makers should seek to discover the customers who buy the sick product; what other items in the mix they buy; in what quantities; and how much profit they contribute.

The firm using direct marketing channels can do this with precision and at relatively little cost. The firm marketing through indirect channels will find it more difficult, and the information will be less exact; but it still may be worth-while. If the stakes are high enough, marketing research may be conducted to discover the extent to which the customer purchases of profitable items actually are associated with that of the sick product. Although the results may not be precise, they may supply an order-of-magnitude idea of the interlocking patronage situation.

Product interrelationships in marketing constitute a significant factor in making deletion decisions, but should never be accepted as the deciding factor without careful study to disclose at least the extent of the hazards they involve.

Other Possibilities

The fact that a product's market is declining or that its profit performance is substandard does not mean that deletion is the only remedy.

Profits can be made in a shrinking market. There are things other than elimination of a product that can be done about deteriorating profit performance. They tend to fall into four categories.

1. *Costs.* A careful study may uncover ways of reducing factory costs. This may result from improved processes that either eliminate manpower or equipment time or else increase yield; or from the elimination of forms or features that once were necessary or worth-while but are no longer needs. The natural first recourse of allocating joint and overhead costs on a basis that is "kinder" to the doubtful product is not to be viewed with enthusiasm. After reallocation, these costs still remain in the business; and the general profit picture has not been improved in the least.

2. *Marketing.* Before deleting a product, management will be wise to examine the methods of marketing it, to see if they can be changed to improve its profit picture.

Can advertising and sales effort be reduced without serious loss of volume? A holding operation requires much less effort and money than a promotional one.

Are services being given that the product no longer needs?

Can savings be made in order handling and delivery, even at some loss of customer satisfaction? For example, customers may be buying the product in small orders that are expensive to handle.

On the other hand, by spending more marketing effort, can volume be increased so as to bring about a reduction in factory cost greater than the added marketing expense? In this attempt, an unexpected "assist" may come from competitors who delete the product and leave more of the field to the firm.

By remodeling the product, "dressing it up," and using a new marketing approach, can it be brought back to a state of health and profit? Here the decision-makers must be careful not to use funds and facilities that could be more profitably invested in developing and marketing new products.

3. *Price.* It is natural to assume that the price of a failing product cannot be raised. At least in part, its plight is probably due to the fact that it is "kicked around" by competition, and thus that competition will not allow any increases.

But competitors may be tired of the game, too. One company that tried increasing prices found that wholesalers and retailers did not resent a larger cost-of-goods-sold base on which to apply their customary gross profit rates, and that consumers continued to buy and competitors soon followed suit.

Although a price rise will not usually add to the sum total of user happiness, it may not subtract materially from total purchases. The decision-makers should not ignore the possibility of using a price reduction to gain enough physical volume to bring about a more-than-offseting decline in unit costs, although at this stage the success of such a gambit is not likely.

4. *Cross Production.* In the materials field, when small production runs make costs prohibitive, arrangements may sometimes be made for Firm A to make the *entire* supply of Product X for itself and Competitor B. Then B reciprocates with another similar product. Such "trades," for instance, are to be found in the chemical business.

Summation for Decision

In solving deletion problems, the decision-makers must draw together into a single pattern the results of the analysis of all the factors bearing on the matter. Although this is probably most often done on an intangible, subjective basis, some firms have experimented with the formula method.

For example, a manufacturer of electric motors included in its formula the following factors:
1. Profitability
2. Position on growth curve
3. Product leadership
4. Market position
5. Marketing dependence of other products

Each factor was assigned a weight in terms of possible "counts" against the product. For instance, if the doubtful item promised no profits for the next three years, it had a count of 50 points against it, while more promising prospects were assigned lesser counts. A critical total for all factors was set in advance which would automatically doom a product. Such a system can include other factors—such as recapturability of invested capital, alternate available uses of facilities, effects on labor force, or other variables peculiar to the individual case.

The use of a formula lends an aura of precision to the act of decision-making and assures a degree of uniformity in it. But obviously the weights assigned to different factors cannot be the same in all cases. For example, if the deletion of a doubtful product endangers a large volume of sales of other highly profitable items, that alone should probably decide the matter.

The same thing is true if deletion will force so heavy a writeoff of invested funds as to impair the firm's capital structure. Certainly this will be true if all or most of the investment can be recaptured by the depreciation route if the product stays in the mix.

This kind of decision requires that the factors be weighted differently in each case. But when managers are given a formula, they may tend to quit thinking and do too much "weighing."

The Deletion of a Product

Once the decision to eliminate a product is made, plans must be drawn for its death and burial with the least disturbance of customer relations and of the other operations of the firm.

Such plans must deal with a variety of detailed problems. Probably the most important fall into four categories: timing; parts and replacements; stocks; and holdover demand.

1. *Timing.* It is desirable that deletion be timed so as to dovetail with the financial, manpower, and facilities needs for new products. As manpower and facilities are released from the dying product and as the capital devoted to it flows back into the cash account, it is ideal if these can be immediately used in a new venture. Although this can never be completely achieved, it may be approximated.

The death of a product should be timed so as to cause the least disturbance to customers. They should be informed about the elimination of the product far enough in advance so they can make arrangements for replacement, if any are available, but not so far in advance that they will switch to new suppliers before the deleting firm's inventories of the product are sold. Deletion at the beginning of a selling season or in the middle of it probably will create maximum customer inconvenience, whereas at the end of the season it will be the least disturbing.

2. *Parts and Replacements.* If the product to be killed off is a durable one, probably the deleting firm will find it necessary to maintain stocks of repair parts for about the expected life of the units most recently sold. The firm that leaves a trail of uncared-for "orphan" products cannot expect to engender much good will from dealers or users. Provision for the care and maintenance of the orphan is a necessary cost of deletion.

This problem is much more widespread than is commonly understood. The woman who buys a set of china or silverware and finds that she cannot replace broken or lost pieces does not entertain an affectionate regard for the maker.

The same sort of thing is true if she installs draperies and later, when one of them is damaged, finds that the pattern is no longer available.

3. *Stocks.* The deletion plan should provide for clearing out the stocks of the dying product and materials used in its production, so as to recover the maximum amount of the working capital invested in it. This is very largely a matter of timing—the tapering off of purchase, production, and selling activities. However, this objective may conflict with those of minimizing inconvenience to customers and servicing the orphan units in use after deletion.

4. *Holdover Demand.* However much the demand for a product may decline, it probably will retain some following of devoted users. They are bound to be disturbed by its deletion and are likely to be vocal about it; and usually there is little that management can do to mitigate this situation.

Sometimes a firm can avoid all these difficulties by finding another firm to purchase the product. This should usually be tried before any other deletion steps are taken. A product with a volume too small for a big firm to handle profitably may be a money-maker for a smaller one with less overhead and more flexibility.

Neglect or Action?

The process of product deletion is important. The more dynamic the business, the more important it is.

But it is something that most company executives prefer not to do; and therefore it will not get done unless management establishes definite, clearcut policies to guide it, sets up carefully articulated procedures for doing it, and makes a positive and unmistakable assignment of authority and responsibility for it.

Exactly what these policies should be, what form these procedures should take, and to whom the job should be assigned are matters that must vary with the structure and operating methods of the firm and with its position in the industry and the market.

In any case, though, the need for managerial attention, planning, and supervision of the deletion function cannot be overemphasized. Many business firms are paying dearly for their neglect of this problem, but unfortunately do not realize how much this is costing them.

Any executive is extremely interested in finding the package that will bring the greatest increase in sales. He must find out what the proper combination of packaging attributes is by evaluating each possible combination in terms of the six basic functions of any package. However, the packager is still in need of a final criterion, since no package will do all functions equally well. Emphasizing one may involve limiting or even sacrificing one of the others.

A Theory of Packaging in the Marketing Mix

William R. Mason

It is axiomatic that the job of packaging is to sell. But after that banality has been voiced, what guides to management judgment—what theories, if you will—influence the choice of a package?

This article is not a check list of features that should be built into a package, but a rough guide to basic judgments management must bring to bear in its choice of packaging before the particulars of type face, combination of colors, package count, or printing method are up for decision.

The critical judgments that must be made on the packaging choice concern the "mix" of packaging attributes best able to perform, in different degrees, the particular functions of the package that are believed to be important to sales. The basic judgment in choice of packaging is "What jobs should the package do, and how completely should it do each?" The answers to the lesser decisions can fall into place once the "mix" of desirable packaging attributes has been determined, once the assignment of basic functions desired of the package has been made. Frequently, too much effort and time are devoted to making lesser

Reprinted by permission of the publisher from *Business Horizons,* Vol. 1, No. 3 (Summer, 1958), pp. 91-95 decisions, usually on questions of graphic art, rather than this basic judgment.

The packager may accept as a guide, when making basic decisions on product "mix," that:

The major purpose of any package is to influence or control the location of product storage within the marketing channel.

"Storage," as I am using the term, means the holding of goods for future use at any level along the marketing channel, *including the level of the ultimate consumer.* Even at the ultimate consumer level, the product may be stored in several places—sugar, for example, may be stored on a shelf or on the table. The packager is interested in getting the bulk of his product's storage as near as possible to the point of ultimate use.

The functions of the product's package are:
- Protecting the product
- Adapting to production line speeds
- Promoting the product
- Increasing product density[1]
- Facilitating the use of the product
- Having re-use value for the consumer

The performance of a package in the first two of these basic functions is relatively easy to measure through physical testing procedures. And, because it is comparatively easy to evaluate the degrees to which these functions are fulfilled by any package under consideration, such measurement is very common. Today, it must be a rare package that reaches its market without being rated objectively on its degrees of protection and production line adaptability. However, these ratings seem to be applied too often without consideration of the package's ability to fulfill its other possible functions.

There are four other major jobs that the package can do at least partially; these should be assigned priority by company management, but often they seem to be neglected.

All packages have the opportunity to perform, at least partially, each of these functions. But it is an unusual package that performs each to the same degree. That the package gives a superior performance of one function does not necessarily mean that it will give a superior performance of another. Because he needs to choose a package, the packager, whether he recognizes it or not, must assign priorities to the value of each of these functions to further his product's sale and use.

To illustrate, it is usually easy to create a package that has uniquely promotable features quite aside from graphic arts; that is, a package that could eminently perform the promotional function. But something else has to give. Using such a package may require sacrificing a good job in one of the other areas, for example in adaptability to production line speeds or in failure to

---

[1]   That is, increasing the ratio of product volume to package volume.

increase package density. In like fashion, it is frequently possible to build a feature facilitating product use into a package—but not always without sacrificing some measure of product protection.

After all, when a package is criticized as a poor sales- or use-builder, it can be criticized fairly only when its performance of *each* of the basic functions is evaluated. A product may seem "overpackaged" simply because the packager's assignment of priorities differs from the critic's.

Interrelationships

Let's examine in a little more detail the way each function impinges on the others:

Protecting the Product. Beyond the requirements imposed by various governmental, carrier, and trade practice rulings, there usually are a substantial number of alternatives open to management with regard to product protection—even during the period when the product is in its distribution channel. To illustrate, even though a carrier ruling may require the product's 24-count carton to have a minimum corrugated fiberboard strength of, say, a 100-pound test, a company's management may choose board that meets more severe tests in order to permit higher stacking or use of mechanized materials-handling equipment by certain important handlers at various levels in the product's distribution channel. Accordingly, in such a situation, an opportunity to tailor the product's package to its product-protection job alone is relinquished because of a desire to better the package's performance of its density-increasing and promotional jobs.

But perhaps a more important range of product-protection considerations occurs at the time of product use—especially when the product is partially used. How much protection should the bread wrapper give a partially used loaf of bread? Will incorporating the use-facilitating features of a pouring spout or a tear tape opening require yielding too much product protection?

Adapting to Production Line Speeds. Sometimes the operating speeds of packaging equipment do not match the speeds of other equipment in the production line. Until recently, for instance, the normal operating speeds of wrapping machinery that would handle polyethylene film did not match the normal production line speeds for many products. Two or more wrapping machines were often required in a production line, and the results were poor space utilization, greater capital investment, and sometimes greater labor costs. As an alternative to these wastes, the packager "made do" with other types of film that could be handled by high-speed wrapping equipment but lacked some of polyethylene's protective attributes. New types of wrapping machines have largely corrected this situation. But the point is that the freedom of the packagers to better their packages' protective attributes was limited.

The question of a package's adaptability to production line speeds, however, usually crops up before the package is actually used. The packager's advertising agency or his sales department suggests a new package with striking promise of being able to fulfill the promotional or use-facilitating function better than current packaging; but, upon analysis, the suggested new package is found to require either slowdowns in production line speeds or investment in new packaging equipment. The company's management is then obliged to judge whether or not the suggested package's better performance of the promotional or use-facilitating functions justifies the slower line speed or the different packaging equipment.

Promoting the Product. Features may be built into a package which are promotable to consumers, to customers, and to intermediaries in its product's distribution channel. But sometimes a feature desirable for promotion to one of the three is not desirable for one of the others. Features that minimize a retailer's loss or pilferage are, presumably, important to him; but they are not necessarily of any interest to consumers. Features that minimize a consumer's embarrassment at purchase can increase a retailer's stacking or display difficulties and make inventory control more trying.

Even granting a package feature that is promotable regardless of level in its product's distribution or use, incorporation of the feature into the package frequently requires sacrificing some good package performance of one of the other basic package functions. For example, a gift-wrapped set-up box complete with nosegay of artificial flowers is a highly promotable candy package, as is a rigid plastic, reusable package for razors that is large enough to hold a fishing lure. But both packages sacrifice density for better promotion.

Increasing Product Density. This seems to be the area where the packager's sales department on the one hand, and his purchasing and production departments on the other, are most often in disagreement about the choice of packaging. Except on those occasions when the sales department recommends yielding a package's higher density in order to improve its promotional value, the sales department is usually advocating increased package density. It improves relations with carriers; it permits better utilization of space throughout the distribution channel, thus encouraging fuller inventory stocks in the pipeline; and it permits more units to be displayed per assigned running foot of self-service display space. But it frequently slows production line speeds and increases per-unit packaging cost.

Usually this issue turns on package shape. The cylinder, for instance, is an efficient package shape for liquids; a given measure of liquid can be packaged cylindrically with less material than is necessary for any rectangular container holding the same amount of liquid. But the normal 12-count (3 X 4 put-up) layer of a 24-count carton will occupy significantly less shelf space if it holds rectangular packages rather than the same number of cylindrical packages with the same amount of liquid.

But bettering a package's performance of its density-increasing function can inhibit good performance in other areas too. The density of many candy packages, for instance, could be improved significantly, but not without loss of their value as items specifically tailored for re-use as sewing baskets or cookie tins. Increasing density could also lessen the package's value as a promotional vehicle or as a promotable item in itself. Package designers seem better able to build points of brand differentiation into a 12-ounce beer bottle than into the higher-density 12-ounce beer can.

Facilitating the Use of the Product. Excluding changes in the graphic art of packages, most package changes in recent years have been in facilitating the product's use. All the changes to tear tapes, pouring spouts, squeeze bottles, aerosol cans, and so forth would have to be included here. And, as is obvious to anyone exposed to the mass advertising media, bettering the package's fulfillment of this function has proved to be a means of bettering the package's performance in promotion.

In many cases, however, where the use-facilitating function of a package has been improved, a case can be built that some degree of product protection has been sacrificed. And, bettering the package's use-facilitating job sometimes means relinquishing some package value as a re-use container for the consumer. The flow of a viscous liquid perhaps can be directed a little more accurately or easily from the mouth of a narrow-necked glass jar than from a tin can, but packaging the liquid in the glass jar means sacrificing the protection against impact provided by the tin can. The tear tape makes a corrugated carton easier to open but, for many purposes, lessens its value as a re-usable container. Some shaker openings make cleanser or spice packages easy to use but, once used, leave the product exposed.

Having Re-use Value for the Consumer. Perhaps the competition of the various functions of the package for recognition by company managements is most apparent in this area. In recent years, according much recognition to this function of the package seems not to have been in vogue. Typically, designing a package to do its other jobs well has meant slighting its re-use value—the previous illustrations of candy and razors notwithstanding. A package's re-use value generally has suffered with successive changes unless its re-usability has been very promotable.

The Principle, The Corollary, and Recent Trends

How does management know whether it is better to sacrifice a measure of product protection for a more promotable package or to build a use-facilitating attribute into the package instead of a density-increasing attribute?

Assuming that two "mixes" are in conflict or partial conflict, management may find the answer by deciding which will be more likely to push product storage as far from the packager as possible. This is, of course, another way of saying that the basic purpose of a product's package should be as much as possible to maximize product inventory near the point of use or possible use. If neither "mix" holds promise of increasing product inventory at the point of use, does either hold promise of increasing product storage at the next level back from the point of use? If neither "mix" aids in getting the product stored on the dining-room table, does either help in getting more of the product inventoried on the kitchen shelves? If neither helps there, which encourages the greater amount of well-placed open display at retail? If it is a tie between the two package "mixes" at this level, which of the two has promise of encouraging the greater retailer inventory—regardless whether in open display or not?

It follows, then, that the most successful package changes are those whose impact is greatest at a level in the product's marketing one step forward from the level currently storing the channel's largest share of the product.

Most recent packaging changes can be understood a little better if viewed against the backdrop of these generalizations. Interestingly, they explain current trends in package design that, on the surface, seem to be running in opposite directions. For instance, recently some company managements have been increasing package size or package count. Other managements have unit-packaged, lessened package size, or reduced package count. But both apparently contradictory approaches have the same purpose—*to maximize product inventory as close to a point of use as possible.* Let's examine a few recent package changes in light of these generalizations (I am refering to those changes that typically affect more than just the package's graphic art):

Changes Involving Package Size or Count. Proprietary medicine, soap powder or detergent, beverages, and toilet tissue are among those widely distributed consumer products whose recent package changes have included addition of "king" or "giant economy" size packages to their lines. Table salt, facial tissue, crackers, and cereal on the other hand are among the items, distributed in large part through the same marketing channel, which have added smaller-size packages or "unitized" packages to their lines. In each case, promotion turning on "convenience" to the user frequently has accompanied the introduction of the new package size. Where the move has been to increase the package size, packagers are trying to encourage the consumer to maintain inventories of their particular brands far in excess of the consumer's normal needs for the product during any reasonable time span between shopping trips. In effect, the packagers are trying to move a greater share of their channel's total storage function closer to the point of use—from retailer to consumer in this particular illustration. Where the move has been to lessen package size, it is apparent that the packagers are trying to move storage location further forward: to get facial tissues into purses as well as on the vanity; to get brand-identified salt on the dining-room, breakfast, TV, or barbecue table as well as on the pantry shelf; to get half a dozen varieties of cereal in the home rather than in the store in anticipation of a family's vacillating demands. Again, the packagers are trying to move a greater share of the channel's total storage closer to the point of use.

Changes Involving Package Shape. Ice cream and milk, in both powdered and liquid forms, are examples of items that have been undergoing changes from cylindrical to space-saving rectangular packages. In part, at least, the change has been precipitated by increased recognition of the marketing channel's limited capacity to store items under refrigeration and of its eagerness to husband its shelf space. In effect, the change permits a greater share of the inventory to be moved forward.

Changes Involving Packaging Materials. This is the area where packagers' desires to push storage forward probably have been most apparent. And, incidentally, it is in this area that the lie is put to the belief that a package's prime job is protection of the product. If product protection were the prevailing consideration, few if any of certain kinds of change in packaging materials would ever have taken place. For example:

1. *Changes from opaque to transparent materials* usually have been represented as irrefutable evidence of the packager's good faith in allowing his customers to see his product. Understandably, the suppliers of transparent packaging materials have done what they could to further this impression. But conversion from opaque to transparent packaging typically has meant something else as well; *It has been a means of obtaining favorable open display shelf space at retail,* where the product could be seen by the consumers. In effect, it has meant moving part of the storage function forward in the channel from concealed storage or low-traffic locations to prominent, high-traffic locations. Small wonder that such a premium has come to be placed on transparency—even for products not especially attractive to the eye.

2. *Changes from rigid to flexible materials* have almost always meant relinquishing some measure of product protection—and the recent changes from rigid to flexible packaging are legion. The changes, while requiring some loss of product-protection value, typically have given the product an especially promotable package, one with conspicuous promise of moving product storage closer to a point of use.

Changes Involving Addition of "Ease-of-Opening" or "Ease-of-Use" Attributes. I believe that, where they have been successful, package changes incorporating this kind of feature have tended to move product storage increasingly closer—however slightly— to the point of use. Typically, the movement of storage effected by such "ease-of-opening" package changes has not been at the consumer level in the product's marketing channel; it has been at the retail level. Perhaps it could be argued that the extremely successful rigid flip-top cigarette package has helped move the smoker's storage of his cigarettes a little closer to the point of their use, but the main value of the package with regard to its movement of product storage has been at the retail level. The package, again, was a means of obtaining a good, high-traffic position in open display for the particular brands of cigarette that pioneered this packaging change. It was something distinctively new that could be promoted to the marketing channel itself—quite aside from its being amenable to use in effective promotion to smokers—for brands not having so extensive or complete retail inventories as those enjoyed by more popular brands.

In summary, the choice of a product's package, no less than the choice of the total selling effort brought to bear on the product, has to represent a reconciliation of a variety of functions, each of which has potential merit in furthering the sale of the product, but all of which are, in part at least, mutually exclusive.

The most successful reconciliation will be the one that, to return to our original axiom, produces the most sales. It will emphasize that function which pushes the bulk of product storage one step farther along the marketing channel and one step closer to the ultimate consumer.

All too often management perceives distribution problems within the context of nondistribution areas of marketing such as sales, sales promotion, advertising, and so on. Furthermore, the distribution function within a firm is often scattered in all directions of the company—from manufacturing to marketing. The authors portray some of the characteristics of managerial thinking relative to one of marketing's least managed areas—channel management. Some guideline suggestions are made for rethinking the channel concept and its application to management.

A Look at Channel Management

Reavis Cox

Thomas F. Schutte

A strange anomaly in marketing today is the extent to which both managers and students who accept the idea that marketing efforts should be customer-oriented, overlook the fact that, if efforts so oriented are to be successful, managers must use effective marketing channels. Conventional textbooks speak of the four P's as constituting the variables which management has under its control in working with marketing problems—product, place, price, and promotion. They discuss in great detail some of the things managers can do under these headings, but they offer little more than vague descriptions of the numbers and kinds of agencies through which these things must be done. Only a small number of specialized students—and most of these only in very recent years—have come to grips with what is involved if these agencies are to be organized into combinations and sequences that will do well the whole job of connecting production and consumption. This is a major but largely neglected problem in management. Some of the managers themselves are beginning to see dimly what is required, but they have made little progress in formalizing their ideas into rules or procedures.

Reprinted by permission of the authors and the publisher from *Marketing Involvement in Society and the Economy*, edited by Philip R. McDonald (Chicago: American Marketing Association, 1970), pp. 99-105.

The purpose of this paper and of the panel discussion that will follow is to stimulate a rethinking of the role of management as applied to the channel. Emphasis will be placed upon the problems of the firm rather than the academic discipline of marketing in general. What we hope to do is to help managers, as well as students, develop new perspectives in channel management by providing:

1. Some examples of managerial problems raised by channels.
2. An operational definition of channel management.
3. A look at some characteristics of managerial thinking about channels.
4. Some suggestions for rethinking the channel concept and its application to management.

Examples of Distribution Problems

The scope and magnitude of channel problems may be obscured both by the way marketing or distribution is defined and by the ways in which distribution programs are developed and carried into effect. It is interesting to note how often firms visualize their problems, not as problems in distribution, but as problems in selling, advertising, sales promotion, pricing, product management, or even manufacturing. A good way to see what we mean is to look at some examples of confusion which were selected by the authors without any attempt to be systematic or thorough.

1. A well-known pharmaceutical manufacturer assigns the responsibility for what it calls customer trade relations to its public relations department. The management of finished goods, inventories, warehouses, and physical distribution is a responsibility of the manufacturing department. Customer requests, servicing, returns, and allowances are divided between marketing and finance without a clear assignment to either group. No one is formally responsible for seeing to it that these scattered activities add up to a coordinated overall program. Can one be surprised that the central management is beginning to wonder whether its organization does not automatically produce under-achievement in distribution?

2. A leading manufacturer of toiletry products distributes exclusively through drug wholesalers and drug chains. In response to spending heavily for promotion, advertising, and personal selling, it built up a strong consumer demand for one of its lines. Nearly two-thirds of the potential market for the sorts of goods constituting this line is bought by consumers through non-drug trades, and this proportion is increasing. Members of these trades wanted the product, but the company, dominated by principles derived from other products, would not change its distribution policy. Consequently, sales of the line have been falling for two years as the company refuses to see that products must be sold where consumers expect to find them not where sellers like to put them.

3. A large trucking company receives as many as 300,000 garments in one day from local manufacturers. Through a program of prompt efficient handling and shipping, the firm can put garments on hangers in the receiving rooms of retailers, over a large geographic area, within 24 hours of receipt. The chairman of the board of the trucking company laments, "We get the garment quickly to

the stores, on hangers, and ready to move to the sales floors. Then we discover that they sit around for days or even weeks waiting for someone to attach price tags." One part of a marketing system was done well, but the system, as a whole, faltered.

4. The idea that the economy offers an opportunity for someone to set up a gigantic distributor of automotive parts for competing manufacturers, is relatively new. Until the creation of such a firm, the thousands of manufacturers, producing even more thousands of products, marketed them through a multitude of selling organizations. Customers for these parts, primarily garages and service stations, were constantly badgered by a plethora of salesmen representing manufacturers. Not only was the selling costly, but the complexity of the enormous number of automobiles, the number of parts needed for one vehicle, and the models to be served were all such that parts service centers required an intelligence system, effective inventory control, and sharp reductions in selling costs. But the need was not visualized until the new distributing firm recognized the need for analyzing the entire distribution system, brought it to the consciousness of parts users, and provided a service to meet it.

5. A furniture retailer currently receives many goods from manufacturers that require repair and refinishing. It employs two full-time men to do this work. The president of the retail operation justifies the presence of the two workers because they cost less than he would have to pay for the work involved and the loss of sales incurred in shipping the damaged goods back to the supplier. This retailer is looking for a manufacturer who will help him eliminate the need for having two full-time men. He believes a less costly system is possible. Some supplier that does its homework in looking at the entire channel may find this retailer to be a good, profitable account.

6. A well-known manufacturer of consumer paper products introduced a "giant economy box" of one product. Thanks to heavy promotion, consumers wanted it. So the retailers stocked it, but many supermarkets did so reluctantly because they had to stock it on the floor. They lacked shelf space for it. Thus, the manufacturer was vulnerable to competition from others who could satisfy the consumers' demand without penalizing the retailers. The extensive marketing research done by the producer during product development found a consumer need but failed to recognize that the retailer also had needs to be satisfied.

One could go on and on with such illustrations of the failure of businessmen to recognize the true nature of the channel problems, but these examples are sufficient for our purposes.

What the Channel of Distribution Is

For present purposes, a channel of distribution may be defined as an organized network of agencies and institutions which, in combination, perform all the activities required to link producers with users, and users with producers in order to accomplish the marketing task. From the point of view of the seller, the channel permits him to find and supply users of his goods. From the point of view of the buyer, the channel finds and delivers to him the want-satisfying goods he seeks. Some intangible services, also require the use of channels to connect suppliers with users.

Contrary to many textbooks, a channel of distribution is not a static network. Not only are new channels created for new products as they appear, but also, new channels often are developed for existing products. For example, a manufacturer of proprietary drugs may restrict his distribution of a sun-tan lotion to drug stores and the agencies that serve them until his penetration of the drug store market is optimized, at which time he may revise his distribution system to include variety chains and supermarkets. Likewise, the same proprietary drug manufacturer may decide to modify his policy of distributing exclusively through wholesalers because chain stores that will not buy through wholesalers now hold more of the market than do independent drug stores.

It should be noted that a new channel of distribution normally is created because both buyers and sellers need it in order to fulfill their joint marketing task as effectively as possible. For example, Smith, Kline and French Laboratories relies on over 400 drug wholesalers and over 35,000 drug stores to perform the services required if products such as Contac, Sea and Ski, and Love are to reach and satisfy consumers. On the other hand, the Drug House, Inc., one of the country's largest drug wholesalers of proprietary and ethical products expects SKF to perform a number of services that will facilitate its servicing of individual drug stores; for example, putting inner-packs of six units each in the shipping cases.

Hartz Mountain, Inc., a producer of proprietary health care products for small animals, distributes through numerous rack jobbers to many thousands of pet shops and supermarkets. It does so because these jobbers provide, more cheaply than anyone else, the services of weekly stocking, dusting, and rehabilitation of goods on the shelves. Furthermore, the rack jobber provides the financial service of reimbursing the central offices with their due net profits without any previous billing to the chain and with subsequent dollar pay-out by the chain.

Conventional Thinking About Channels

Although the management of marketing channels has not received the formal attention it deserves from businessmen, a number of ways in which managements tend to view the problem may be discerned. Some of these are not really conscious formulations but rather, what we may call "*as if* propositions." That is, the managers behave *as if* the channel is a certain kind of structure without spelling out their assumptions in detail. At least six such propositions can be stated.

1. *Channels are determined by the characteristics of the product.* A seller of goods following this rule holds that the shape and design of the channel that distributes his products are determined by their characteristics. Thus, goods of high unit-value can absorb high costs but require protection against loss or theft; perishability imposes a need for refrigeration and quick handling; large size or heavy weight calls for special materials handling equipment; and so on. The best channel in this view is the one that minimizes the cost imposed by the products' characteristics. This orientation may cause a seller to become so preoccupied

with his product that he loses sight of other needs felt by intermediate traders and ultimate users.

2. *The channel stops at the loading platform.* Some businessmen seem to see distribution as ending (rather than beginning) when the goods have been shipped. In essence, this notion sees distribution as an activity consisting of loading the product onto a comon or contract carrier at the shipper's dock. What happens thereafter is the buyer's responsibility. The concept, thus baldly stated, may be oversimplified in many cases; but it would be interesting to know how many firms see marketing in effect as a process of getting customers to take goods physically as near to the manufacturing plant as possible and to assume responsibilities for them from that point on.

3. *The channel is primarily, if not exclusively, an agency for the physical distribution of goods.* The literature and traditions of marketing are such that one can easily come to view distribution as physical distribution alone and thus overlook all the other tasks that must be performed by channels. Such a view is really an extension of the loading-platform thesis; but it opens the way to a consideration of choices as to where the seller's loading platform shall be located. Physical distribution is an important component part of the distribution process but viewing it as the distribution process is still a very narrow concept. Too often, sellers who overemphasize physical distribution tend to look upon their channel problem as being that of locating warehouses or selecting a viable form of transportation system for their products.

4. *There is no provision within firms for the management of channels.* This may be called the vacant-chair thesis. Of the many possible conventions followed in channel management, this is one of the most important. It can be stated simply: Nobody serves or is expected to serve as manager of the firm's channels because the firm has no manager of marketing. If the company is well organized functionally, the various aspects of marketing will be handled by a number of officers—the purchasing agent, the customer relations manager, the traffic manager, the sales manager, the warehouse manager, and so on. But there will be no one man who coordinates the relations of the firm with all the agencies that form its marketing channel.

This view carries some significant consequences with it. In the absence of a channel manager one must ask: Who designs the distribution system for new products? Who reviews the needs and resources for existing products in order to make certain that required adjustments are made in the channel system? Who speaks for the company in dialogues with members of the channel?

Somehow or other, management gets questions answered; but the officers who answer them remain unidentified, and the chair of the distribution manager seems to remain vacant.

5. *The manufacturer constructs and manages the channel.* This concept can be called the dominant force thesis. It sees the manufacturer as both the architect and the captain of the channel. His is the dominant force. Textbooks commonly look at the distribution function almost as if the manufacturer presents all the stimuli and the distributive agencies (whether wholesalers, agents, or retailers) merely respond to what he does.

The fact that some manufacturers seem to act according to the dominant force theory may cause strain and conflict within the channel. The chairman of the board of the Rawlings Corporation says of the relationship between manufacturers and retailers, "I have been surprised and appalled at the *bad feelings, complete misunderstanding, and even distrust that exist between the manufacturers and the retailer.*"[1] He explains his concept of the relationships between the two by offering an analogy:

The situation reminds us a little of the climax of a "Western". Two cowboys silently face each other in the middle of a hushed Front Street, each waiting for the other to draw.
Each of our "heroes" feels that the other has done him dirt. The manufacturer is telling himself that the dealer hasn't been loyal, while the dealer firmly believes that the manufacturer has gotten just what he deserves.
So they stand there—each waiting for the other to draw. Meanwhile back on the ranch, nobody is minding the cows and someone else is selling the beefsteak.[2]

6. *Nobody manages the channel.* Earlier in the paper we definded a channel as an organized network of agencies. But who organizes and manages the channel as a whole? One answer is that nobody does. The channel works as free competition is said to work in that the play of market forces attracts people to the performance of needed services and drives them to cooperate with one another in the absence of formal management. Somehow or other, the distribution task is accomplished even though no agency has any authority to command others.

Some students deplore this situation. They ask how a channel manager can be created, apparently assuming that formal management would improve the efficiency of the distribution system. A few writers seem to think that in practice, channel systems, even though they usually do not have formally recognized managers sometimes do have *de facto* managers or captains. They achieve their position by virtue of their firm's having market power and the will to lead.

Rethinking the Concept of Channel Management

We can now consider some suggestions as to how the marketing manager can develop a better understanding by his firm of the channel problems it faces. The central principle to be followed is that the firm must think not solely in terms of its own operation within the channel but rather in terms of relationships of its own operations to the operations of all other agencies within the channel. It also must keep in mind the fact that effectiveness in its own activities is not enough.

Somehow, matters must be worked out so that everything done by everybody

[1] R.D. Brown, "Selling Through—Not to—Retailers," in Malcolm P. McNair and Mira Berman, Eds., *Marketing Through Retailers* (New York: American Management Association, 1967), p. 59.
[2] *Ibid.,* p. 60.

in the channel adds up to effectiveness at the point where the final user chooses it over the offerings made to him by competing channels.

Thinking in Terms of Systems

Systems analysis is in danger of becoming a superficial "buzz word" in the study of marketing today, but there is real merit in applying the concept to channel management. It must be admitted that very often, little rationale is apparent in a firm's distribution system. The utility of systems analysis may be demonstrated if we look upon it as being helpful in the following sorts of studies:

1. A description of existing structure of a firm's channel or channels.
2. An assessment of needs and responses of each agency in the actual or desired channel for each product.
3. An evaluation of each specific channel and the flows it embodies from the joint or common viewpoint of *all* the agencies concerned.
4. A consideration of modifications and adjustments that might be made in the channels for given products.

The Existing Structure. All too often, a seller of goods views his channel relationship as one between himself and his immediate customer or alternatively, as one between himself and the final user of his product, without regard to intermediate buyers. The first task in assessing a channel management system is to develop a critical-path description of the agencies performing the various channel services for given products. The assessment can often be made most effectively by considering the work done by the channel members as being that of conducting a number of "flows," i.e., the physical flow of the good, the flow of ownership, the flow of information, and so on.

The importance of this orientation has been stressed by one well known channel theorist, Professor Ralph Breyer. In an interview with one of the authors, he emphasized what he thought to be the most critical problems in distribution today. One of these was "the channel overview" problem. Here, he noted:

One must examine the channel from a total-channel point of view—not just the manufacturer's, or the wholesaler's, or the retailer's. Without this commitment to the study and management of channels as a whole, little progress can be made toward the optimizing of distribution. It is entirely *wrong* to view a channel from the standpoint of the manufacturer only or to think that what is good for the manufacturer is good for the channel.

A simplistic version of a channel from the viewpoint of the manufacturer can be seen in Figure 1. A similar simplistic version from the viewpoint of the wholesaler can be seen in Figure 2. In Figure 1, the channel is for one product or line produced by one manufacturer. In Figure 2, the channel is for competing products made by several manufacturers but handled by one wholesaler. The charts are familiar enough but they ordinarily are used with little imagination. It takes little insight to see that the ideas of manufacturer and wholesaler as to what constitutes "effective" operation of a "good" channel can differ sharply.

Anyone who sets himself up to be the channel leader or captain will need to keep this fact in mind.

Just recently, a Madison Avenue creative enthusiast has advocated that manufacturers take a more adventuresome approach to couponing ads.[3] He advocates the "wild" use of all shapes and sizes of the consumer "cents-off" tear-out coupons placed in print media. Uniformity of coupons in terms of the familiar rectangular approach would go by the wayside. Instead, a cents-off coupon for dog food would be shaped like a French Poodle or a cents-off coupon for wet soup would be shaped like a bowl of soup. While such new adventures may be eye catching and even appealing to consumers, we wonder if the Madison Avenue creative genius has ever appraised the consequences of the new shapes from the standpoint of the retailers who redeem the coupons. Imagine the stacking, sorting, cataloguing, and storing problems faced by retailers and redemption centers! Here is where some application of Figure 1 and Figure 2 might be helpful to manufacturers.

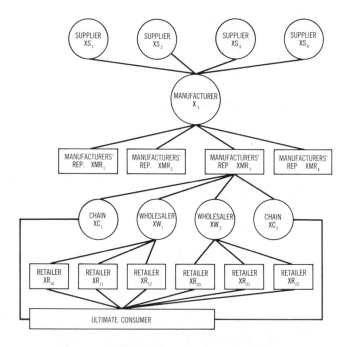

Figure 1   A simplistic structure of a trade channel from the viewpoint of a manufacturer (Due to the simplistic nature of the illustrated channel and the lack of space, the identification of the physical ownership, information and money flows was omitted.)

[3] Stephen Baker, "Wild Shapes, Sizes Are Today's Look in Coupons," Advertising Age, August 4, 1969.

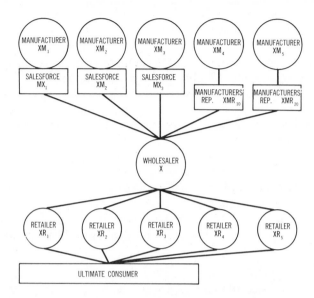

Figure 2   A simplistic structure of a trade channel from the viewpoint of a wholesaler (Due to the simplistic nature of the illustrated channel and the lack of space, the identification of the physical ownership, information and money flows was omitted.)

In trying to sort out the tasks performed by each agency in a channel, much less simplistic approaches are required. One of these is to use what has been called the "flow" approach. This elaborates the structures charted in Figure 1 and 2 by visualizing what happens in a channel not as one flow but as a group of several interrelated flows. In a book on channel management being prepared by the present authors, channels are viewed as conducting four flows:

1. *The physical flow of the goods*, i.e., a sequence of agencies or (more precisely) facilities through which the goods move for transportation, storage, sorting, and so on.

2. *The flow of ownership or control*, i.e., a sequence of agencies through which moves the authority to decide what shall be done with the goods.

3. *The flow of information*, i.e., a sequence of agencies through which users tell producers and distributors what they want, while producers and distributors simultaneously tell users what they have to sell and try to persuade users to buy it.

4. *The flow of money*, i.e., a sequence of agencies through which capital is assembled and brought into the marketing process and an overlapping sequence of agencies through which buyers pay sellers for what they buy.

Application of the flow concept to channel management makes it possible to determine the precise role of each agency or facility in the channel of distribution. Discrepancies in the effectiveness with which agencies perform specific activities may be observed. For example, one firm has developed a critical-path appraisal of its physical distribution system. In doing so it has found that its three public warehouses were handling in a dissimilar manner; customers' original orders, the shipping orders, bills of lading, and the informational feedback to the sales (carbons of various order papers). As a result, customers were receiving inconsistent and often poor service.

Assessing the Needs and Responses of Each Firm Within the Channel. One of the saddest shortcomings in channel management is the seller's frequent failure to consider the marketing needs and responses of his customers. How often does a seller objectively determine what his customers need in each of the flows? The manufacturer, if he makes any guess at all, is likely to decide intuitively what the customers want to do, or even can do, relative to each of the flows. There is nothing unusual about a firm that thinks one or two reports by salesmen will tell what its wholesalers are thinking.

Very unusual is a carefully designed, thorough, and systematic effort to find out the facts. An example is what one company calls its "Dealer Forum":

I write from some experience. In the Office Machines Division we created a Dealer Forum, and this proved very effective. We rotated our members on this Dealer Forum every two years. The meetings were held with the top management of the Division, including the manufacturing, engineering, financial, and marketing heads, as well as the general manager. Many fine programs came out of the Dealer Forum, and it was so successful . . . We . . . are going to adopt the same type of program with our sporting goods retailers.[4]

In a recent informal study, a drug manufacturer found the one of its advertising agencies not only failed to understand the nature of the management system for the total channel but did not really understand the role of its detail men. The agency was aiming its promotional pieces at the doctors without realizing that these pieces must also meet the needs and wishes of the detail men. For many of the pieces, there was no opportunity to test their effectiveness with doctors because the detail men never used them. The moral to be drawn from this simple illustration is that knowing the needs and responses of channel members is just as important as knowing the needs and responses of ultimate consumers.

Evaluation of the Channels as a Whole. As Professor Breyer's comments suggested earlier, what is good for the manufacturer or any other seller is not necessarily good for all other sellers and buyers within the channel. Once the needs and responses of all the components within the trade channel have been assessed, it becomes possible to evaluate the viability of the present channel system. Here, numerous questions might serve as a guideline in evaluation. Such questions as the following might be raised: Are there discrepancies in the performance of the flows among members of the channel? Are there alternative firms or agencies that might be more effective than those now used in carrying the product through the channel and to the ultimate consumer? What will be the

[4] Brown, *op. cit.,* p. 60.

impact on the channel structure and the requisite channel flows if new agencies or firms are added to the channel? Are there conventional ways of acting that inhibit the marketing effectiveness of sellers and buyers within the channel?

Possible Modifications and Adjustments of the Channel. After evaluation of a channel system comes the problem of making whatever modifications or adjustments seem to be needed. The appropriate guideline should be: "Observe the consequences of any change upon all agencies in the entire structure." Also, it should be emphasized that modifications or adjustments ought to occur *only after* the preceding three steps in the systems procedure have been taken.

The Managerial Responsibility for Channels

Despite the fact that every businessman and every consumer needs effectiveness in the operations of every complete channel of which he is a member, formal management of the system can rarely be established by any method other than vertical integration. However, one tremendous service can be performed by each member of a non-integrated channel. This is to make someone in its corporate hierarchy responsible for doing what can be done to achieve full channel efficiency. Thus, the channel function would become just as distinct an operating assignment as sales, advertising, or promotion.

The responsibilities should include at least the following:

1. *Systems management.*
   (a) Reviewing the existing structure of specific flows (ownership, physical movement, information, and money).
   (b) Developing an inventory of the needs and each agency within the channel.
   (c) Modifying and adjusting the channel to meet the needs for change.
2. *Channel relations*
   (a) Informing channel members of marketing programs and changes in any facet of marketing and non-marketing programs.
   (b) Receiving information and questions from trade customers relative to any facet of marketing and non-marketing programs.
3. *Internal coordination of distribution, as affected by:*

   (a) Manufacturing.
   (b) Finance.
   (c) Marketing.

The above list of responsibilities is not definitive. It nevertheless provides a start towards the development of a well organized channel management function within the firm. It thus offers business management an opportunity to make a significant contribution to the strengthening of what is unquestionably one of the least managed areas of marketing today.

Forces leading to conflict and cooperation within marketing channels are explored in this article. Several conclusions and hypotheses concerning marketing channels are advanced, including one emphasizing the importance of the various institutions comprising a channel to act in unity.

Conflict and Cooperation in Marketing Channels

Bruce Mallen

The purpose of this paper is to advance the hypotheses that between member firms of a marketing channel there exists a dynamic field of conflicting and cooperating objectives; that if the conflicting objectives outweigh the cooperating ones, the effectiveness of the channel will be reduced and efficient distribution impeded; and that implementation of certain methods of cooperation will lead to increased channel efficiency.

Definition of Channel

The concept of a marketing channel is slightly more involved than expected on initial study. One author in a recent paper[1] has identified "trading" channels, "non-trading" channels, "type" channels, "enterprise" channels, and "business-unit" channels. Another source[2] refers to channels as all the flows extending from the producer to the user. These include the flows of physical

Reprinted by permission of the authors and the publisher from *Progress in Marketing*, edited by L. George Smith (Chicago: American Marketing Association, 1964), pp. 65-85.

[1] Ralph F. Breyer, "Some Observations on Structural Formation And The Growth of Marketing Channels," in *Theory in Marketing,* Reavis Cox, Wroe Alderson, Stanley J. Shapiro, Editors. (Homewood, Illinois: Richard D. Irwin, Inc., 1964), pp. 163-175.

[2] Ronald S. Vaile, E.T. Grether, and Reavis Cox, *Marketing In the American Economy* (New York: Ronald Press, 1952), pp. 121 and 124.

possession, ownership, promotion, negotiation, financing, risking, ordering, and payment.

The concept of channels to be used here involves only two of the above-mentioned flows: ownership and negotiation. The first draws merchants, both wholesalers and retailers, into the channel definition, and the second draws in agent middlemen. Both, of course, include producers and consumers. This definition roughly corresponds to Professor Breyer's "trading channel," though the latter does not restrict (nor will this paper) the definition to actual flows, but to "flow-capacity." "A trading channel is formed when trading relations, making possible the passage of title and/or possession (usually both) of goods from the producer to the ultimate consumer, is consummated by the component trading concerns of the system."[3] In addition, this paper will deal with trading channels in the broadest manner and so will be concentrating on "type-trading" channels rather than "enterprise" or "business-unit" channels. This means that there will be little discussion of problems peculiar to integrated or semi-integrated channels, or peculiar to specific channels and firms.

Conflict

Palamountain isolated three forms of distributive conflict.[4]

1. Horizontal competition—this is competition between middlemen of the same type; for example, discount store *versus* discount store.
2. Intertype competition—this is competition between middlemen of different types in the same channel sector; for example, discount store *versus* department store.
3. Vertical conflict—this is conflict between channel members of different levels; for example, discount store *versus* manufacturer.

The first form, horizontal competition, is well covered in traditional economic analysis and is usually referred to simply as "competition." However, both intertype competition and vertical conflict, particularly the latter, are neglected in the usual micro-economic discussion.

The concepts of "intertype competition" and "distributive innovation" are closely related and require some discussion. Intertype competition will be divided into two categories; (a) "traditional intertype competition" and (b) "innovative intertype competition." The first category includes the usual price and promotional competition between two or more different types of channel members at the same channel level. The second category involves the action on the part of traditional channel members to prevent channel innovators from establishing themselves. For example, in Canada there is a strong campaign, on the part of the traditional department stores, to prevent the discount operation from taking a firm hold on the Canadian market.[5]

---

[3] *op. cit.*, p. 165.

[4] Joseph C. Palamountain, *The Politics of Distribution* (Cambridge: Harvard University Press, 1955).

[5] Isaiah A. Litvak and Bruce E. Mallen, *Marketing: Canada* (Toronto: McGraw-Hill of Canada, Limited, 1964), pp. 196-197.

Distribution innovation will also be divided into two categories; (a) "intrafirm innovative conflict" and (b) "innovative intertype competition." The first category involves the action of channel member firms to prevent sweeping changes within their own companies. The second category "innovative intertype competition" is identical to the second category of intertype competition.

Thus the concepts of intertype competition and distributive innovation give rise to three forms of conflict, the second of which is a combination of both: (1) traditional intertype competition, (2) innovative intertype competition, and (3) intrafirm innovative conflict.

It is to this second form that this paper now turns before going on to vertical conflict.

Innovative Intertype Competition

Professor McCammon has identified several sources, both intrafirm and intertype, of innovative conflict in distribution, i.e., where there are barriers to change within the marketing structure.[6]

Traditional members of a channel have several motives for maintaining the channel status quo against outside innovators. The traditional members are particularly strong in this conflict when they can ban together in some formal or informal manner—when there is strong reseller solidarity.

Both entrepreneurs and professional managers may resist outside innovators, not only for economic reasons, but because change "violates group norms, creates uncertainty, and results in a loss of status." The traditional channel members (the insiders) and their affiliated members (the strivers and complementors) are emotionally and financially committed to the dominant channel and are interested in perpetuating it against the minor irritations of the "transient" channel members and the major attacks of the "outside innovators."

Thus, against a background of horizontal and intertype channel conflict, this paper now moves to its area of major concern; vertical conflict and cooperation.

Vertical Conflict—Price

The Exchange Act. The act of exchange is composed of two elements: a sale and a purchase. It is to the advantage of the seller to obtain the highest return possible from such an exchange and the exact opposite is the desire of the buyer. This exchange act takes place between any kind of buyer and seller. If the consumer is the buyer, then that side of the act is termed shopping; if the manufacturer, purchasing; if the government, procurement; and if a retailer, buying. Thus, between each level in the channel an exchange will take place (except if a channel member is an agent rather than a merchant).

One must look to the process of the exchange act for the basic source of conflict between channel members. This is not to say the exchange act itself is a conflict. Indeed, the act or transaction is a sign that the element of price conflict has been resolved to the mutual satisfaction of both principals. Only along the

---

[6] This section is based on Bert C. McCammon, Jr., "Alternative Explanations of Institutional Change And Channel Evolution," in *Toward Scientific Marketing,* Stephen A. Greyser, Editor. (Chicago: American Marketing Association, 1963), pp. 477-490.

road to this mutual satisfaction point or exchange price do the principals have opposing interests. This is no less true even if they work out the exchange price together, as in mass retailers' specification-buying programs.

It is quite natural for the selling member in an exchange to want a higher price than the buying member. The conflict is subdued through persuasion or force by one member over the other, or it is subdued by the fact that the exchange act or transaction does not take place, or finally, as mentioned above, it is eliminated if the act does take place.

Suppliers may emphasize the customer aspect of a reseller rather than the channel member aspect. As a customer the reseller is somebody to persuade, manipulate, or even fool. Conversely, under the marketing concept, the view of the reseller as a customer or channel member is identical. Under this philosophy he is somebody to aid, help, and serve. However, it is by no means certain that even a large minority of suppliers have accepted the marketing concept.

To view the reseller as simply the opposing principal in the act of exchange may be channel myopia, but this view exists. On the other hand, failure to recognize this basic opposing interest is also a conceptual fault.

When the opposite principals in an exchange act are of unequal strength, the stronger is very likely to force or persuade the weaker to adhere to the former's desires. However, when they are of equal strength, the basic conflict cannot so easily be resolved. Hence, the growth of big retailers who can match the power of big producers has possibly led to greater open conflict between channel members, not only with regard to exchange, but also to other conflict sources.

There are other sources of conflict within the pricing area outside of the basic one discussed above.

A supplier may force a product onto its resellers, who dare not oppose, but who retaliate in other ways, such as using it as a loss leader. Large manufacturers may try to dictate the resale price of their merchandise; this may be less or more than the price at which resellers wish to sell it. Occasionally, a local market may be more competitive for a reseller than is true nationally. The manufacturer may not recognize the difference in competition and refuse to help this channel member.

Resellers complain of manufacturers' special price concessions to competitors and rebel at the attempt of manufacturers to control resale prices. Manufacturers complain of resellers' deceptive and misleading price advertising, nonadherence to resale price suggestions, bootlegging to unauthorized outlets, seeking special price concessions by unfair methods, and misrepresenting offers by competitive suppliers.

Other points of price conflict are the paper-work aspects of pricing. Resellers complain of delays in price change notices and complicated price sheets.

Price Theory. If one looks upon a channel as a series of markets or as the vertical exchange mechanism between buyers and sellers, one can adapt several theories and concepts to the channel situation which can aid marketing theory in this important area of channel conflict.[7] For example, the exchange mechanism

---

[7] Bruce Mallen, "Introducing The Marketing Channel To Price Theory," *Journal of Marketing*, July, 1964, pp. 29-33.

between a manufacturer as a seller and a wholesaler as a buyer is one market. A second market is the exchange mechanism between the wholesaler as a seller and the retailer as a buyer. Finally, the exchange mechanism between the retailer as a seller and the consumer as a buyer is a third market. Thus, a manufacturer-wholesaler-retailer-consumer channel can be booked upon as a series of three markets.

The type of market can be defined according to its degree of competitiveness, which depends to a great extent on the number of buyers and sellers in a market. Some possible combinations are shown in Table 1.

A discussion of monopoly in a channel context may show the value of integrating economic theory with channel concepts.

If one channel member is a monopolist and the others pure competitiors, the consumer pays a price equivalent to that of an integrated monopolist; and the monopolist member reaps all the channel's pure profits; that is, the sum of the pure profits of all channel members. Pure profits are, of course, the economist's concept of those profits over and above the minimum return on investment required to keep a firm in business.

Table 1
Classification of Economic Markets

Suppliers (sellers)	Middlemen (buyers)	Market situation
Pure competitor	Pure competitor	Pure competition
Oligopolist	Pure competitor	Oligopoly
Monopolist	Pure competitor	Monopoly
Pure competitor	Oligopsonist	Oligoposony
Pure competitor	Monopsonist	Monopsony
Oligopoly	Oligopsonist	Bilateral oligopoly
Monopolist	Monopsonist	Bilateral monopoly
Monopolist	Monopolist	Successive monopoly

Assume that the retailer is the monopolist and the others (wholesalers and manufacturers) are pure competitors, as for example, a single department store in an isolated town. Total costs to the retailer are composed of the total cost of the other levels plus his own costs. No pure profits of the other levels are included in his costs, as they make none by definition (they are pure competitors).

The retailer would be in the same buying price position, so far as the lack of suppliers' profits are concerned, as would the vertically integrated firm. Thus, he charges the same price as the integrated monopolist and makes the same profits.

If the manufacturer were the monopolist and the other channel members pure competitors, he would calculate the maximizing profits for the channel and then charge the wholesaler his cost plus the total channel's pure profits—all of which would go to him since the others are pure competitors. The wholesaler would take this price, add it on to his own costs, and the result would be the price to retailers. Then the retailers would do likewise for the consumer price.

Thus, the prices to the wholesaler and to the retailer are higher than in the first case (retailer monopoly), since the channel's pure profits are added on before the retail level. The price to the consumer is the same as in the first case. It is of no concern to the consumer if the pure profit elements in his price are added on by the manufacturer, wholesaler, or retailer.

Thus, under integrated monopoly, manufacturer monopoly, wholesaler monopoly, or retailer monopoly, the consumer price is the same; but the prices within the channel are the lowest with the retailer monopoly and the highest with the manufacturer monopoly. Of course, the nonmonopolistic channel members' pure profits are not affected by this intrachannel price variation, as they have no such profits in any case.

Vertical Conflict–Non Price

Channel conflict not only finds its source in the exchange act and pricing, but it permeates all areas of marketing. Thus, a manufacturer may wish to promote a product in one manner or to a certain degree while his resellers oppose this. Another manufacturer may wish to get information from his resellers on a certain aspect relating to his product, but his resellers may refuse to provide this information. A producer may want to distribute his product extensively, but his resellers may demand exclusives.

There is also conflict because of the tendency for both manufacturers and retailers to want the elimination of the wholesaler.

One very basic source of channel conflict is the possible difference in the primary business philosophy of channel members. Writing in the *Harvard Business Review*, Wittreich says:

In essence, then, the key to understanding management's problem of crossed purpose is the recognition that the fundamental (philosophy) in life of the high-level corporate manager and the typical (small) retail dealer in the distribution system are quite different. The former's (philosophy) can be characterized as being essentially dynamic in nature, continuously evolving and emerging; the latter, which are in sharp contrast, can be characterized as being essentially static in nature, reaching a point and leveling off into a continuously satisfying plateau.[8]

While the big members of the channel may want growth, the small retail members may be satisfied with stability and a "good living."

Anarchy[9]

The channel can adjust to its conflicting-cooperating environment in three

[8] Warren J. Wittreich, "Misunderstanding The Retailer," *Harvard Business Review*, May-June, 1962, p. 149.

[9] The term "anarchy" as used in this paper connotes "no leadership" and nothing more.

distinct ways. *First*, it can have a leader (one of the channel members) who "forces" members to cooperate; this is an autocratic relationship. *Second*, it can have a leader who "helps" members to cooperate, creating a democratic relationship. *Finally*, it can do nothing, and so have an anarchistic relationship. Lewis B. Sappington and C. G. Browne, writing on the problem of internal company organizations, state:

The first classification may be called "autocracy." In this approach to the group the leader determines the policy and dictates or assigns the work tasks. There are no group deliberations, no group decisions . . .

The second classification may be called "democracy." In this approach the leader allows all policies to be decided by the group with his participation. The group members work with each other as they wish. The group determines the division and assignment of tasks . . .

The third classification may be called "anarchy." In anarchy there is complete freedom of the group or the individual regarding policies or task assignments, without leader participation.[10]

Advanced in this paper is the hypothesis that if anarchy exists, there is a great chance of the conflicting dynamics destroying the channel. If autocracy exists, there is less chance of this happening. However, the latter method creates a state of cooperation based on power and control. This controlled cooperation is really subdued conflict and makes for a more unstable equilibrium than does voluntary democratic cooperation.

Controlled Cooperation

The usual pattern in the establishment of channel relationships is that there is a leader, an initiator who puts structure into this relationship and who holds it together. This leader controls, whether through command or cooperation, i.e., through an autocratic or a democratic system.

Too often it is automatically assumed that the manufacturer or producer will be the channel leader and that the middlemen will be the channel followers. This has not always been so, nor will it necessarily be so in the future. The growth of mass retailers is increasingly challenging the manufacturer for channel leadership, as the manufacturer challenged the wholesaler in the early part of this century.

The following historical discussion will concentrate on the three-ring struggle between manufacturer, wholesaler, and retailer rather than on the changing patterns of distribution within a channel sector, i.e., between service wholesaler and agent middleman or discount and department store. This will lay the necessary background for a discussion of the present-day manufacturer-dominated *versus* retailer-dominated struggle.

Early History

The simple distribution system of Colonial days gave way to a more complex

[10] Lewis B. Sappington and C. G. Browne, "The Skills of Creative Leadership," in *Managerial Marketing*, rev. ed., William Lazar and Eugene J. Kelley, Editors. (Homewood, Ill.: Richard D. Irwin, Inc., 1962), p. 350.

one. Among the forces of change were the growth of population, the long distances involved, the increasing complexity of new products, the increase of wealth, and the increase of consumption.

The United States was ready for specialists to provide a growing and widely dispersed populace with the many new goods and services required. The more primitive methods of public markets and barter could not efficiently handle the situation. This type of system required short distances, few products, and a small population, to operate properly.

19th Century History

In the same period that this older system was dissolving, the retailer was still a very small merchant who, especially in the West, lived in relative isolation from his supply sources. Aside from being small, he further diminished his power position by spreading himself thin over many merchandise lines. The retailer certainly was no specialist but was as general as a general store can be. His opposite channel member, the manufacturer, was also a small businessman, too concerned with production and financial problems to fuss with marketing.

Obviously, both these channel members were in no position to assume leadership. However, somebody had to perform all the various marketing functions between production and retailing if the economy was to function. The wholesaler filled this vacuum and became the channel leader of the 19th century.

The wholesaler became the selling force of the manufacturer and the latter's link to the widely scattered retailers over the nation. He became the retailer's life line to these distant domestic and even more important foreign sources of supply.

These wholesalers carried any type of product from any manufacturer and sold any type of product to the general retailers. They can be described as general merchandise wholesalers. They were concentrated at those transportation points in the country which gave them access to both the interior and its retailers, and the exterior and its foreign suppliers.

Early 20th Century

The end of the century saw the wholesaler's power on the decline. The manufacturer had grown larger and more financially secure with the shift from a foreign-oriented economy to a domestic-oriented one. He could now finance his marketing in a manner impossible to him in early times. His thoughts shifted to some extent from production problems to marketing problems.

Prodding the manufacturer on was the increased rivalry of his other domestic competitors. The increased investment in capital and inventory made it necessary that he maintain volume. He tended to locate himself in the larger market areas, and thus, did not have great distances to travel to see his retail customers. In addition, he started to produce various products; and because of his new multiproduct production, he could reach—even more efficiently—these already more accessible markets.

The advent of the automobile and highways almost clinched the manufacturer's bid for power. For now he could reach a much vaster market (and they could reach him) and reap the benefits of economics of scale.

The branding of his products projected him to the channel leadership. No longer did he have as great a need for a specialist in reaching widely dispersed customers, nor did he need them to the same extent for their contacts. The market knew where the product came from. The age of wholesaler dominance declined. That of manufacturer dominance emerged.

Is it still here? What is its future? How strong is the challenge by retailers? Is one "better" than the other? These are the questions of the next section.

Disgareement Among Scholars

No topic seems to generate so much heat and bias in marketing as the question of who should be the channel leader, and more strangely, who is the channel leader. Depending on where the author sits, he can give numerous reasons why his particular choice should take the channel initiative.

Authors of sales management and general marketing books say the manufacturer is and should be the chief institution in the channel. Retailing authors feel the same way about retailers, and wholesaling authors (as few as there are), though not blinded to the fact that wholesaling is not "captain," still imply that they should be, and talk about the coming resurrection of wholesalers. Yet a final and compromising view is put forth by those who believe that a balance of power, rather than a general and prolonged dominance of any channel member, is best.

> The truth is that an immediate reaction would set in against any temporary dominance by a channel member. In that sense, there is a constant tendency toward the equilibrium of market forces. The present view is that public interest is served by a balance of power rather than by a general and prolonged predominance of any one level in marketing channels.[11]

John Kenneth Galbraith's concept of countervailing power also holds to this last view.

For the retailer:

> In the opinion of the writer, "retailer-dominated marketing" has yielded, and will continue to yield in the future greater net benefits to consumers than "manufacturer-dominated marketing," as the central-buying mass distributor continues to play a role of ever-increasing importance in the marketing of goods in our economy . . .

> . . . In the years to come, as more and more large-scale multiple-unit retailers follow the central buying patterns set by Sears and Penneys, as leaders in their respective fields (hard lines and soft goods), ever-greater benefits should flow to consumers in the way of more goods better adjusted to their demands, at lower prices.[12]

[11] Wroe Alderson, "Factors Governing The Development of Marketing Channels," in *Marketing Channels For Manufactured Products,* Richard M. Clewett, Editor. (Homewood, Richard D. Irwin, Inc., 1954), p. 30.

[12] Arnold Corbin, *Central Buying in Relation To The Merchandising of Multiple Retail Units* (New York, Unpublished Doctoral Dissertation at New York University, 1954), pp. 708-709.

... In a long run buyer's market, such as we probably face in this country, the retailers have the inherent advantage of economy in distribution and will, therefore, become increasingly important.[13]

The retailer cannot be the selling agent of the manufacturer because he holds a higher commission; he is the purchasing agent for the public.[14]

For the wholesaler:

The wholesaling sector is, first of all, the most significant part of the entire marketing organization.[15]

... The orthodox wholesaler and affiliated types have had a resurgence to previous 1929 levels of sales importance.[16]

... Wholesalers have since made a comeback.[17] This revival of wholesaling has resulted from infusion of new management blood and the adoption of new techniques.[18]

For the manufacturer:

... the final decision in channel selection rests with the seller, manufacturer and will continue to rest with him as long as he has the legal right to choose to sell to some potential customers and refuse to sell to others.[19]

These channel decisions are primarily problems for the manufacturer. They rarely arise for general wholesalers ...[20]

Of all the historical tendencies in the field of marketing, no other is so distinctly apparent as the tendency for the manufacturer to assume greater control over the distribution of his product ...[21]

... Marketing policies at other levels can be viewed as extensions of policies established by marketing managers in manufacturing firms; and, furthermore, ... the nature and function can adequately be surveyed by looking at the relationship to manufacturers.[22]

Pro-Manufacture

The argument for manufacturer leadership is production oriented. It claims

[13] David Craig and Werner Gabler, "The Competitive Struggle for Market Control," in *Readings in Marketing,* Howard J. Westing, Editor. (New York, Prentice-Hall, 1953), p. 46.

[14] Lew Hahn, *Stores, Merchants and Customers* (New York, Fairchild Publications, 1952), p. 12.

[15] David A. Revzan, *Wholesaling in Marketing Organization* (New York: John Wiley & Sons, Inc., 1961), p. 606.

[16] *Ibid.,* p. 202.

[17] E. Jerome McCarthy, *Basic Marketing* (Homewood, Illinois: Richard D. Irwin, Inc., 1960). p. 419.

[18] *Ibid.,* p. 420.

[19] Eli P. Cox, *Federal Quantity Discount Limitations and Its Possible Effects on Distribution Channel Dynamics* (Unpublished Doctoral Dissertation, University of Texas, 1956), p. 12.

[20] Milton Brown, Wilbur B. England, John B. Matthews Jr., *Problems in Marketing,* 3rd ed. (New York: McGraw-Hill Book Co., Inc., 1961), p. 239.

[21] Maynard D. Phelps and Howard J. Westing, *Marketing Management,* Revised Edition. (Homewood, Ill.: Richard D. Irwin, Inc., 1960), p. 11.

[22] Kenneth Davis, *Marketing Management* (New York: The Ronald Press Co., 1961), p. 131.

that they must assure themselves of increasing volume. This is needed to derive the benefits of production scale economies, to spread their overhead over many units, to meet increasingly stiff competition, and to justify the investment risk they, not the retailers, are taking. Since the retailers will not do this job for them properly, the manufacturer must control the channel.

Another major argumentative point for manufacturer dominance is that neither the public nor retailers can create new products even under a market-oriented system. The most the public can do is to select and choose among those that manufacturers have developed. They cannot select products that they cannot conceive. This argument would say that it is of no use to ask consumers and retailers what they want because they cannot articulate abstract needs into tangible goods; indeed, the need can be created by the goods rather than vice-versa.

This argument may hold well when applied to consumers, but a study of the specification-buying programs of the mass retailers will show that the latter can indeed create new products, and need not be relegated to simply selecting among alternatives.

Pro-Retailer

This writer sees the mass retailer as the natural leader of the channel for consumer goods under the marketing concept. The retailer stands closest to the consumer; he feels the pulse of consumer wants and needs day in and day out. The retailer can easily undertake consumer research right on his own premises and can best interpret what is wanted, how much is wanted, and when it is wanted.

An equilibrium in the channel conflict may come about when small retailers join forces with big manufacturers in a manufacturer leadership channel to compete with a small manufacturer-big retailer leadership channel.

Pro-Wholesaler

It would seem that the wholesaler has a choice in this domination problem as well. Unlike the manufacturer and retailer though, his method is not mainly through a power struggle. This problem is almost settled for him once he chooses the type of wholesaling business he wishes to enter. A manufacturers' agent and purchasing agent are manufacturer-dominated, a sales agent dominates the manufacturer. A resident buyer and voluntary group wholesaler are retail-dominated.

Methods of Manufacturer Domination

How does a channel leader dominate his fellow members? What are his tools in this channel power struggle? A manufacturer has many domination weapons at his disposal. His arsenal can be divided into promotional, legal, negative, suggestive, and, ironically, voluntary cooperative compartments.

Promotional. Probably the major method that the manufacturer has used is the building of a consumer franchise through advertising, sales promotion, and packaging of his branded products. When he has developed some degree of consumer loyalty, the other channel members must bow to his leadership. The more successful this identification through the promotion process, the more assured is the manufacturer of his leadership.

Legal. The legal weapon has also been a poignant force for the manufacturer. It can take many forms, such as, where permissible, resale price maintenance. Other contractual methods are franchises, where the channel members may become mere shells of legal entities. Through this weapon the automobile manufacturers have achieved an almost absolute dominance over their dealers.

Even more absolute is resort to legal ownership of channel members, called forward vertical integration. Vertical integration is the ultimate in manufacturer dominance of the channel. Another legal weapon is the use of consignment sales. Under this method the channel members must by law sell the goods as designated by the owner (manufacturer). Consignment selling is in a sense vertical integration; it is keeping legal ownership of the goods until they reach the consumer, rather than keeping legal ownership of the institutions which are involved in the process.

Negative Methods. Among the "negative" methods of dominance are refusal to sell to possibly uncooperative retailers or refusal to concentrate a large percentage of one's volume with any one customer.

A spreading of sales makes for a concentrating of manufacturer power, while a concentrating of sales may make for a thinning of manufacturer power. Of course, if a manufacturer is one of the few resources available and if there are many available retailers, then a concentrating of sales will also make for a concentrating of power.

The avoidance and refusal tactics, of course, eliminate the possibility of opposing dominating institutions.

Suggestives. A rather weak group of dominating weapons are the "suggestives." Thus, a manufacturer can issue price sheets and discounts, preticket and premark resale prices on goods, recommend, suggest, and advertise resale prices.

These methods are not powerful unless supplemented by promotional, legal, and/or negative weapons. It is common for these methods to boomerang. Thus a manufacturer pretickets or advertises resale prices, and a retailer cuts this price, pointing with pride to the manufacturer's suggested retail price.

Voluntary Cooperative Devices. There is one more group of dominating weapons, and these are really all the voluntary cooperating weapons to be mentioned later. The promise to provide these, or to withdraw them, can have a "whip and carrot" effect on the channel members.

Retailers' Dominating Weapons

Retailers also have numerous domination weapons at their disposal. As with manufacturers, their strongest weapon is the building of a consumer franchise through advertising, sales promotion, and branding. The growth of private brands is the growth of retail dominance.

Attempts at concentrating a retailer's purchasing power are a further group of weapons and are analogous to a manufacturer's attempts to disperse his volume.

The more a retailer can concentrate his purchasing, the more dominating he can become; the more he spreads his purchasing, the more dominated he becomes. Again, if the resource is one of only a few, this generalization reverses itself.

Such legal contracts as specification buying, vertical integration (or the threat), and entry into manufacturing can also be effective. Even semiproduction, such as the packaging of goods received in bulk by the supermarket can be a weapon of dominance.

Retailers can dilute the dominance of manufacturers by patronizing those with excess capacity and those who are "hungry" for the extra volume. There is also the subtlety, which retailers may recognize, that a strong manufacturer may concede to their wishes just to avoid an open conflict with a customer.

Voluntary Cooperation

But despite some of the conflict dynamics and forced cooperation, channel members usually have more harmonious and common interests than conflicting ones. A team effort to market a producer's product will probably help all involved. All members have a common interest in selling the product; only in the division of total channel profits are they in conflict. They have a singular goal to reach, and here they are allies. If any one of them fails in the team effort, this weak link in the chain can destroy them all. As such, all members are concerned with one another's welfare (unless a member can be easily replaced).

Organizational Extension Concept

This emphasis on the cooperating, rather than the conflicting objectives of channel members, has led to the concept of the channel as simply an extension of one's own internal organization. Conflict in such a system is to be expected even as it is to be expected within an organization. However, it is the common or "macro-objective" that is the center of concentration. Members are to sacrifice their selfish "micro-objectives" to this cause. By increasing the profit pie they will all be better off than squabbling over pieces of a smaller one. The goal is to minimize conflict and maximize cooperation. This view has been expounded in various articles by Peter Drucker, Ralph Alexander, and Valentine Ridgeway.

Together, the manufacturer with his suppliers and/or dealers comprise a system in which the manufacturer may be designated the primary organization and the dealers and suppliers designated as secondary organizations. This system is in competition with similar systems in the economy; and in order for the system to operate effectively as an integrated whole, there must be some administration of the system as a whole, not merely administration of the separate organizations within that system.[23]

Peter Drucker[24] has pleaded against the conceptual blindness that the idea of

---

[23] Valentine F. Ridgeway, "Administration of Manufacturer-Dealer Systems," in *Managerial Marketing,* rev. ed., William Lazer and Eugene J. Kelley, Editors. (Homewood, Ill.: Richard D. Irwin, Inc., 1962), p. 480.

[24] Peter Drucker, "The Economy's Dark Continent," *Fortune,* April 1962, pp. 103 ff.

the legal entity generates. A legal entity is not a marketing entity. Since often half of the cost to the consumer is added on after the product leaves the producer, the latter should think of his channel members as part of his firm. General Motors is an example of an organization which does this.

Both businessmen and students of marketing often define too narrowly the problem of marketing channels. Many of them tend to define the term channels of distribution as a complex of relationships between the firm on the one hand, and marketing establishments exterior to the firm by which the products of the firm are moved to market, on the other ... A much broader more constructive concept embraces the relationships with external agents or units as part of the marketing organization of the company. From this viewpoint, the complex of external relationships may be regarded as merely an extension of the marketing organization of the firm. When we look at the problem in this way, we are much less likely to lose sight of the interdependence of the two structures and more likely to be constantly aware that they are closely related parts of the marketing machine. The fact that the internal organization structure is linked together by a system of employment contracts, while the external one is set up and maintained by a series of transactions, contracts of purchase and sale, tends to obscure their common purpose and close relationship.[25]

Cooperation Methods

But how does a supplier project its organization into the channel? How does it make organization and channel into one? It accomplishes this by doing many things for its resellers that it does for its own organization. It sells, advertises, trains, plans, and promotes for these firms. A brief elaboration of these methods follows.

Missionary salesmen aid the sales of channel members, as well as bolster the whole system's level of activity and selling effort. Training of resellers' salesmen and executives is an effective weapon of cooperation. The channels operate more efficently when all are educated in the promotional techniques and uses of the products involved.

Involvement in the planning functions of its channel members could be another poignant weapon of the supplier. Helping resellers to set quotas for their customers, studying the market potential for them, forecasting a member's sales volume, inventory planning and protection, etc., are all aspects of this latter method.

Aid in promotion through the provision of advertising materials (mats, displays, commercials, literature, direct-mail pieces), ideas, funds (cooperative advertising), sales contests, store layout designs, push money (PM's or spiffs), is another form of cooperation.

The big supplier can act as management consultant to the members, dispensing advice in all areas of their business, including accounting, personnel, planning, control, finance, buying, paper systems or office procedure, and site

[25] Ralph S. Alexander, James S. Cross, Ross M. Cunningham, *Industrial Marketing*, rev. ed. (Homewood, Ill.: Richard D. Irwin, Inc., 1961), p. 266.

selection. Aid in financing may include extended credit terms, consignment selling, and loans.

By no means do these methods of coordination take a one-way route. All members of the channel, including supplier and reseller, see their own organizations meshing with the others, and so provide coordinating weapons in accordance with their ability. Thus, the manufacturer would undertake a marketing research project for his channel, and also expect his resellers to keep records and vital information for the manufacturer's use. A supplier may also expect his channel members to service the product after the sale.

A useful device for fostering cooperation is a channel advisory council composed of the supplier and his resellers.

Finally, a manufacturer or reseller can avoid associations with potentially uncooperative channel members. Thus, a price-conservative manufacturer may avoid linking to a price-cutting retailer.

E. B. Weiss has developed an impressive, though admittedly incomplete list of cooperation methods (Table 2). Paradoxically, many of these instruments of cooperation are also weapons of control (forced cooperation) to be used by both middlemen and manufacturers. However, this is not so strange if one keeps in mind that control is subdued conflict and a form of cooperation—even though perhaps involuntary cooperation.

Extension Concept Is the Marketing Concept

The philosophy of cooperation is described in the following quote:

The essence of the marketing concept is of course customer orientation at all levels of distribution. It is particularly important that customer orientation motivate all relations between a manufacturer and his customer—both immediate and ultimate. It must permeate his entire channels-of-distribution policy.[26]

Table 2
Methods of Cooperation as Listed[27]

1. Cooperative advertising allowances
2. Payments for interior displays including shelf-extenders, dump displays, "A" locations, aisle, displays etc.
3. P.M.'s for salespeople
4. Contests for buyers, salespeople, etc.
5. Allowances for a variety of warehousing functions
6. Payments for window display space, plus installation costs
7. Detail men who check inventory, put up stock, set up complete promotions, etc.
8. Demonstartors
9. On certain canned food, a "swell" allowance
10. Label allowance
11. Coupon handling allowance
12. Free goods
13. Guaranteed sales
14. In-store and window display material
15. Local research work
16. Mail-in premium offers to consumer
17. Preticketing
18. Automatic reorder systems
19. Delivery costs to individual stores of large retailers

[26] Hector Lazo and Arnold Corbin, *Management in Marketing* (New York: McGraw-Hill Book Company, Inc., 1961), p. 379.

[27] Edward B. Weiss, "How Much of a Retailer is the Manufacturer," in *Advertising Age*, July 21, 1958, p. 68.

Table 2 (Continued)

20. Studies of innumerable types, such as studies of merchandise management accounting
21. Payments for mailings to store lists
22. Liberal return privileges
23. Contributions to favorite charities of store personnel
24. Contributions to special store anniversaries
25. Prizes, etc., to store buyers when visiting showrooms—plus entertainment, of course
26. Training retail salespeople
27. Payments for store fixtures
28. Payments for new store costs, for more improvements, including painting
29. An infinite variety of promotion allowances
30. Special payments for exclusive franchises
31. Payments of part of salary of retail salespeople
32. Deals of innumerable types
33. Time spent in actual selling floor by manufacturer, salesmen
34. Inventory price adjustments
35. Store name mention in manufacturer's advertising

This quote synthesizes the extension-of-the-organization system concept of channels with the marketing concept. Indeed, it shows that the former is, in essence, "the" marketing concept applied to the channel area in marketing. To continue:

The characteristics of the highly competitive markets of today naturally put a distinct premium on harmonious manufacturer-distributor relationships. Their very mutuality of interest demands that the manufacturer base his distribution program not only on what he would like from distributors, but perhaps more importantly, on what they would like from him. In order to get the cooperation of the best distributors, and thus maximum exposure for his line among the various market segments, he must adjust his policies to serve their best interest and, thereby, his own. In other words, he must put the principles of the marketing concept to work for him. By so doing, he will inspire in his customers a feeling of mutual interest and trust and will help convince them that they are essential members of his marketing team.[28]

Summary

Figure I summarizes this whole paper. Each person within each department will cooperate, control, and conflict with each other (notice arrows). Together they form a department (notice department box contains person boxes) which will be best off when cooperating (or cooperation through control) forces weigh heavier than conflicting forces. Now each department cooperates, controls, and conflicts with each other. Departments together also form a higher level organization—the firm (manufacturer, wholesaler, and retailer). Again, the firm will be better off if department cooperation is maximized and conflict minimized. Finally, firms standing vertically to each other cooperate, control, and conflict. Together they form a distribution channel that will be best off under conditions of optimum cooperation leading to consumer and profit satisfaction.

[28] Lazo and Corbin, *loc. cit.*

Conclusions and Hypotheses

1. Channel relationships are set against a background of cooperation and conflict; horizontal, intertype, and vertical.

2. An autocratic relationship exists when one channel member controls conflict and forces the others to cooperate. A democratic relationship exists when all members agree to cooperate without a power play. An anarchistic relationship exists when there is open conflict, with no member able to impose his will on the others. This last form could destroy or seriously reduce the effectiveness of the channel.

3. The process of the exchange act where one member is a seller and the other is a buyer is the basic source of channel conflict. Economic theory can aid in comprehending this phenomenon. There are, however, many other areas of conflict, such as differences in business philosophy or primary objectives.

4. Reasons for cooperation, however, usually outweigh reasons for conflict. This has led to the concept of the channel as an extension of a firm's organization.

5. This concept drops the facade of "legal entity" and treats channel members as one great organization with the leader providing each with various forms of assistance. These are called cooperating weapons.

6. It is argued that this concept is actually the marketing concept adapted to a channel situation.

7. In an autocratic or democratic channel relationship, there must be a leader. This leadership has shifted and is shifting between the various channel levels.

8. The wholesaler was the leader in the last century, the manufacturer now, and it appears that the mass retailer is next in line.

9. There is much disagreement on the above point, however, especially on who should be the leader. Various authors have differing arguments to advance for their choice.

10. In the opinion of this writer, the mass retailer appears to be best adapted for leadership under the marketing concept.

11. As there are weapons of cooperation, so are there weapons of domination. Indeed the former paradoxically are one group of the latter. The other groups are promotional, legal, negative, and suggestive methods. Both manufacturers and retailers have at their disposal these dominating weapons.

12. *For maximization of channel profits and consumer satisfaction, the channel must act as a unit.*

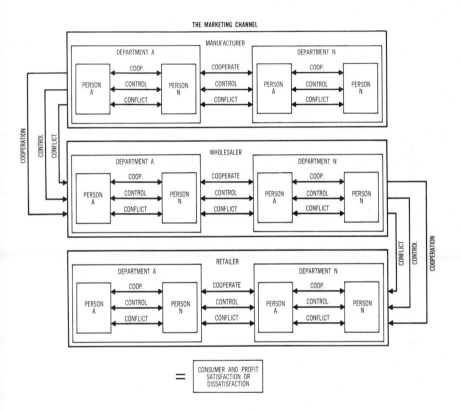

Figure 1   Organizational extension concept

What guides are available to aid the retailer in developing his marketing strategy? The author shows that the traditional concepts of shopping, convenience, and specialty goods may be updated and integrated with the idea of patronage motives and how they provide the retailer with a new means of evaluating his strategy.

Retail Strategy and the Classification of Consumer Goods

Louis P. Bucklin

When Melvin T. Copeland published his famous discussion of the classification of consumer goods, shopping, convenience, and specialty goods, his intent was clearly to create a guide for the development of marketing strategies by manufacturers.[1] Although his discussion involved retailers and retailing, his purpose was to show how consumer buying habits affected the type of channel of distribution and promotional strategy that a manufacturer should adopt. Despite the controversy which still surrounds his classification, his success in creating such a guide may be judged by the fact that through the years few marketing texts have failed to make use of his ideas.

The purpose of this article is to attempt to clarify some of the issues that exist with respect to the classification, and to extend the concept to include the retailer and the study of retail strategy.

Reprinted by permission of the author and the publisher from the *Journal of Marketing*, published by the American Marketing Association, Vol. 27, No. 1 (January, 1963), pp. 50-55.

[1] Melvin T. Copeland, "Relation of Consumers' Buying Habits of Marketing Methods," *Harvard Business Review*, Vol. 1 (April, 1923), pp. 282-289.

Controversy Over the Classification System

The starting point for the discussion lies with the definitions adopted by the American Marketing Association's Committee on Definitions for the classification system in 1948.[2] These are:

Convenience Goods: Those consumers' goods which the customer purchases frequently, immediately, and with the minimum of effort.
Shopping Goods: Those consumers' goods which the customer in the process of selection and purchase characteristically compares on such bases as suitability, quality, price and style.
Specialty Goods: Those consumers' goods on which a significant group of buyers are habitually willing to make a special purchasing effort.

This set of definitions was retained in virtually the same form by the Committee on Definitions in its latest publication.[3]

Opposing these accepted definitions stands a critique by Richard H. Holton.[4] Finding the Committee's definitions too imprecise to be able to measure consumer buying behavior, he suggested that the following definitions not only would represent the essence of Copeland's original idea, but be operationally more useful as well.

Convenience Goods: Those goods for which the consumer regards the probable gain from making price and quality comparisons as small compared to the cost of making such comparisons.
Shopping Goods: Those goods for which the consumer regards the probable gain from making price and quality comparisons as large relative to the cost of making such comparisons.
Specialty Goods: Those convenience or shopping goods which have such a limited market as to require the consumer to make a special effort to purchase them.

Holton's definitions have particular merit because they make explicit the underlying conditions that control the extent of a consumer's shopping activities. They show that a consumer's buying behavior will be determined not only by the strength of his desire to secure some good, but by his perception of the cost of shopping to obtain it. In other words, the consumer continues to shop *for all goods* so long as he feels that the additional satisfactions from further comparisons are at least equal to the cost of making the additional effort. The distinction between shopping and convenience goods lies principally in the degree of satisfaction to be secured from further comparisons.

[2] Definitions Committee, American Marketing Association, "Report of the Definitions Committee," *Journal of Marketing*, Vol. 13 (October, 1948), pp. 202-217, at p. 206, p. 215.

[3] Definitions Committee, American Marketing Association, *Marketing Definitions*, (Chicago: American Marketing Association, 1960), pp. 11, 21, 22.

[4] Richard H. Holton, "The Distinction Between Convenience Goods, Shopping Goods, and Specialty Goods," *Journal of Marketing*, Vol. 23 (July, 1958), pp. 53-56.

The Specialty Good Issue

While Holton's conceptualization makes an important contribution, he has sacrificed some of the richness of Copeland's original ideas. This is essentially David J. Luck's complaint in a criticism of Holton's proposal.[5] Luck objected to the abandonment of the *willingness* of consumers to make a special effort to buy as the rationale for the concept of specialty goods. He regarded this type of consumer behavior as based upon unique consumer attitudes toward certain goods and not the density of distribution of those goods. Holton, in a reply, rejected Luck's point; he remained convinced that the real meaning of specialty goods could be derived from his convenience goods, shopping goods continuum, and market conditions.[6]

The root of the matter appears to be that insufficient attention has been paid to the fact that the consumer, once embarked upon some buying expedition, may have only one of two possible objectives in mind. A discussion of this aspect of consumer behavior will make possible a closer synthesis of Holton's contribution with the more traditional point of view.

A Forgotten Idea

The basis of this discussion is afforded by certain statements, which the marketing profession has largely ignored over the years, in Copeland's original presentation of his ideas. These have regard to the extent of the consumer's awareness of the precise nature of the item he wishes to buy, *before* he starts his shopping trip. Copeland stated that the consumer, in both the case of convenience goods and specialty goods, has full knowledge of the particular good, or its acceptable substitutes, that he will buy before he commences his buying trip. The consumer, however, lacks this knowledge in the case of a shopping good.[7] This means that the buying trip must not only serve the objective of purchasing the good, but must enable the consumer to discover which item he wants to buy.

The behavior of the consumer during any shopping expedition may, as a result, be regarded as heavily dependent upon the state of his decision as to what he wants to buy. If the consumer knows precisely what he wants, he needs only to undertake communication activities sufficient to take title to the desired product. He may also undertake ancillary physical activities involving the handling of the product and delivery. If the consumer is uncertain as to what he wants to buy, then an additonal activity will have to be performed. This involves the work of making comparisons between possible alternative purchases, or simply search.

There would be little point, with respect to the problem of classifying the consumer goods, in distinguishing between the activity of search and that of

[5] David J. Luck, "On the Nature of Specialty Goods," *Journal of Marketing,* Vol. 24 (July, 1959), pp. 61-64.

[6] Richard H. Holton, "What is Really Meant by 'Specialty' Goods?" *Journal of Marketing,* Vol. 24 (July, 1959), pp. 64-67.

[7] Melvin T. Copeland, same reference as footnote 1, pp. 283-284.

making a commitment to buy, if a consumer always performed both before purchasing a good. The crucial point is that he does not. While most of the items that a consumer buys have probably been subjected to comparison at some point in his life, he does not make a search before each purchase. Instead, a past solution to the need is frequently remembered and, if satisfactory, is implemented.[8] Use of these past decisions for many products quickly moves the consumer past any perceived necessity of undertaking new comparisons and leaves only the task of exchange to be discharged.

Redefinition of the System

Use of this concept of problem solving permits one to classify consumer buying efforts into two broad categories which may be called shopping and nonshopping goods.

Shopping Goods

Shopping goods are those for which the consumer *regularly* formulates a new solution to his need each time it is aroused. They are goods whose suitability is determined through search before the consumer commits himself to each purchase.

The motivation behind this behavior stems from circumstances which tend to perpetuate a lack of complete consumer knowledge about the nature of the product that he would like to buy.[9] Frequent changes in price, style, or product technology cause consumer information to become obsolete. The greater the time lapse between purchases, the more obsolete will his information be. The consumer's needs are also subject to change, or he may seek variety in his purchases as an actual goal. These forces will tend to make past information inappropriate. New search, due to forces internal and external to the consumer, is continuously required for products with purchase determinants which the consumer regards as both important and subject to change.[10]

The number of comparisons that the consumer will make in purchasing a shopping good may be determined by use of Holton's hypothesis on effort. The consumer, in other words, will undertake search for a product until the perceived value to be secured through additional comparisons is less than the estimated cost of making those comparisons. Thus, shopping effort will vary according to the intensity of the desire of the consumer to find the right product, the type of product and the availability of retail facilities. Whether the consumer searches diligently, superficially, or even buys at the first opportunity, however, does not alter the shopping nature of the product.

[8] George Katona, *Psychological Analysis of Economic Behavior* (New York: McGraw-Hill Book Co., Inc., 1951), p. 47.

[9] Same reference, pp. 67-68.

[10] George Katona and Eva Mueller, "A Study of Purchase Decisions in Consumer Behavior," Lincoln Clark, editor, *Consumer Behavior* (New York: University Press, 1954), pp. 30-87.

Nonshopping Goods

Turning now to nonshopping goods, one may define these as products for which the consumer is both willing and able to use stored solutions to the problem of finding a product to answer a need. From the remarks on shopping goods it may be generalized that nonshopping goods have purchase determinants which do not change, or which are perceived as changing inconsequentially, between purchases.[11] The consumer, for example, may assume that price for some product never changes or that price is unimportant. It may be unimportant because either the price is low, or the consumer is very wealthy.

Nonshopping goods may be divided into convenience and specialty goods by means of the concept of a preference map. Bayton introduces this concept as the means to show how the consumer stores information about products.[12] It is a rough ranking of the relative desirability of the different kinds of products that the consumer sees as possible satisfiers for his needs. For present purposes, two basic types of preference maps may be envisaged. One type ranks all known product alternatives equally in terms of desirability. The other ranks one particular product as so superior to all others that the consumer, in effect, believes this product is the only answer to his need.

Distinguishing the Specialty Good

This distinction in preference maps creates the basis for discriminating between a convenience good and a specialty good. Clearly, where the consumer is indifferent to the precise item among a number of substitutes which he could buy, he will purchase the most accessible one and look no further. This is a convenience good. On the other hand, where the consumer recognizes only one brand of a product as capable of satisfying his needs, he will be willing to bypass more readily accessible substitutes in order to secure the wanted item. This is a specialty good.

However, most nonshopping goods will probably fall in between these two polar extremes. Preference maps will exist where the difference between the relative desirability of substitutes may range from the slim to the well marked. In order to distinguish between convenience goods and specialty goods in these cases, Holton's hypothesis regarding consumer effort may be employed again. A convenience good, in these terms, becomes one for which the consumer has such little preference among his perceived choices that he buys the item which is most readily available. A specialty good is one for which consumer preference is so strong that he bypasses, or would be willing to bypass, the purchase of more accessible substitutes in order to secure his most wanted item.

It should be noted that this decision on the part of the consumer as to how much effort he should expend takes place under somewhat different conditons than the one for shopping goods. In the nonshopping good instance the consumer has a reasonably good estimate of the additional value to be achieved by purchasing his preferred item. The estimate of the additional cost required to

[11] Katona, same reference as footnote 8, p. 68

[12] James A. Bayton, "Motivation, Cognition, Learning–Basic Factors in Consumer Behavior," *Journal of Marketing*, Vol. 22 (January, 1958), pp. 282-289, at p. 287.

make this purchase may also be made fairly accurately. Consequently, the consumer will be in a much better position to justify the expenditure of additional effort here than in the case of shopping goods where much uncertainty must exist with regard to both of these factors.

The New Classification

The classification of consumer goods that results from the analysis is as follows:

Convenience Goods: Those goods for which the consumer, before his need arises, possesses a preference map that indicates a willingness to purchase any of a number of known substitutes rather than to make the additional effort required to buy a particular item.

Shopping Goods: Those goods for which the consumer has not developed a complete preference map before the need arises, requiring him to undertake search to construct such a map before purchase.

Specialty Goods: Those goods for which the consumer, before his need arises, possesses a preference map that indicates a willingness to expend the additional effort required to purchase the most preferred item rather than to buy a more readily accessible substitute.

Extension to Retailing

The classification of the goods concept developed above may now be extended to retailing. As the concept now stands, it is derived from consumer attitudes or motives toward a *product*. These attitudes, or product motives, are based upon the consumer's interpretation of a product's styling, special features, quality, and social status of its brand name, if any. Occasionally the price may also be closely associated with he product by the consumer.

Classification of Patronage Motives

The extension of the concept to retailing may be made through the notion of patronage motives, a term long used in marketing. Patronage motives are derived from consumer attitudes concerning the retail establishment. They are related to factors which the consumer is likely to regard as controlled by the retailer. These will include assortment, credit, service, guarantee, shopping ease and enjoyment and usually price. Patronage motives, however, have never been systematically categorized. It is proposed that the procedure developed above to discriminate among product motives be used to classify consumer buying motives with respect to retail stores as well.

This will provide the basis for the consideration of retail marketing strategy and will aid in clearing up certain ambiguities that would otherwise exist if consumer buying motives were solely classified by product factors. These ambiguities appear, for example, when the consumer has a strong affinity for some particular brand of a product, but little interest in where he buys it. The manufacturer of the product, as a result, would be correct in defining the product as a specialty item if the consumer's preferences were so strong as to cause him to eschew more readily available substitutes. The retailer may regard it as a convenience good, however, since the consumer will make no special effort to purchase the good from any particular store. This problem is clearly avoided by separately classifying product and patronage motives.

The categorization of patronage motives by the above procedure results in the following three definitions. These are:

Convenience Stores: Those stores for which the consumer, before his need for some product arises, possesses a preference map that indicates a willingness to buy from the most accessible store.

Shopping Stores: Those stores for which the consumer has not developed a complete preference map relative to the product he wishes to buy, requiring him to undertake a search to construct such a map before purchase.

Specialty Stores: Those stores for which the consumer, before his need for some product arises, possesses a preference map that indicates a willingness to buy the item from a particular establishment even though it may not be the most accessible.

The Product-Patronage Matrix

Although this basis will now afford the retailer a means to consider alternative strategies, a finer classification system may be obtained by relating consumer product motives to consumer patronage motives. By cross-classifying each product motive with each patronage motive, one creates a three by three matrix, representing nine possible types of consumer buying behavior. Each of the nine cells in the matrix may be described as follows:

1. *Convenience Store–Convenience Good*: The consumer, represented by this category, prefers to buy the most readily available brand of product at the most accessible store.
2. *Convenience Store–Shopping Good*: The consumer selects his purchase from among the assortment carried by the most accessible store.
3. *Convenience Store–Specialty Good*: The consumer purchases his favored brand from the most accessible store which has the item in stock.
4. *Shopping Store–Convenience Good*: The consumer is indifferent to the brand of product he buys, but shops among different stores in order to secure better retail service and/or lower retail price.
5. *Shopping Store–Shopping Good*: The consumer makes comparisons among both retail controlled factors and factors associated with the product (brand).
6. *Shopping Store–Specialty Good*: The consumer has a strong preference with respect to the brand of the product, but shops among a number of stores in order to secure the best retail service and/or price for this brand.
7. *Specialty Store–Convenience Good*: The consumer prefers to trade at a specific store, but is indifferent to the brand of product purchased.
8. *Specialty Store–Shopping Good*: The consumer prefers to trade at a certain store, but is uncertain as to which product he wishes to buy and examines the store's assortment for the best purchase.
9. *Specialty Store–Specialty Good*: The consumer has both a preference for a particular store and a specific brand.

Conceivably, each of these nine types of behavior might characterize the buying patterns of some consumers for a given product. It seems more likely, however, that the behavior of consumers toward a product could be represented by only three or four of the categories. The remaining cells would be empty, indicating that no consumers bought the product by these methods. Different cells, of course, would be empty for different products.

The Formation of Retail Strategy

The extended classification system developed above clearly provides additional information important to the manufacturer in the planning of his marketing strategy. Of principal interest here, however, is the means by which the retailer might use the classification system in planning his marketing strategy.

Three Basic Steps

The procedure involves three steps. The first is the classification of the retailer's potential customers for some product by market segment, using the nine categories in the consumer buying habit matrix to define the principal segments. The second requires the retailer to determine the nature of the marketing strategies necessary to appeal to each market segment. The final step is the retailer's selection of the market segment, and the strategy associated with it, to which he will sell. A simplified, hypothetical example may help to clarify this process.

A former buyer of dresses for a department store decided to open her own dress shop. She rented a small store in the downtown area of a city of 50,000, ten miles distant from a metropolitan center of several hundred thousand population. In contemplating her marketing strategy, she was certain that the different incomes, educational backgrounds, and tastes of the potential customers in her city meant that various groups of these women were using sharply different buying methods for dresses. Her initial problem was to determine, by use of the consumer buying habit matrix, what proportion of her potential market bought dresses in what manner.

Table 1
Proportion of Potential Dress
Market in Each Matrix Cell

Buying Habit	% of Market
Convenience store—Convenience good	0
Convenience store—Shopping good	3
Convenience store—Specialty good	20
Shopping store—Convenience good	0
Shopping store—Shopping good	35
Shopping store—Specialty good	2
Specialty store—Convenience good	0
Specialty store—Shopping good	25
Specialty store—Specialty good	15
	100

By drawing on her own experience, discussions with other retailers in the area, census and other market data, the former buyer estimated that her potential market was divided, according to the matrix, in the following proportions.

This analysis revealed four market segments that she believed were worth further consideration. (In an actual situation, each of these four should be further divided into submarket segments according to other possible factors such as age, incomes, dress size required, location of residence, etc.) Her next task was to determine the type of marketing mix which would most effectively appeal to each of these segments. The information for these decisions was derived from the characteristics of consumer behavior associated with each of the defined segments. The following is a brief description of her assessment of how elements of the marketing mix ought to be weighted in order to formulate a strategy for each segment.

A Strategy for Each Segment

To appeal to the convenience store-specialty good segment she felt that the two most important elements in the mix should be a highly accessible location and a selection of widely-accepted brand merchandise. Of somewhat lesser importance, she found, were depth of assortment, personal selling, and price. Minimal emphasis should be given to store promotion and facilities.

She reasoned that the shopping store-shopping good requires a good central location, emphasis on price, and a broad assortment. She ranked store promotion, accepted brand names and personal selling as secondary. Store facilities would, once again, receive minor emphasis.

The specialty store-shopping good market would, she believed, have to be catered to with an exceptionally strong assortment, a high level of personal selling and more elaborate store facilities. Less emphasis would be needed upon prominent brand names, store promotions, and price. Location was of minor importance.

The specialty store-specialty good category, she thought, would require a marketing mix heavily emphasizing personal selling and highly elaborate store facilities and services. She also felt that prominent brand names would be required, but that these would probably have to include the top names in fashion, including labels from Paris. Depth of assortment would be secondary, while least emphasis would be placed upon store promotion, price, and location.

Evaluation of Alternatives

The final step in the analysis required the former dress buyer to assess her abilities to implement any one of these strategies, given the degree of competition existing in each segment. Her considerations were as follows. With regard to the specialty store-specialty good market, she was unprepared to make the investment in store facilities and services that she felt would be necessary. She also thought, since a considerable period of time would probably be required for her to build up the necessary reputation, that this strategy involved substantial risk. Lastly, she believed that her experience in buying high fashion was somewhat limited and that trips to European fashion centers would prove burdensome.

She also doubted her ability to cater to the specialty store-shopping good market, principally because she knew that her store would not be large enough to carry the necessary assortment depth. She felt that this same factor would limit her in attempting to sell to the shopping store-shopping good market as well. Despite the presence of the large market in this segment, she believed that she would not be able to create sufficient volume in her proposed quarters to enable her to compete effectively with the local department store and several large department stores in the neighboring city.

The former buyer believed her best opportunity was in selling to the convenience store-specialty good segment. While there were already two other stores in her city which were serving this segment, she believed that a number of important brands were still not represented. Her past contacts with resources led her to believe that she would stand an excellent chance of securing a number of these lines. By stocking these brands, she thought that she could capture a considerable number of local customers who currently were purchasing them in the large city. In this way, she believed, she would avoid the full force of local competition.

Decision

The conclusion of the former buyer to use her store to appeal to the convenience store-specialty good segment represents the culmination to the process of analysis suggested here. It shows how the use of the three-by-three matrix of consumer buying habits may aid the retailer in developing his marketing strategy. It is a device which can isolate the important market segments. It provides further help in enabling the retailer to associate the various types of consumer behavior with those elements of the marketing mix to which they are sensitive. Finally, the analysis forces the retailer to assess the probability of his success in attempting to use the necessary strategy in order to sell each possible market.

Marketing decision-makers need to view the problems and functions of physical distribution in terms of an organized system in order to improve the efficiency of one of marketing's most underdeveloped areas.

The Logistics of Distribution

John F. Magee

American business is awakening to a new, exciting opportunity to improve service and reduce costs—better management of the flow of goods from plant to user. Capitalizing on this opportunity means:

• Thinking of the physical distribution process as a *system* in which, just as in a good hi-fi system, all the components and functions must be properly balanced.

• Taking a fresh look at the responsibilities, capabilities, and organizational positions of executives in traffic, warehouse management, inventory control, and other functions which make up the overall system.

• Re-examining the company's physical plant and distribution procedures in the light of technical advances in such areas as transportation, data processing, and materials handling.

In this article I shall first examine the pressing need for improved management of companies' distribution systems. Then I shall outline some of the most promising ways by which progress in "industrial logistics" can be achieved, with special attention to the implications of technological advances for policy, the problems of getting started with a new look at a company's system, and the steps that should be taken in making a good distribution study.

Stubborn Pressures

The need for progress in distribution is a product of not one but several

Reprinted by permission of the publisher from *Harvard Business Review*, Vol. 38 (July-August, 1960), pp.89-101. ©1960, by the President and Fellows of Harvard College; all rights reserved.

trends—trends in costs, in product-line policy, and in the market place. More often than not, the challenge posed is to the system as a whole, not just to the particular part or function where trouble is most obvious.

Rising Costs

For years, businessmen and economists have looked with mixed feelings on the increase in distribution costs in our economy. Over the past half century, tremendous strides have been made in reducing the costs of production, but these feats have not been duplicated in other areas. If the over-all efficiency of companies is to continue to improve, management must turn its attention increasingly to holding distribution costs in line. Physical distribution costs in particular, estimated by some to represent the third largest component in the total cost of business operation, are a logical center for management attention.

The problems of cutting these costs pose certain new and interesting questions for business. Whereas in many production operations it has been possible in the past to substitute a machine for human labor and to cut the cost of one operation without seriously disturbing the rest of the production system, this is hardly the case in efforts to cut physical distribution costs. Indiscriminate cost reduction in any one of the individual cost elements, such as inventory maintenance, warehousing, transportation, or clerical activities, can have a disastrous effect on the efficiency of the system as a whole. To illustrate this point:

● Suppose we cut inventories. Certainly a reduction in inventories will save capital investment and the costs of supplying capital, and it may save some expenses in storage, taxes, and insurance. On the other hand, an indiscriminate reduction in inventory levels may seriously impair the reliability of delivery service to customers and the availability of products in the field. An inventory reduction which saves money but destroys competitive position is hardly a contribution to a more effective distribution system.

● We can cut transportation costs, perhaps, by changing to methods showing lower cost per ton-mile, or by shipping in larger quantities and taking advantage of volume carload or truckload rates. But if lower transportation costs are achieved at the expense of slower or less frequent movement of goods, we face the risk of: (a) cutting the flexibility and responsiveness of the distribution system to changes in customer requirements; (b) requiring greater field inventories to maintain service; (c) creating greater investment requirements and obsolescence risks.

Similarly, blanket refusal to allow cost increases in any one part can wipe out opportunities to make the system as a whole more efficient. For instance:

New methods of high-speed data communications and processing may in fact increase the clerical costs of operating the distribution system. On the other hand, they may cut down delays in feeding information back to govern production operations and to control lags in getting material moving into the distribution system in response to customer demand. Thus, they may actually cut *total* distribution system costs because of their impact on improved production and inventory control.

It takes a careful analysis of the total physical distribution system to know whether net costs will be increased or decreased by efforts to cut the cost of any one component.

Proliferating Product Lines

Physical distribution systems in recent years have been put under tremendous pressure induced by changes in product-line characteristics. Until recently, for example, products like typewriters, light bulbs, appliances, and plumbing fixtures were largely utilitarian, with differences in product characteristics rather closely related to function. A typewriter manufacturer did not have to worry about matching typewriter color to office decor or type style to company "image." Light bulbs used to be white and sometimes clear, and they varied by wattage. Now, however, typewriters come in pastels and two-tones. Light bulbs are sold not only to provide light but atmosphere, with a corresponding increase in the number of products that have to be shipped, stocked, and controlled. Appliances and plumbing fixtures are available to customers not only in the classical antiseptic white, but in a wide range of color and style combinations. In short, style and individuality have become strong competitive weapons.

In an almost unending list of products in the consumer field, variations in color, packaging, and other features have imposed heavy burdens on the distribution system. In the marketing of industrial goods, variations in grade, color, and size have had a similar impact. In paper manufacture, for example, the wide variety of package sizes required for consumer products has led carton manufacturers to demand correspondingly wide ranges of kraft board roll widths from paper manufacturers, and these demands have created difficult problems of scheduling, inventory control, and distribution.

The growth and change in product-line characteristics in both consumer and industrial products have meant that manufacturing plants have had more items to make, and the distribution system has had more items to handle and stock. More items mean lower volume per item and storage costs. Take, for example, just the impact on inventory requirements of substituting three items for one:

Suppose we had substituted items B,C, and D for an old item A. If sales among these items are broken down 60% to B, 30% to C, and 10% to D, with no over-all increase in sales compared to the volume on the old item A, then Exhibit 1 shows what is likely to happen to field inventory requirements—an increase of more than 60%. (This figure is based on characteristic relationships between inventory and sales in companies with which I am familiar. In general, the larger the sales the lower inventory can be relative to sales. Thus, product D with 10% of sales needs a much higher proportion of inventory than product B, with 60% of the sales.)

At a carrying cost of 20% a year, this increase represents a handsome expense for maintaining competitive position.

Let us be optimistic, however, and assume that items B, C, and D do more than yield the same total volume; let us assume that total volume increases by 50%. Even so, the inventory requirements would double, and inventory cost per

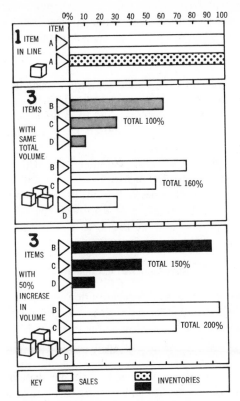

Exhibit 1   What happens to inventories when the product line is broadened?

unit sold would increase over 30%—a substantial source of pressure on the distribution system.

These figures illustrate the impact of small-volume items on the cost of operating the distribution system. Yet diversity of product sales is characteristic in American businesses, whether selling in consumer or industrial markets. Exhibit 2 shows the typical relationship between the number of items sold and the proportion of sales they account for. The figures are based on the records of a large number of firms in the consumer and industrial products fields. The exhibit reveals that while 10%–20% of total items sold characteristically yield 80% of the sales, half of the items in the line account for less than 4% of the sales. It is the bottom half of the product line that imposes a great deal of the difficulty, expense, and investment on the distribution system.

Alternative Courses

Increased cost, selling, and product-line pressures suggest that management should take a hard look at alternative distribution patterns, as a means of cutting logistics costs without a major sacrifice in service. Here are a few of the possibilities.

● The company can carry central stocks of low-selling items only. To get the right balance of transportation costs, handling costs, and service, it may be necessary to stock these items at one central point and ship them against individual customer orders as the latter arise, perhaps by expedited service or air freight.

● For many items in the line, a good compromise may be to carry some low- or middle-volume items in only a few large regional warehouses, as a compromise between the excessive storage costs incurred from broad-scale stocking and the transportation and service penalties incurred by attempting to meet demand from manufacturing points alone.

● Warehouse points can be consolidated. With improvements in transportation and in mechanical material- and data-handling methods, large opportunities exist in many businesses for cutting down on the number of field warehouse points. With increased volume through the individual warehouses, carrying a broader product line at the local points begins to make greater economic sense.

Sales-Generating Capacity

The first and most basic job of the distribution system is to get customers, to turn interest and orders into sales. As business has grown more competitive and the public has become harder to please, management has focused increasing attention on the *quality* of its logistical operations. What can be done to make products more readily available for purchase in local markets? What improvements can be made in backing up product merchandising and advertising programs with adequate deliveries and service? Obviously, questions like these are affected by cost considerations, but as marketing objectives they deserve individual attention.

In analyzing the capacity of a distribution system to produce sales, executives will do well to examine three key characteristics:

1. *Location*—It has been estimated, for example, that from 5 distribution points a company can reach 33% of the U.S. consumer market within a day; while from 25 warehouse locations, 80% can be reached in one day.

2. *Inventories*—Judging from my own and associates' experience, approximately 80% more inventory is needed in a typical business to fill 95% of the customers' orders out of stock than to fill only 80%.

3. *Responsiveness*—The ability of a system to transmit needs back to the supplying plant and get material needed into the field determines how quickly the business can shift with changes in customer preferences to meet demand with minimum investment and cost.

Revolution in Technology

The pressures on distribution methods have led to exciting new technological advances for getting goods to the user at lower cost to the company—with less labor and materials expended and less capital tied up in inventories and facilities. When these advances are introduced in proper balance, the distribution process

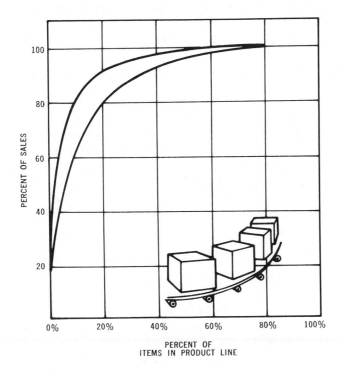

PERCENT OF
ITEMS IN PRODUCT LINE

Exhibit 2   What fraction of total sales is accounted for by what fraction of total items in the product line?

can better meet the needs of the consumer. Major technological changes are now taking place in transportation, information handling, and material handling. Let us examine each of then in turn.

Costs vs. Transport Time

Transportation thinking has been dominated too long by preoccupation with the direct traffic bill. Too much attention has been paid to transport cost per ton-mile and not enough to the contribution transportation makes to the effectiveness of the distribution system as a whole.

Railroad rate structures are to an outsider an eye-opening illustration of what can happen when a transportation system is put under the cost-per-ton-mile pressure for too long. Rail rate structures, despite frequent attempts to introduce some rationale, have degenerated into an unbelievable hodgepodge of unrealistic and uneconomic rate compromises as the roads have succumbed to the pressure of giving each shipper the lowest cost per ton-mile, often at the expense of service. While improvements in equipment, such as the introduction of the diesel locomotive, have lead to greater efficiency on the track, in some cases at least the longer trains and increased classification problems that have resulted have meant little or no net increase in over-all distribution efficiency. The gap between traffic and marketing thinking is painfully evident in many companies' distribution methods; little has been done to relate transportation methods and service to the objectives of the distribution system in support of marketing efforts.

Transportation costs are important indeed, but they are only part of the story. For example, think of the value of materials in transit:

• Data collected on sample shipments in various parts of the country indicate that material may spend one to two weeks in transit and that the capital value of assets tied up in the transportation system may, depending on the pressure for capital, add as much as 1% to the economic cost of the goods.

• Service, or reliability of the transport system, is also important. Goods must get to the user promptly and reliably, to permit him to operate systematically with low inventories.

• The direct and indirect costs of damages in transport are another large item in the traffic bill that at times get overlooked in the pressure for low cost per ton-mile.

. Clearly, transport time is one of the key determinants of the efficiency of the distribution system. Its impact is not vivid or dramatic, and executives do not always appreciate what a difference it makes, but in a great many companies it is a significant factor in financing. To take a simple illustration:

Suppose that in a company doing an annual business of $100 million, time in transit is reduced from 14 days to 2. Time between reorders is 14 days, communication and processing time is 4 days, and field stocks average $12.5 million. In such a situation the reduction in transit time might well lead to a reduction in distribution inventory investment of $6 million, made up of: (1) a reduction of $3.3 million in transit, i.e., 12 days' sales; (2) a reduction of $2.7 million in inventories required to protect customer service resulting from a faster, more flexible distribution system response.

Speeding up Service

Changes in transportation leading to improved opportunities in distribution have been truly revolutionary since World War II. Major superhighway systems have been built, truck speeds have increased substantially and so have trailer capacities. The growth in the use of trucking for industrial distribution is now well known. The stimulus from subsidies is only part of the story; trucks have been able to compete at characteristically higher ton-mile costs because they have offered speed, reliability, and flexibility to shippers.

Without doubt, railroads are responding to this challenge. A recent survey showed that almost all Class I railroads are offering some form of piggyback or expedited motor-carrier service. At least some railroads are showing new merchandising awareness in concentrating on customer service. Whether the industry will be able, in the face of inherent limitations, to reverse the decline in its share of manufacturers' freight business is still an open question.

Air freight represents a challenge to both rail and over-the-road haulers. Today most industry executives still tend to view air freight as a luxury, as a service available for "orchids and emergencies." However, the trend in air freight rates has been sharply downward in recent years. With new planes coming into service, even further reductions can be projected—down to 8 cents to 12 cents a ton-mile from present-day rates of approximately 22 cents. Much depends on the success of efforts to develop aircraft equipped for freight handling and for flexible operation under a wide range of conditions (for example, modest runway lengths), and to build up the ground service needed to match air-handling speeds so as to avoid the danger faced by the railroads—the collapse of service as a result of concentration on mass, low-cost, terminal-to-terminal movement.

Impact of New Methods

What is the significance of the ferment in transportation methods? For one thing, improvement in local truck service opens up opportunities to serve wide-flung markets through fewer and larger distribution points. With larger distribution centers, the chance that mechanized material handling and storage systems will pay off is enhanced, and inventory requirements are reduced through consolidation.

To suggest the size of the opportunity, one analysis with which I am familiar showed that cutting the number of field distribution points for a national product line from 50 to 25 would increase total transport costs 7% but cut inventories 20% and cut *total* physical distribution cost 8% (the latter representing roughly a 1% cut in the total cost of delivered product). This was accomplished at the cost of serving a few small markets—about 5% of the total—with second-day instead of first-day delivery.

Rapid truck or air service increases the feasibility of relying on shipments from a few central points to back up service. Here are two ways in which this can be employed:

1. The many low-volume items in the typical product line, the items on which local storage and handling costs outweigh the penalty costs of expedited shipment, can be held centrally and moved to the market where they are needed, as needed. For example, the bottom 50% of the product line, which as Exhibit 2 shows often accounts for only 4% of sales, may require 25% or more of the warehousing costs and inventory capital charges. Turnover of the stocks of these items is often only one eighth that of the high-volume half of the line. In a *relatively* high number of cases, special shipments could be made at a cost well below that of storing the items at local distribution centers.

2. If there are substantial reserve stocks designed to protect customer service located in the field, it is possible to pare them down in the knowledge that additional supplies can be moved in promptly to meet sudden customer demands.

In a typical distribution system a large share of the inventory—as much as 90%—is carried to protect delivery service to customers in the face of fluctuating demand and system delays. This safety stock is almost likely to be used at the end of the reorder cycle, when stocks hit their low point before new receipts. Exhibit 3 illustrates a common situation, with safety stocks being partly

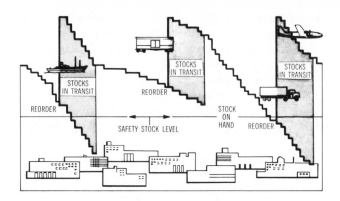

**Exhibit 3   What   is   the   characteristic
inventory pattern of stocks on hand in the
typical company?**

depleted at intervals just before a new shipment arrived. During the period of the
first reorder, demand has been heavy. In many reorder cycles, however, stocks
will not be touched at all; this is the case before the second reorder in the
illustration (middle of the chart) comes in. Note that inventory in transit
represents a fairly significant proportion of the whole.

How much of safety stocks is actually used depends on the reorder system
and level of service maintained. Typically, the last 10% may be needed only once
or twice a year—a turnover rate roughly one sixth the average; and the last 30%
may be needed only two to four times a year. Warehouses and inventory
carrying charges on this portion of inventory, then, may easily run to 10%—20%
of the sales they make possible.

There is an opportunity in many companies for management to cut material
held in the field and back up customer service through regularized high-speed
delivery service. This possibility will deserve increasing attention from
management as the cost of high-speed transport, communication, and data
processing drop.

Information Processing

Revoluntionary data-processing methods were noisily battering at established
business methods some six or seven years ago, but the impact was more in noise
generated than in accomplishment. Now that a lot of the superficial excitement
has died away, however, a broad and solid structure of accomplishment in
modern data-processing techniques is quietly being built.

For one thing, computers seem to have become much more broadly accepted
than anticipated. When the earliest internally programed machines were
announced, computer manufacturers' optimistic estimates were in the dozens.
Today the number of machines installed or in the process of installation is in the
thousands. In support of computing or processing facilities, great improvements

are taking place in communications systems, especially systems designed to feed into or out of computers. In distribution management, fast, reliable communication is equally as important as fast, reliable processing.

The *use* being made of modern information-processing equipment in distribution is just as significant as its broad market acceptance. For instance, machines are being used to maintain local inventory balances, forecast near-term demand, employ forecasts and inventory balances as inputs in calculating item orders, prepare tentative purchase orders, allocate item balances among stock points, and draw up production schedules and work force requirements. These are not mere compiling and accounting functions, nor is it fair to call them "decision making." In these functions, the machine systems are interpreting rules or procedures to work out the decisions implicit in them in light of the facts of the situation. In other words, the equipment is doing what we would like intelligent clerks to do: diligently following policy and weighing costs to arrive at day-to-day actions.

The forecasting function in particular deserves special attention. I refer not to the longer term economic forecasts, annual business forecasts, or even short-term (e.g., quarterly) business predictions, but to short-term forecasts of sales, item by item, over the replenishment lead time. These forecasts are made implicitly or explicitly in every inventory control system. In most companies they are left up to the individual stock clerk or inventory controller to make as best he can, usually with little or no training or guides. Management will spend hundreds of hours of industrial engineering time simplifying or improving a job method here and there to take a few pennies out of labor cost. Yet the stock clerk making inventory control forecasts may, through his control over product distribution and assets tied up in inventories, be costing his company many pennies indeed.

Many people still argue that one cannot forecast routinely because intuition and background knowledge count too heavily. They fail to recognize that objective procedures for short-term prediction of item sales have the same merits as, say, routing and tooling lists in a shop. Experience leaves little doubt that great gains can be made by substituting powerful systematic methods for casual or unrecognized ones.[1]

Changes in Material Handling

Mechanization is slowly spreading from the making of things to their handling in distribution. For instance:

One company in the clothing industry has installed a new data-processing system first to handle sales orders and then inventory control and production-scheduling systems. At the same time, it has been developing a bin-and-conveyer system which will permit economical mechanization of order-filling activities. The goal toward which both of these efforts are directed is a unified system in which the customer order not only serves as an input in automatic order handling but will also, after suitable internal mechanical

[1] See Robert G. Brown, "Less Risk in Inventory Estimates," HBR July–August 1959, p. 104.

processing, activate the warehouse system to select and consolidate the customer's order. This customer order data will also be processed internally for inventory management and production planning purposes.

How will such changes in warehousing and materials handling influence the planning of distribution systems? The effects will take at least three forms:

1. *Integration of systems for (a) material storage and transport and (b) information handling*—This development should create opportunities for significant "automation" of the distribution function and for reduction of manual drudgery. Ultimate full-scale mechanization of materials handling will not only require redesign of warehouse and transport facilities, but will have an impact on design of products and packages as well.

2. *Pressure to reduce the number of distribution points or warehouses*—Mechanized warehouses cost money. One way to improve the efficiency of capital utilization is of course to increase throughput.

3. *Pressure to concentrate ownership of warehousing facilities*—Mechanization takes capital. This factor will be another force behind the tendency for manufacture, distribution, and maintenance service to become integrated under one ownership roof.

Getting Started

Some managers view the opportunities presented by changes in distribution technology with about the same air with which a bear views a porcupine: the possibilities look interesting, but where can you start to get your teeth in?

Improvements in distribution efficiency cost money. Higher speed, more flexible transport generally costs more per ton-mile. Mechanized warehousing systems or material-handling systems are not cheap. The cost of working out, installing, and testing new information-processing systems may make direct clerical cost savings look like a rather thin return on investment. In fact, direct payoffs from distribution changes (e.g., modified transport methods leading to a direct cut in transport costs) may often be small or nonexistent. The payoffs, often handsome ones, are likely to be indirect, coming about from "tradeoffs" such as paying a higher transport bill to save material investment, putting in warehouse investment to cut over-all shipping costs, and so on.

Because tradeoffs so often are involved, it is not always easy for management to get an aggressive, functionally operated group of people to think *through* the problems. It is not easy for men in production, sales, warehousing, traffic, merchandising, and accounting to grasp other functions' needs or express their own needs in terms which make the advantages of tradeoff and balance clear. Many times the distribution *system* has been run too long as a collection of more or less independent *functions*. Any changes, any tradeoffs to get the system into better, more economical balance, any modifications to take advantage in the whole system of new technical developments—these are bound to be disruptive and to some extent resisted.

The difficulties in facing up to a searching look at the distribution system are not confined to the individual functions concerned. Some of the toughest questions arise at the general management level. For example:

- What degree of sales service is the system to provide? How far will the firm go to meet customers' service desires?

- What standards are to be used to judge investment in facilities and inventory so that it can be weighed against any cost savings that are made possible?

- What policy will the company take toward ownership and operation of the distribution, transport, warehousing, and information-processing facilities? Will the company operate its own facilities, lease them, contract for services, or rely on independent businesses to perform some or all of the necessary distribution system functions?

- What is the company's policy toward employment stabilization? To what extent is the company prepared to pay higher distribution costs to absorb demand variations and to level employment?

Approach to the Issues

Grappling with all of these problems is like untangling a tangled skein of yarn. Each decision has an impact on other choices and for this reason is hard to pin down. The distribution problem is a system problem, and it must be looked at as such. If it is examined in total and if the experience and methods available for studying it are used, the issues just mentioned can be resolved in an orderly, mutually compatible way.

In my experience, three key conditions have, when present, made for a sound distribution system study and an effective implementation program:

1. Recognition by company management that improving distribution means examining the full physical distribution system.

2. Use of quantitative systems analysis or operations research methods to show clearly the nature of tradeoffs and the relation between system operation and company policies.

3. Cooperative work by men knowledgeable in sales and marketing, transportation, materials handling, materials control, and information handling.

In the following sections we shall see the need for these conditions asserting itself again and again as we go through the steps of making a good distribution study.

Making the Study

How should a distribution system study be made? What principal steps should be taken? As far as I know, there is no formula for the approach. The relative emphasis put on different phases of the study can vary, as can also the degree of detail; the order of analysis can be changed; and so on. But there are important steps to take at some point in any study, and I shall discuss them in logical order.

1. *Data on the company's markets should be organized in a helpful way.*

The distribution system study starts with a study of customers. This does not need to be a field interview program; to a large extent what is required is the organization of market facts which are available. Occasionally, a moderate amount of skilled field interview work may be desirable to obtain customers' estimates of service requirements and their comparison of the company with its competition.

A great deal of useful information can be obtained by analysis of sales data. Here are some of the key questions of interest:

• Are we servicing several fundamentally different markets through different distribution channels? Are these markets located differently? Do they buy in different patterns, in different quantities, and with different service and stock availability requirements?

• How are our sales distributed among customers? We have found that the top 10% of a company's customers characteristically account for from 60% to 80% or even more of its business.

• Do the same customers tend to buy our high-volume items as well as slow-moving items? The answer to this question has an important bearing on how the slow-moving items, for which distribution and sales service costs are often relatively high, should be handled. Few companies seem to have really examined this problem, though strong opinions on it exist in most.

2. *Statistical analyses of product characteristics should be made, with special attention to the nature of sales fluctuations.*

Sometimes the facts about products can be established fairly readily. An example is the susceptibility of items in the line to spoilage or damage. The degree to which sales volume is concentrated among a few fast-moving items (as illustrated in Exhibit 2) can often be ascertained rather quickly, too. But data of this kind do not tell us nearly enough.

Statistical analysis is needed to establish certain key sales characteristics of the product line, all related to the *variability* of item sales. The significance of variability must be emphasized. Business managers are used to thinking in terms of averages or average rates, but the answers to many important questions affecting distribution system design depend on the characteristics of short-term sales variations about the average.

Most items exhibit unexpected day-to-day variations in sales about the average or expected level. In some cases the fluctuations are extremely wide and short-term in character; in other cases they are quite steady and predictable. The statistical characteristics of these variations determine in a very significant way how a distribution system will work and how it should be designed to operate economically.

3. *In analyzing sales variations, special attention should be paid to size, time, area, and volatility.*

Executives interested in the practical implications of short-term sales variations might focus on the following questions:

• How big are the ups and downs? The magnitude of sales variations *over the replenishment lead time* will determine how large the inventory of an item must be to maintain a desired level of delivery service. The amount of an item on hand at a field point or on order must always equal the maximum reasonable demand over the lead time. Thus, the bigger the sales fluctuations, the more inventory of an item must be carried in the distribution system—at local warehouses, at the factory—to provide a given level of delivery service.

• Are the variations correlated from one time period to the next? If one day's sales are above or below average, are the chances considerably better than 50-50 that the next day's sales will be above or below average, too? If sales are highly correlated from one week to the next, or from one month to the next, this means that the range of accumulated variation over the replenishment lead time increases nearly in proportion to the lead time itself. Doubling the warehouse lead time would nearly double the range of sales variations and the inventory requirements, while cutting the lead time in half would cut inventory requirements nearly in proportion. If sales are *not* correlated from one period to the next, chance variations tend to offset to some degree; doubling the lead time would increase inventory requirements only 40%–50%, while cutting it in half would cut inventories 30% or so.

High correlation in sales puts a premium on cutting lead times to make the distribution system react faster, perhaps through more expensive but higher speed transport, communications, and sales-information processing. By contrast, lower correlation means it may be more economical to let lead times lengthen and save expense in information handling and transport at the cost of somewhat higher inventories. Exhibit 4 illustrates all this graphically for a hypothetical firm: The dotted line represents transport, handling, and data-processing costs, tending to fall as a longer lead time permits less frequent reordering and slower, less expensive methods of shipment. The solid lines represent unit inventory costs, increasing nearly in proportion to lead time in the case of high sales correlation (dashed color line) and at a slower rate in the case of low correlation (black dashed line). The higher the correlation, the further the point of minimum total cost is shifted toward the left—that is toward a shorter lead time—even in the face of higher transport, handling, and proccessing costs.

• Are sales variations correlated between areas or markets? Is an unexpected increase in an item's sales in, say, the Pittsburgh area likely to coincide with an increase in Cleveland, or are variations unrelated from one market to another? Some causes of expected sales variations may affect a wide geographic region (e.g., weather, rumors); others may be related entirely to local conditions (e.g., individual customers' plans).

The degree of cross-correlation in chance sales variations occurring in different markets has a significant influence on warehouse location decisions. For example, if the cross-correlation is low, so that chance variations in sales in one market tend to offset those in another, there is a potentially substantial economy in consolidation warehouses, in having fewer distribution points to serve the same total market. But if the cross-correlation is high, little would be saved to offset possibly greater transportation costs.

• How do sales variations compare among items? Are sales of high-volume items relatively more stable than sales of low-volume items? Generally (but not always), one finds evidence that the higher the sales volume of an item, the more

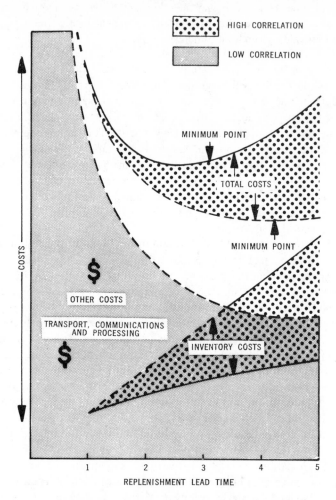

**Exhibit 4   Impact of sales correlation on
lead time cost**

stable will be sales, relatively speaking. Differences in the sales volatility of
products influence distribution system choices. The more changeable the sales of
an item, other things being equal, the better the chances that centralized
stocking in regional distribution centers or plants will be advantageous.

4. *Inventory functions should be examined and related to other company
needs.*

Characteristically inventories are made up of: (a) stock in transit; (b) supplies
arising from periodic shipments; (c) reserves carried to protect service in the face
of unusual demand (safety stock). In some businesses, inventories are also
carried to accommodate seasonal sales patterns and to permit a smoothed load
to be put on manufacturing. These inventory functions and methods for

analyzing have already been discussed in HBR[2] and there is no need to outline them again here. Suffice it to say that one important job in a distribution study is to identify the functions actually served by inventories and to characterize the factors—e.g., transport times, reordering principles used, and service requirements—that are responsible for existing inventory levels and costs.

5. *The costs of warehouse storage and handling, traffic or freight, and clerical procedures should be determined.*

Many of these costs are difficult to obtain from normal company accounting records or engineering studies; direct unit costs often just are not maintained in these records. However, statistical analyses of operating cost records can often serve quite adequately.

Warehouse costs are as good an illustration as any of the approach I have in mind. Included here are: (a) *The cost of holding inventory*—These are generally related to the average or maximum inventory level in a distribution center and include space rent (including maintenance and janitor services, heat, and so on) and inventory costs (taxes, obsolescence and spoilage, and especially the cost of capital tied up in inventory). In our experience, careful study of the storage bill typically yields costs of 20%—35% per year on the capital value of the inventory, depending on the financial resources and policies of the company. (b) *The cost of handling*—These include the costs of physically moving material into and out of storage or through terminal marshaling areas.

What is wanted here are cost factors which can be used to calculate the warehousing and handling costs under different system plans. These factors usually take the form of:

- A fixed charge per warehouse per year x number of warehouses (the fixed charge is generally $5,000—$10,000 per warehouse per year, depending on the character of space.
- Warehousing cost per year unit in inventory x average inventory in the system.
- Handling cost per year per unit through the warehouse.

These cost factors can be built up from an engineering study or derived from statistical analysis of existing cost data. They will, of course, differ for different types of facilities and operating methods. For example, a mechanized warehouse operation will of course have a quite different order of costs from a nonmechanized operation.

Clerical cost factors for alternate operating systems can be derived in similar fashion. Transport costs must also be collected, usually in the form of specimen rates collated with shipment volumes for alternate transport methods. Such possibilities as in-transit privileges, "marriage" of shipments, and forwarding schemes should be reviewed.

---

[2] See John F. Magee, "Guides to Inventory Policy: Part I. Functions and Lot Size," January-February 1956, p. 49; "Part II. Problems of Uncertainty," March—April 1956, p. 103; "part III. Anticipating Future Needs," May—June 1956, p. 57; and Robert G. Brown, op. cit. See also John F. Magee, *"Production Planning and Inventory* (New York, McGraw-Hill Book Company, Inc., 1958) and Robert G. Brown, *Statistical Forecasting for Inventory Control* (New York, McGraw-Hill Book Company, Inc., 1959).

6. *Management should analyze alternative distribution plans on paper.*

The effect of alternative numbers of warehouses, changed locations, different transport methods, and different response times should be tested, using the methods of inventory analysis and programming techniques. Existing manufacturing capacities and locations may be used as a starting point. Alternatively—or as a second step in the analysis—the effect of changes in manufacturing facilities, in capacities, or in the product assigned to individual plants can be tested.

The first broad system studies are used to see where the biggest payoffs or traps may be. On paper, it is possible to make some arbitrary changes in lead times, warehouse locations, plant capacities, flexibility, and so on to see what the gross impact on distribution costs will be and thus whether detailed implementation studies are justified. It is important that the system study be based on current demand conditons, such as gross volume, product mix, and regional balance, as well as demand conditions projected roughly five to ten years ahead.

The facilities analysis is a step-by-step process. As the studies proceed, they will indicate potentially useful modifications in the distribution system. For example, a high concentration of sales among a few customers may indicate the need for special distribution plans, or the degree of concentration among products and the statistical characteristics of demand will suggest the need for regional stocking, changed warehouse numbers or locations, or similar alternatives. Again, an inventory study may indicate payoff possibilities in reducing lead times, in modifying service standards, or in introducing new, more flexible transport and handling methods.

Generally, as a result of broad analyses of facilities and operations, special studies will be indicated. Such studies as these may be in order:

• Detailed analysis of the information-processing methods and costs to (a) take advantage of advancing technology to improve forecasting and control and (b) cut replenishment lead times.

• Investigation of the costs of employment variations and manufacturing changes. Additional inventory—or changes in production technology—may be justified to minimize these costs. If so, however, the additions or changes should be clearly recognized; "manufacturing cost" is too often a lame excuse for careless, inefficient management of materials in distribution.

• Study of product redesign or regrouping, especially where the product line may have evolved without much thought having been given to logistics concepts.

• Analysis of special ordering procedures, stock locations, and transport methods for handling low-volume items.

Organization Plans

Distribution system management poses some puzzling organization problems to the typical, functionally organized firm. Distribution is not a sales function; it is not traffic management; it is an aspect of *all* of these functions. At the same time, the effectiveness of its managers will determine the conditions under which men in the individual functions must work.

Most companies prefer not to put all aspects of distribution management—sales order processing and analysis, field stock control, warehouses, traffic, production control—under one organizational unit, but to divide responsibility among several interested units. Such a division leads, however, to difficulty principally because of failure to (a) recognize the need for specific coordinated distribution systems planning, (b) specify planning and control responsibilities, and (c) set up performance measures consistent with over-all system efficiency and with assigned responsibilities.

In revising an organization to meet current needs and in keeping it up to date, executives should try to have five questions uppermost in their minds:

1. What are the necessary planning steps, policy decisions, and operating decisions to be made?

2. Who is the right person to make each of the decisions?

3. What information does he need, and how can he get it most expeditiously?

4. Does each person know how to recognize an emergency calling for nonroutine action? Does he know how to resolve it?

5. What performance measures reflect what is expected of each person in terms of the operation of the whole system?

Conclusion

To sum up, a number of pressures have piled up on today's distribution systems. As manufacturing efficiency has increased and product cost has come down, costs have grown. Physical distribution costs are a significant share of these.

Business in many fields is becoming increasingly competitive, with competition taking new forms, including availability of goods and reliability of delivery. Product changes are forcing new pressures on the distribution system—more items to carry, faster obsolescence, lower unit sales and inventory turnover. In particular, changes in merchandising practices, such as the introduction of style as a merchandising weapon, have significantly complicated the distribution problem. Pressures for improvement in logistics also include internal forces—for example, the need to stabilize production and insulate production levels from short-term fluctuations in sales.

In the face of these trends, a number of revolutionary changes have taken place. Substantial improvements have come about in essentially all forms of transportation methods. Tremendous strides forward have been made in information-handling methods, including schemes for assimilating and processing data dealing with product demand and with the need for replenishment. Materials-handling methods, ranging from mechanized stock keeping to extensions of the pallet concept to eliminate item-by-item handling, have been gaining acceptance. Finally, and perhaps as important as improvement in physical facilities and concepts, there has been progress in ways of looking at the logistics problem and at methods for analyzing distribution systems.

So far, we have seen farsighted companies taking advantage of the changes I have described by redesigning their distribution systems to cut costs and increase the support given to sales programs. The next step is now beginning to be felt—the insinuation of distribution concepts into certain aspects of long-term planning and capital budgeting, especially the analysis of facility requirements, the location of distribution points, and the determination of financial requirements to support distribution.

Of course, we must avoid the trap of thinking that all management problems will be resolved in terms of efficient distribution. Nevertheless, the long-range impact of distribution-system thinking on production, on product design, and on manufacturing location may be substantial. Perhaps one of the most significant changes will be in concepts of organization, in the assignment of functions and responsibilities. Efficient physical distribution poses a challenge to business in integrating what is essentially a system approach with the functional approaches that hitherto have tended to govern business organization planning.

In the long run, at least two possible directions are open for making a wide variety of products available in local markets. On the one hand, manufacturers can move toward centralized manufacture, with the specialty or small-volume items being made in enough volume to permit reasonable manufacturing economy and then being moved rapidly, perhaps by air freight, to the local markets as needed. On the other hand, management can try to achieve diversity through superificial differences built into a few basic product lines. Low-cost mass transport methods, perhaps rail freight, can be used to move parts and components from centralized manufacturing points with heavy equipment into widespread local assembly or modification plants. At the local points, the final touches can be put on the product to meet customer demand.

One thing seems sure: the choice of distribution system each company makes will have a significant impact on product design, plant investment, and organization. Industrial logistics and trends in logistics technology will receive increasing attention from business, along with markets, capital resources, and product development, in the formation of corporate plans for the decade ahead.

Advertising is more than a mere extension of personal selling techniques to the printed page or the television screen. The author maintains that it is a special form of propaganda, designed to gain and hold the allegiance of mass market. Its function is to persuade, not to present a balanced judgment. Advertising must convey its message through the use of symbols which stir the emotions and lead to action; but it forces the improvement of products to fit the changing needs of consumers.

The Propaganda Function in Marketing

Edmund D. McGarry

The most controversial aspect of marketing is advertising. Ever since advertising began to appear, moralists and critics have complained that it distorted people's natural desires, misinformed them as to the products they needed, played upon their emotions, and led to waste of resources.

Proponents of advertising, on the other hand, have argued that it is an economical method of distributing goods advertised. The purpose here is not to discuss these issues directly, but rather to place the advertising process in its proper perspective as a function of marketing.

Advertising as used today is primarily a type of propaganda. The essence of propaganda is that it conditions people to act in a way favorable to or desired by the propagandist. It deliberately attempts to influence, persuade, and convince people to act in a way that they would not otherwise act. Propaganda had its birth in the attempt of the church to propagate the faith. It is used by leaders

Reprinted by permission of the author and the publisher from the *Journal of Marketing*, published by the American Marketing Association, Vol. 23, No. 2 (October, 1959), pp. 131-139.

who seek a following in politics, in religion, and in all affairs which require action by large bodies of people.

In business it is used primarily by sellers to obtain a market by conditioning people in the market to accept the particular products offered. The growth of new techniques of communication has greatly extended the range of propaganda penetration, has expanded the number of products advertised, and has increased the total amount of propaganda disseminated; but the aim of the messages carried is essentially unchanged since the beginning of civilization.

In fact, the use of force of argument instead of physical force marked the change from savagery to civilized living. "The creation of the world," said Plato, "is the victory of persuasion over force."

The use of persuasion is part of man's apparatus to adapt his way of life to change. Without some stimulus to action, man tends to be indifferent and apathetic to change, and unwilling to exert the effort which change necessitates. He prefers to follow his preconditioned routines rather than direct his effort in some different way. There must be some extra stimulus to action; and this stimulus is afforded either by compulsion of force or the threat of force, or by persuasion in the form of the written or spoken word.

Propaganda versus Education

Propaganda differs from education in that education presumably is oriented toward the dissemination of "truth" —dispassionate, objective, and unbiased. Pure education takes an impartial non-partisan point of view. It is not prejudiced; it has no slant. Yet all of us know that education must persuade to get students to study; it must propagandize to get funds.

Propaganda, on the other hand, by definition is biased, partial, and one sided. It has an axe to grind; therefore, it is always controversial. But unlike education, in which there is no sponsor, the sponsor of propaganda, particularly advertising propaganda, is known. And everyone knows what the sponsor is trying to do, what his motives are, and how he would like others to act. The sponsor of commercial propaganda must identify himself and the product he advertises and he must take the responsibility for it; otherwise, his propaganda cannot be directed to his purpose.

Every advertisement is designed to predispose its readers to a favorable consideration of its sponsor and his product. It is deliberately planned to make its readers and listeners take sides—to affiliate and ally themselves under its banner and to ignore all others.

Advertising is the obtrusive display of the conflict of interests in the market place. It represents a parade of the contestants in the battle for market supremacy, each imploring the audience to follow him. By its very nature advertising must be prejudiced in order to be potent.

The Barrage Effect of Propaganda

Commercial propaganda is a social phenomenon, and its analysis must necessarily be in a social framework. It is, in fact, a part of our culture and at the same time exercises a considerable influence on that culture. Professor David M. Potter speaks of it "as an instrument of social control comparable to the school and the church in the extent of its influence upon society."[1]

Like other types of propaganda, advertising has a barrage effect. Although it is designed primarily to induce people who have the money and the need to buy the product, its effect cannot usually be confined to these. It creates a pattern of thought in a much larger population. Its results are diffuse and pervasive rather than selective. Because of this diffusion, many who are not in a position to buy, read, or listen to the advertisement, and many others who do not see or hear the message directly, learn of it from others by word of mouth.

Moreover, the pattern of thought created by advertising is likely to last for an indefinite period. If consecutive appeals are used, the effect tends to be cumulative both because of the widening group which sees it and because of the intensification of the impression it makes. This cumulative effect continues to a point of diminishing returns which is reached either through saturation of the market, through the counteracting influence of competing messages, or through the saturation of receptivity.

There is another sense in which there is a spill-over of advertising effectiveness. This is what might be called the cross-product influence. It is said, for instance, that when vacuum cleaners were first advertised the demand for brooms increased; the inference is that the promotion of cleanliness in the home leads to the increased sales of any product that enhances cleanliness.

Still another type of spill-over effect is seen in the case of the firm selling a family of products in which the advertising of any one will increase to some extent the sales of all other products in the same use-class, even if they are marketed by competitors.

It would seem logical to assume that, when two competing advertisers attempt to promote their individual brands for a particular use, the impact will be greater than if only one is advertised; and, if the market can be expanded, the advertising of each will have a complementary effect on that of the other. If this is true, then there is a cumulative effect of advertising generally in the sense that, as more advertising is published, there is developed a greater propensity to purchase advertised goods of all kinds. The increase may be at the expense of non-advertised goods it may be at the expense of savings, or it may result in greater effort on the part of consumers to secure more income.

Advertising versus Personal Selling

Advertising today has to take a large part of the responsibility for making sales. To a great extent salesmen, particularly at the retail level, have become anonymous persons—unknown either to the selling firm or to the buyer—who merely facilitate the sale by formally presenting the product and accepting payment. The real job of adjusting the consumer to the product is done by the mass propaganda called advertising.

[1] David M. Potter, *People of Plenty* (Chicago: University of Chicago Press, 1954), p. 168.

In taking over the task formerly performed by the salesman, advertising must substitute symbolic language for the personal appeal of man-to-man at a point where the merchandise is itself present and the transaction takes place. The task of persuading the customer is pushed back in time to a point where it can be planned and partly executed months before the product reaches the market. It is removed in space from the point of sale to the business office, where the entire selling technique is planned and developed without benefit of the presence of the buyer. The sale must thus consist of an impersonalized message to thousands of unidentified potential customers, who have no way of communicating their impressions.

· Modern advertising has many tasks to perform, which do not arise when selling is done face-to face at the point of sale:

1. It must create or point out a need by identifying the circumstances under which it arises.
2. It must link the need to the possibility of fulfilling it with a general product, so that when the need arises the respondent will think of the product that will fulfill it.
3. It must differentiate the particular brand and its sponsor from other products which might satisfy the need approximately as well.
4. It must connect the particular branded product with the place and the conditions under which it can be obtained.
5. It must show that the need is urgent and that the task of buying is easy.
6. It must give a rational basis for action, for people do not like to buy goods which they cannot justify to their own consciences.
7. It must stimulate the respondent to make a firm decision on which he will act at a later time.

In accomplishing these tasks, advertising acts under the kleiglights of publicity. Unlike personal selling, where the promotion is carried on in private between two or more people, the messages publicized in advertising are conspicuous and cannot escape observation. This is one of the reasons why advertising comes in for a great deal of criticism that is equally relevant to selling on a personal basis. The so-called abuses which are concealed and disguised in the personal sales transaction are flaunted in the face of the public when they are published on the printed page or appear on the television screen. There is little doubt that there is more misrepresentation, deceit, and fraud in person-to-person sales relationships than in advertising.

The Purpose of Advertising.

Commercial propaganda or advertising had its genesis in the need of the mass producer to sell goods in large quantities, and competition of other goods forced him to resort to an anonymous market: an aggregation of people scattered geographically, and unknown and unidentified as individuals. These conditions, and the growing separation of the locus of production in time and space from the locus of consumption, necessitated some means of making an individual manufacturer's product known and thus assuring it a continuous market.

Through the use of propaganda it was possible to create markets that were more stable than their component parts; for, although individual consumers are notoriously whimsical in changing their minds, their reactions in the market as a whole tend to cancel each other out.[2]

In order to accomplish these results the advertiser must use all the tools at his disposal. He must have an intimate understanding of the product advertised and be able to sense these characteristics whether inherent or inferred, which will fulfill the hopes and expectations of the potential owner and user. He must envisage the product in its use-setting. He must comprehend and appreciate the nature of human behavior. And he must be able to use the tricks of his trade—often the same as, and always closely akin to, those used on the rostrum and in the pulpit.

If the propaganda which the advertiser writes is to be effective, it must be expressed in terms in which the consumer thinks, with the same overtones and exaggerations of the product that the well-disposed consumer will attribute to it. It must recognize that the consumer to whom it appeals is but imperfectly rational, that he hates the labor of rational thinking, and that he is sometimes more impressed by what seems to others to be superficial than by the real merits of the product.

Rational versus Emotional Appeals

In a broad, general sense advertising appeals either to man's reason or to his emotion or to both. It is difficult, of course, to differentiate in any precise way between these; but generally speaking rational appeals seem more effective in deciding alternative means to ends rather than the ends themselves. Emotion, on the other hand, is usually the trigger to action, particularly when the actions mean a change of attitude on the part of the person.

There are many road-blocks to actions based on rational appeals; for rational arguments tend to raise questions rather than to answer them. Emotional appeals, on the other hand, attempt to stimulate the individual to carry through impulses which he already has. Assuming that this is true, the rational appeal is likely to be more lasting and its secondary effect to be stronger, because people are more likely to repeat rationalizations than they are to communicate their emotional feelings.

Advertising is highly concentrated on marginal products, things that one can do without, things that can be purchased with free income after the more austere basic needs such as necessary food, housing, clothing, etc., are taken care of.[3] It is these marginal products that give the real satisfactions in life. Even in the case of basic products, it is the exotic, the unusual elements—the fringe benefits—that set one off from his fellow creatures and thus claim the attention of consumers.

[2] Compare Neil H. Borden, *The Economic Effects of Advertising* (Chicago: Richard D. Irwin, 1942).

[3] F. P. Bishop, *The Ethics of Advertising* (London: Robert Hale, Ltd., 1949), p. 48.

The Most Common Motives

Some years ago Victor Schwab suggested that there were ten leading motives or desires of the average consumer to which advertising must appeal in order to be effective:[4]

1. *Money and a better job.* "There must always be some kind of short-cut to getting ahead faster."
2. *Security in old age.* "When I get along in years, I want to be able to take it easy."
3. *Popularity.* "It's fun to be asked out all the time, to be wanted by everybody."
4. *Praise from others.* "Praise from others is a nice thing to get and I like to get it when I deserve it, and I often do".
5. *More comfort.* "A lot of people who are not as industrious or as capable as I am seem to have more comforts, so why shouldn't I spread myself once in a while?"
6. *Social advancement.* "Where would a person be if he never tried to better himself and to meet and associate with better people?"
7. *Improved appearance.* "It is awfully nice to have people tell you how attractive and well-dressed you are. If I had the time and money some people spend on themselves, I would show them."
8. *Personal prestige.* "I am going to see to it that my children can prove that they have parents they need never be ashamed of."
9. *Better health.* "I don't feel any older than I did years ago, it's just that I don't seem to have the drive and energy I used to have."
10. *Increased enjoyment.* "I work hard, I do the best I can about things so why shouldn't I get as much enjoyment as I can?"

Advertisers have found by trial and error that these types of appeals are effective. It is evident that each appeal contains a bit of rationality with a large dose of sentimentality. The fact that these appeals are effective simply indicates that "the average human mind is a montage of hasty impressions, fuzzy generalities, bromidic wall-motto sentiments, self-justifications and sentimentalities."[5] It is out of this "jumble of ideas and feelings" that the advertiser must find a background for his appeals.

More and Better Wants

"The chief thing which the common sense individual actually wants," wrote Professor Frank H. Knight, "is not satisfactions for the wants which he has, but more and better wants. There is always really present and operative, though in the background of consciousness, the idea of, and desire for a new want to be striven for when the present objective is out of the way."[6] Advertising attempts to present goods which are new or additional in the consumers' inventory of wants and to indicate how they can be realized. In doing this, it both creates a want and the means of satisfying it.

The fact that advertising concentrates its efforts on changing people's customary wants has given rise to the contention that it corrupts people's desires

---

[4] Victor Schwab, "Ten Copy Appeals," *Printers' Ink (December 17, 1943), pp. 17ff.*

[5] Same reference, p. 17.

[6] Frank H. Knight, *The Ethics of Competition* (New York: Harpers, 1935), p.22.

and stimulates so-called "artificial" consuming habits. But this argument is beside the point for, as Professor Knight has indicated, "there is no issue as between natural and artificial wants. All human wants are more artificial than natural, and the expression 'natural wants,' if it has any meaning, can only refer to those of beasts. By the same token, human wants are more sentimental than real."[7]

Most people have always lived rather drab and unimaginative lives. The so-called golden ages of history were golden only to the few. The great masses lived by drudgery, and thought in terms of only the elemental emotions such as hunger and comfort. The so-called "democratic way of life" rests simply on the idea that our present economy is oriented to change the thinking of these masses. Propaganda, if it is to be effective, must appeal to the masses in the terms of their own mental processes.

It is sometimes alleged also that, through advertising, businessmen foist on people goods they do not want. This, of course, is sheer nonsense. There are, in fact, few acts necessarily more deliberate than that of the consumer's action in response to advertising.

Picture the consumer in his living room reading a magazine advertisement. He has had to choose the particular magazine, and pay for it; he has had to select from among the hundreds of pages those he wishes to read, and he can either accept or reject the arguments presented. Assuming that he accepts them and resolves to make the purchase, he must still wait hours or even days before an opportune time arises to make the purchase. During the interval between the time he reads the advertisement and the time he undertakes the overt act of buying, he is entirely outside the influence of the message and may deliberate and search his soul to his heart's content either in private or in consultation with his friends. There is not even mass psychology to influence him. He is a free agent and there is no possibility of coercion, duress, or constraint of any kind.

But the impossibility of advertising to force consumers to buy what they do not want should not be confused with the fact that advertisers sometime overstep the bounds of propriety to make claims for their products which cannot be justified. In some product areas effective protection has been provided by law, but in general the chief defense of the consumer lies in his own discrimination of whom he will patronize or refuse to patronize.

The Larger System of Beliefs

In discussing propaganda generally, psychologists Krech and Crutchfield state that "suggestions which are accepted as a consequence of propaganda tend to be in harmony with some larger system of beliefs or some already existing predisposition, and therefore presumably with the major needs and interests of the subject."[8]

[7] Same reference, p. 103.

[8] D. K. Krech and R.S. Crutchfield, *Theory and Problems of Social Psychology* (New York: McGraw-Hill, 1948), p. 347.

To put this another way, at any given time the subject of propaganda has many prejudices, beliefs, and attitudes of different intensities. Some are deeply entrenched, while others are at a superficial level. The more deeply entrenched these predispositions are, the more difficult it will be to change them, and some seem to be entrenched so deeply that they cannot be changed by propaganda at all.

Since it is easier and less expensive to modify existing predispositions than to oppose them, propagandists find it expedient to fit their messages into the current pattern of thinking rather than oppose it head on. It is for this reason that most changes in attitudes and wants achieved by advertising are almost imperceptible, and can be objectively observed only over a period of time.

Both in the selection of the characteristics of the product to promote and in the framing of appeals, the advertiser must give attention to consumers' preconceived ideas of what they want. He develops his product and its appeals to fit into these ideas and to project them further. If his advertising is successful in selling his product, competitors will find it necessary to discover other new products or new characteristics of old products, likewise in line with consumers' ideas, as a basis for their counter-propaganda. Thus, competition in advertising tends to develop a constantly increasing improvement of the product to fit consumers' wants, while at the same time it raises the standards of wants in the consumers' minds.

Discounting the Message

The very mass of advertising and the great amount that comes to the attention of consumers is often open to criticism. Critics ask, for instance, "Is there no limit to the increasing din of the market place?" "Will it continue until all businesses are wasting their substance and crying their wares?" "Are there no antidotes for this infectious disease?" We suspect there are.

The editor of *Harper's Magazine,* puts it this way: "Perhaps, however, we will in the long run have reason to be grateful to the copywriters and press agents, even the worst of them. It may turn out that thanks to advertising and public relations, the American people will become the first people in the history to be impervious to propaganda. Maybe it isn't such a bad thing that the advertisers and other word-manipulators have got us to the point that we never take words quite at their face value. In all events, it is hard to imagine that people inured to American advertising would wholeheartedly believe the kind of promises and assurances, whereby Hitler and Stalin have enslaved two great nations in our time."[9]

When two advertisers say approximately the same things about their product, the message of one tends to neutralize that of the other, and the public learns to discount what is said by both. In a free world the right to persuade and be persuaded is one of the essential freedoms. We assume that each of us has the

[9] Robert Amory, Jr., "Personal and Otherwise," Harper's Magazine (September, 1948), p. 6.

mentality and the fortitude to choose—to accept or reject what he hears or what he reads.

Each has the right to act or to refuse to act on the basis of all the propaganda he absorbs, whether it is in the form of advertising or word-of-mouth gossip. That he often rejects propaganda is a matter of record. But we assume that, whether a person acts wisely or foolishly, he will take the responsibility for the act and that he himself will reap the benefits or the penalties of his action. For this reason he will eventually learn to listen more discriminatingly and act more wisely in the light of all the information available.

Effect on Media Content

It is sometimes alleged that advertising, because it pays most of the cost of magazines and newspapers, dominates and controls the information in these media. It is said that, since the advertiser pays the piper, he must call the tune.

Actually this is seldom true because the medium that publishes biased or slanted news tends to lose its circulation when its bias becomes known, and in this way it ceases to be an effective means of communication. Even the most severe critics of advertising admit that this type of direct and overt influence is pretty well eliminated by the intense competition among media themselves.

The effect of advertising on news content and editorial opinion is far more indirect and subtle. Editors themselves are human and they live in the same environment as the rest of us. They, too, are subject to the propaganda which all of us read; and it would be too much to expect that they are not influenced in a general way by what they read. As a part of the total environment it tends to set a point of view which is not unfavorable to advertising.

The Function of Media

From the advertiser's point of view, the function of the newspaper, the magazine, the broadcasting station, or any other medium of publication is to gather a crowd or furnish an audience.[10] Once the crowd has gathered, it must be entertained, amused, or at least interested enough to hold together while the advertiser's message is being delivered. The need for holding the audience arises from the fact that advertising is selective, in the sense that a specific message is likely to have an appeal only to a scattered few among the many in the crowd. As for the many others who have no need or interest in the particular product, they become bored and resentful that their attention has been disrupted.

The fact that advertising is selective in its expectations, though not in its aims, means that its impact on those to whom the message does not apply or who do not care to listen ranges from irritation to exasperation. From the listener's point of view, it is an unwarranted intrusion on their privacy, by some "jerk" who wants to sell something.

Therefore, the advertiser must use every art he can contrive to make his

[10] See G. B. Hotchkiss, *Milestones of Marketing* (New York: Macmillan, 1938), p. 10.

message palatable, even to those who do not want to listen; and at the same time
he searches for a vehicle which will capture and hold his audience while he gives
them "the works." In rare cases he is able to convert his message into news
which is interesting and entertaining in itself; but often there is a trail of
resentment left in the listener's mind, and he deliberately tries to develop some
means of shutting out the message from his consciousness. The result is that a
great deal of advertising never passes the threshold of the reader's or the
listener's consciousness.

Although there is danger of exaggerating the importance of advertising in
causing certain changes in our culture, it would be erroneous to conclude that its
influence is negligible. Advertising is so prevalent, so pervasive, so extensive, and
so conspicuous that it would be absurd to argue that it does not affect our
attitudes.

On the other hand, the fact that advertising, in order to be successful and
economical, "must be in harmony with some larger system of beliefs or some
already existing predisposition" indicates that its influence is tangential rather
than direct, that it tends to fit in with and supplement other motivational
influences rather than act as an independent force.

Effect on Consumer Standards

Advertising, both for individual products and in the aggregate, appeals to the
anticipatory aspirations of the group.[11] It offers goals of attainment that would
not otherwise be thought of. It sets up ideals to be sought after. Its appeals are
designed to stimulate action which will result in a more comfortable, congenial,
and satisfying life.

Thus, in the aggregate it creates an ever-expanding series of aspirations for the
future. In doing this, it shapes the standards of living for the future; and, since
man lives largely in a world of anticipation, it lays the basis for much of his
enjoyment.

In American business, commercial propaganda is part and parcel of the
mass-production process. Our present American business could no more operate
without advertising than it could without the automatic machine or the
assembly line. By means of this propaganda, the millions of people coming from
many nations and races and diverse backgrounds are conditioned to want
sufficient amounts of a given standardized product to make it possible to
produce that product at a fraction of the cost which would otherwise be
necessary.

If left without such propaganda as is found in advertising, people would not
choose the same products they do choose. Whether they would choose the same
product at a later date is purely a matter of conjecture, but it seems unlikely. If
it is assumed that without advertising they would choose something different,
then no producer would be able to secure sufficient production to provide these

[11] See Wroe Alderson, *Marketing Behavior and Executive Action* (Homewood, Ill.:
Richard D. Irwin, 1957), p. 276ff.

diverse things at prices people could afford to pay. This is another way of saying that standarization of wants through advertising is in part the basis for the economies which come through mass production.

In spite of the necessity that people's wants be so standardized as to secure mass production, the enormous market and the high-level purchasing power available in America have enabled firms to proliferate these standards and to offer a wider variety of goods for sale than would be possible even under a handicraft system where goods are presumably made to fit the consumer's specifications.

Incidentally, the assumption sometimes made, that people would make wiser choices if there were no advertising, ignores the fact that preconceived notions of what they want have themselves been formed by other types of propaganda and other influences no less biased and no more rational than the propaganda used by sellers.

As people get more income, and as competition becomes stronger among sellers for a share of this income, adjustment of goods to the consumer becomes finer. More attention is given to the marginal aspects of goods. New quality standards are developed in terms of their psychological rather than their utilitarian values. For instance, people in buying shoes are often more interested in style and how they look to others than in comfort and durability, which are likely to be taken for granted.

These types of desires are often hidden and so subtle that sellers are faced with a continuously changing market, difficult to interpret and almost impossible to predict. They are thus forced to offer their products with infinite variations in characteristics and appeals. To the consumer, the opportunity to choose from this vast variety of products is itself a major element in his standard of living.

This humorous article describes how the author's life was affected on that imaginary day when all advertising was outlawed.

The Day the Ads Stopped

George G. Kirstein

The day the advertising stopped began just like any other day—the sun came up, the milk was delivered and people started for work. I noticed the first difference when I went out on the porch to pick up *The New York Times*. The newsdealer had advised me that the paper would now cost 50c a day so I was prepared for the new price beneath the weather forecast, but the paper was thinner than a Saturday edition in summer. I hefted it thoughtfully, and reflected that there really was no alternative to taking the *Times*. The *News* had suspended publication the day before the advertising stopped with a final gallant editorial blast at the Supreme Court which had declared the advertising prohibition constitutional. The *Herald Tribune* was continuing to publish, also at 50c, but almost no one was taking both papers and I preferred the *Times*.

As I glanced past the big headlines chronicling the foreign news, my eye was caught by a smaller bank:

1 KILLED, 1 INJURED IN
ELEVATOR ACCIDENT AT MACY'S

The story was rather routine; a child had somehow gotten into the elevator pit and his mother had tried to rescue him. The elevator had descended, killing the woman, but fortunately had stopped before crushing the child. It was not so much the story as its locale that drew my attention. I realized that this was the first time in a full, rich life that I had ever read a newspaper account of an accident in a department store. I had suspected that these misfortunes befell stores, as they do all business institutions, but this was my first confirmation.

Reprinted by permission of the author from *The Nation*, Vol. 198, No. 23 (June 1, 1964), pp. 555-557.

There were other noticeable changes in the *Times*. Accounts of traffic accidents now actually gave the manufacturers' names of the vehicles involved as, "A Cadillac driven by Harvey Gilmore demolished a Volkswagen operated by ... " The feature column on "Advertising" which used to tell what agencies had lost what accounts and what assistant vice president had been elevated was missing. As a matter of fact, the whole newspaper, but particularly the Financial Section, exhibited a dearth of "news" stories which could not possibly interest anyone but the persons mentioned. Apparently, without major expenditures for advertising, the promotion of Gimbels' stocking buyer to assistant merchandise manager was not quite as "newsworthy" as it had been only yesterday. Movies and plays were listed in their familiar spot, as were descriptions of available apartments in what used to be the classified section. The women's page was largely a catalogue of special offerings in department and food stores, but no comparative prices were given and all adjectives were omitted. One could no longer discover from reading the *Times*, or any other paper, who had been named Miss National Car Care Queen or who had won the Miss Rheingold contest.

Driving to work, I observed workmen removing the billboards. The grass and trees behind the wall of signs were beginning to reappear. The ragged posters were being ripped from their familiar locations on the walls of warehouses and stores, and the natural ugliness of these structures was once more apparent without the augmenting tawdriness of last year's political posters or last week's neighborhood movie schedules.

I turned on the car radio to the subcription FM station to which I had sent my $10 dues. The music came over the air without interruption, and after awhile a news announcer gave an uninterrupted version of current events and the weather outlook. No one yet knew which radio stations would be able to continue broadcasting. It depended on the loyalty with which their listeners continued to send in their subscription dues. However, their prospects were better than fair, for everyone realized that, since all merchandise which had previously been advertised would cost considerably less on the store counter, people would have funds available to pay for the news they read or the music or other programs they listened to. The absence of the familiar commercials, the jingles, the songs and the endless repetition of the nonsense which had routinely offended our ears led me to consider some of these savings. My wife's lipsticks would now cost half as much as previously; the famous brand soaps were were selling at 25 percent below yesterday's prices; razor blades were 10 percent cheaper; and other appliances and merchandise which had previously been nationally advertised were reduced by an average of 5 per cent. The hallowed myth that retail prices did not reflect the additional cost of huge advertising campaigns was exploded once and for all. Certainly these savings should add up to enough for me to pay for what I listened to on my favorite radio station or read in the newspaper of my choice.

After parking my car, I passed the familiar newsstand between the garage and the office. *"Life* $1," the printed sign said. *"Time* and *Newsweek,* 75c." Next to these announcements was a crayon-scrawled message, *"Consumer Reports* sold out. Bigger shipment next week." I stopped to chat with the newsie. "The mags like *Consumer Reports* that tell the truth about products are selling like crazy," he told me. *"Reader's Digest* is running a merchandise analysis section next month." I asked about the weekly journals of opinion. He said, "Well now they are half the price of the news magazines—*The Nation* and *The New Republic* prices have not gone up, you know, but I don't think that will help them much. After all, a lot of magazines are going to begin printing that expose-type stuff. Besides, people are buying books now. Look!" He pointed across the street to the paperback bookstore where a crowd was milling around as though a fire sale were in progress.

I walked over to the bookstore and found no special event going on. But books represented much better value than magazines or newspapers, now that the latter were no longer subsidized by advertisements, and the public was snapping up the volumes.

Sitting in my office, I reviewed the events and the extraordinary political coalition that had been responsible for passing the advertising prohibition law through Congress by a close margin. The women, of course, had been the spearhead of the drive. Not since the Anti-Saloon-League days and the militant woman-suffrage movement at the beginning of the century had women organized so militantly or expended energy more tirelessly in pursuit of their objective. Their slogans were geared to two main themes which reflected their major grievances. The first slogan, "Stop making our kids killers," was geared mainly to the anti-television campaign. The sadism, killing and assorted violence which filled the TV screens over all channels from early morning to late at night had finally so outraged mothers' groups, PTAs and other organizations concerned with the country's youth that a massive parents' movement was mobilized.

The thrust of the women's drive was embodied in their effective two-word motto, "Stop lying." Women's organizations all over the country established committees to study all advertisements. For the first time in history, these common messages were analyzed in detail. The results were published in anti-advertising advertisements, by chain letter and by mouth. The results were devastating. No dog-food manufacturer could claim that pets loved his product without having the women demand, "How in the name of truth do you know? Did you interview the dogs?" No shampoo or cosmetic preparation could use the customary blandishments without having the women produce some witch who had used the particular product and who had lost her hair, developed acne or had her fingernails curl back.

Women led the attack, but the intellectuals soon joined them, and the clergy followed a little later. The intellectuals based their campaign largely on the argument that the English language was losing its usefulness, that word meanings were being so corrupted that it was almost impossible to teach youth to read to any purpose. One example commonly cited was the debasement of the superlative "greatest." The word had come to mean anything that didn't break down; viz., "the greatest lawn mower ever," interpreted realistically, was an instrument that, with luck, would cut grass for one summer. The clergy's campaign was geared simply to the proposition that it was impossible to teach people the virtues of truth when half-truths and lies were the commonly accepted fare of readers and viewers alike.

Opposition to the anti-advertising law was impressive, and at the beginning it looked as if all the big guns were arrayed against the women. Spokesmen for big business contended throughout the campaign that elimination of advertising meant elimination of jobs. The fallacy of this argument was soon exposed when all realized that it was not men's jobs but simply machine running time that was involved. By this decade of the century, the cybernetic revolution had developed to a point where very few men were involved in any of the production or distribution processes. No one could feel sympathy for the poor machines and their companion computers because they would be running only four hours daily instead of six.

Some merchants tried to blunt the "stop lying" slogan by telling the absolute truth. One San Francisco store advertised:

2,000 overcoats—only $12. Let's face it—our buyer goofed! These coats are dogs or you couldn't possibly buy them at this price. We're losing our shirt on this sale and the buyer has been fired. But, at least, many of these coats will keep you warm.

The trouble with this technique was that it backfired in favor of the women. The few true ads, by contrast, drew attention to the vast volume of exaggeration, misrepresentation and outright lies that were printed as usual. The advertising industry published thirteen different editions of its "Advertisers Code" in the years preceding the law's passage, but few could detect any difference from the days when no code at all existed.

The press, of course, was the strongest opponent and loudest voice against the advertising prohibition. Its argument was largely legalistic, based on the First Amendment to the Constitution, for the publishers had decided at the outset of their defense not to emphasize the fact that if advertising stopped, readers would actually have to pay for what they read, rather than have America's largest corporations pay for the education and edification of the public. However, the words "Free Press" came to have a double meaning—both an unhampered press and a press that charged only a nominal fee for the publications.

The constitutional argument was really resolved in the final speech on the floor of the Senate before a gallery-packed audience, by Senator Thorndike of Idaho. His memorable ovation, certainly among the greatest in the Senate's distinguished history, concluded:

And so, Mr. President, the opponents of this measure [the advertising prohibition] claim that the founders of this republic, our glorious forefathers, in their august wisdom, forbade the Congress to interfere with the freedom of the press to conduct itself in any way it found profitable. But I say to you, that the framers of our Constitution intended to protect the public by permitting the press, without fear or favor, to examine all of the institutions of our democracy. Our forefathers planned a press free to criticize, free to analyze, free to dissent. They did not plan a subsidized press, a conformist press, a prostitute press.

The applause was thunderous and the bill squeaked through the Senate by four votes. Three years later, the Supreme Court upheld Senator Thorndike's interpretation. That was two days ago, and today the advertising stopped.

All morning I worked in the office, and just before noon I went uptown for lunch. The subway cars were as drab as ever and seemed a little less bright because of the absence of the familiar posters. However, in one car the Camera Club of the Technical Trades High School had "hung" a show of New York City photographs chosen from student submissions. In another car, the posters on one side carried Session I of a course in Spanish for English-speaking riders, while the opposite side featured the same course in English for those speaking Spanish. This program was sponsored by the Board of Education which had subcontracted the administration of it to the Berlitz School. A poster in both languages in the middle of the car explained that the lessons would proceed on a weekly basis and that by sending $1 to the Board of Education, sheets and periodic tests would be available upon request.

On Madison Avenue, the shopping crowds were milling around as usual, but there was a noticeable absence of preoccupied and hatless young men hurrying along the street. The retirement plan that the advertising industry had worked out through the insurance companies was fairly generous, and the majority of key personnel that had been laid off when the agencies closed were relieved not to have to make the long trek from Westport or the nearer suburbs each day. Some of the copywriters who had been talking about it since their youth were now really going to write that novel.

Others had set up shop as public relations counselors, but the outlook for their craft was not bright. Without the club of advertising, city editors looked over mimeographed press releases with a new distaste, and it is even rumored that on some newspapers the orders had come down to throw out all such "handouts" without exception. On the magazines, the old struggle between the editorial staff and the advertising sales staff for dominance had finally been resolved by the elimination of the latter. There were even some skeptics who believed that public relations counseling would become a lost art, like hand basket weaving. So most former advertising copywriters planned to potter about in their gardens, cure their ulcers and give up drinking. They were not so many. It was a surprise to most people to learn that the advertising industry, which had had such a profound effect on the country's habits and moral attitudes, directly employed fewer than 100,000 people.

Outside 383 Madison Avenue, moving vans were unloading scientific equipment and laboratory accessories into the space vacated by Batten, Barton, Durstine & Osborn. The ethical drug industry had evolved a plan, in the three-year interim between the passage of the advertising prohibition and the Supreme Court's validation of it, to test all new drugs at a central impartial laboratory. Computers and other of the latest information-gathering machinery were massed in the space vacated by this large advertising agency to correlate the results of drug tests which were being conducted in hospitals, clinics, laboratories and doctors' offices throughout the world.

The Ford Foundation had given one of its richest grants, nearly three-quarters of a billion dollars, to the establishment of this Central Testing Bureau. The American Medical Association had finally agreed, under considerable public pressure, to take primary responsibility for its administration. It was pointed out to the doctors that when the drug companies could no longer make their individual claims through advertisements in the AMA bulletin or the medical society publications, a new and more reliable method of disseminating information would be required. At the outset, the AMA had joined the drug companies in fighting bitterly against the prohibition, but the doctors now took considerable pride in their centralized research and correlation facilities. The AMA bulletin, once swollen to the bulk of a small city's telephone directory, was now only as thick as a summer issue of *Newsweek*. Doctors no longer would find their mail boxes stuffed with throw-away material and sample pills; but they would receive the weekly scientific report from Central Testing Bureau as to the efficacy of and experience with all new preparations.

Late in the afternoon, I began to hear the first complaints about the way the new law worked. One of the men came in and picked up a folder of paper matches lying on my desk. "I'm swiping these; they're not giving them out any more, you know." Someone else who had been watching TV said that the two channels assigned to the government under a setup like that of the B.B.C., were boring. One channel showed the ball game, but the other had been limited to a short session of the Senate debating the farm bill, and a one-hour view of the UN Security Council taking up the latest African crisis. My informant told me the Yanks had won 8 to 0, and the Senate and the UN weren't worth watching. I reminded him that when the channel that was to be supervised by the American Academy of Arts and Sciences got on the air, as well as the one to be managed by a committee of the local universities, things might improve. "Cheer up," I told him, "At least it's better than the Westerns and the hair rinses."

Oh, there were some complaints, all right, and I suppose there were some unhappy people. But personally I thought the day the advertising stopped was the best day America had had since the last war ended.

Does advertising represent a dissipation of economic resources or their efficient use? Economists generally have been lined up on one side of this question and marketing men on the other. In this article, an economist disagrees with his colleagues. The main criticisms are reviewed and analyzed. The informational role of advertising is emphasized. The fact that advertising is used generally when it is the most efficient tool in the marketing arsenal is underlined. The quantitative dimensions of so-called competitive or persuasive advertising are indicated. The relationships to competition, costs, economic growth, and the degree of affluence of a society are reviewed.

Is Advertising Wasteful?

Jules Backman

With some exceptions, economists generally have criticized advertising as economically wasteful. All the criticisms are not so extreme as one widely used economics text which states:

Overall, it is difficult for anyone to gain more than temporarily from large advertising outlays in any economy in which counteradvertising is general. The overall effect of advertising, on which we spent $14 billion [actually $15 billion—JB] in 1965, is to devote these productive resources (men, ink, billboards, and so forth) to producing advertising rather than to producing other goods and services.[1]

Reprinted by permission of the author and the publisher from the *Journal of Marketing,* published by the American Marketing Association, Vol. 32, No. 1 (January, 1968), pp.2-8.

[1] George Leland Bach, *Economics,* Fifth Edition (Englewood Cliffs, New Jersey: Prentice-Hall, Inc., 1966), p. 437. See also Kenneth Boulding, "Economic Analysis," Volume 1, *Microeconomics,* Fourth Edition, Vol. 1 (New York: Harper and Row, 1966), p. 513.

Most critics do not go this far in condemning advertising. However, they do emphasize that advertising may be wasteful in several ways: by adding unnecessarily to costs, by an inefficient use of resources, by promoting excessive competition, and by causing consumers to buy items they do not need. This article brings together the scattered criticisms of advertising and answers to them and thus presents an overview of the debate in this area. The nature of these criticisms and the significance of waste in a competitive economy are first reviewed. Attention is then given to the vital informational role played by advertising, particularly in an expanding economy. Advertising is only one alternative in the marketing mix, and hence its contribution must be considered among alternatives rather than in absolute terms.

Variations on a Theme

The criticism that advertising involves economic waste takes several forms.

Competition in Advertising

The attack usually is centered on competition in advertising which some critics state flatly is wasteful.[2] Others have been concerned about the relative cost of advertising as a percentage of sales. Sometimes an arbitrary percentage, such as 5%, is selected as the dividing line between "high" and more "reasonable" levels of expenditure.[3]

Such cutoff points are meaningless, since the proper relative expenditures for advertising are a function of the product's characteristics. It is not an accident that relative advertising costs are highest for low-priced items which are available from many retail outlets and subject to frequent repeat purchases (for example, cosmetics, soaps, soft drinks, gum and candies, drugs, cigarettes, beer, etc.).

Particularly criticized are emotional appeals, persuasion, and "tug of war" advertising where it is claimed the main effect is to shift sales among firms rather than to increase total volume of the industry. For example, Richard Caves states: "At the point where advertising departs from its function of informing and seeks to persuade or deceive us, it tends to become a waste of resources."[4]

In a competitive economy competitors must seek to persuade customers to buy their wares. We do not live in a world where a company stocks its warehouse and waits until customers beat a path to its doors to buy its products. If this is all that a business firm did, we would have economic waste in terms of products produced but not bought as well as in the failure to produce many items for which a market can be created. In the latter case, the waste would take the form of idle labor and unused resources.

[2] Nicholas H. Kaldor, "The Economic Aspects of Advertising," *The Review of Economic Studies,* Vol. 18 (1950-51), p. 6.

[3] Joe S. Bain, *Industrial Organization* (New York: John Wiley & Sons, 1959), pp. 390-91. See also *Report of a Commission of Enquiry Into Advertising* (London, England: The Labour Party, 1966), P. 42. The Reith Report defined "substantially advertised products" at 5% or more.

[4] Richard Caves, *American Industry: Structure, Conduct, Performance* (Englewood Cliffs, New Jersey: Prentice-Hall, Inc., 1964), p. 102.

Inefficient Use of Resources

Economists have criticized advertising most vigorously as involving an inefficient use of resources. This criticism has been directed particularly against advertising where the main effect allegedly is a "shuffling of existing total demand" among the companies in an industry. Under these conditions, it is stated, advertising merely adds to total costs and in time results in higher prices. There undoubtedly is shifting of demand among firms due to many factors including advertising. But this is what we should expect in a competitive economy. Moreover, there are many products for which total demand is increased (for example, television sets, radio sets, cars, toilet articles) for multiple use in the same home. In the sharply expanding economy of the past quarter of a century there are relatively few industries in which total demand has remained unchanged.

It must also be kept in mind that the resources devoted to competitive advertising usually are considered to be wasteful "in a full-employment economy" because they may be utilized more efficiently in other ways. Thus, the extent of "waste" involved also appears to depend upon whether the economy is operating below capacity. This point is considered in a later section.

Adds to Costs

Sometimes, it is stated that if advertising succeeds in expanding total demand for a product, the result is a shift of demand from other products, the producers of which will be forced to advertise to attempt to recover their position. The net result of such "counter-advertising" is to add to costs and to prices.

But all increases in demand do not necessarily represent a diversion from other products. Thus, an expanded demand for new products is accompanied by an increase in income and in purchasing power flowing from their production. Moreover, during a period of expanding economic activity, as is noted later, the successful advertising may affect the rate of increase for different products rather than result in an absolute diversion of volume.

Creates Undesirable Wants

Another variation is the claim that advertising is wasteful because it " . . . creates useless or undesirable wants at the expense of things for which there is greater social need. When advertising makes consumers want and buy automobiles with tail fins, tobacco, and movie-star swimming pools, there is less money (fewer resources) available to improve public hospitals, build better schools, or combat juvenile delinquency."[5] It is claimed that many of these types of products are useless and anti-social. Criticism of advertising is nothing new. In the late 1920s Stuart Chase claimed: "Advertising creates no new dollars. In fact, by removing workers from productive employment, it tends to depress output, and thus lessen the number of real dollars."[6]

[5] "Advertising and Charlie Brown," *Business Review,* Federal Reserve Bank of Philadelphia (June, 1962), p. 10.

[6] Stuart Chase, *The Tragedy of Waste* (New York:Macmillan Company, 1928), p. 112.

These are value judgments reached by the critics on the basis of subjective "standards" which they set up. "What is one man's meat is another man's poison," as the old saying goes. The real question is who is to decide what is good for the consumer and what should he purchase?

In a free economy, there is a wide diversity of opinion as to what combinations of goods and services should be made available and be consumed. Obviously, tastes vary widely and most persons do not want to be told what is best for them. In any cross section of the population of the country there will be a wide disagreement as to what constitutes the ideal components of a desirable level of living. Each one of us must decide what purchases will yield the greatest satisfactions. We may be misled on occasion by popular fads, advertising, or even advice of our friends. But these decisions in the final analysis are made by the buyers and not by the advertisers, as the latter have found out so often to their regret.

Competition and "Waste"

The critics of advertising are really attacking the competitive process. Competition involves considerable duplication and "waste." The illustrations range from the several gasoline stations at an important intersection to the multiplication of research facilities, the excess industrial capacity which develops during periods of expansion, and the accumulations of excessive inventories.

There is widespread recognition that inefficiencies may develop in advertising as in other phases of business.[7] Mistakes are made in determining how much should be spent for advertising—but these mistakes can result in spending too little as well as too much.

We cannot judge the efficiency of our competitive society—including the various instrumentalities, such as advertising—by looking at the negative aspects alone. It is true that competition involves waste. But it also yields a flood of new products, improved quality, better service, and pressures on prices. In the United States, it has facilitated enormous economic growth with the accompanying high standards of living. The advantages of competition have been so overwhelmingly greater than the wastes inherent in it that we have established as one of our prime national goals, through the anti-trust laws, the continuance of a viable competitive economy.

Informational Role of Advertising

Advertising plays a major informational role in our economy because (1) products are available in such wide varieties, (2) new products are offered in such great numbers, and (3) existing products must be called to the attention of new consumers who are added to the market as a result of expansion in incomes, the population explosion, and changes in tastes.

[7] Committee on Advertising, *Principles of Advertising* (New York: Pitman Publishing Corp., 1963), p. 34; and Neil H. Borden, "The Role of Advertising in the Various Stages of Corporate and Economic Growth," Peter D. Bennett, editor, *Marketing and Economic Development* (Chicago, Illinois: American Marketing Association, 1965), p. 493.

The most heavily advertised products are widely used items that are consumed by major segments of the population. This does not mean that everyone buys every product or buys them to the extent that he can. Some of these products are substitutes for other products. For example, it will be readily recognized that cereals provide only one of many alternatives among breakfast foods. In some instances, heavily advertised products compete with each other like, for example, soft drinks and beer. In other instances, additional consumers can use the products so that the size of the total market can be increased (for example, toilet preparations).

Potential markets also expand as incomes rise and as consumers are able to purchase products they previously could not afford. As the population increases, large numbers of new potential customers are added each year. Continuous large-scale advertising provides reminders to old customers and provides information to obtain some part of the patronage of new customers. The potential market is so huge that large scale advertising is an economical way to obtain good results.

In addition, the identity of buyers changes under some circumstances and new potential buyers must be given information concerning the available alternatives. It has also been pointed out that some of these products are " . . . subject to fads and style changes" and that " . . . consumers become restive with existing brands and are prepared to try new varieties." Illustrations include cereals, soaps, clothing, and motion pictures.[8]

The consumer has a wide variety of brands from which to choose. Product improvements usually breed competitive product improvements; the advertising of these improvements may result in an increase in total advertising for the class of products.

When any company in an industry embarks on an intensified advertising campaign, its competitors must step up their advertising or other sales efforts to avoid the possible loss of market position. This is a key characteristic of competition.

On the other hand, if any company decides to economize on its advertising budget, its exposure is reduced and its share of market may decline if its competitors fail to follow the same policy. Thus, for some grocery products it has been reported that " . . . competition within a sector may have established a certain pattern with regard to the extent of advertising, and any company dropping below this level faces possible substantial loss of market share.[9]

These results flow particularly if the industry is oligopolistic, that is, has relatively few producers who are sensitive to and responsive to actions of competitors. However, as the dramatic changes in market shares during the past decade so amply demonstrate, this does not mean that the companies in such oligopolistic industries will retain relatively constant shares of the market.[10]

[8] Lester G. Telser, "How Much Does It Pay Whom To Advertise?," *American Economic Review, Papers and Proceedings* (December, 1960), pp. 203-4.

[9] National Commission on Food Marketing, *Grocery Manufacturing,* Technical Study No. 6 (Washington, D.C.: June, 1966), p. 14.

[10] Jules Backman, *Advertising and Competition* (New York: New York University Press, 1967), Chapters 3 and 4.

The informational role of advertising has been succinctly summarized by Professor George J. Stigler:

" ... Under competition, the main tasks of a seller are to inform potential buyers of his existence, his line of goods, and his prices. Since both sellers and buyers change over time (due to birth, death, migration), since people forget information once acquired, and since new products appear, the existence of sellers must be continually advertised ...
"This informational function of advertising must be emphasized because of a popular and erroneous belief that advertising consists chiefly of nonrational (emotional and repetitive) appeals."[11]

Elsewhere, Professor Stigler has pointed out that " ... information is a valuable resource," that advertising is "the obvious method of identifying buyers and sellers" which "reduces drastically the cost of search," and that "It is clearly an immensely powerful instrument for the elimination of ignorance ... "[12]

Often this information is required to create interest in and demand for a product. Thus, it has been reported:

" ... to a significant degree General Foods and the U.S. food market created each other. Before a new product appears, customers are rarely conscious of wanting it. There was no spontaneous demand for ready-to-eat cereals; frozen foods required a sustained marketing effort stretching over many years; instant coffee had been around for decades, supplying a market that did not amount to a tenth of its present level. General Foods' corporate skill consists largely in knowing enough about American tastes to foresee what products will be accepted."[13]

Similarly, J. K. Galbraith, who has been very critical of advertising, has recognized that:

A new consumer product must be introduced with a suitable advertising campaign to arouse an interest in it. The path for an expansion of output must be paved by a suitable expansion in the advertising budget. Outlays for the manufacturing of a product are not more important in the strategy of modern business enterprise than outlays for the manufacturing of demand for the product.[14]

We live in an economy that has little resemblance to the ideal of perfect competition postulated by economists. However, one of the postulates of this ideal economy is perfect knowledge. Advertising contributes to such knowledge.

---

[11] George J. Stigler, *The Theory of Price,* Third Edition (New York: The Macmillan Company, 1966), p. 200.

[12] George J. Stigler, "The Economics of Information," *The Journal of Political Economy* (June, 1961), pp. 213, 216, 220. See also S. A. Ozga, "Imperfect Markets Through Lack of Knowledge," *Quarterly Journal of Economics* (February, 1960), pp. 29, 33-34, and Wroe Alderson, *Dynamic Market Behavior* (Homewood, Illinois: Richard D. Irwin, Inc., 1965), pp. 128-31.

[13] "General Foods is Five Billion Particulars," *Fortune* (March, 1964), p. 117.

[14] J. K. Galbraith, *The Affluent Society* (Boston, Massachusetts: Houghton Mifflin Company, 1958), p. 156.

Thus, in such an idealized economy, even though advertising may be wasteful it would still have a role to play. But in the world of reality, with all its imperfections, advertising is much more important. Advertising is an integral and vital part of our growing economy and contributes to the launching of the new products so essential to economic growth.

How Much Is Informational?

In 1966, total expenditures for media advertising aggregated $13.3 billion.[15] It is impossible to determine exactly how much of this amount was strictly informational. However, the following facts are of interest.

Classified advertising was $1.3 billion.
Other local newspaper advertising, largely retail, was $2.6 billion.
Business paper advertising was $712 million.
Local radio and TV advertising was $1.1 billion.
Spot radio and spot TV advertising was $1.2 billion.
National advertising on network TV, network radio, magazines and
    newspapers was $3.7 billion.
Direct mail was $2.5 billion.

Classified advertising and local advertising are overwhelmingly informational in nature. Certainly some part of national advertising also performs this function. These figures suggest substantially less than half of total advertising is of the type that the critics are attacking as wasteful;[16] the exact amount cannot be pinpointed. Moreover, it must be kept in mind that a significant part of national advertising is for the promotion of new products for which the informational role is vital.

From another point of view, even if there is waste, the social cost is considerably less than suggested by these data. Thus, in 1966 about $10 billion was spent on advertising in newspapers, magazines, radio, and television; another $746 million was spent on farm and business publications. Without these expenditures, these sources of news and entertainment would have had to obtain substantial sums from other sources. It has been estimated that " . . . advertising paid for over 60% of the cost of periodicals, for over 70% of the cost of newspapers, and for 100% of the cost of commercial radio and TV broadcasting."[17] Thus, advertising results in a form of subsidization for all media of communication. Without it, these media would have to charge higher subscription rates or be subsidized by the government or some combination of both.

Advertising and Expanding Markets

Economic growth has become a major objective of national economic policy

[15] This total excludes a miscellaneous category of $3.3 billion.

[16] For the United Kingdom, the "disputed proportion" of advertising expenditures has been estimated at about 30% of the total. Walter Taplin, *Advertising, A New Approach* (Boston, Massachusetts: Little, Brown & Co., 1963), p. 126.

[17] Fritz Machlup, *The Production and Distribution of Knowledge in the United States* (Princeton, New Jersey: Princeton University Press, 1962), p. 265.

in recent years. Rising productivity, increasing population, improving education, rates of saving, and decisions concerning new investments are the ingredients of economic growth. In addition, there must be a favorable political climate including tax policies and monetary policies designed to release the forces conducive to growth.

Advertising contributes to economic growth and in turn levels of living by complementing the efforts to create new and improved products through expenditures for research and development. One observer has described the process as follows:

... advertising, by acquainting the consumer with the values of new products, widens the market for these products, pushes forward their acceptance by the consumer, and encourages the investment and entrepreneurship necessary for innovation. Advertising, in short, holds out the promise of a greater and speedier return than would occur without such methods, thus stimulating investment, growth, and diversity.[18]

Among the most intensive advertisers have been toilet preparations (14.7% of sales), cleaning and polishing preparations (12.6%), and drugs (9.4%). The markets for these· products have been expanding at a faster rate than all consumer spending.

Between 1947 and 1966, personal consumption expenditures for these products increased as follows:[19]

	1947	1955	1966
		(millions of dollars)	
Toilet articles & preparations	1,217	1,915	4,690
Cleaning, polishing & household supplies	1,523	2,480	4,487
Drug preparations & sundries	1,313	2,362	5,062

As a share of total personal consumption expenditures, the increases from 1947 to 1966 were as follows:

Toilet articles and preparations
from 0.76% to 1.01%
Cleaning, polishing and household
supplies from 0.94% to 0.97%
Drug preparations and sundries
from 0.82% to 1.09%

These increases in relative importance are based upon dollar totals. However, the retail prices of these products rose less than the consumer price index during the postwar years.

[18] David M. Blank, "Some Comments on the Role of Advertising in the American Economy—A Plea for Revaluation," L. George Smith, editor, *Reflections on Progress in Marketing* (Chicago, Illinois: American Marketing Association, 1964), p. 151.

[19] *The National Income and Product Accounts of the United States, 1929-1965, Statistical Tables* (Washington, D.C.: United States Department of Commerce, August, 1966), pp. 44-49: and *Survey of Current Business* (July, 1967), pp. 23-24.

Between 1947 and 1966, the price increases were as follows:

Total consumer price index	45.4%
Toilet preparations	14.6
Soaps and detergents	2.6
Drugs and prescriptions	22.8

Thus, the increase in relative importance of these highly advertised products has been even greater in real terms than in dollars.

Between 1947 and 1966, the increase in *real* personal consumption expenditures has been:

Toilet articles and preparations from 0.68% to 1.12%
Cleaning, polishing and household supplies from 0.87% to 1.05%
Drug preparations and sundries from 0.82% to 1.24%

Clearly, advertising appears to have contributed to an expansion in the demand for these products and to the growth of our economy with the accompanying expansion in job opportunities and in economic well-being. There may have been some waste in this process—although all of such expenditures cannot be characterized as wasteful—but it appears to have been offset in full or in part by these other benefits.

The charge of large-scale waste in advertising appears to reflect in part a yearning for an economy with standardized, homogeneous products which are primarily functional in nature. An illustration would be a refrigerator that is designed solely to be technically efficient for the storage of food. However, customers are also interested in the decor of their kitchens, in convenience and speed in the manufacture of ice cubes, in shelves that rotate, and in special storage for butter. These are additions to functional usefulness which "an affluent society" can afford but which a subsistence economy cannot.

Advertising in a High Level Economy

The concept of waste must be related to the level achieved by an economy. Professor John W. Lowe has observed that "Perhaps a good deal of the 'wastefulness' assigned to advertising springs from the fact that a large part of the world's population cannot consider satisfying *psychological wants* when most of their efforts must be devoted to *needs.*"[20] (Italics added.)

In a subsistence economy, scarcity is so significant that advertising might be wasteful, particularly where it diverts resources from meeting the basic necessities of life. Such an economy usually is a "full employment economy" in the sense that everyone is working. But the total yield of a full employment subsistence economy is very low, as is evident through Asia, Africa, and South America.

Professor Galbraith has noted that "The opportunity for product differentiation . . . is almost uniquely the result of opulence . . . the tendency for

[20] John W. Lowe, "An Economist Defends Advertising," *Journal of Marketing,* Vol. 27 (July, 1963), p. 18.

commercial rivalries . . . to be channeled into advertising and salesmanship would disappear in a poor community."[21]

In the high level American economy, there usually are surpluses rather than scarcity. The use of resources for advertising to differentiate products, therefore, is not necessarily a diversion from other uses. Rather, it frequently represents the use of resources that might otherwise be idle both in the short run and the long run and thus may obviate the waste that such idleness represents.

The Marketing Mix

The concept of waste cannot ignore the question—waste as compared with what alternative? Advertising cannot be considered in a vacuum. It must be considered as one of the marketing alternatives available. Generally it is not a question of advertising or nothing, but rather of advertising or some other type of sales effort.

It is a mistake to evaluate the relative cost of advertising apart from other marketing costs. It is only one tool in the marketing arsenal which also includes direct selling, packaging, servicing, product planning, pricing, etc. Expenditures for advertising often are substituted for other types of selling effort. This substitution has been readily apparent in the history of the discount house. These houses have featured well-advertised brands which were presold and, hence, virtually eliminated the need for floor stocks and reduced the need for space and many salesmen.

Advertising is undertaken where it is the most effective and most economical way to appeal to customers. It is a relatively low cost method of communicating with all potential customers and this explains its widespread adoption by many companies. To the extent that less efficient marketing methods must be substituted for advertising, we would really have economic waste.

Summary and Conclusions

There is wide agreement that the informational role of advertising makes a significant contribution to the effective operation of our economy. There is also agreement that inefficiency in the use of advertising is wasteful, as are other types of inefficiencies that are part and parcel of a market-determined economy. The gray area is so-called competitive advertising, largely national, which is the main target of those who insist advertising is wasteful. Although precise data are not available, the estimates cited earlier indicate that the charge of competitive waste applies to substantially less than half of all advertising expenditures.

Competition unavoidably involves considerable duplication and waste. If the accent is placed on the negative, a distorted picture is obtained. On balance, the advantages of competition have been much greater than the wastes.

Advertising has contributed to an expanding market for new and better products. Many of these new products would not have been brought to market

[21] John K. Galbraith, *American Capitalism: The Concept of Countervailing Power* (Boston, Massachusetts: Houghton Miflin Company, 1952), pp. 106-07.

unless firms were free to develop mass markets through large-scale advertising. There may be some waste in this process, but it has been more than offset by other benefits.

Where burgeoning advertising expenditures are accompanied by expanding industry sales, there will tend to be a decline in total unit costs instead of increase, and prices may remain unchanged or decline. In such situations, it seems clear that advertising, while adding to total costs, will result in lower total *unit* costs, the more significant figure. This gain will be offset to some extent if the increase in volume represents a diversion from other companies or industries with an accompanying rise in unit costs. Of course, such change is inherent in a dynamic competitive economy.

Advertising expenditures have risen as the economy has expanded. At such times, the absolute increase in sales resulting from higher advertising expenditures need not be accompanied by a loss in sales in other industries. This is particularly true if a new product has been developed and its sales are expanding. In that event, new jobs probably will be created and help to support a higher level of economic activity generally.

The claim that resources devoted to advertising would be utilized more efficiently for other purposes ignores the fact that generally we have a surplus economy. All of the resources used for advertising are not diverted from other alternatives. Rather, it is probable that much of the resources involved would be idle or would be used less efficiently. Even more important would be the failure to provide the jobs which expanding markets create.

Finally, advertising does not take place in a vacuum. It is one of several marketing alternatives. The abandonment of advertising could not represent a net saving to a company or to the economy. Instead, such a development would require a shift to alternative marketing techniques, some of which would be less efficient than advertising since companies do not deliberately adopt the least effective marketing approach. On balance, advertising is an invaluable competitive tool.

We do not have an adequate answer to the question, "What is the role of selling in modern marketing?" Because of the extreme flexibility and adaptability of personal selling, it is often regarded as the residual *element in the promotion or selling mix. It is necessary to take a deeper look at the role of personal selling as a prelude to developing new techniques of research and analysis to this area of marketing.*

The Role of Selling in Modern Marketing

Wendell R. Smith

The topic to which my remarks are to be addressed is perhaps better stated in the form of a question, "What is the role of selling in modern marketing?" I suggest that this is a question to which we do not have an adequate answer. However, it is a question of critical importance—a question to which an answer is urgently needed if the advancement of science in marketing is to continue in a logical and balanced way.

To put it another way, the area of *personal selling* is becoming one of the relatively dark corners in marketing. It stands in danger of being by-passed by the "new breed" of mathematical and quantitative research specialists who are bringing excitement, increased precision, and more ambitious goals into other segments of the field. Most particularly they are concerning themselves with the measurement and analysis of other ways of performing the *selling function* in marketing-advertising and some forms of sales promotion.

Let's examine some of the reasons why this is happening and review the courses of action that are available to those who feel that effective, well planned

Reprinted by permission of the author and the publisher from *Emerging Concepts in Marketing,* edited by William S. Decker (Chicago: American Marketing Association, 1962), pp. 174-178.

and organized, ethical, personal selling is worth saving, and that its future has not been pre-empted by alternative ways of getting the selling function performed. Let me hasten to add that I am not one who believes that the quantitative approach—model building, simulation techniques, and the use of computers—is going to take over. It seems clear, however, that this approach to marketing research and analysis will have a greater staying power and lasting impact upon the field than some other approaches that quickly skyrocketed into popularity by holding out false hopes to eager students, researchers, and businessmen. Now let's anticipate some semantic difficulties and get them out of the way.

As Arno Johnson has so effectively pointed out, "The coming changes in our labor force and productivity, accompanied by economic and social changes in the next ten years, will make the role of selling and advertising assume increasing importance in our economy." I think we will all agree that the *selling function* in marketing includes personal selling, advertising, sales promotion and related activity. Selling, or more properly *personal selling,* is concerned with direct, person-to-person persuasive communication. While this aspect of marketing is the oldest form of selling, its scientific content and development has lagged materially behind that of the newer, more impersonal ways of communicating persuasively with the market.

It overstates the case but slightly to conclude that marketing men have become preoccupied with increasing effectiveness in the management of *things* as opposed to the management of *people* or the human element involved in performance of the selling function.

As some of the people with whom I have discussed this matter put it, we have experienced a tremendous improvement in the development of education and training for the management of aspects of marketing other than personal selling. Much has been done in the development of research and advisory techniques designed to help managers of marketing make decisions with more confidence because they are based on better accumulations and analyses of facts. The danger implicit in this situation has been the temptation to emphasize education for staff activities as contrasted with line activities. As a result, personal selling has suffered. However, the future looks brighter by virtue of the fact that formal and specific attention is now being paid to the process of decision-making itself which is the essence of line activity and responsibility.

In my opinion, there are two major reasons why the "new breed" has deemed the personal selling area as less appropriate for the application of their techniques.

1. Because of the extreme flexibility and adaptability of personal selling effort, it is often regarded as the *residual* element in the promotional or selling mix. As a result of the greater ability and tendency of managers of advertising to develop specific plans and programs for the future, personal selling often comes to be regarded as the dependent variable. Admittedly, this generalization is dangerous because the relative rigidity or flexibility of the personal selling element of a marketing program varies significantly from product class to product class and even from company to company. Suffice it to say that

newcomers to the field often interpret this residual status assigned to personal selling by management as an indication of relative weakness and unimportance.

2. For one reason or another, personal selling or *salesmanship* has not been too successful in establishing for itself a clearly defined role in the marketing curricula of schools of business. It is no secret that courses in salesmanship have all but disappeared from the offerings of many schools. In other institutions, they are little respected by the academic community and this lack of respect extends to some segments of the business community. The subject matter of many such courses lacked intellectual excitement from the point of view of students and faculty alike because they frequently attempted to do in the classroom what is better done on the job, while neglecting the rationale of selling and the 'why' of activities associated with it. At the other end of the continuum, some courses in sales management became so broad and inclusive that only a title change was necessary to follow the trend toward emphasis on the broader area of *marketing management*. An unfilled gap was thus created.

We should also admit that while marketing as an entity has had considerable difficulty in establishing itself as a candidate for designation as a science, the difficulty has been overwhelming in connection with selling. The roots of this are to be found deeply imbedded in the high-pressure selling tactics of the twenties. It appears that these activities occurred, not because marketing men thought this was the way to do the job, but because of inept production and general management that brought to the market unwanted or relatively undesired goods that had to be pushed through the channels of distribution if they were to be sold at all. In retrospect, this chastening experience was good for marketing in that it made crystal clear the role that marketing should assume in product planning and product development activities. However, it made personal selling or salesmanship the leading candidate for the role of "whipping boy."

Thus far I have been negative and critical of the way in which academicians and practitioners alike have responded to the continuing challenge of personal persuasive communication as an essential and productive marketing activity. I plead guilty to doing this as a means of preparing the ground for offering some constructive suggestions regarding the future.

There is an obvious case to be made for the re-establishment of personal selling as a full-ranking member of the family of activities that in total comprise the whole of marketing. Just as physical distribution has re-entered the spotlight by means of solid accomplishment in the application of new and more sophisticated techniques of inventory control and determining the logistics of product movement, a similar opportunity exists in the personal selling area. Even the most ardent critics of personal selling as we have known it in the past must concede that persuasive communication on a personal basis is essential as a catalyst to the process by means of which our productive capabilities can be translated into an improved standard of living and a more predictable and smoothly operating economic system. One needs only to look at many of the areas of industrial marketing to recognize the substantial payoff that can result from carefully planned and administered use of salesmen to accomplish sales, service, and two-way communication objectives. Substantial progress is observable in other areas of our economy. The selling of life insurance, for example, has made substantial progress as evidenced by its increased effectiveness, its increased acceptability to the general public, and its ability to attract able people. Much can be learned, too, from advertising's current response to criticism evidenced by the high level of interest in measurements of effectiveness as a step toward increased accountability to management.

It is now both feasible and necessary to take a more intensive look at the personal selling function in marketing: *feasible* because needed techniques and tools of investigation are now available, *necessary* because of a need to break with the past and to define and orient the activity anew within the context of an emerging science of marketing. What are the steps that will be necessary to attain this deeper understanding?

1. First it will be necessary to look at personal selling, not as a discrete activity, but as a part of a system by means of which the marketing job is accomplished. This spotlights the all-important allocation decision that commits the marketer to a specific mix of personal selling, advertising, and promotional effort. Put another way, it is imperative to discover, as a starting point, the irreducible minimum role of persuasive personal communication, taking fully into account the developments and advances that have been made in the impersonal methods of selling that have developed. It is unrealistic to assume that the role of personal selling can or should continue unchanged by technological progress. Just as the work of the agricultural segment of the economy is currently accomplished with a substantially lower human involvement than ever before, it is obvious that the substitution of capital for labor in the supermarket and similar developments will have an impact upon both the kind and quantity of personal selling required. While it was once reasonably correct to think of people employed in retailing as being primarily engaged in personal selling, this does not appear to be true today. It is imperative, then, to find and identify the hard core areas where personal selling does now and may be expected to continue to bear responsibility of such magnitude as to offer both challenge and opportunity to people professionally trained for the job. We need to do some market research to identify those situations where the need for tailored, personal selling is both substantial and rewarding.

2. Then we must review the exciting new developments in marketing, in the other business disciplines, and in the behavioral sciences for the purpose of developing an understanding of the task that can be performed by personal selling and discovering a technology that will enable this job to be performed in the most efficient and effective way. In this connection we may have to part with the very comfortable notion that "experience is the best teacher." It is well within the realm of feasibility that what is now going on in the development of search theory, decision theory, organization theory, game theory, and in other areas may have applicability to the selling situation.

The salesman today is a new kind of man doing a new kind of job. He no longer merely drums a particular product but helps tailor merchandise to the customer's desire, aids in promoting it, assures its delivery and proper use. He knows more about the customer's needs and his own company's best interests.

The Salesman Isn't Dead—He's Different

Carl Rieser

There is no more abused figure in American life than the salesman. One group of critics scorns him for certain qualities that another group sneers at him for losing. To many novelists, playwrights, sociologists, college students, and many others, he is aggressively forcing on people goods that they don't want. He is the drummer, with a dubious set of social values—Willy Loman in the Arthur Miller play. The second group of critics, which includes the Secretary of Commerce and many business executives all over the U.S., charges the salesman with lacking good, old-fashioned, hard-hitting salesmanship. He was spoiled by the postwar days when competition was easy. If only he would get up off his duff, and get out and *sell,* the goods would move and business would be in fine shape.

Both sets of critics are swatting at a target that doesn't matter much any more. The plain fact is that, as one Boston sales executive recently said, "The old drummer type of salesman has gone by the board." Nor are his talents especially needed in today's economy. To be sure, there are plenty of aggressive, hard-hitting salesmen still around, and there will always be a place for their brand of selling. But this kind of man is no longer the archetype.

From bits and pieces of evidence in all sectors of U.S. business, it is now possible to discern the emergence of a new dominant type, a man with a softer touch and greater breadth, a new kind of man to do a new—much more

Reprinted by permission of the publisher from *Fortune* Magazine, Vol. 66 (November, 1962), pp. 124 ff.

significant—kind of job. Whereas the old-time salesman devoted himself primarily to pushing a product, or a line of products, the new-era salesman is involved with the whole distribution pipeline, beginning with the tailoring of products to the customer's desire and extending through their promotion and advertising to final delivery to the ultimate consumer.

The salesman has been cast in his new role by "the marketing concept," a term that originated at General Electric around 1950 and has gained wide currency recently. It means essentially that companies are orienting their organization and effort toward the market, toward the ever changing needs of the customer, and the ever shifting calculations of their own production costs and opportunities. The emphasis is less concentrated on the isolated point-of-sale; it is spread forward, into the buyer's operations, and backward into the seller's operations. The profound consequences of this trend have been suggested by Orm Henning, marketing manager of industrial products at Texas Instruments:

"One should remind oneself that selling is only part of marketing—particularly in the scientific-industrial world. Marketing is communicating back to your factory your individual customer's needs and particular problems. When you realize and practice this, you open an entirely new vista in the area of sales. You cannot afford to sell a product, a static product—not in our business."

And what's true today in the electronics business—and many others—is going to be true of more and more businesses tomorrow.

The great change in selling affects practically all industries and all kinds of goods, whether they are what the marketing profession calls "pull-through" or "push-through" products. Pull-through refers generally to mass-produced consumer items, where a sort of siphon is already working. Pull-through products and services are pre-sold by the manufacturer to the final consumer by mass advertising and promotion, which in effect creates a demand that almost literally pulls the goods through the distribution pipeline. Push-through products are wholly new consumer goods for which the siphon has not yet begun to work or, more commonly, they are industrial materials and equipment. Since the latter are usually highly technical in nature, they must be explained to the buyer and they require more personal selling so as to generate in the buyer the idea that he needs the product.

The distinction between pull-through and push-through is becoming less important. The retailer now stocks Kleenex tissues, for example, because he is persuaded that Kimberly-Clark Corp. will maintain public recognition of the brand and will see to it that thousands of boxes are siphoned rapidly and profitably right through his warehouse and off his store shelves. The job of the Kimberly-Clark salesman is to service the account so that the buyer will keep buying. He expedites and consolidates the shipments, keeps track of the retailer's inventory, sees that the goods get the greatest display and promotion possible, keeps himself available in case of any trouble or emergency. The job of the man who sells computers is much the same. The computer is one element in a whole system of mechanical devices and programing techniques, which is sold on the basis of what the customer is persuaded it can do for him.

The salesman's responsibility becomes greater as technology advances and producers offer products of ever mounting complexity. "We are tending toward the marketing of systems and services," says James Jewell, marketing vice president of Westinghouse. "The customers want to buy greater production—not equipment. We take the full responsibility for engineering and installing, and we are moving further into servicing."

This orientation toward the customer's needs is pointed up in a recent book that has received wide attention in the trade—*Innovation in Marketing,* by Theodore Levitt, a management consultant and a member of the faculty of Harvard Business School. Levitt, who speaks for a new generation of believers in "the marketing concept," states flatly that "a strictly sales-oriented approach to doing business can be suicidal. The difference between selling and marketing is more than semantic. Selling focuses on the needs of the seller, marketing on the needs of the buyer. Selling is preoccupied with the seller's need to convert his product or service into cash; marketing with the idea of satisfying the needs of the customer by means of the product or service and by the whole cluster of customer-getting value satisfactions associated with creating, delivering, and finally consuming it."

In this quotation Levitt seems to be oversimplifying the contrast between selling and marketing. Any implication that "the marketing concept" isn't motivated by the seller's desire for profits is, of course, mistaken. While his motives remain the same, the seller now sees marketing as a more elaborate link between production and consumption, a link that has to be carefully constructed and maintained.

Two situations may illustrate the change. In the past, a factory would over-produce the market and unload on the sales force the responsibility for un-loading the goods on the customers. In the other situation, the salesmen kept their volume up by selling those products in their line that were easiest to sell—even those that were the least profitable. The incidence of both these cases tends to be diminished by the new trend with its more delicate alignment of markets and production, and its careful analysis of product profitability. The salesman is less often stuck with the necessity of a fast, hard sell. But he is steadily pressed to make the sales where the profit lies. Altogether, the marketing concept has played a vital role in developing the enormous velocity in the flow of goods, a phenomenon that has been described earlier in this series as the "short-order economy" (Fortune, August, 1962).

The Mirror of the Markets

There is little doubt that the impact of "the marketing concept" has reduced the stature of the sales manager in sources of companies. He has lost his former autonomy and now reports to the marketing vice president rather than directly to the president. He has less say over such vital matters as pricing and credit policies. The sales force must fit its work into an over-all corporation marketing policy. Furthermore, over the decade, the autonomy of the sales manager has been further trimmed in many companies by the creation of the job of product manager, who has both line and staff authority for a given product or group of products and coordinates production with advertising, research, and field selling.

The marketing concept has had very decided and significant structural effects on sales forces. This can be seen very clearly at General Electric, father of the marketing concept. G.E.'s salesmen used to be essentially product specialists, each selling only the line of a specific manufacturing department, even though it went into a variety of markets. It took time for G.E. to orient its sales forces toward markets rather than products, but this process finally began seven years ago in the company's electrical-apparatus business. Instead of specializing in one product, e.g., cord sets, fan motors, push buttons, the salesman began selling a whole group of products to a particular market—for example, the air-conditioning industry. Early this year more than a dozen separate departments selling G.E.'s biggest single customer, the government, were reorganized into one defense sales force. In other words, instead of being product-oriented, the sales organizations have become "mirrors" of the markets G.E. serves.

Recently, Westinghouse reorganized its entire 13,600-man field sales organization along somewhat similar lines, in accord with what the company calls the "province concept." The company wants to be represented wherever possible by a "Mr. Westinghouse" rather than by a confusing bevy of different salesmen from various production divisions. (Significantly, in reorganizing, Westinghouse also seized the opportunity to put more salesmen in jobs where they actually meet customers and eliminated virtually an entire "staff" layer of some 104 sales managers who never called on customers.)

The same kind of reorganization has gone on in scores of companies in such diverse fields as motor trucks and optical equipment. At American Optical Co., for example, salesmen who used to be product specialists now sell a line that includes every piece of furniture and equipment for the doctor's office, from lenses to tables.

Thus the kind of man needed for this new kind of sales job has to be a generalist. The trend is away from the "sales engineer," the technically trained salesman, of a few years ago. His successor is a man capable of absorbing stacks of information churned out by the marketing department, and of applying it to his customers' problems. He goes forth armed with a tremendous amount of data on his customers' needs, their products, their corporate organizations, and their supply and delivery schedules.

He is also a man with more executive ability than the salesman of yesterday. A Boston sales manager describes the new salesmen as simply "businessmen who travel." One Milwaukee executive notes that increasingly the new salesman is being given the authority and stature to make important decisions in the field without having to go back to corporate headquarters for an O.K. General Foods has adopted a new title of prestige for its senior salesmen, each of whom lives with one food-chain customer and attends to its needs. They are called "account executives" and they command the services of junior salesmen, who do the routine housekeeping chores of servicing the customers' stores.

In the new order of things there is obviously still a need for hard-selling, aggressive salesmen to open up new accounts, to introduce new and untried products, to sell the wares of new companies that have no national reputation. Since the service-oriented sales staff has turned away from this kind of pioneering effort, the door has been opened to a new kind of pioneering effort, the door has been opened to a new kind of specialist, typified by a New York firm called the George N. Kahn Co. This company provides a crew of highly aggressive young salesmen who open up new territories for companies that don't want to retrain their own sales forces for such sporadically necessary missions. (Kahn is not a manufacturer's representative; it works on a flat-fee basis rather than a commission and, after pioneering the sale of a product, expects that the manufacturer will take it back for handling by his own sales staff.) There is now some thought in the top management of a number of companies that the way to deal with this basic problem is to set up special sections of sales staffs with the specific function of going after new business. Thus what has been commonly thought of as the primary function of all salesmen is now becoming the specialty of a few.

The Service Troops

The new salesman has a tremendous advantage over his predecessors. Not only does he have access to much more information about his customers, but he is also backed up by formidable technical and other kinds of assistance. For example, in reshaping its inorganic-chemical sales recently, FMC Corp. (formerly Food Machinery & Chemical Corp.) has beefed up the number of its technical people directly behind the salesmen by some 20 per cent. The present ratio: one technical man to every four salesmen. The great pioneer in this development was du Pont, which years ago saw the close connection between selling and customer service: Today, at Chestnut Run, outside Wilmington, du Pont has an impressive $20-million, campus-like complex of laboratories and workshops, employing 1,700 scientists, technicians, and others devoted to providing sales literature, solving technical problems, providing all kinds of services for customers or potential buyers of du Pont products, and otherwise aiding the sales effort. Companies selling all kinds of goods have developed similar assistance, though, naturally, the more complex the technology, the more elaborate the technical backup.

The development of sophisticated electronic data-processing systems, which was described earlier in this series, is revolutionizing inventory handling, ordering, warehousing, and other physical aspects of marketing. This, in turn, relieves the salesman of a great deal of detail that used to absorb valuable hours of his time—writing up orders and reports, checking whether goods are available and how soon they can be delivered, and performing other niggling drudgery.

At the same time, the computer also introduces an element of impersonality in the relations between a seller and a buyer. Much of today's ordering of goods and materials, from packaged foods to industrial chemicals, is done, as it were, by a computer, which tells the buyer when to reorder; the transaction is handled routinely and a salesman never enters into it. This disencumbering of the salesman releases him to function on a new level of performance, to use his time more creatively. At Allis-Chalmers, which has just set up a department of marketing, an executive says, "Now our salespeople won't get bogged down in a lot of detail that goes hand in hand with selling, like the preparation of presentations, charts, convention exhibits, and whatnot. We'll do all the work, including the training of salesmen, in cooperation with company divisons."

"You lose one of the big babies. . ."

The rise of the new salesman is the result of changes in the marketplace that have drastically altered the relationship of buyer to seller. One of the most significant developments has been the growing importance of the big customer. In almost every line of business, fewer and bigger customers are responsible for an increasingly large part of any given company's sales. Twenty-five years ago, when independent grocers were an important factor in food retailing, food processors did the bulk of their business with thousands upon thousands of chains and stores. Today, with the concentration of business in the hands of a relatively few big chains, some 300 buying offices throughout the U.S. account for 80 per cent of all good bought at wholesale. Preoccupation with the "key customer" affects every industry, from steel to office supplies. Sighs an officer of the Acme Chemical Co. in Milwaukee, "You lose one of the big babies and you're in trouble."

This whole trend is building up momentum as smaller buyers band together to increase their purchasing power and efficiency by buying cooperatively. It affects suppliers of school equipment, for example, because schools are consolidating on a county basis. Independent hardware stores and even hospitals are doing it.

How this has affected the food business has been fully explored in a new book with a provocative title, *The Vanishing Salesman,* by E. B. Weiss, a New York marketing specialist in the consumer-goods field. Actually, Weiss does not believe that the salesman is vanishing; his point is that the shift to the service-oriented sales function has so greatly altered the nature of personal selling that companies are faced with entirely new conditions in the hiring, training, and organization of salesmen. Weiss also notes that as retail food chains have become bigger and bigger, and their purchases have reached stupendous volume, the position of the individual buyer, once regarded as the salesman's opposite number, has greatly diminished. The buyer in a food chain used to be an important figure; he made the decisions on what the chain was going to buy. Now his power has been usurped by buying committees. The buyer has become merely a technician who interviews the salesmen from the food processor and passes on his findings to his superiors. Says Weiss: "Members of the buying committee tend not to be buying specialists. Moreover, they make decisions covering the entire range of merchandise inventoried by the organization. Since they tend to be at executive levels considerably higher than that of the buyer who appears before them, they are more apt to depend on their own judgment than that of the buyer. And, by the same token, the buyer is not apt to put up much of a battle . . . In buying committee sessions, it is presumably the majority that rules. But since it is traditional in large organizations for so many committee members to vote with the head of the table, the majority rule prevails more in theory than in fact."

So the man that the seller must get to is the man at the head of the table. And this is true not only in the food field. Throughout U.S. industry, key buying power has steadily risen up through the corporate structure to higher echelons of authority. In industrial selling, an increasing number of purchasing decisions tend to involve bigger and bigger outlays of capital. In large part this is the result of the rise of what is now commonly called *systems selling*. Instead of buying components from many suppliers, a company often buys a whole integrated system, be it a system for heating and air conditioning, protecting a plant from theft and fire, automating a production line, or handling materials. As technology becomes more complex, users, intent on eliminating technical headaches, are ever more anxious to buy such systems, while suppliers, intent on greater profit, are ever more anxious to design and sell a whole package. Naturally, the final approval for such an expenditure or commitment moves up the line, from the plant superintendent or manager, to the corporate controller or treasurer, perhaps all the way to the president or board chairman.

"The President's Project"

Not only has this created the need for salesmen with sufficient stature to talk to the customer's top management, but it has also drawn top executives more directly into the selling act. In company after company, higher officials now make a very determined effort to get out in the field and call on the big customers, and even to do considerable pioneer work with potential customers. This kind of thing, of course, is not new. Many companies were built by star salesmen at the top, a very good example being the late Thomas J. Watson Sr. at I.B.M. ("What my father used to do when people began to talk about the great complexity of the products," says Tom Watson Jr., the present head of the company, "would be to sweep his hand and say, 'It's all so simple. All it does is add, subtract, and multiply!'") And in industries where enormous capital investment is required, such as the utility business, intimate and continued contact between seller and buyer at a high level has always been important. But now personal selling by top executives is becoming much more common. Raytheon, for example, has divided up its list of big customers among managers and officers of the company, and assigned each the responsibility of keeping in touch with a few accounts, with a view to bolstering the salesman's efforts.

General Foods was one of the pioneers in this. When Charles Mortimer was president of the company, he started "The President's Project," a series of meetings with customers all over the country. "In the beginning the meetings started out 100 per cent social," explains Wayne Marks, now president of the company. "They were strictly for pleasure—and we invited more than one customer to a meeting. But we found that nothing *happened*. Except that we got acquainted. We didn't find out what to improve in our business operation. So the format was quickly changed."

Now Marks's office sets up his customer-visiting schedule at least a month in advance. The customer is requested to have all his key people at the meeting, and several weeks before the encounter, G.F. sends along a "questionnaire" to elicit comments on G.F.'s performance and suggestions for items to discuss. In the past eighteen months Marks, accompanied by a team of executives and salesmen, has visited fifty-four customers throughout the U.S.

Marks has found the customers "avid" for this kind of contact. Not only does G.F. come out of these encounters (some of them lasting for five or six hours over dinner and drinks) with a fuller idea of what it should be doing—but the customers learn a great deal about their own organizations that they weren't aware of. Says Marks: "Many a meeting, at the end of the boss man will say, 'Why don't *we* go out and find out what's happening in our own stores?' At the end of a recent meeting the top man told me, 'I've been frank with you and told you what I don't like about your operations. Would you be willing to report back to us on what you think of us?' "

The "Sellingest" Firm

Personal selling is now a company-wide endeavor, and the contact with the customer takes place at many levels in an organized, formal way. The best illustration of how this has changed fundamentally the relations between buyer and seller is offered by National Cash Register, long known as perhaps the "sellingest" firm in the country. N.C.R.'s founder, the late John H. Patterson, has been called the father of many of the standard techniques of modern selling. He established the first formal training courses for salesmen, the first yearly sales quotas, the first guaranteed sales territories for salesmen, the first annual sales convention. Patterson's earlier sales methods were comparatively crude; cash registers were sold to storekeepers by appealing to their fear that dishonest clerks were pocketing money out of the till. But over the years the company refined its appeals, and forty years ago, when it began selling accounting machines, it even evolved a primitive kind of systems selling. But its big leap came about five years ago when the company introduced, somewhat belatedly as compared with the competition, its first electronic computer.

N.C.R. had to set up a whole new sales force for the computer, and in doing so it made a profound discovery: it was not easy to make a salesman of accounting machinery into a computer salesman. Says one N.C.R. senior salesman: "It was the death of salesmen like Willy Loman. At N.C.R. a few were left behind. They couldn't make the switch. It wasn't that they were too old—some were in their forties. But men's intellectual capabilities get set at various ages, and some *were* too old at that age." The company also found that it had to alter its time-honored compensation system. Normally, the N.C.R. salesman collects an advance that is charged against the commission he makes on his sales. Says marketing director Harry Keesecker, "Computer selling is still incentive selling, but due to the kind of product—sometimes the long time between sales—we have to compensate the salesmen by salary plus commission."

At the same time N.C.R. set up an elaborate organization to give the salesmen technical support. This now includes 325 mathematicians and technical people; the number has doubled in size in the past twelve months. They develop manuals and presentations, help the customer define his problems, train his computer operators for him, set up his E.D.P. system, and produce the programming for it. The support organization also trains the computer salesman, a departure for N.C.R., which years ago built its whole sales-training program around the use of experienced salesmen, borrowed from the field, as instructors. (The total computer sales and support staff numbers about 500 people, as against 2,100 in accounting machines, but the company is supplementing the small computer force by training as many of the accounting-machine men as possible to sell both kinds of equipment.)

The Willy Lomans Are No Longer Feasible

The difference between the old and new eras at N.C.R.—and in salesmanship in general—is dramatically illustrated by the story of how the company landed a rather sensational contract for the sale of a computer to the Dime Savings Bank of Brooklyn, New York, the country's second-largest mutual savings bank. The bank and the company had long-standing ties dating back to 1929, when the Dime bought its first N.C.R. posting machines for the tellers' windows. In subsequent decades the bank bought other N.C.R. equipment. In those years the chief link between the two was an N.C.R. salesman, Anthony de Florio, now district manager of sales for accounting and computer systems, and Karl Stad, who is now vice president of methods and systems at the Dime. The relationship was a cordial one, and N.C.R., which is mainly known for its experience in retailing and banking, was solidly in with the Dime.

In the late 1950's, however, there was a sudden change in the old easygoing ways. The bank decided, in 1957, that it was time to think about tying its entire bookkeeping operations into a computer to keep up with its bounding growth, and Stad was told to set up a task force to study the entire field and to recommend the "ideal" system. De Florio observes, "This was the beginning of group selling. The salesman had to understand the problems and systems of the customer. The staff at the bank had to define what was required. And we at N.C.R. had to be sure that the bank wasn't running away from us in know-how." (To N.C.R., as to many another company, the growing sophistication of the buyer has become an important factor to reckon with.) N.C.R. also had to reckon with competition; every other computer manufacturer came in for the kill at Dime. For the next two years Stad and his team studied the field and enlarged their expertise. By 1959 they had winnowed the choice down to four systems, including N.C.R.'s, and asked the competitors for feasibility studies. (Says de Florio: "By the time you get to feasibility studies, the Willy Lomans are no longer feasible.")

Now the contacts between the company and the bank multiplied. N.C.R. sent teams of technical people from Dayton headquarters to confer with Stad—they submitted a technical proposal two inches thick—and Stad went out to Dayton to talk to N.C.R.'s research people. He was put up at N.C.R.'s plush Moraine

Farm, the estate of a former board chairman, which the company now uses to entertain groups of customers and potential customers. (Like du Pont and other companies, N.C.R. uses its factories and laboratories as a sales showcase.) By the end of 1959, Stad decided that N.C.R.'s 304 computer, then just being delivered to the first purchasers, was the one for the Dime.

Thereupon the Dime's board of trustees decided that Stad's decision ought to be second-guessed by an independent consultant in the electronic data-processing field. This, of course, opened up the whole matter again, and brought the competitors back in. Fortunately for N.C.R., the consultant confirmed the decision, and the affair between the bank and the company again resumed, in a deliberate and measured way. The Dime's board selected a committee of three trustees to study the proposal. They went out to Dayton—staying at an even more posh N.C.R. guest house, the old home of Orville Wright—and they talked with everyone from technicians to N.C.R.'s president, R. S. Oelman, and its then board chairman, S. C. Allyn. On the way back in the plane, the trustees decided to sign with N.C.R. It was an $800,000 decision, and it was a key one not only to the bank but to N.C.R., which closed some other bank contracts on the strength of the Dime's decision.

N.C.R. was in the middle of a training program for the Dime's employees when, early in 1960, a crisis arose. N.C.R.'s technicians reached the chilling conclusion that the 304 computer would not have the capacity to do what the Dime eventually would require—i.e., a direct linkage from the posting machines at the tellers' windows to the computer without the intermediate use of tabulating equipment. The next model in the design stage, the 315 random-access computer, would do the job—but not the 304. De Florio had to come clean with the bank. "I called up Karl and said, 'Let's have lunch at the Brooklyn Club,' " recalls de Florio, still wincing at the ensuing conversation. De Florio offered to tear up the contract for the 304. The Dime's board accepted the proposal, and the whole computer question was back in the soup again.

Rival manufacturers had another chance to make presentations, and N.C.R. had to start all over again selling its 315 model, then two years from delivery. De Florio kept pounding on one main point: the bank already was using N.C.R. machines at its windows, and any company that finally got the computer contract would have to tie in to N.C.R.'s equipment. In the end the argument prevailed; Stad recommended the 315 computer on the grounds that it would be "just as good" as other computers—though no better—and that N.C.R. had "window experience." Along with the computer, the bank also agreed to use other N.C.R. equipment in its integrated system, so the total package came to $2 million. Says de Florio, looking back on the whole transaction, "In this kind of selling you can't see everything you buy. A lot has to be bought on faith. Therefore a company likes to work with big companies. Come hell or high water, they have to deliver."

One of N.C.R.'s brightest and most successful young computer salesmen recently expanded this doctrine. "A salesman is important," he remarked, "because the policy makers today come from a previous generation of doing business. They don't have the technical equipment necessary to make a decision about a computer that requires technical sophistication. So the salesman has to take the language of the computer man and turn it into language his customer understands. I used to think that those decisions would be made on a scientific basis—but it's a gross act of faith." The salesman's job, he said, is "to create an environment in which an act of faith can take place."

The "Foot Soldiers" Need Upgrading

There is doubtless still plenty of faith in sales transactions. But as the Dime Savings Bank affair shows, there is a great deal more. And this is the fact that salesmen do not seem to realize when they talk about their jobs. They are still trained to have a kind of emotionalism about their craft, and they carry with them a heavy load of outworn notions about their role. They view selling as both warfare and love, hostility and benevolence. They see themselves as "the men on the firing line," and "the foot soldiers of democracy." The combative nature of selling is stressed in almost every book on the subject, as in one of the most famous and widely sold of all books on selling, *Open the Mind and Close the Sale,* by John M. Wilson, who recently retired as N.C.R.'s sales manager. Wilson speaks of the "tension in every buyer-seller reationship," of the "challenge" in each encounter, of the need for "handling" the customer—though, of course, "in the way he wants to be handled."

This lag in the recognition of what has happened to selling is harmful, because the sales profession is still held in low esteem by the public. Just how low was indicated recently in a survey by *Sales Management* magazine of college students and their attitude toward selling. Selling ranked a very poor fourth, after teaching, law, and medicine, as a choice for a career. Only 6 per cent of the students favored it. (Of seventy-one students whose fathers are in sales, only *five* wanted to go into selling.)

The students did not particularly object to the working conditions in selling; relatively few said they were put off by too much traveling, for example. Nor did many feel that the financial reward was inadequate. The chief objections to a selling career (some even denied that selling *is* a career) were these: "I don't want to force people to buy things they don't need." "Job security is poor." "I'm not extrovert enough." "Selling has no prestige."

One student unwittingly put his finger on the ironic predicament business faces. He remarked that selling simply does not require "a college education or intelligence." The main feature of the new kind of personal selling, of course, is that it does require men who are able and intelligent; the new salesmen, quite obviously, must be recruited from among the better college graduates. But how are they going to be recruited if the better college graduates think selling is beneath them? The experience of Scott Paper illustrates the difficulties business has in luring these men into selling. The company prides itself on the fact that 95 percent of its sales staff are college graduates. Each year, to keep the staff replenished, it interviews some 2,000 students, invites about 100 of these men to visit its Philadelphia headquarters, makes offers to about seventy-five—and lands thirty-five or forty of them.

The trouble is that business has signally failed to get across the idea that there has been a tremendous change in selling. (The *Sales Management* poll shows that this generation of students has not grasped one of the simplest and most fundamental changes—i.e., that by and large salesmen are no longer paid on commission but are salaried.) Business has a massive educational job to do. Perhaps as a start it might throw a lot of the old inspirational literature on selling and let the facts of the new situation do the inspiring.

The author contends that the discrepancy between economic theory and actual pricing policies of business firms is more apparent than real. He argues that current pricing practices are consistent with the general theory of monopolistic competition and that most "price policies" described by students of marketing are merely special cases of the theory of monopolistic competition.

Price Policies and Theory

Edward R. Hawkins

Although the theory of monopolistic competition is now over thirty years old it remains virtually unused by marketing students, even those who are attempting to develop theory in marketing. In particular, "marketing price policies" are still treated as though they have no relation to economic theory of any sort. In the leading marketing text books there are sections describing such pricing policies as "odd prices," "customary prices," "price lining," "psychological prices," etc. [1] These are presented as descriptions of market behavior, presumably discovered by marketing specialists and unknown to economists. Even the one marketing text that explains the basic pricing formula

Reprinted by permission of the publisher from the *Journal of Marketing,* published by the American Marketing Association, Vol. 18, No. 3 (January, 1954), pp. 233-240.

[1] R.S. Vaile, E.T. Grether, and Reavis Cox, *Marketing in the American Economy* (New York: Ronald Press, 1952), ch. 22; E.A. Duddy and D.A. Revzan, *Marketing* (New York: McGraw-Hill, 2nd ed. 1953), ch. 29; P.D. Converse, H.W. Huegy, and R.V. Mitchell *Elements of Marketing* (New York: Prentice-Hall, 5th ed. 1952) ch. 10; H.H. Maynard and T.N. Beckman *Principals of Marketing* (New York: Ronald Press 5th ed. 1952) ch. 35, 36; R.S. Alexander, F.M. Surface, R.E. Elder, and Wroe Alderson, *Marketing* (Boston: Ginn & Co., 1940) ch 16. Since these policies are fully described in marketing texts the explanation of them in this article will be brief. The attempt, rather, is to express the policies in terms of demand curves in order that the relationship to the theory of monopolistic competition may be seen.

under conditions of monopolistic competition fails to use it in the discussion of price policies. [2] Since text book writers treat the subject in this way it is not surprising that practitioners writing on pricing do not attempt to relate their policies to economic theory. [3]

It is the purpose of this article to show that these price policies are special cases of the general theory of monopolistic competition. Perhaps clarification of this point will serve to narrow the gap between the economic and marketing conceptions of price policies in marketing literature.

The thesis is that each of the familiar price policies represents an estimate of the nature of the demand curve facing the seller. It is not possible, on the basis of available evidence, to generalize on the validity of these estimates in various situations. The point merely is that a seller using one of these policies is implicitly assuming a particular demand curve. In the following sections various price policies are discussed in these terms, after a brief review of the general theory of pricing which is basic to all of the policies discussed.

The General Theory of Pricing

The theory of correct pricing under conditions of monopolistic competition, as developed by Chamberlin and Robinson is illustrated in Figure 1. Each seller with some degree of monoploy created by product differentiation has his own negatively-inclined average revenue curve, AR. From this he derives the marginal revenue curve, MR, and determines his price by the intersection of MR and MC, his marginal cost. Marginal cost can be derived from either average cost, AC, or average variable cost, AVC, since it would be the same in either case. In practical terms this means that for correct pricing the seller does not need to allocate overhead cost to individual items. For that matter, he does not even need to compute MR and MC, for the same correct price can be derived from AR and AVC by maximizing the total of the spread between them multiplied by the volume.

An alternative solution which may be more understandable to business men can be obtained from break-even charts. The customary break-even chart is deficient for pricing purposes because it is based on only one price and reveals nothing but the quantity that would have to be sold at that price in order to break even. A modification can be devised that remedies this shortcoming of the break-even chart, and even has some advantages over the MC-MR formula. Figure 2 shows such a chart, in which a number of different total revenue (TR) curves are drawn, indicating the total volumes at different prices. On each such TR curve a point can be estimated showing the sales volume that would actually be obtained at that price. If these points are connected a type of demand curve results (DD'), indicating total revenue rather than average revenue as in the usual

---

[2] Charles F. Phillips and Delbert J. Duncan, *Marketing, Principles and Methods* (Chicago: Richard D. Irwin, Inc., rev. ed. 1952), ch. 29, 30, 31.

[3] For example, Oswald Knauth, "Considerations in the Setting of Retail Prices," *Journal of Marketing,* v. XIV, no. 1, July 1949, pp. 1-12; Q. Forrest Walker, "Some Principles of Department Store Pricing." *Journal of Marketing.* XIV no. 4, April 1950, pp. 529-537.

demand curve.[4] The objective of correct pricing is to maximize the vertical distance between DD' and the TC (total cost) curve. This formulation has an advantage over the MC-MR one in that in addition to indicating the correct price and volume it also shows total cost, total revenue, and total net profit. It may also be more acceptable to business men and engineers who are accustomed to break-even charts.

In the following discussion of marketing price policies, however, the AR curve will be used because it more clearly illustrates the points made.

Marketing Price Policies

Odd Prices

The term "odd prices" is used in two ways in marketing literature; one refers to a price ending in an odd number, while the other means a price just under a round number. If a seller sets his prices according to the first concept it means that he believes his AR curve is like the one shown in Figure 3.[5] In this case each price ending in an odd number will produce a greater volume of sales than the next lower even-numbered price. Many sellers appear to believe this is true, although the only large-scale test ever reported was inconclusive.[6]

[4]Cf. Joel Dean, *Managerial Economics* (New York: Prentice-Hall, Inc., 1951), p. 405. Dean shows a total revenue curve without, however, indicating its relationship to break-even charts.

[5] This curve might be regarded as discontinuous, especially since the difference between points is only one cent. But it is customary to draw demand curves as continuous even though, as Chamberlin has said, *any* demand curve could be split into segments. E.H. Chamberlin, "Comments," *Quarterly Journal of Economics,* v. XLIX, November, 1934, p. 135; and A.J. Nichol, although drawing important conclusions from the supposed discontinuity of certain demand curves, states that the curves would be continuous if it were feasible to change prices by small amounts. A.J. Nichol, "The Influence of Marginal Buyers on Monopolistic Competition," *Quarterly Journal of Economics,* v. XLIX, November, 1934, footnote 7, p. 126. Henry Smith believes that discontinuous demand curves might result from such heavy advertising of a certain price that the product would be unsalable at any other price. Cf. "Discontinuous Demand Curves and Monopolistic Competition: A Special Case," *Quarterly Journal of Economics,* v. XLIX, May, 1935, pp. 542-550. This would not seem to be a very common case, however, since marketing literature reveals heavily advertised products selling at various prices.

[6] Eli Ginsberg, "Customary Prices," *American Economic Review,* v. XXVI, no. 2, 1936, p. 296. Some economists doubt the validity of positively-inclined segments of demand curves, believing either (a) that the case could happen only if consumers regard price as one of the qualities of the product, thus making it improper to show these "different" products on one demand curve, or (b) that it simply does not happen that consumers will buy more of a product at a higher price than they will at a lower one. In regard to the first view, the important thing for purposes of the seller's pricing policy is the shape of the AR curve for what *he* knows is the same product. And while he may be interested in the psychology lying behind the consumer's demand curve he is not committed to the belief that it must be capable of explanation in terms of indifference curves. In regard to the second point, many marketing writers have commented on the view that a higher price will sometimes sell more than a lower one. For example, Phillips and Duncan say it may be possible to sell a greater number of a 15-cent item at 19 cents than at 15 cents *(op. cit.,* p. 656). Q. Forrest Walker, *loc. cit.,* suggests that 98 cents may sell better than 89 cents. Maynard and Beckman state "It is said that more articles can be sold at 17 cents than at 14 cents." *(op. cit.,* p. 209). A Converse and Huegy say "Some sellers feel that odd prices are better than even prices; others, feel that it makes little difference" *(op. cit.,* p. 209). A New England supermarket

The second concept of odd-pricing implies an AR curve like the one shown in Figure 4, with critical points at prices such as $1, $5, and $10.[7] The presumption is that sales will be substantially greater at prices just under these critical points, whether ending in an odd or even number.

Psychological Prices

Some of the marketing text books give the name of "psychological pricing" to policies quite similar to the one just discussed. It has been found in some pricing experiments that a change of price over a certain range has little effect until some critical point is reached. If there are a number of such critical points for a given commodity the AR curve would look like the one in Figure 5, resembling a series of steps. This differs from the concept of odd pricing in that the curve does not necessarily have any segments positively inclined, and the critical points are not located at each round number but only at the prices psychologically important to buyers. Pricing tests at Macy's have disclosed such step-shaped AR curves.[8]

Customary Prices

Another pricing policy usually described as though it has no relationship to theory is the one using "customary prices." This is most frequently associated with the five-cent candy bar, chewing gum, soft drink, or subway fare. The chain stores have experimented, apparently successfully, with combination cut prices on some such items, and inflation has brought about upward changes in others. In the main, however, the five-cent price on items for which it has been customary has persisted. To the extent that the policy is correct it merely means that the AR curve is like the one shown in Figure 6, with a kink at the customary price.[9]

Pricing at the Market

Figure 6 also illustrates the estimate of the AR curve which results in a policy of "pricing at the market." A firm that adopts this policy believes that a price above those of competitors would curtail sales sharply, while a lower price

---

chain reports that their meat prices never end in the figure "1" because their price tests show they can sell more at a price ending in "3". And a U.S. Department of Commerce study reports a price of 79 cents selling more than a price of 75 cents, and a case where silk underwear sold more readily at $2 or $5 than at $1.95 or $4.95 respectively. Cf F. M. Bernfield, "Time for Businessmen to Check Pricing Policies," *Domestic Commerce*, XXXV (March, 1947), p. 20.

. [7]This idea is applied even to very high prices. Thus, an automobile may be sold at $1995 rather than at $2,000.

[8] Oswald Knauth, "Some Reflections on Retail Prices," in *Economic Essays in Honor of Wesley Clair Mitchell* (New York: Columbia University Press, 1935), pp. 203-4. Although these tests involved changes in price, the important thing is that changes that reduced price below the critical points produced much greater increases in sales than changes that did not. In other words, the demand curve had very different elasticities at different points.

[9] Of course where the policy of customary pricing is not correct, as may be true in some of the chainstore cases mentioned, the demand curve would be quite elastic below the customary price.

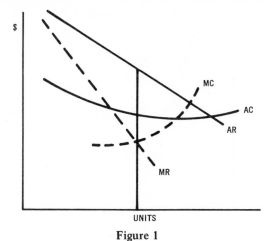

Figure 1

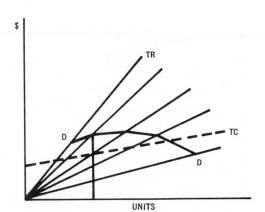

Figure 2

would not significantly increase them. This pricing policy is one of the most common, possibly because ignorance of the true shape of the AR curve suggests that the safest policy is to imitate competitors.

The policy of pricing at the market is also designed to avoid price competition and price wars. But a rule-of-thumb policy is not the correct solution to this problem, for the theory of monopolistic competition provides the bases for the proper calculation. What is required is an estimate of the AR curve after competitors have made whatever response they would make to the firm's pricing moves. In Figure 7 this is indicated by AR_2, while AR is the customary curve based on an assumption of "all other things remaining the

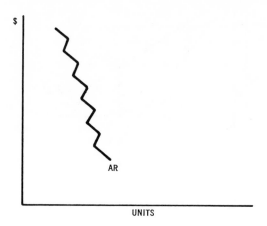

Figure 3

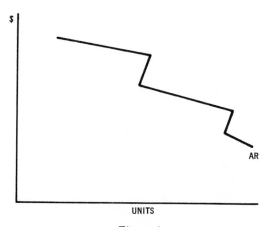

Figure 4

same." While it is very difficult for a seller to guess what competitors will do, the theory of correct oligopoly pricing along the AR_2 curve is quite clear, and does not necessarily call for "pricing at the market."

Prestige Pricing

It has often been pointed out in marketing literature that many customers judge quality by price. In such cases sales would be less at low prices than at high ones. This idea was the original legal basis for Fair Trade laws. While most manufacturers appear to be less impressed by this possibility than retailers are,

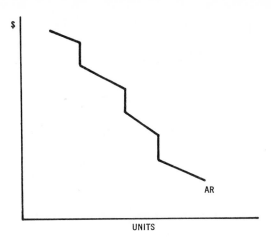

Figure 5

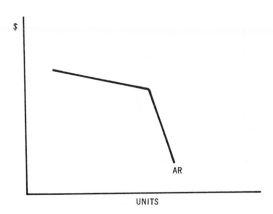

Figure 6

there have been cases reported in which low prices led to reduced sales. The shape of the AR curve illustrating this situation has already been indicated in economic literature.[10] See Figure 8.

[10] F. R. Fairchild, E. S. Furniss, and N. S. Buck, *Elementary Economics* (New York: Macmillan Co., 1939), 4th ed., v. 1 p. 166. Converse and Huegy cite an instance of aspirin being tried out at different prices, 19c, 29c, 39c, and 49c, with the highest sales resulting at 49c (op. cit., p. 207). And they comment on this reason for positively inclined demand curves, "Thus merchandise can be priced too low as well as too high. Customers may fear that at the low price it cannot be of good quality, and will actually buy more at a somewhat higher price than they would at a lower price" (p. 206).

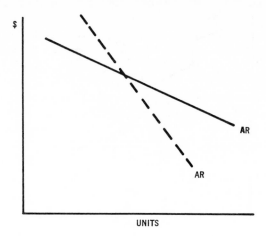

Figure 7

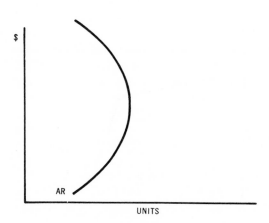

Figure 8

Price Lining

Many retailers when questioned about their pricing policies seem to feel they have avoided the problem entirely by adopting customary price "lines." Once the lines are decided upon, prices may be held constant over long periods of time; changes in market conditions are met by adjustments in the quality of the merchandise.

While this policy does not require pricing decisions, except initially and in case of special sales, it does present the seller with exactly the same choice as a variable price policy does in respect to the question of whether to equate marginal cost and marginal revenue, or to use a customary per cent of markup.

This decision is made with reference to the prices paid for merchandise rather than the prices at which it will be sold. Although manufacturers and wholesalers dealing in types of merchandise which is customarily price-lined at retail usually tailor their own prices to fit the retail prices, the retailer does have some choice in regard to the quality of goods he buys. Presumably, the more he pays the more he can sell, at any given price line. That is, the lower his per cent of markup the higher his sales volume should be. Figure 9 illustrates this situation, where P is the established price at retail, and CG shows the various quantities that could be sold at different costs of goods to the retailer. The retailer should equate his marginal cost with marginal revenue (the price), paying NM for the goods and selling quantity OM. If instead he buys at a price that provides a customary or arbitrary per cent of markup it would be purely accidental if he would obtain the maximum gross margin.

Since there are few variable costs associated with the sale of most items at retail, except the cost of goods, the retailer's aim in general should be simply to maximize his gross margin dollars. If, however, other variable costs are significant they can be added to the cost of goods and a calculation made of the average variable costs, from which marginal cost can be computed. In Figure 9 the curve CG would merely be replaced by an AVC curve.

Resale Price Maintenance

Another situation in which the retailer feels he has no pricing problem is when the manufacturer maintains resale prices by means of Fair Trade contracts. Even here, however, the retailer may find it advantageous to sell above the Fair Trade price in some cases, in states where the Fair Trade laws call for minimum rather than specified prices. In any case the retailer must decide whether to equate marginal cost and marginal revenue or to insist upon a customary per cent of markup. If he selects the latter he may refuse to handle, or to push, many low markup items which would actually be very profitable to him.

The price policy appropriate for a manufacturer using resale price maintenance is illustrated in Figure 10. At any given retail price, P, which he may set, he will have an AR curve determined by the retailers' attitudes towards the amount of markup resulting from the price at which he sells to them. At low markups some dealers will refuse to handle the item, and others will hide it under the counter. At relatively high markups dealers will push the item and will be able to sell more than consumers would otherwise take at the given retail price. The manufacturer should calculate his optimum price by computing MR from this AR curve and equating this with his MC. He should do this with the AR curve associated with each retail price and then select the combination of retail and wholesale prices that will result in maximum profit for him.[11]

Quantity Discounts

Quantity discounts are usually described in marketing texts, and explained in

[11] For a fuller discussion see E. R. Hawkins, "Vertical Price Relationships," ch. 11 in Reavis Cox and Wroe Alderson (ed.), *Theory in Marketing* (Chicago: Richard D. Irwin, Inc., 1950).

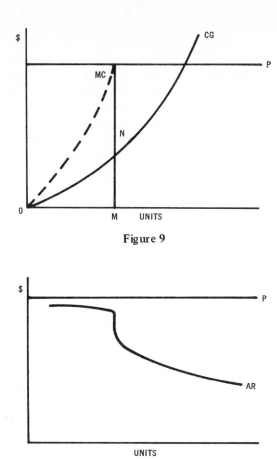

Figure 9

Figure 10

terms of the lower unit cost of handling large orders, or simply the desire to increase sales volume. Economic analysis of the quantity discount policy would focus on the theory of price discrimination. With reference to this theory, a quantity discount schedule, open to all buyers, is a very rough device for price discrimination, and should not be used if the laws allowed freedom of discrimination. Instead, the seller should estimate the demand curve of each buyer, and offer each the price (or prices) that would maximize the seller's revenue in respect to that buyer.[12] This might well mean lower prices for some small buyers than for some large ones, depending on the elasticity of their demand curves.

Figure 11 illustrates a case in which the large buyer's demand curve is inelastic in the significant range, while the small buyer's curve is quite elastic. It

[12] If the buyer is in a monopsonistic position he does not have a demand curve in the Marshallian sense, but it is possible to estimate how he will respond to various price offers.

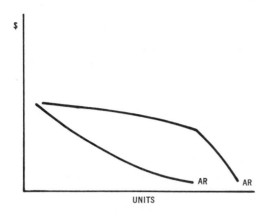

Figure 11

would therefore be foolish to offer them a quantity discount schedule that would give the large buyer lower prices than the small one. The large buyer would take almost as large a quantity at high prices as at low ones, while the small buyer will not. This may not be a usual situation, but it is a possible one, and indicates that the seller should consider the elasticities of demand rather than adopt an arbitrary discount schedule.

The correct theory of price discrimination, where each buyer is to be offered a different price, has been outlined by Mrs. Robinson.[13] It indicates that the seller should equate the marginal revenue from each buyer with the marginal cost of the entire output.

Different costs of selling to different buyers can be taken into account by computing the AR curves as *net* average revenue curves, after deduction of the variable costs associated with the particular sales. And it would still be possible that the large buyer should be charged a higher price than the small one.

Some economists have used the term "quantity discount" to refer to a situation, unusual in marketing practice, in which each buyer is offered a quantity discount scale tailored to his own demand curve.[14] Of course a "quantity discount" of this kind would usually produce more net profit for the seller than a single price to each buyer, since it is an approach toward the maximum profit situation of perfect price discrimination, in which each buyer would be charged the highest price he would be willing to pay for each successive unit he bought. A seller may be attempting to gain some of the advantages of this type of pricing when he constructs a general quantity discount schedule with an eye to its effects on certain large buyers. In so doing, he would have to take care that the

---

[13] Joan Robinson, *The Economics of Imperfect Competition* (London: Macmillan Co., 1933), p. 182.

[14] James M. Buchanan, "The Theory of Monopolistic Quantity Discounts," *Review of Economic Studies*, v. XX, no. 3, 1952-3.

gain would not be cancelled by the adverse effect of the schedule on his net profits from other buyers.

Geographic Pricing

While some economists have long been concerned with the geographic aspects of pricing, and this interest has recently been spreading, on the whole marketing specialists and economic geographers have regarded the spatial aspects of economics as their own province. Unfortunately they have developed theories which do not include the essential economic aspects of the problem. Figure 11 may be used to illustrate some of the problems of geographic pricing. If the AR curve of each buyer is taken as a *net* average revenue curve, after deduction of transportation costs, then it is clear that the nearer buyer should not necessarily be given the lower delivered price. The elasticity of each buyer's demand curve is the important factor which should be considered. As has been indicated by Mrs. Robinson, the correct net price to each buyer would equate the seller's marginal revenue with the marginal cost of his entire output.[15]

While the Robinson-Patman Act does not permit the free price discrimination that would maximize the seller's profit, it does allow some discretion in pricing. The seller is not permitted to employ price differentials greater than his cost differentials, but he is free to give discounts less than the amount of cost saving to him. Moreover, he is allowed some discretion to employ price differentials when the buyers are not in competition with each other, or where he himself is "meeting competition." He may also, of course, discriminate by selling slightly different products, under different brand names.

Conclusion

The discrepancy between economic theory and actual pricing policies, as observed by marketing specialists, is more apparent than real. Most of the pricing behavior reported by marketing students is quite consistent with the general theory of monopolistic competition, and can be integrated with that theory. A considerable gain can be made on both sides if this integration is accomplished. Economists need to know more about the pricing policies actually used by businessmen. On the other hand, marketing students can understand these policies better if they appreciate the theoretical basis for them. Most of the "price policies" described by marketing specialists are merely special cases of the general theory of monopolistic competition. If so regarded, not only would clarification result, but perhaps additional insight would be gained regarding the advantages and disadvantages of each policy, and the situations to which they are appropriate.

[15] John Robinson, *loc. cit.*

Most economic theory relating to business behavior emphasizes pricing. Also, the economist traditionally attempts to explain marketing strategy in terms of monopolistic and competitive market structures. This approach is challenged by the author of this article whose research shows that the product and the customer are the determining factors in a company's marketing strategy.

How Important Is Pricing in Competitive Strategy?

Jon G. Udell

In an effort to ascertain the key elements of business success in the market place, the author conducted a study among 200 producers of industrial and consumer goods. A sample of fairly well-known and successful manufacturing companies was selected from *Martindell's Manual of Excellent Management*. Listed are companies which are supposedly well managed, evaluated according to the criteria developed by the American Institute of Management. The use of the manual seemed appropriate in that the two most heavily weighted criteria are sales vigor and management efficiency.

The present study attempted to answer the question: "What are the key policies and procedures common to successful marketing managements in various manufacturing industries?"

Management's interest in the study was reflected by a 75% response to a 4-page mail questionnaire. The first section of the questionnaire listed 12 general policy areas of marketing management—among them, sales research and sales planning, pricing, management of sales personnel, and product service. The respondent, usually the vice president in charge of marketing, was asked to select

Reprinted by permission of the author and the publisher from the *Journal of Marketing*, published by the American Marketing Association, Vol. 28, No. 1 (January, 1964), pp. 44-48.

the five areas which he regarded as most vital in his company's marketing success.

Importance of Product Development

The results indicate that product research and development, selected by almost 80% of the respondents, is most important in modern-day competitive strategy. Four other policy areas, relating to either product or sales effort, were selected by more than half of the respondents. Table 1 presents a percentage analysis of the responses.

It appears that business management did not agree with the economic views of the importance of pricing—one-half of the respondents did *not* select pricing as *one of the five* most important policy areas in their firm's marketing success.

Also, the two major facets of nonprice competition (product and sales effort) were subdivided into a number of policy areas; for example, sales effort was subdivided into sales research and sales planning, management of sales personnel, and advertising and sales promotion. In short, *the competitive activities relating to the product and to sales effort were selected as most important in the success of these firms.*

Pricing

The emphasis on product and sales effort does not imply that price is unimportant. Three factors probably account for the relatively low ranking of pricing:

1. In today's competitive economy, *supply*—or production capacity—*generally exceeds demand;* and, therefore, nearly all sellers are forced to be either completely competitive or almost collusive in their pricing. Because there may be little or no freedom for a company to deviate from the market price, heavy reliance must be placed on product differentiation and sales effort.

2. *The relatively well-to-do consumers of today are interested in more than just price.* They are interested in product quality, distinctiveness, style, and many other factors which lead to both physical and psychological satisfaction. Consumers not only can afford but want product differentiation and sales promotion. From them the consumer receives a great deal of psychological satisfaction and utility. It is only logical that consumer-oriented managements would choose to emphasize products and sales efforts in an attempt to satisfy consumer desires.

3. *It is through successful product differentiation that a manufacturer may obtain some pricing freedom.* Products known to be identical must be priced identically in the market place. A departure from identical prices would result in all patronage going to the seller or sellers with the lowest price.

Marketing Strategies According to Products and Customers

Economists have proposed several theories that give recognition to the nonprice factors of competitive strategy.[1] However, they have not credited the nature of the product and the characteristics of the buyers as the dominant factors in explaining how companies organize to market their products. Instead, the dominant factor is usually assumed to be the market structure of the industry (competitive, oligopolistic, or monopolistic).

A producer of machine tools would not be expected to compete in the same manner as a producer of perfume; and a comparison of the structures of the machine-tool and perfume industries would not explain the differences in their marketing strategies. *Common business sense would lead one to believe that a company's use of nonprice competitive strategy should vary according to the nature of a firm's product and the characteristics of the buyers for that product.*

Accordingly, the data were classified according to the respondents' type of industry: industrial goods, consumer durable goods, and consumer nondurable goods.

Table 1
How Management Ranks the Factors
of Marketing Success

Rank	Policy areas	% of firms selecting the policy area[a]
1	Product research and development	79
2	Sales research and sales planning	73
3	Management of sales personnel	59
4	Advertising and sales promotion	56
5	Product service	52
6	Pricing	50
7	Organizational structure	44
8	Distribution channels and their control	41
9	Marketing cost budgeting and control	17
10	Financing and credit	14
11	Transportation and storage	7
12	Public relations	7

[a] Based on a tabulation of 135 usable questionnaires. Percentages here are rounded.

Producers of Industrial Goods

The producers of industrial goods stressed the product facet of competitive strategy.

Two of the policy areas listed in the marketing management study pertain directly to the product—product research and development, and product service. (Product service refers to those activities performed by a manufacturer in the attempt to guarantee that a product gives satisfactory performance to its users.)

As shown in Table 2, both of these policy areas were selected by about 80% of the industrial users.

[1] Lawrence Abbott, *Quality and Competition* (New York: Columbia University Press, 1951); Hans Brems, "The Interdependence of Quality Variations, Selling Effort and Price," *Quarterly Journal of Economics,* Vol. 62 (May, 1948), pp. 418-440; C.A. Stocking, "Advertising and Economic Theory," *American Economic Review,* Vol. 21 (March, 1931), pp. 43-55.

The policy areas relating to sales effort were relegated to a lesser role by the successful manufacturers of industrial goods. The average selection for the policy areas pertaining to sales effort was 50%, as compared with the average product selection of 80%.

The industrial-goods producers' primary emphasis on the product facet of marketing strategy was also emphasized in letters received from various respondents. A Pratt & Whitney Aircraft executive said: "Our two most valuable assets sales-wise are the technical excellence of our products, and our policy of rendering the best possible product service to our customers both before and after the sale."

Table 2
Policy Areas Selected by Industrial
Goods Producers

Policy areas	% of firms selecting the policy area[a]
Product:	
Product research and development	79
Product service	79
Average product selection ratio	79
Sales efforts:	
Sales research and sales planning	63
Management of sales personnel	49
Advertising and sales promotion	37
Average sales efforts selection ratio	50
Pricing	47
Other areas:	
Organizational structure	50
Distribution channels and their control	34
Financing and credit	18
Marketing cost budgeting and control	12
Transportation and storage	9
Public relations	7

[a] Based on the questionnaires of 68 industrial goods producers. Percentages here are rounded.

Producers of Consumer Goods

The manufacturers of consumer goods placed a much greater emphasis on the sales effort facet of competitive strategy. This emphasis was especially great in the case of the firms producing nondurable goods.

As shown in Table 3, the nondurable goods producers had an average sales effort selection of 85%, as compared with an average product selection of 45%. Durable goods producers had an average sales efforts selection of 79%, as compared with the product selection of 60%.

The differences were accounted for by the low selection ratios for product service, in that most consumer goods manufacturers selected product research and development.

It is understandable that consumer-goods producers selected product research and development with such a high degree of frequency in light of their emphasis

Table 3
Policy Areas Selected by Consumer
Goods Manufacturers

Policy areas	Manufacturers of nondurable goods	Manufacturers of durable goods[a]
Sales efforts:		
Advertising and sales promotion	89	73
Management of sales personnel	64	91
Sales research and sales planning	82	73
Average sales efforts selection ratio	85	79
Product:		
Product research and development	83	75
Product service	14	36
Average product selection ratio	45	60
Pricing	50	46
Other areas:		
Distribution channels and their control	54	46
Organizational structure	39	27
Marketing cost budgeting and control	29	9
Financing and credit	11	9
Transportation and storage	4	9
Public relations	7	

[a] Based on the questionnaires of 28 nondurable goods producers and 11 durable goods producers. Figures here are rounded.

on sales efforts. It is less difficult to promote a differentiated product than it is to promote an undifferentiated product.

Product research and development are important, but sales efforts are *most* important to manufacturers of consumer goods.

Product research and development was not broken down into research related to physical (real) product improvement and research related to psychological (fancied) product improvement. It would be immaterial to the consumer-goods manufacturer if a product change were *real* or *fancied,* so long as the change was regarded as an improvement by his customers.

The second section of the questionnaire subdivided the general areas of policies and procedures into more specific categories of business activities. When product research and development was subdivided into three categories of activities, the following selections were obtained:

		Manufacturers of	
	Inaustrial goods	Consumer nondurables	Consumer durables
Technical research and development	75	54	56
Marketing research related to new products	30	62	56
Product evaluation	16	19	22

As might be expected, the technical development of products was most emphasized by the industrial-goods producers, whereas marketing research related to new products was most emphasized by the consumer-goods producers.

The analysis indicates that all three groups of manufacturers—industrial, consumer durable, and consumer nondurable—stressed the nonprice facets of competitive strategy, and that *the relative emphasis on product and sales efforts varied according to the nature of the products and the characteristics of the buyers.*

To further test this proposition, the questionnaires were grouped according to specific industries. If the proposition were valid, there should have been a high degree of similarity in the marketing strategies of respondents of a specific industry. That is, the respondents of a given industry producing similar products for like customers, should select similar policy areas as most important in their marketing success.

Here are three examples that demonstrate the validity of this proposition.

Table 4
Selection of Major Policy Areas
Twelve Producers of Major Installations

Rank	Policy areas	Selection ratio—%
1	Product research and development	100
2	Product service	100
3	Distribution channels and their control	67
4	Organizational structure	42
5	Management of sales personnel	42
6	Sales research and sales planning	42
7	Advertising and sales promotion	33
8	Pricing	25
9	Financing and credit	17
10	Public relations	17
11	Marketing cost budgeting and control	8
12	Transportation and storage	8

Table 5
Selection of Major Policy Areas by
Eight Producers of Metals

Rank	Policy areas	Selection ratio—%
1	Product service	100
2	Product research and development	75
3	Sales research and sales planning	63
4	Pricing	63
5	Distribution channels and their control	50
6	Management of sales personnel	38
7	Organizational structure	25
8	Transportation and storage	25
9	Financing and credit	25
10	Public relations	13
11	Advertising and sales promotion	13
12	Marketing cost budgeting and control	–

Case No. 1—Capital Goods Industry

The most homogeneous grouping of companies with similar products and similar customers consisted of 12 producers of major installation—capital goods. As Table 4 illustrates, *all 12 producers selected product research and development and product service.*

Distribution channels and their control was selected by 8 of the 12 producers.

Table 6
Selection of Major Policy Areas by
Chemical and Drug Producers

Policy areas	Selection ratio of industrial chemical producers (3)		Selection ratio of consumer chemical producers (3)	
Product research and development	100		100	
Product service	67		–	
Average product selection ratio		83		50
Advertising and sales promotions	–		100	
Sales research and sales planning	100		67	
Management of sales personnel	33		67	
Average sales efforts selection ratio		44		78

This may be because sales servicing before and after is often performed by the distributors of capital goods.

The 100% selection for product research and development and for product service were high. Statistically one would expect such an occurrence only twice in 100,000 trials due to random sampling error.

Assuming that each policy area is actually of equal importance, there is a .00002 probability of getting a policy area with a 100% selection ratio due to random sampling error (binomial theorem used). The fact that *both* of the policy areas pertaining to product were selected by all 12 respondents provides further statistical proof that the selection ratios are *not* due to chance.

Case No. 2—Metals Industry

Another grouping of companies was comprised of producers of steel, zinc, aluminum, and other processed metals. The companies have similar markets and similar products, in that their products are the raw materials for the manufacture of other goods.

It would be anticipated that the product facet of competition would have prevailed in the competitive strategies of these companies; and Table 5 shows that this was true.

Case No. 3—Chemical Industry

A third grouping of companies highlights the importance of customers in determining marketing strategy. Of the six chemical manufacturers participating in the study, three produced for the consumer market and three of the industrial market.

All six firms responded by selecting product research and development, but at this point the similarities ceased.

As shown in Table 6, the average product selection ratio of the industrial chemical manufacturers was much higher than that of the consumer chemical manufacturers. The average sales effort selection ratio of the consumer products manufacturers was higher than that of the industrial producers.

How Important Is Size?

To ascertain the influence of company size on management's selection of the facets of marketing strategy, the responses were classified according to the sales volume of each company: less than $50 million, $50 to $100 million, $100 to $500 million, and over $500 million.

The differences among the selection ratios of the various size classifications were so small that none was found to be statistically significant. Apparently size had little influence on the relative importance that a company attached to the various facets of its marketing mix.

In Conclusion

The ranking method provided only a rough measure of the importance of price, product, and sales efforts; *but it was a measurement.*

As for another possible limitation—lack of differentiation between responses related to "what is" and what the respondents felt "should be"—one might ask, "Who is better qualified to select the most important areas of a successful firm's marketing program than the firm's marketing management?"

The study reported illustrates two major points:

1. In today's market, the nonprice facets of competition occupy a prominent role.
2. The explanation of the roles of nonprice competitive facets does *not* lie solely in the structure of the industry (or the size of the firm) but instead primarily in the nature of the product and its market.

The importance of the nonprice aspects of the marketing mix and the variations among industries can be explained by the nature of today's economy. To compete successfully in a setting characterized by oligopolistic firms offering rival products to a customer-dominated market, the firm must be customer-oriented. In appealing to the customer, management finds success in utilizing the nonprice facets of competitive activity, adjusting its strategy to the needs and desires of the buyer.

A seven-step approach to new product pricing is proposed: (1) approximate the impact of price on projected volume; (2) appraise marketing requirements; (3) plot growth curves at several price levels; (4) calculate the approximate cost data; (5) appraise capabilities of competitors; (6) estimate competitors' costs; (7) decide on the price.

A Planned Approach to New Product Pricing

Stephen J. Welsh

New products, for the purpose here, are defined as those which represent a major innovation and which are new to the industry. This definition excludes products which are new only in the sense that a specific company has not manufactured them before. The market for such a new product is undefined at the outset; not all the potential applications are known; there is no available market experience on directly competing products; channels of distribution have yet to be chosen; appropriate markups are undetermined; and there is an almost complete lack of cost experience. Moreover, potential customers are full of questions about a new product: Will it really work? How long will it work, and how reliable will it be? How soon might major improvements be made, and how would these improvements affect the value of the purchase? Will prices come down substantially, and how soon?

Uncertainties such as these can materially influence the price a customer may be willing to pay, and the amount of time, effort, and expense involved in selling customers. Offsetting these many difficulties peculiar to new product pricing is at least one advantage: Putting a price on a new product is a task that cannot be

Reprinted by permission of the author and the publisher from *New Product Development,* edited by Joseph Eastlack (Chicago: American Marketing Association, 1966), pp. 67-81.

ducked. Too often, with established products, we manage to avoid a systematic review of our pricing problems and opportunities, rationalizing that, after all, we do have the product priced and that since the price has served us for sometime, let's carry it on a little longer. A new product, obviously, does not permit us this luxury. It is quite literally priceless, and before we can go to the market, we must put a price on it—for better or worse, wisely and deliberately, or by cut and try.

Preliminary Considerations

The pricing job should start very early—ideally, when the product is in the concept stage. If someone hands us a prototype and says: "Here, put a price on it," it is too late, for much of our money has been spent. The price determines the return on investment, and the estimated return should determine our decision to invest in the development in the first place. Logically, therefore, price planning should start at the very beginning.

We should have clearly in mind the reasons for bringing out a new product before we attempt to price it. It is easy to jump to the conclusion that our objective is to maximize profit. Although this is an important element in any pricing situation, a company may have other objectives.

1. For example, it may want to load a manufacturing facility more fully, or eliminate or reduce a seasonal load problem. The manufacturer of television antennas may decide to introduce a novel item of tubular lawn furniture.

2. Again, a company may wish to broaden the line and thereby make better use of a selling or distribution facility or asset. This is common practice in the food field: A truck that delivers bread and cake might as well deliver a line of cookies also.

3. A company may wish to use the new product as an entree into new markets for other, broader lines. A manufacturer of conveyors may develop a better rock-crusher primarily as a way of getting into the construction market.

4. A company may want to complete a line in order to remove a competitive disadvantage represented by present gaps.

5. Finally, the company may chiefly be interested in a vehicle for the sale of complementary products.

In some of these situations, a price structure designed to maximize profit could work against the accomplishment of the company's real objectives. Hence, first of all, price structure or policy must be clearly related to overall marketing objectives and strategies.

Steps in New Product Pricing

Assuming that this relationship has been defined, we are ready to approach our new-product pricing decision. Let us assume that our primary objective is achieving maximum profit for a single line or product. This goal is suggested not because it is the commonest, but because it involves us in the full range of complexities inherent in most new-product pricing problems.

The approach involves seven steps, which are designed to develop, in logical sequence, the answers to the following three key questions:

1. How much will many customers be willing to pay for how much of the product? In other words, how would our sales volume vary as a function of our price?

2. What is the least we can profitably charge? That is, what does our cost picture look like at various levels of output?

3. What risks are involved? More specifically, what threats should we anticipate from our competitors, and what might they be able to do to us and when?

Perhaps one day our operations researchers and computer people will develop formulas which will take all of these factors precisely into account and come up with a single "best answer." But for the present, all we can hope to do is to secure as much information as possible to guide us in formulating sound human judgments.

Step 1: Approximate the Impact of
Price on the Volume We Might Expect
to Achieve

We know that there is a relationship between the price we set on our product and the volume we might hope to achieve with it. The economist tells us that a typical price volume relationship theoretically looks like the diagram in Exhibit 1. At a high price, only a small volume can be expected—probably to the point of market saturation—beyond which there will be no additional volume. Although this is a highly theoretical representation of the relationship, it can be a useful starting point for our thinking, since by definition our new product (at least for a time) permits us to enjoy the monopolistic position the economist had in mind.

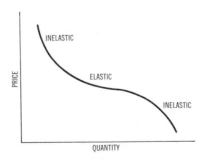

Exhibit 1   Single-stage demand curve

Getting practical mileage out of this concept depends on recognizing the fact that any new product, however novel it may be, does have alternative or indirectly competitive products. This fact introduces a few variations into the original demand curve, at or near price levels of these alternative products, as Exhibit 2 shows. These alternatives are key elements in our thinking, because what a customer will pay us for a new product necessarily reflects the price-performance package which we offer him as compared with that of competing products.

Exhibit 2   Two-stage demand curve

For our new product and for each competing product, two primary factors determine relative attractiveness to potential customers—performance and price. We can develop reasonably accurate information on our performance, competitor performance, and competitor price, and this will enable us to reason in at least approximate terms about the remaining unknown, namely, the price of our new product. We go about this by taking the following substeps:

1. What is our product? We must define our product, not in terms of its construction, chemical formulation, or any similar physical description, but rather in terms of what it will do—that is, its performance characteristics. How durable is it? How beautiful? How convenient? How efficient?

2. What are the applications for our new product? Obviously, the advantages or disadvantages of our product in comparison with alternative products depend upon the use to which it will be put. A new fabric, for example, which will pass water vapor but shed water droplets is one thing in rainwear applications, another in battery separators, something else in bandages or surgical dressings, and still another when used as a filtering medium. The performance requirements differ in major ways, and the products with which our new product will be competing will be different for each of these application areas.

3. What are the alternative products the customer can use? We don't have to consider each one, but it is important to spot the principal ones from which we can expect competition in each of our use areas.

4. In each of these applications, what are the customer's performance requirements and what is their relative importance? In other words, which major product characteristics appear likely to govern his selection of the product to be used?

5. What are the prices of the alternatives, and how well do they fulfill the

product requirements of our customers? With some few exceptions, reliable price information on these products is easy to acquire. On product performance, extensive field research with users may be necessary to give us the answers we need.

6. How does our product perform in comparison with these alternative products? Here, comparative engineering tests and the whole range of product testing techniques can come into play.

7. On the basis of this information, what would seem to be the "threshold" price for our product? Threshold price may be defined as that price which appears likely to obtain the customer's real consideration of our product. It includes the premium a customer would be willing to pay for the performance characteristics of our product compared with those of the alternative products.

Exhibit 3 is a threshold price chart for a real industrial product which we have studied and which we can call "super synthetic resin." The chart summarizes a good deal of the information developed in the preceding steps. For each of the two applications, it shows present price levels of two alternative materials and a judgment on maximum threshold price for super synthetic resin, in the markets represented by these two uses. In one application, super synthetic resin is clearly inferior to both alternatives, and the magnitude of the inferiority finds expression in the 4- to 6-cent cut in price the company would have to take to get consideration for super synthetic. In the other application, super synthetic resin would seem potentially worth 4 to 6 cents a pound more than the alternatives.

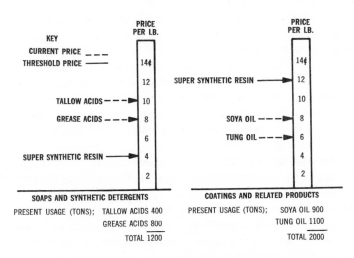

Exhibit 3   Threshold price comparison

Actually, fourteen different application areas were individually examined in this study, and nine major alternative materials were involved. Nearly 300 extensive and highly technical interviews were conducted. This sounds like a lot of work, and it was. However, an investment of some $8 million was involved.

Of course analysis of a proposed product may never have reached this stage. If the pricing job started very early, as has been suggested, the program may already have been jettisoned as impractical, obviously too expensive, or for some other reason.

By the time the analysis has got this far the chances are that the product has been subjected to many comparative engineering tests and appropriate product testing in the field. We may have accumulated a mass of detailed data from salesmen. In essence, we have been applying to our product, in advance, the kinds of appraisal involved in value analysis, to borrow a notion from the purchasing field.

Step 2: Appraise Marketing Requirements and Broadly Define a Marketing Plan

We now should have some idea of the size of the market which might exist for us at several price levels. We have no idea, however, of the timing required to penetrate this market. This element of timing is of crucial importance, first, because we must later consider the impact of competition upon our pricing strategy, and second, because the rate at which we develop sales volume could materially influence our costs.

To some extent, the rate at which we can penetrate a market depends on the characteristics of both the product and the market. For example, if our product requires a long period of testing by customers, our rate of developing significant commercial volume would be relatively slow. Similarly, seasonal variations of our proposed market might have a bearing on the matter.

Over and above these inherent timing determinations, the rate at which we can develop sales volume depends on our marketing plan, the formulation of which is our second step. This, in turn, should begin with an appraisal of the requirements for successful entry into the market.

Assume that the new product is a novel business machine, an improved collator based on a new principle and having substantially superior operating characteristics. First of all, we must recognize that, besides the engineering of the product itself, there are a number of other features to be decided. These include such matters as service contracts, guarantees, and whether the collator should be sold or leased.

Next, obviously, we must decide which segment of the market (the various application segments of the total market as well as the geographic segments) to approach first and in what sequence to approach the remainder. We must determine who has the principal influence in purchases of equipment of this kind—systems, purchasing, engineering, management personnel. Finally, the message we should use to reach those who will purchase should be determined.

With this kind of information in hand, we are prepared to start thinking about appropriate channels of distribution and to appraise the kinds of activity required to set up this distribution. Simultaneously, we will be making our judgments on the role and relative importance of advertising, promotional activities, publicity, field sales, participation in trade shows and conventions, and other means to be used in introducing the product into the market.

Outlining the marketing plan will give some insight into selling costs and expenses, which will become important to use later as a significant cost factor, and it will also give a basis for judgment regarding the rate at which we might expect to penetrate the market under this plan.

Step 3: Plot Growth Curves at Several
Selected Price Levels

When we have pulled together our tentative marketing plan, including its timing, we are then ready to prepare a chart like the one in Exhibit 4. Since we

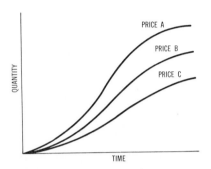

Exhibit 4   Projected product sales patterns

have now introduced the time element, this chart shows several growth curves, one for each price level, summarizing our judgments concerning the rate at which we might be able to develop sales volume at these different prices. These growth curves assume that our tentative marketing plan will be carried out, and that present competitive conditions will continue. More specifically, they assume that in the future, as at present, we will have no directly competing products, and that there will be no changes in competing products, their performance specifications, or their prices.

Step 4: Calculate the Approximate
Cost Data

There is some evidence that the importance of cost has been overemphasized in pricing situations. Many companies still use formulas based almost entirely on cost considerations. Although cost certainly is an important factor in new product pricing, a better balanced viewpoint recognizes that cost is principally significant in determining whether the new product is economically feasible and whether it should be introduced at all. It is, in short, principally important in developing a price floor. However, since cost obviously has an important bearing on pricing, we must consider this factor.

Developing approximations of unit manufacturing cost is a relatively simple job, if we have estimates of sales volume and rate and if no undue precision is required at the time. The manufacturing costs of direct labor, materials and supplies, purchased components, equipment required, and overhead can be developed in approximate terms on the basis of the predicted volume levels. The basis for estimating the elements of sales and administrative expense is provided in the action program which has already been broadly defined.

Exhibit 5 shows the kind of chart that can be prepared from the foregoing information. It represents our unit costs plotted against time. Although the basic

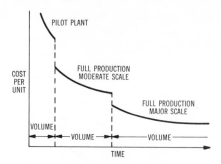

Exhibit 5   Our projected cost patterns

data would necessarily be developed in terms of volume, we have already developed approximations of volume against time, and consequently this form of presentation can be readily prepared.

The time factor is important, since we must now appraise competitive capabilities, and here time is essential.

Step 5: Appraise Capabilities of Competitors, Including Timing

In the previous step, we were proceeding on the assumption that there would be no change in the competitive environment, but we know that this is wishful thinking. Sooner or later, competitors will be attracted to our market, and there is always the possibility that additional alternative products or materials may be developed, or that changes may be made in the offerings or price of the alternative materials currently available.

In trying to evaluate these threat or risk factors, we obviously cannot tell what course future events will take. However, we can at least try to forecast the impact that future competition would have. As in the military world, endeavoring to appraise our rival's intentions is a philosophical pursuit of dubious value. But we can appraise his capabilities, usually with fair accuracy.

There are two key questions in appraising the capabilities of a potential competitor.

1. What will he do to us and how long will it take him to do it?
2. How effectively and at what cost does it appear likely he can do it?

In Step 5 we are looking primarily for an answer to the first of these questions—the timing on which we might anticipate competition. In Step 6 we will turn our attention to the relative advantages or disadvantages that competitors may have in our market and the costs at which they might be able to operate.

In trying to estimate the timing with which competitive forces may come into play, we will find the "requirements" for successful operation in the business a useful place to start. If our competitor is to operate successfully in the market, he must meet the same requirements that we do. Consequently, we must consider each major function—research and development, manufacturing, and sales—and form some judgments about the amount of time our competitor might need to spend in each activity if he is going to enter and operate in our market.

In the research and development area, we can readily evaluate the patent situation, which may give us some clue regarding the probable timing or conditions of direct competition. Further, by appraising realistically the magnitude of the technological innovation which our product represents, and by putting together what we know about our competitor's research, we can arrive at a reasonably good estimate of the amount of time he should require to duplicate our accomplishment. Another point in this appraisal is how much opportunity for additional product research and development is available to us. In other words, is it possible that, while our competitor is getting to where we are now, we can go on to further exploration of the field and consequently stay a jump or more ahead of him?

In a similar way, we need to appraise his capabilities to meet the manufacturing and sales requirements of the operation. An interesting question in the sales area is the extent to which we might have been able, by virtue of being first, to sew up key distribution agencies or facilities.

As the result of such analysis, it is possible to prepare a chart like the one in Exhibit 6. In this hypothetical example, our competition is in a more favorable

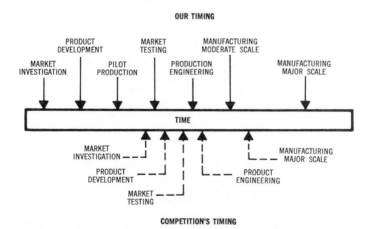

Exhibit 6   Competitive timing program

position than we are. It is assumed that whereas we are entering a new field, our competition is well-established and has specific product and marketing capabilities and know-how superior to ours. As a result, even though we have the advantage of starting our market investigation and product development phases first, our competition can reach the stage of manufacturing on a major scale ahead of us. Such an analysis of competitive capabilities needs to be made as objectively as possible. We should be careful not to overestimate the amount of time it would take our competitors to match us. On the other hand, it is important not to sell short the accomplishment made by our own technical or manufacturing people.

Step 6: Estimate Competitors' Costs

At this point, we need for comparison with our own costs some estimates of the unit costs our competitors might incur. While this might seem an almost impossible assignment, fortunately we do not need to be precise. What we chiefly have to be able to evaluate is the major points of difference between their costs and our costs in meeting the requirements for successful operation in this business. If, for example, it appears likely that a competitor can copy or otherwise match our performance without duplicating the extensive research and development we have put into it, this is certainly an important plus for him. If his manufacturing equipment will permit him to manufacture much more economically than we can and perhaps with a smaller added investment, this also becomes significant. Or if either of us has major advantages in distribution or in marketing organization, or has marketing contacts which would be extremely time consuming and costly to duplicate, these, too, should be appraised in broad but useful terms. On the basis of judgments of this kind, it is possible to prepare a chart something like the one in Exhibit 7.

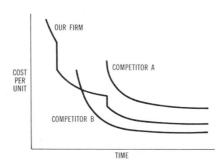

Exhibit 7   Our projected costs vs. those of competitors

Step 7: Decide on the Price

By this time, we have surrounded ourselves with a good deal of information, even if it is only approximate. Now we are prepared for the big push, which is to make the pricing decisions. Here, as always, we are faced with some choices.

1. We can decide between a skimming strategy or a penetration strategy.

2. We can decide to get as much profit as we can as soon as we can, or, if our

estimate of the competitive situation gives us enough time, we can attempt to maximize our profit with a somewhat lower price schedule.

3. We can establish a price that will discourage competitors and yet not discourage ourselves.

Some of the bases for our decisions have been assumed. For example, in Step 2 we tentatively established a marketing plan which predicted both costs and the rate of market development we might achieve. At this point, it would be desirable to review the proposed plan and, if necessary, devise several alternative plans leading to different costs and rates of penetration, so that the profitability of the various plans may be compared.

This kind of analysis should be continued during the stage of actual introduction of the product. As additional information accumulates, it can be plotted in the same way, to review the correctness of our pricing strategy on a continuing basis.

Pricing Guideposts

The following suggestions may help summarize the points we have been discussing.

1. Begin your pricing analyses early in the product-development process. Ideally, price thinking should begin before any money is invested, and preferably as soon after the product idea is conceived as possible.

2. Consider cost, certainly, but as a limit or floor on price. In itself, cost is not a sound basis for determining price.

3. Do not try to be precise at this point. Only substantial differences should be considered. The best approach is a series of successive approximations. In this way, obvious disqualifiers come to the fore quickly, before a great deal of time and effort has been expended.

4. Take a broad view of pricing. Since there is no facet of the business which is not reflected in the pricing process, representatives of all functions must participate in the program.

5. Get, and maintain on a continuing basis, detailed information about competitive products, prices, markets, and strategies. The sales organization is a good source of information of this kind, and it is all too often overlooked in a company's over-all planning for new product development and introduction. The intelligence function of many companies is very weak.

6. Don't try to avoid using your judgment. While the pricing procedure described requires judgment, it has the advantage of requiring a number of small judgments rather than a few large ones, thereby reducing the number of broad jumps involved in the process.

7. Get your product-line policies and plans in order. Most pricing binds grow out of unsound or poorly policed product-line policies or faulty business objectives. A lack of such policies and objectives is behind most situations in which there is a failure to set a price which will yield an adequate profit before competitors get under way.

The approach suggested here is difficult, complex, and time consuming. But the problem is a crucial one, and we should be willing to devote to it an effort which is commensurate with the magnitude of the individual project. The alternative is guessing. We all like to guess with a few dollars, but guessing wrong with hundreds of thousands or millions of dollars is another matter. The cost of not performing this task in a rational, comprehensive manner can be very high indeed, and probably explains in part the magnitude of the statistics about the proportion of failures in new product ventures.

The complexity of the problem and the scope and difficulty of handling all of the manifold considerations makes a persuasive argument for limiting new product development to projects of substantial significance. The effort required to evaluate a product or establish a sound pricing policy for a $20 million product line does not substantially exceed the scope of work required for a $50,000 line.

The seven steps outlined above are not a method, but an approach involving a logical order and rational sequence for considering a wide range of highly important factors. They cannot substitute for executive judgment, but they can furnish the kinds of materials that people who make the judgments will need for soundly based decisions on new product pricing.

VI INTERNATIONAL MARKETING

American business firms are increasingly discovering the existence of marketing opportunities outside the boundaries of the United States. Concomitant with these opportunities are the challenges created by the diversity of the various countries.

In some cases businessmen have committed the fatal mistake of visualizing markets in terms of preconceived stereotypes rather than analyzing and treating them as market segments with unique characteristics. Each market may require special decisions regarding product planning, channels of distribution, promotion, and physical distribution. Currency differences create pricing problems. Language differences result in major communications barriers. Buying habits vary between—and within—countries.

Ernest Dichter provides valuable insight into the behavior patterns of the world's inhabitants in the first selection, "The World Customer." He compares and contrasts the international consumer's buying habits, his national pride, self illusions, and the differences and similarities from nation to nation.

Warren J. Keegan discusses the formulation of an international marketing strategy in the next selection. He evaluates two strategic alternatives: exporting the firm's domestic marketing strategy without changes or adjusting the firm's marketing mix to fit conditions in each foreign market. Keegan suggests that prospective markets be grouped by stage economic development for purposes of analysis.

The final article in Part VI concentrates on marketing in the less-developed countries and points out how marketers must adapt their policies and practices to meet the socioeconomic circumstances of national and regional overseas markets.

This article examines the world customer's behavior patterns, his national pride, and his differences and similarities from one nation to the next. Understanding of consumers in each country is necessary if marketing managers are to profitably serve them.

The World Customer

Ernest Dichter

- Only one Frenchman out of three brushes his teeth.
- Automobiles have become a must for the self-esteem of even the lowliest postal clerk in Naples or the Bantu streetcleaner in Durban.
- There is a supermarket in Apia, the capital of Western Samoa (which received its independence in January of this year). I found can openers and the cans to go with them in a remote village on the island of Upolu.
- Four out of five Germans change their shirts but once a week.
- Amazon Indians use outboard motors in deep green water alleyways.

What do these facts, and many others like them, portend for the future marketing manager? For top management in companies with foresight to capitalize on international opportunities? They mean that an understanding of cultural anthropology will be an important tool of competitive marketing. They mean that knowledge of the basic differences, as well as basic similarities, among consumers in different parts of the world will be essential. They mean that the successful marketer of the future will have to think not of a United States customer, nor even of a Western European or Atlantic community customer, but of *a world customer.*

For Western European countries, it is specific marketing facts and consumer purchasing behavior patterns which are of moment to today's businessman seeking new customers. At present, these countries comprise the biggest potential overseas market for most products. They are also the countries about whose consumers the most research information has been gathered. However, as some of the above examples illustrate, other parts of the world too are becoming potential markets, as human desires break the barricades of centuries in South America, Africa, and Asia.

Emergence of the European Common Market has forced businessmen and philosophers alike to take a look at the European as a distinct species. We now see the European as more than a Frenchman or an Austrian. The Atlantic community market and the world market may make us yet take a fresh look at what is alike and what is really different in humans, their desires, hopes, fears—in short, their motivations. Close observation of customers, and potential customers, all over the world reveals that there *are* some striking similarities, yet at the same time a considerable degree of permanent difference. From objective examination of these basic cultural similarities and differences, one may discern clues for serving the World Customer today.

In this article, I shall first point to a number of consumer behavior patterns relevant to international marketing, particularly within the Western European market but also in some of the less developed areas. Then I shall examine the differential role of national pride, which obviously affects and will affect the success of American-made products in Western European and other countries in the Atlantic market. Finally, in an effort to define and interpret the economic and psychological differences among world customers, I shall postulate six world market groups of nations, measured by the yardstick of middle class development.

The Distinctive European

The U.S. company going into Europe has to study the culture and the psychology of the people of the country, not just its manufacturing facilities and markets in the technological sense. The advertising and sales managers have to learn that reaching customers in a given country involves a real understanding of the basic motivations which operate within that country.

In dealing with various European markets. the American businessman must open his eyes to certain paradoxes, stereotypes, and hidden competitors.

Apparent Paradoxes

There are paradoxes between the way in which American products are perceived and the way they are used. Thus, anti-Americanism is strongly coupled with a desire for many U.S. products, often out of pure snobbery, often because they are symbols of an affluent society. The Italian housewife considers her American sister a poor cook and a lady of leisure, but dreams day and night of owning a Hollywood kitchen.

A similar paradox is that of the West German businessman who scoffs at American know-how, pointing out the technical superiority of many of his national products, but proudly puts his elegantly uniformed chauffeur in a Ford, polished up to the last fold of its lacquered steel hull tuxedo.

Ingrained Stereotypes

The American businessman must cast off deeply ingrained stereotypes in analyzing the purchasing behavior of European consumers, in reference to product meaning, "purchasing morality," and quality consciousness.

We all "know" that French women are very fashion conscious. Yet a study recently showed that this was exactly one of those glib stereotypes that have little if any basis in reality. The purchase of a dress or coat is much more of an investment for the Frenchwoman than for the American women. This results from differences both in income and in prices of fashion products. It is not enough, therefore, to tell a French shopper that a garment is fashionable. She also wants to know, in a way, the "trade-in-value" of the dress or blouse. How long will the fabric last? How many years will she be able to wear it? These are promises and appeals which have to a very large extent lost their attraction to the American woman.

The European is very conscious of preservation. He collects and retains things. The only parallel that we have had in this country was during the period of World War II, when we developed a new kind of pride, a pride in doing without, a pride in not having bought a new car for several years, for example. This pride did not last very long. Just as soon as cars became available again, we reverted to our somewhat affluent American habit of replacing models quite rapidly. Yet this concept of "purchasing morality" still exerts influence in the United States for some products. For example, the average male still hesitates to buy two or three suits at one time because he feels that suits, together with many other articles of clothing, are highly overvalued, and therefore it is extravagant to buy more than one at the same time. On the other hand, most of us have learned that it no longer pays to resole shoes more than twice.

As for quality consciousness, as well as confidence in the trustworthiness of the manufacturer, this is quite different in different countries. In Australia or South Africa—and for that matter in England—you find on most toilet tissues the reassuring message that the manufacturer guarantees that the paper was not made out of secondhand rags, but only new rags and new raw materials.

Such a promise has become completely unnecessary in North America. Whatever advertising may be accused of, in many areas it provides the consumer, particularly in branded merchandise, with an assurance that he will not be cheated as long as he buys a well-known brand. It is true today that whether we buy a Westinghouse, a General Electric, or a Kelvinator refrigerator, we get more or less equal values as long as we pay about the same amount of money. What we have learned to buy is the freedom of individual choice. We buy images; we buy the sizzle because we have been reassured that the steak itself is of generally good quality. *In many European countries this confidence,* this almost blind reliance on the promise of the manufacturer, *has not yet been established.* Therefore, advertising approaches have to be based much more on definite proofs of quality.

Hidden Competitors

Another problem facing Atlantic marketers is that in many areas they are still dealing with hidden competitors, lurking in places unfamiliar in domestic marketing. Taking toilet tissue again, in some recent motivational research done in West Germany I found it was much too premature to promise the German consumer luxury softness or colors compatible with the bathroom fixtures. Instead, the hidden but real competitor with which the toilet tissue manufacturer has to contend is the newspaper and the old standby of the German equivalent of the Sears, Roebuck catalog. The West German family feels that toilet tissue, particularly the American luxury type, is wasteful and unnecessary. The advertising approach, then, has to deal much more with providing absolution and selling the concept that good quality toilet tissue is a part of modern life.

Ethos of Nationalism

Nationalism obviously plays a major role in determing consumer acceptance of nondomestically made products. Understanding its manifold aspects is a *sine qua non* for U.S. businessmen operating overseas.

National feeling manifests itself in many ways. Some of these have already been touched on briefly before. In this section, I shall show in greater detail how: (1) national pride can be a motivating sales factor employable by the astute overseas marketer as an asset; (2) long-standing cultural traditions in one nation can dictate the *discard* of advertising approaches proven successful in another nation; (3) stereotyped national *self*-illusions can alter the direction of marketing strategy.

National Pride

Admiration of foreign products often goes together with *hidden inferiority feelings* which are overcompensated by tearing the foreigner down. These products are the tangible symbols of foreign superiority, For example:

● In Venezuela, despite various forms of anti-Yankee sentiment, it is considered chic to smoke U.S. cigarettes. Even when the American brand name is used and the Venezuelan smoker can discover the little phrase "Hecho en Venezuela" on his package the almost completely identical cigarette suffers at least a 50% prestige loss. A successful approach used in overcoming this problem was to convince Venezuelans that the people they secretly admired in a form of love-hatred—the Americans—indeed liked Venezuelan tobacco, used it for their own cigarettes, and had no negative feeling toward Venezuelan cigarettes.

A similar solution was found in connection with Venezuelan rum by serving this rum in hotels in Caracas frequented by U.S. businessmen and tourists. The Venezuelan could be convinced that if it was good enough for the supposed foreign connoisseur, then it certainly ought to be good enough for him.

● The French gasoline, *Total*, had a domestic marketing problem arising from a national inferiority complex. Gasoline, to the Frenchman, was for a long time represented by American and British companies. Gasoline and oil (to a lesser extent) are symbols of power. The Frenchman was not convinced that his own gasoline would have the same power as the foreign brands. The approach calculated to overcome this sentiment was to present *Total* as an international brand that happened to originate in France and the Sahara, but was accepted and well-liked in many other countries.

● In Morocco, sales of French pasteurized milk had dropped considerably with the advent of Morocco's independence. This stemmed partly from the exodus of the French army with its families, and also from Moroccan unfamiliarity with drinking pasteurized milk.

But the drop in milk sales was also due to other factors, psychological in nature. One was the lack of confidence in the quality of pasteurized milk—Moroccan women were accustomed to buying from street vendors who milked the cows in front of their own eyes and then ladled the milk out of the pail. The soulless, odorless, clean pasteurized milk in bottles was simply too far removed from the original natural source of milk for the women to realize that they were still receiving the same quality of product.

But even more interesting was a factor dealing again with the phenomenon of national pride. The company had changed the lettering on its milk bottles and milk cartons from French to Arabic. The purpose was to please the newly independent consumers. Research showed, however, that instead of being pleased, consumers reacted negatively to this attempt at flattery. They stated it in the following way: "What is good enough for the French people is good enough for us. We don't want Arab milk. We want good French milk that the Frenchmen drink themselves."

For *marketing purposes* it thus was necessary to re-establish confidence in the naturalness of pasteurized bottled milk by showing cows and having street vendors also peddle pasteurized milk. A second measure was to change the lettering on the milk bottles back to French. Both steps resulted in increased sales.

The little phrase "Made in ..." can have a tremendous influence on the acceptance and success of products over and above the specific advertising techniques used by themselves.

In a recent study in West Germany, this query was posed as part of a projective test: "An important discovery has been made in the technical field which has a great influence on our daily life. Which country has made this discovery?" As many as 78% answered: "Germany." (The study is being repeated in other countries. It will be interesting to examine the answers.) We also asked the Germans to think of a new product which through an error in production caused the death of several hundred people. The task of the respondents was to indicate which country would be most likely to manufacture such a product. We found that Germans considered this most likely to happen in the East zone, Russia, or the satellite countries, and then up to 30% in Italy or France.

The strong positive attitude evidenced by Germans toward their own technical product influenced an advertising approach developed for Ford in

Germany. Research showed that the name Ford had a strong American association. The reaction of Germans was: "Americans drive our cars, Volkswagen and Mercedes; therefore they must be convinced that German cars are better than their own; so why should we buy their cars?" When the German Ford was presented as an example of cooperation between American ingenuity and know-how and German thoroughness efficiency, considerable sales success was achieved.

"Inverted Morality"

The influence of cultural traditions permeates a host of consumer behavior patterns.

The fact that 64% of Frenchmen don't brush their teeth is in part caused by the lack of running water in many communities. But a far more interesting aspect of this behavior could be explained on the basis of what I call "inverted morality." Here is an illustration of what can happen:

In Puritanical cultures it is customary to think of cleanliness as being next to godliness. The body and its functions are covered up as much as possible.

But, in Catholic and Latin countries, to fool too much with one's body, to overindulge in bathing or toiletries, has the opposite meaning. It is *that* type of behavior which is considered immoral and improper. Accordingly, an advertising approach based on Puritanical principles, threatening Frenchmen that if they didn't brush their teeth regularly, they would develop cavities or would not find a lover, failed to impress.

To fit the accepted concept of morality, the French advertising agency changed this approach to a permissive one. The new approach presented the brushing of teeth as modern and chic but not as an absolute necessity which when neglected would result in dire consequences.

In line with the "inverted morality" notion is the fact that deodorant sales in France are lower than in most of other countries. The majority, up to 80% of French housewives, use laundry soap instead of toilet soap. Only 20% of them have discovered perfumed, feminine soap which in the United States is frequently referred to as a "French type" of soap.

Self-Illusions

Often nationals of a particular country are completely mistaken themselves about their own main characteristics. Successful marketers must be as cognizant of these national self-illusions as they must be aware of the mistaken sterotypes noted earlier. For example:

• Germans still refer to themselves as a nation of poets and thinkers; yet the largest selling newspaper, *The Bildzeitung,* has a circulation of 2½ million based largely on sensationalism and tabloid treatment of news. Even German *advertisers* had to be shown that this circulation, although proven by audits, was indeed psychologically possible. The only way this could be done was to force the German advertiser to look at his own people, including himself, without hypocrisy and in the harsh light of reality.

• All references to economy, comfort, and warmth had only a minimal effect in getting Englishmen to install central heating. They all ran up against a barrier of traditional self-illusion that Englishmen are of a hardy race that does not need the softening and effeminate effect of central heating. Inroads could be made only when the health of babies was used as a rationalization and after reassurance was given to the English "he-man ' that to feel comfortably warm would not be detrimental to his self-image of virility.

• Most Europeans are convinced that they are individualists and nonconformists. Studies have shown that this is to a very large extent an illusion. There is a widely expressed fear of losing individuality, but right now it is the European who is becoming the representative of the mass market while it is the American market which in turn relies more and more on psychological segmentations. U.S. manufacturers may produce individuality on a mass scale, but individuality has become the decisive appeal in many products and services.

National self-illusions are hardly restricted to other nations. In the United States, as in quite a few other countries, many of our ethical principles are still based on the concept that we have to work by the sweat of our brow. In Germany, this is even more so. *The more you work, the more moral you feel.* Yet at the same time our modern psychological development and automation have resulted in a situation where fewer and fewer people work with their hands. Service fields are increasing, and we have more and more leisure time. The recent victory of the electricians' union in New York introducing a five-hour day aroused the nation for many reasons. Particularly pertinent here is that it clashed with most of our cherished beliefs of the importance of achieving happiness through work.

We are now confronted with increasing leisure time. Our discomfort results to a large extent from a lack of hedonistic morality such as prevailed among the Greeks for whom life was here to be enjoyed by a few people who did not have to work and did not have to feel guilty about it.

Leisure pursuits are spreading rapidly. Labor-saving devices are multiplying, and they are being adopted all over the world. The major differences lies in the degree of manifest or latent guilt feelings which are aroused:

• Instant coffee is used by the Dutch housewife accompanied by the verbal protests that she only uses it in an emergency. What happens, however, is that the number of emergencies has increased amazingly.

• French farmwives are inclined to say that they need large kitchen stoves in order to do the cooking for their large farm families. Young farmwives, however, have begun to admire and gradually buy the smaller units used by their city sisters. They have discovered that they do not have to stay as long behind the stove, and so are finding interests in other roles than that of a kitchen slave.

Breaking Boundaries

Politically, in recent years we have watched a host of new nations emerge from erstwhile colonial status. It may be argued that many colonies would have been better off staying under the protection of enlightened colonial powers. Yet their desire for independence, no matter how premature we consider it to be, is so impulsive, explosive, and uncontrollable that no other solution remains than to satisfy this emotionally, humanly understandable hunger.

More important to the marketer is the fact that the same desire which spurred these political events has another dimension—viz., *in terms of consumption, whole centuries are being skipped in a world revolution of human expectations.*

Thus, from the viewpoint of the international psychologist's concern with the people still living in national units, we see the gradual development of the World Customer who breaks all boundaries:

- When a South African clothing manufacturer asks how to sell more long pants to previously half-naked Bantus, he is the first one to smash the barrier of apartheid, no matter how segregationistic his views may be. The moment one starts thinking of 10 million natives as consumers, one has to concern himself with their emotions and motivations.

Research revealed a greater psychological parallel between the emancipated Zulu and the emancipated white worker than between the nonemancipated Zulu and his emancipated tribal brother. The latter is ashamed when visited by his former ethnic peers. He has learned to speak English Afrikaans, has started to wear long pants, and often owns a car—a secondhand, dilapidated car, but nevertheless a car. He represents in many ways the same emotional conflict as that which existed between the first- and second-generation immigrants during the period of heavy immigration in the United States.

- In Australia until a few years ago 10% of the population was represented each year by newcomers, migrants, or—more euphemistically—"new Australians." These new Australians will change the basic Australian character in unrecognizable fashion within another ten years or so. As consumers, on the one hand, they want to eat, drink, and use the same products as the established Australians; on the other hand, they bring in their own customs and often superimpose Italian, German, or Spanish culture on the Australians.

Six Market Groups

How can we locate the World Customer at various stages of development? How can we measure nations?

The "consumer revolution" which we are witnessing is basically not a proletarian one, but *is a revolution of the middle class.* It is the degree of development of a large middle class which makes the difference between a backward and a modern country both economically and psychologically. That is the clue for appraising and interpreting different cultures, for measuring their achievement.

The most important symbol of middle class development in the world today is the automobile. It is the automobile which represents achievement and personal freedom for the middle class. And this restless middle class is the most important factor in the constructive discontent which motivates people's desires and truly moves them forward. In some countries, like the United States, West Germany, Switzerland, Sweden, and Norway, most people have enough to eat and are reasonably well housed. Having achieved this thousand-year-old dream of humanity, they now reach out for further satisfactions. They want to travel, discover, be at least physically independent. The automobile is the symbol of mobility; the automobile has become the self-mobile!

Using middle class development as a measure of achievement, if we were to visualize the social composition of each country in terms of a scale showing the size of its middle class, upper class, and lower class, we could probably define some six groups.

Group One: The Almost Classless Society, Contented Countries. In this group we would include primarily the Scandinavian countries. The middle class takes up almost all of the scale, with very few people left who could be considered really poor and few who are really rich. We are dealing with a socialistic security and equalization which sounds like paradise, but often leads to loss of incentives.

In these countries, products are viewed in a rather sober fashion. The car, for instance, is strictly utilitarian, and showing off with one's auto is not considered correct.

Studies have shown that reliability and economy are very important. Attitudes toward products are rational: they do not represent a special status value. There is generally a conservative attitude toward new gadgets and styles. Second cars are practically nonexistent.

Group Two: The Affluent Countries. This group includes the United States, West Germany, Switzerland, Holland, and Canada. Few people starve, and there is still some room at the top. The top of the middle class itself, however, often is high and desirable enough so that there is no need to break through and trespass into the unpopular and threatened class of financial aristocracy.

Among these countries the most advanced is the United States. What happens in many areas in the United States represents the latest and leading trends and permits us to predict what will happen in the next few years in the other affluent countries. People in affluent countries want greater individuality in their products. They dream of high-quality, repair-proof, almost custom-tailored articles.

While the German still uses his car for prestige purposes, in the United States the status value of cars has substantially diminished and has been shifted to other products and services such as swimming pools, travel, and education. The average American considers his car more like an appliance than a status symbol. Conspicuous cars like the Cadillac or the Lincoln try to emphasize their quiet elegance to avoid being considered cars for show-offs. There is increased attention to functional values and integration in car designs. Cars are not pampered; they are expected to do their job.

Group Three: Countries in Transition. In this group we may place England, France, Italy, Australia, South Africa, and Japan. These countries still have a working class in the nineteenth century sense. But this class is trying to break out of its bondage and join the comfortable middle class. The upper classes still have privileges and can afford maids, Rolls-Royces, and castles; but their privileges are being rapidly whittled away. These countries have not had complete social revolutions. (The Labor government in England represented such an attempt but failed.) Servants are still cheap but rapidly getting more expensive and less easily available. Many wage-earning groups suffer from low wages. Living standards are behind those of the United States and West Germany. The white-collar worker often makes less money than the factory worker, but he has not integrated yet with the developing labor-based middle class. Prestige still plays an important role.

Cars are pampered in these countries. They are an extension of one's personality. They are given pet names. They represent major investments. Cars are outward symbols of success. There are still many first-car people, who have only now bought their first proof of "having arrived." Price plays an important role as an invitation to enter the automobile world—upgrading the buyer from bicycles and motorcycles. For top classes, some very expensive cars are available. Style plays a role with certain groups; there is much experimentation, curiosity, and desire for product adventure. Markets are still fluid, have not stabilized yet. There is resistance in all these countries against planned obsolescence. A lot of people hold onto their cars for six to ten years or more. American cars are considered to be too flashy and also too expensive.

Group Four: Revolutionary Countries. Venezuela, Mexico, Argentina, Brazil, Spain, India, China, and the Philippines are in this group. In these areas large groups of people are just emerging from near-starvation and are discovering industrialization. Relatively speaking, there are more extremely rich people, a small but expanding middle class, and a very large body of depressed economic groups that are beginning to discover the possibilities of enjoying life through the revolution in industry.

In these countries large sections of the population have not even reached the level of being consumers. These are the Indians living in many South American countries, the people living in villages in India and Indonesia, and so on.

Automobiles are available only to a relatively small group. They are expensive and considered a luxury. They are taxed so highly that they are beyond the reach of most people. American cars are considered the idea. People want to show off. Small cars are bought as a way to get started. As the middle class develops, there should be an even further increase in the sale of small and compact cars, with the really rich people preferring big American cars.

Group Five: Primitive Countries. The newly liberated countries of Africa and the remaining colonies comprise the fifth group. In these countries there exists only a very small group of wealthy indigenous and foreign businessmen, new political leaders, and foreign advisers. The rest of the population is most often illiterate and ignorant and exists in a preconsumer stage, characterized either by barter or by almost complete primitive "self-sufficiency." The few cars that are sold are primarily for the government bureaucracy. There is no real car market as yet:

Group Six: The New Class Society. In Russia and its satellite countries, there is emerging a class of bureaucrats who represent a new form of aristocracy, while everybody else represents a slowly improving, low middle class. True, in these countries the extremely low income and the starving proletarians have disappeared.

The automobile, the modern home with its mechanized kitchen and mass-produced food items, and supermarket distribution represent the symbols of a new industrial society. By understanding the basic position of a country on this scale of development one can understand the role of products at present and one can also predict their future possibilities.

There is an interest in prestige cars. All the bourgeois symbols of capitalist countries are being copied—particularly those of the United States.

Our Greatest Opportunity

Many recent stories in the press—most of them picked up in foreign countries—make it appear that we ought to be ashamed of the good life we are leading. This recanting has its origin in a deep-seated guilt feeling which is unhealthy and dangerous. Some of the recanting is directed against a number of specific products, such as electrical gadgets, big cars, luxury and leisure time, and merchandise.

The real measuring rod of the success of one system over another should be based on the happiness of the citizens, their creativeness, and their constructive discontent. The desire to grow, to improve oneself, and to enjoy life to the fullest is at least equal, if not decidedly superior, to the goal of being ahead in a missile or a satellite program.

Our present life, therefore, should be presented as a challenge to the outside world—not in a boastful way, but as a life attainable by everyone through democratic and peaceful pursuits.

Conclusion

In most countries I have visited, I find that human desires are pretty much alike. The big difference lies in the level of achievement, in its many different forms.[1]

In Iquitos, on the Amazon River, I recently visited an Indian tribe. They live in blissful fashion, hunting and planting bananas and yuccas. Who is smarter—we, the hard-working "civilized people"—or the contented Indians? Part of the answer was provided by the fact that our guide complained that there were fewer and fewer Indians for tourists to see. They were becoming "too civilized." In other words, these primitive people who were supposed to be happy are caught in the inevitable maelstrom of development. They smoke cigarettes and are beginning to wear jeans and shirts.

Growth and progress are the only possible goals of life. I believe that the clue to man's destiny lies in his relentless training toward independence, not only politically, but also in the psychological sense. We are beset by fears, by inhibitions, by narrow-minded routine thinking. Step by step, year by year, we free ourselves more and more. Jets reduce physical distances; international trade and mass communications break down barriers. The world is opening up. The Common Market will broaden into an Atlantic Market and finally into a World Market. In order to participate effectively in this progressive development of mankind, it is essential to have a creative awareness of human desire and its strategy throughout the world—to understand and prepare to serve the New World Customer.

[1] See David C. McClelland, "Business Drive and National Achievement," page 99 of this issue.—*The Editors*

*In formulating world product policy, a
multinational company has two broad
strategic alternatives. It may extend its
domestic product line to world markets
without adjusting to foreign market
conditions, or it may adjust its product and
marketing communications to respond to
different foreign marketing environments.*

Multinational Marketing Strategy and Organization: An Overview

Warren J. Keegan

One of the most striking business developments in recent years has been the emergence of the multinational manufacturing corporation as an important factor in the international economy. Natural resource extraction, transportation, utility, and financial companies have been operating directly in foreign countries for many decades; so have a limited number of manufacturing companies. But for the most part, it has only been since World War II that large numbers of manufacturing companies have extended the scope of their international operations to anything more extensive than a domestically based export operation selling through a network of independent agents and distributors. Today, increasing numbers of United State corporations look abroad for substantial proportions of their profits and sales, and indeed, it is not uncommon to find companies whose sales and profits from abroad exceed those from the United States. The investments of United States companies abroad are now six times greater than at the end of World War II. Increasingly, they include not only manufacturing facilities, but research facilities as well as extensive marketing organizations.

A small but growing number of U.S. companies have substantial proportions of assets and sales outside the United States. To reflect this foreign involvement,

Reprinted by permission of the author and the publisher from *Changing Marketing Systems,* edited by M. S. Moyer (Chicago: American Marketing Association, 1967), pp. 203-209.

and the change it has brought about, the terms "international," "worldwide," "multi-national" corporation have appeared and are now frequently used to describe the company whose scope of operations encompasses many countries and regions, and whose management considers the entire world as the company's potential area of operations.

The Problem

One of the most important challenges to a headquarters executive of a multi-national firm is the formulation of an effective world marketing strategy. This objective is by no means an accepted goal. There is a widespread view current among international executives that it is impossible to plan the marketing function at the headquarters level in a multi-national corporation. Advocates of this position argue that the variations in local markets are so great in so many different dimensions—economic, social and political—that it is imperative that the marketing function be handled entirely at the local level.

In this article, we shall show that in a multi-national corporation, important elements of marketing strategy must be formulated at the headquarters level. In a multinational company, the organizational framework and extent of decision-making decentralization will vary from company to company, but at a minimum, the headquarters executive group is responsible for formulating company strategy, that is, for the determination of overall objectives and the allocation of financial and manpower resources to achieve these objectives. Marketing strategy at the headquarters level includes the indentification of areas of operation, both in geographic and product terms, the formulation of strategy regarding marketing communications (advertising, sales promotion, direct mail) which will be prepared for the areas of operation, the formulation of a strategic pricing policy to set limits upon pricing tactics employed by subsidiary companies, and the allocation of corporate resources to support formulated programs.

A Conceptual Framework for Multi-National Marketing Strategy Formulation

The strategic marketing task of the headquarters-based international executive is formidable. He must identify worldwide opportunities and risks in both geographic and product dimensions. He must appraise the company's internal resources, competence, and response capability. In the light of these factors, he must adjust the mix of controllable marketing factors to formulate a marketing program designed to achieve the maximum level of profitable product adoption in the world marketplace. Conceptually, this strategic process can be represented as a hexagon within a hexagon within a pentagon (Exhibit 1). The sides of the hexagon represent the controllable elements of a marketing program, or the marketing mix. These elements are the product, price, marketing communications, channels of distribution, the marketing information system, which includes feedback from marketing operations as well as marketing intelligence operations designed to gather environmental information, and marketing organization.

The marketing executive, as he adjusts the controllable elements of the marketing mix, responds to relevant observable and measurable independent variables which together form the environment for marketing decisions. These directly relevant variables are shown as the sides of the hexagon enclosing the hexagon in Exhibit 1. These variables include prescriptions, or any ruling affecting a company from "guidelines" to decisions of administrative tribunals, to laws or decrees. Prescriptions may originate with voluntary associations, national or regional governmental or para-governmental institutions, or with legal authority. These are the "rules of the game" which provide the parameters of the marketing decision framework. The other sides of the pentagon include the distribution system, customers, competition, technology and cost. These relevant independent variables are themselves manifestations of underlying basic forces which are represented in Exhibit 1 as the sides of the outer pentagon. The underlying basic macro-forces (economic, social, political, geographic, and scientific) are more important in the context of long-range planning than in the formulation of current programs.

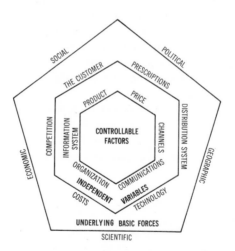

Exhibit 1   Multi-national marketing strategy: a conceptual framework

Multi-National Marketing: Strategic Alternatives

Given this conceptual framework in the product and communications policy areas there are two broad strategic marketing alternatives open to the manufacturing company in international markets: extension or adjustment. The extension approach takes the home marketing mix as given and extends it without adjustment to foreign markets. The product is unchanged, marketing communications are unchanged except for translation, and factory selling price is unchanged. This strategy is frequently employed by companies which are entering foreign markets for the first time. It is also employed by companies which have been involved in international operations for many years and which fail to appreciate the marketing opportunities they have foregone by not pursuing a strategy of adjustment in international markets. The extension strategy in world markets assumes that the need satisfied by a product is the same in all cultures and that the appeals to this need are universal. Perhaps the most notable example of the successful application of this strategy are the soft-drink franchisers. Pepsico's Vice President for Research has expressed this position as follows:

We do not believe that each country requires an individual advertising and product approach. Our experience and our relative success tell us otherwise. Each one of our 530 bottlers in the U.S. will claim at one time or another that their franchise is different. Yet we do not set up an advertising department in Shreveport, Louisiana to set up a separate plan or campaign for that market. No, we develop our plans and general strategy for all fifty states from a central headquarters. In developing our international marketing strategy, we believe in the basic psychological truth that there are greater differences within groups than between groups. It is the sameness in all human beings on which we believe we must base our selling appeals.[1]

Another Pepsi Cola official described that company's international marketing strategy as "one product, one image, and one sound, worldwide."

There are other products for which the extension approach has been applied with apparent success in international markets. American-blend cigarettes and U.S. bourbon are examples of products which have succeeded abroad because foreign consumers have adopted U.S. tastes. Still another application of this strategy is the case of clothing companies which have extended U.S. styles to foreign markets. A notable example is Levi-Strauss, which has sold the famous Levi blue jean without adapting to foreign markets. Indeed, the appeal of the Levi jean has been its close identification with the U.S. market and the Far West.

Unfortunately, however, there are even more examples of the unsuccessful application of the extension strategy to international marketing. The failure of the extension strategy can be traced to basic differences in foreign markets which may be reflected in different needs, or in different characteristics in foreign consumers and customers which require different marketing appeals. Food products extended from the U.S. to the British market provide a sobering record of market failure for the U.S. executive who believes that the British market is no different from the U.S. market. Campbell's found, for example, that its fabulously successful U.S. tomato soup formulation was not accepted in Britain, where consumers prefer a less sweet taste. Another U.S. company spent several million dollars in an unsuccessful effort to introduce U.S. style cake mixes to the British market. Closer to home is Philip-Morris' experience in attempting to take advantage of U.S. television advertising campaigns which have a sizable

---

[1] Norman Heller, "How Pepsi Cola Does It in 110 Countries," Address delivered at the 1966 World Congress, American Marketing Association, Chicago, page 11,13 (duplicated).

Canadian audience in border areas. The Canadian cigarette market is a Virginia or straight tobacco market in contrast to the U.S. market, which is a blended tobacco market. Philip-Morris officials decided that they would ignore market research evidence which indicated that Canadians would not accept a blended cigarette and went ahead with programs which achieved retail distribution of U.S. blended brands in the Canadian border areas served by U.S. television. Unfortunately, the Canadian preference for the straight cigarette remained unchanged. American-style cigarettes sold right up to the border but no further. Philip-Morris was forced to withdraw its U.S. brands.

One of the major strengths of the extension strategy is its lower cost. There are two sources of cost savings which follow from this approach. One, manufacturing economies of scale, is well known and understood. Less well known are the substantial economies associated with the standardization of marketing communications. For a company with worldwide operations, the cost of preparing separate print and TV-cinema films for each market would be enormous. Pepsi Co., International marketers have estimated, for example, that production costs for specially prepared advertising for foreign markets would cost them $8 million per annum, which is considerably more than the amounts now spent by Pepsi Co., International for advertising production. Although these cost savings are important, they should not distract executives from the more important objective of maximum profit performance, which may require the use of an adjustment strategy.

However, the many failures of the extension strategy in international marketing support the utility of considering a second strategic approach to international markets which is extension with adjustment. This approach takes the U.S. or home marketing mix as the base, and makes adjustments to this mix where it is believed desirable to do so. The adjustments may be in the product or marketing communications or in both. The decision of whether or not to adjust is based upon a comparison of estimates of market response to specified adjustments and of estimates of cost that would be involved in making such adjustments. (The argument that international marketers should adjust both product and communications to the different environmental conditions which exist around the world is clearly superficial, for it does not take into account the cost of adjusting or adapting a product or a communication program.)

The adjustment strategy in international marketing assumes that a product will either: (1) serve the same function in foreign markets under different use conditions, or (2) serve a new function or fill a different need under the same use conditions, or (3) serve a different function or fill a different need under different environmental conditions. These market conditions and indicated adjustment responses are illustrated in Table 1.

The international marketer pursuing the adjustment strategy adjusts his marketing mix abroad to fit the conditions which exist in foreign markets. For example, in markets where a product serves the same function under different conditions (Situation A), the international marketer will change or adjust the product while maintaining the same program of marketing communications. Gasoline refiners, for example, adjust their formulations to meet the weather conditions prevailing in market areas, but make no adjustments in marketing communications. Thus, Esso has successfully extended its U.S. "tiger in your tank" campaign to markets around the world. International soap and detergent manufacturers have adjusted their product formulations to meet local water conditions and the characteristcs of washing equipment. Marketing communications, again, have remained unchanged. Other examples of products which have been adjusted to perform the same function internationally under different environmental conditions are agricultural chemicals, which have been adjusted to meet different soil conditions and different types and levels of insect resistance, household appliances which have been scaled to sizes appropriate to different use environments, and clothing, which is adjusted to meet fashion criteria.

Table 1
Alternative Adjustment Situation In
Multi-National Marketing

Adjustment Situation	Market	Conditions	Adjustment Response
	Function or Need Satisfied	Use Conditions	
A	Same	Different	Change product
B	Different	Same	Change communications
C	Different	Different	Change both product and communications

When a product fills a different need or serves a different function under the same use conditions, (Situation B), the adjustment indicated is in marketing communications. There are many illustrations of market conditions which suggest this approach. Bicycles and motorscooters, for example, satisfy needs for basic transportation in many foreign countries and for recreation in the United States. Outboard motors are sold mainly to a recreation market in the United States, while the same motors in many foreign countries are sold mainly to fishing and transportation fleets. There are many examples of food products which serve entirely different needs in different markets. Many dry soup powders, for example, are sold mainly as soups in Europe and as sauces or cocktail dips in the United States. The products are identical; the only change is in marketing communications. In this case, the main communications adjustment is in the labeling of the powder. In Europe, the label illustrates and describes how to make soup out of the powder. In the United States, the label illustrates and describes how to make sauce and dip as well as soup. The appeal of the same product/different communication strategy is its cost of implementation. Since the product in this strategy is unchanged, there is no cost for product research and development or product adjustment. The only costs of the strategy are in identifying different product functions and reformulating marketing communications (advertising, sales promotion, point of sale material, etc.) around the newly identified function.

A third market condition indicating an adjustment strategy occurs when there are differences in environmental conditions of use and in the function which the product serves (Situation C). U.S. greeting card manufacturers have faced this set of circumstances in Europe, where the function of a greeting card is to provide a space for the sender to write his own message in contrast to the U.S. card, which contains a prepared message, or what is known in the greeting card industry as "sentiment." The conditions under which greeting cards are purchased in Europe are also different than in the United States. Cards are handled frequently by customers, a practice which makes it necessary to package the greeting card in European markets in cellophane. American manufacturers pursuing an adjustment strategy have changed both their product and their marketing communications in response to this set of environmental differences.

Sources of Strategic Information

When a headquarters executive in a multi-national corporation decides to formulate an international marketing strategy, he requires information to answer two basic questions. First, should I make an adjustment in the marketing mix for product x in international markets? And second, if I should adjust, what should be adjusted, and in what direction? The headquarters executive wishing to answer such questions must keep informed about the complex and changing world market environment by acquiring information from other people, both inside and outside his company, from publications and other documentary sources, and by directly observing the world in which he operates. Research we have recently conducted indicates the relative importance to high level headquarters executives in U.S. based multi-national corporations of different sources of strategic information about the world environment.

In our study, we classified all sources of information utilized by executives into three basic types: human, documentary and physical sources combined. Three important factors explain the commanding relative importance of human sources. The first is the opportunity to interact with a person. Interaction with an information source results in a focusing of the message flow upon the recipients' information needs, a process which is impossible with a single documentary source, and cumbersome with a collection of documents. The more focused a message, the more likely it is to be information, as opposed to meaningless data.

A second characteristic of human sources is that they can, like documentary sources, be checked over a period of time for accuracy and reliability. One executive, in talking about company representatives as a source of information, identified this factor in these words:

You learn to evaluate the company's representative in an area. If he is good, you rely on him for all your information. If he is not good, say, for example, he has a history of mis-interpreting or holding back information, you double-check, and use additional or even alternative sources.

Another and very important characteristic of human in contrast to documentary sources is the "off the record" nature of word of mouth communication. The same source may be less candid in print than in conversation for perfectly justifiable and understandable reasons. Bank newsletters, for example, when commenting on the situation in a particular country, must be somewhat guarded in their observations to avoid backlash against the sponsoring bank.

The single most important source of external information for executives are company executives based abroad in company subsidiaries, affiliates, and branches. The importance of executives abroad as a source of information about the world environment is one of the most striking features of the modern multi-national corporation. When a headquarters executive in an international corporation with operations abroad acquires external information, the most likely single source of this information is the company's own staff abroad. The general view of headquarters executives is that company executives overseas are the people who know best what is going on in their areas.

For the most part, we found, company executives abroad are in the same functional area as the headquarters executive acquiring information. The international divison head tends to get information from the head of operating companies abroad, the headquarters marketing executive from the overseas company's top marketing executive, and so on. There is a notable absence of information gained from lower level employees such as salesmen whose work brings them into everyday contact with the environment. (This pattern is by no means unique to international operations. In most domestic business operations, there is little or no direct information flow from lower level field sales people to headquarters executives and product engineers.)

The presence of an information network abroad in the form of company people is a major strength of the international company. It may also, paradoxically, be a weakness in the scanning posture of a company that has only partially extended the limits of its geographical operations because inside sources abroad tend to scan only information about their own countries, or at best their own region. Even though there may be more attractive opportunities outside of existing areas of operation, the chances of their being picked up by inside sources abroad is very low for their horizons tend to end at their national borders.

Competitors are an important human source of information for international executives. There is a much greater willingness and openess about exchanging information with competitors among international U.S. executives than among domestic executives, particularly those representing other U.S. international companies. There is a feeling among international executives that "we are all in this boat together" and indeed, there is some truth in this view. Overseas, U.S. executives often face well-developed patterns of "cooperation" among established national firms. At home, many international executives are still, or have been until very recently, engaged in a struggle to gain recognition, support, and understanding of international operations from corporate management. In addition, international U.S. companies that are intensely competitive in the United States are often less competitive abroad, particularly in the lower and middle income areas of the globe.

All of these factors, plus of course the social factor of common experiences, language, and attitudes, serve to create a climate of relatively free information exchange among U.S. international executives.

Documentary Sources

Documentary information sources, we found, are secondary to humans as sources of strategic information. Publications are the single most important source of documentary information. The second most important outside documentary source is information services. If these two outside documentary categories are combined, they are of equal relative importance to international division executives abroad.

Inside the company, letters and reports, mainly from executives abroad, are the most important documentary sources of information. Together, they are the source of as much important information as publications. Another documentary source category inside a company is information storage, which we conceive of as broadly inclusive of any kind of documentary, mechanical, or electrical storage of information outside of the human mind. We found this source to be of almost negligible importance. This finding underlines the difficulties of external information storage and transfer outside of the human memory, yet it suggests an opportunity for development of a major new source of external information. This finding is also a reminder that in spite of the broad label "comprehensive" which is applied to computer-based information systems in many companies, these systems are today almost exclusively concerned with internal information and are thus irrelevant to the task of keeping informed about the outside environment.

Many executives express frustration at the difficulty in trying to keep up with the outpouring of publications. Executives have responded in different ways to the publications explosion. In our investigation, a standard technique encountered was intensive use of the proverbial circular file. A few companies rely upon an internal routing arrangement for publications which permit readers to flag articles of particular interest for subsequent readers. Of far greater importance are the informal systems of cooperative publications scanning. Executives pass things on to other executives who they feel might be interested. These arrangements are reciprocal when executives are at the same level. In superior-subordinate cooperative scanning, however, the flow is mainly upward.

None of the management groups we studied employed a formal system for monitoring published information. This absence of formalized publications surveillance is somewhat surprising in light of the size of the larger companies in our sample. When questioned about the absence of such a system, executives were split between those who expressed some interest in the possibilities of such a system, and those who felt that an expenditure on such an effort would not be worth the gain.

The absence of a formal publications monitoring system has resulted in a considerable amount of reading duplication in many of the companies we studied. For example, in three companies, the high proportions of executives reading information services were *all* reading the same service. If only one executive in each of these companies would read a different service, the scope of the information service scanning in each company would be considerably extended.

Physical Phenomena

The direct perception of physical phenomena is a relatively limited but important source of strategic information acquired by executives. Thus, a major independent variable in the utilization of this source is travel. The instances cited are of two types—one is where the information gained by the executive was easily available from other sources but which required sensory perception of the actual phenomena to register the information in the executive's mind. An example of such an instance was the case of the executive who recalled his astonishment when he realized that his flight from Australia to New Zealand had taken three hours. This observation caused him to realize that the distance from Australia to New Zealand is much greater than he had thought. His image of the relative closeness of the two countries (based upon looking at maps and globes) had led him to suggest that New Zealand be placed under the operating control of the Australian manager. The direct perception of the physical distance led him to recommend that authority for New Zealand be transferred from Australia to New Zealand.

The other type of physical phenomena instances were those where the information gained was *not* readily available from alternative sources. An example of such an instance was the information that a company was erecting a plant in a country that was capable of producing directly competitive product x. Local executives in the country in question drove by the new plant every day on their way to their offices, but were unaware of the product x potential of the plant under construction. The company erecting the plant had announced that it was for product y, and local executives had accepted this announcement. The headquarters executive realized immediately as he was driven by the plant in question that it was potentially capable of producing product x. He possessed technical knowledge which enabled him to perceive information in a physical object—the plant—which his local executives, because they lacked this knowledge, were unable to perceive.

Source Location

Although for organizations as a whole, all external information comes originally from outside, this is not the case for the individual executive within an organization who gets much of his external information from sources located inside his company. The *relative* inportance of inside sources, however, is frequently exaggerated. For our overall sample, *two-thirds* of the important external information acquired came from sources located outside the executive's company. This overall reliance upon outside sources is one of the important findings of our study. For some executives, the reliance upon outside sources is a deliberate strategy.

For many executives and students of organizations, the finding of heavy reliance upon outside sources will come as a surprise. For example, one writer, after emphasizing that the executive is within an organization, maintains that:[2]

> What goes on outside is usually not even known firsthand. It is received through an organizational filter of reports, that is, in an already pre-digested and highly abstract form that imposes organizational criteria of relevance on the outside reality.

An explanation for the tendency of observers and practitioners alike to overestimate the relative importance of sources inside the company might be the result of a failure to distinguish between external and internal information. The sheer volume of internal data and information contained in regularly presented reports that make up a management information system far exceed the very limited amount of external information contained in such reports. Many executives have erronously assumed that because inside sources are the most important sources of internal information that they are also the most important sources of external information. As we have shown, this is a serious error.

Organization and Multi-National Marketing Strategy

Organizations should be structured to respond to the most important dimensions of the environment. In the international operations area, the most important dimension has been distance or geography. Thus, the typical international organization today is structured around geography. Europe, Africa and the Middle East; Japan, Australia and Southeast Asia; and all of Latin America are frequently combined in the same regional group. This structure, we submit, is more related to the era of steamboat surface travel and carrier pigeon communications than it is to the contemporary world of countries at vastly different stages of economic and market development. When it took weeks to travel, or send a letter, from one continent to the next, the geographic organization structure made sense. The cost, in time and money, of attempting any other grouping, given the need for face to face contact between local and headquarters executives, would have been prohibitive. Today, with 600 m.p.h. jet aircraft and instant world-wide communications, geography is no longer the barrier it once was. Moreover, future developments in travel and communications are expected to continue to raise speeds and lower costs.

---

[2] Peter F. Drucker, *The Effective Executive* (New York: Harper and Row, 1966), page 13.

Today, the crucial factor in international markets is their socio-economic and not their geographic distance from each other. Japan has less in common with Malaysia than with the U.K. and EEC countries. South Africa has more in common with Australia than with Tanzania. The emergence of countries at vastly different stages of market development in the same geographic region is a development which calls for a new organizational approach by companies whose international operations are spread over markets at different socio-economic stages of development on many continents.

One approach which may prove to be viable is organization by stages of market development. A stages-of-market-development organization would assemble the countries in its system into groups which reflected similar market conditions. An example of the categories and country assignments that a multinational company might utilize is shown in Table 2. The advantage of the stage of market development organization is its ability to focus the efforts of executives at the headquarters and sub-headquarters level upon strategic problems and opportunities associated with most significant dimensions of today's international environment.

The weakness of the geographic organizational structure is its failure to focus company skills and efforts on markets in underdeveloped or intermediate stages of development. This failure to perform is most evident in the product dimension. For example, there are an estimated 600 million women in the world who still scrub their clothes by hand. These women have been served by multi-national soap and detergent companies for decades, yet until this year, none of these companies had attempted to develop an inexpensive manual washing device.

Table 2
Stages of Market Development
Hypothetical Grouping

Underdeveloped	Intermediate	Advanced
Tanzania	Southern Italy	U.S.A.
Malaysia	Portugal	U.K.
Tunisia	Ghana	France
Laos	Philippines	Germany
Gabon	Venezuela	Northern Italy
Peru	Argentina	Japan, etc.

Colgate Palmolive has shown what can be done when product development efforts are focused upon market needs. A vice president of Colgate asked the leading inventor of modern mechanical washing processes to consider "inventing backwards"—to apply his knowledge not to a better mechanical washing device, but to a much better manual device. The device developed by the inventor is an inexpensive (selling price: under $10), all plastic, hand powered washer that has the tumbling action of a modern automatic machine. The response to this device in less-developed country markets has been enthusiastic.

Organization by stages of market development would, by focusing organizational efforts on market needs, encourage not only product development but pricing and communications strategies tailored to market needs. The important question for a company considering a market stages organizational structure is whether or not the scale of company operations in markets at different stages of development is, or is expected to be, sufficient to justify the creation of separate organizational units.

The cost in time and money of travel and communications has dramatically fallen in recent years, but it is still significant. In companies where organizational adjustments are expected to justify themselves on an immediate payback basis, there is a certain minimum size which must be achieved in order to cover the additional travel and communications expenditures of the stages of market development type of organization. Only larger companies can justify this type of organization on an immediate payback basis. However, companies which view organizational structure as a capital investment may decide to move to a stages-of-market-development organization as part of a strategic plan to develop business in middle and lower income markets.

Conclusion

Marketing strategy and organizational structure in the multi-national company are closely interrelated. Decisions regarding market goals and objectives, product, price, and communication strategies, and resource commitments to implement these strategies are the basic elements of the strategic process. These decisions are a function of the information available to executives, and information flows are directly related to the job relationships and direct perception experiences of executives. Since these relationships and perception experiences are a function of organizational structure, strategic decisions and adjustments will be, in our judgment, more market oriented when markets are grouped according to stages of socio-economic development. This structure will mass the organization's marketing and technical resources around environmental differences. These differences are essential dimensions of response for companies whose products (1) serve a different function, (2) fill a different need or (3) are used under significantly different conditions in foreign markets.

There are profitable markets in the less-developed countries (LDCs) of the world. To lump all of these markets together into something called international marketing is a mistake. Profits will be made by those marketers understanding the real differences in each of these markets. This article points out how marketers must adapt their policies and practices to meet the socioeconomic circumstances of national and regional markets overseas.

Marketing Policy Decisions Facing International Marketers in the Less-developed Countries

Harry A. Lipson

Douglas F. Lamont

Marketers ask the following questions in making policy decisions to create profitable returns for their firms.[1] What are the market opportunities? What market goals can be set? What type of market organization can be established? What market resources are available? What are the possible market offerings? How can control over market performance be maintained? What type of market audits will show future profit-making possibilities?

International marketers make these policy decisions within national market economies whose sectoral capabilities to produce high-level standards of living for a majority of the population range from highly developed, as in the United

Reprinted by permission of the author and the publisher from the *Journal of Marketing*, published by the American Marketing Association, Vol. 33, No. 4 (October, 1969), pp. 24-31.

[1] For a discussion of the responsibilities of administrators of business systems, see Harry A. Lipson and John R. Darling, Jr., *Introduction to Marketing Administration*, John Wiley & Sons, Inc., forthcoming.

States, to very poorly developed, as in Nigeria. Marketing policies employed in a mass consumption economy cannot be transferred to less-developed economies without a great deal of change. As a consequence, international marketers face the difficult task of adapting marketing policies to fit the peculiar requirements of local national markets.

This article will show marketers how to make proper marketing decisions within the less-developed countries (LDCs) of the world. LDCs are those countries which have a per capita national income of less than $500 per year. Their middle class is small; the majority of the people are poor. Markets are highly fragmented in terms of income, social class, language and tribal differences, and other socioeconomic characteristics. The institutional structure needed to integrate these markets is organized on a very inefficient basis or is nonexistent.

Marketers have to deal with these conditions in setting policy decisions that will lead to profits. They are faced with impoverished economies whose governments seek change. National economic plans drawn up to formalize the desire for greater economic prosperity give marketers an indication as to how they can support the public goals of the country in which they are doing business, and at the same time find new avenues for marketing success. Examples of adaptations in marketing policies to fit local governmental and cultural circumstances are presented below from experiences actually encountered within the underdeveloped world. India, Nigeria, and Mexico were selected for presentation simply because they show that the marketing adaptation problem is not bound by geography, cultural differences, or stages of economic growth. The problem exists for markets in Asia, Africa, and Latin America.[2] These examples may be interpreted as a running account of the "game of marketing adaptation" in the three countries and are designed to give marketers some guidance as to how they might better carry out their jobs within the LDCs.[3]

Analysis of Market Opportunities

In the LDCs, an analysis of possible market opportunities is a three-fold procedure. First, given the paucity of information and its relative unreliability, marketers are faced with problems of estimating customer markets from gross data sources. Means are available to do so,[4] and estimates of potential markets through production figures converted into apparent consumption figures provide

---

[2] The results presented in this paper are a part of a research project carried out in the International Business Program of the Graduate School of Business at the University of Alabama. Two graduate students, John W. Roquemore and Richard H. Kenyon, were responsible for the basic findings on India and Nigeria.

[3] The "game of marketing in adaptation" was first suggested in a paper presented by one of the authors, Douglas F. Lamont, at the 1968 Southern Marketing Association meetings held in Washington, D.C. It has been published under the title of "Opportunities for Marketing Growth in the Mexican Market," *Southern Journal of Business*, Vol. 4 (April, 1969), pp. 272-278.

[4] Reed Moyer, "International Market Analysis," *Journal of Marketing Research*, Vol. 5 (November, 1968), pp. 353-361.

a marketer with useful analytical information. The knowledge that 5% of India's 520 million population, or 26 million people, have incomes that give them the buying power of the average American should suggest to marketers that it is imperative for them to get in early in India's industrialization and market development. Such a market size in fact represents an affluent market that is just a little larger than the Canadian market. If marketers only had a knowledge of India's per capita national income, they more than likely would have overlooked this "well-to-do" potential consumer market within the sea of a traditional society.

Second, such national estimates must be tempered with a qualitative understanding of the real regional and cultural differences that exist within the LDCs. The boundaries of most Indian states were drawn to represent the local dominance of a particular subcultural language. Before the present war between Nigeria and Biafra, Nigeria had been divided into four regional areas; although in each area one major tribe dominated the others, 200 different languages are still spoken among the 40 million people of Nigeria. In West Africa, language differences reflect such wide cultural differences that only a very few products can bridge the gap successfully. Such simple things as the print on cotton fabrics fail to gain sufficient consumer acceptance for economy-of-scale purposes, because there are so many ideas to what is right and proper. Market size in Nigeria is so small that marketers develop a market at their own peril if they do not know beforehand the *real* size of their potential market.

English is used as the *lingua franca* along with Hindi in India and Hausa in Nigeria. Spanish has played the same role in Mexico, but now it is slowly coming into full time use among the remaining three or four million Mexicans who speak different Indian languages. Language, therefore, plays a different role in Mexico for marketers. Marketers can be sure that the areas in which the Indian languages predominate are for the most part outside the developing sectors of the Mexican market economy. These would be areas that marketers should leave until last when planning new marketing activity within an LDC.

The real opportunities for marketers lie in regional and cultural market segments rather than in thinking about a broad national market opportunity. For each market segment, marketers should determine available income, effective buying power, propensity to buy, economic awareness for consumption increases, and those other socioeconomic characteristics that will give them the size of their potential market within highly fragmented national economies.

Third, an analysis of market opportunities will be complete only when marketers take into consideration the current shifts in governmental attitude on import-substitution industries, incentives for new investment, taxes and social security payments, and the many other items that will markedly affect whether the business operates at a profit or at a loss. Marketers should pay careful attention to changes in the administrative rules governing market entry. For example, by reading India's Second Five Year Plan (1956-1961), marketers found that certain industries were to be the exclusive responsibility of the Indian government. (This group includes munitions, atomic energy, iron and steel, heavy engineering and heavy electrical plant, coal, oil, most mining, aircraft, air transport, railways, shipbuilding, communications, and electrical generation and distribution.) A second group was listed for gradual state ownership. (This group includes some mining, aluminum, machine tools, ferro-alloys and tool steels, heavy chemicals, essential drugs, fertilizers, synthetic rubber, and road and sea transport.)[5] All other industries were left to private-sector enterprises for competitive market behavior. As the plan was carried out, it became apparent that the Indian government's Hindustan Antibiotics factory and Tata's, an Indian private-sector drug enterprise, could not meet the growing demand for drugs; Merck Sharpe and Dohme was given permission to enter a market that formerly had been closed to foreign private-sector enterprises.[6] A similar situation developed in the production and distribution of fertilizers. The demand for fertilizers increased as the need for Indian agriculture increased, and Armco was brought into the fertilizer business to service the growing demand.[7] These are only two examples of why marketers should carefully study the developmental plans and administrative rulings of the governments in the LDCs.

Nigeria's first developmental plan, published in 1964, did not present any involved schedules of industries that would become government owned. It simply defined the priorities for investment. If marketers wished to make investments in those industries that were on the top of the priority list, then they would be given special benefits by the Nigerian government. Knowledge about Mexico's plans for the improvement of irrigation, agriculture, public retail markets, and towns along the American border tells marketers about potential profit-making opportunities.[8] Many development plans such as those of INPI (Peru's National Planning Institute) or CORFO (Chile's Development Corporation) simply state the objectives to be achieved through the government's support of specific private-sector enterprises. A few plans, such as those of CORDIPLAN (the national plan of the Central Planning Agency of Venezuela) and the regional development plan of its offspring CVG (the Guyana Development Corporation), detail how new industry and new services will be brought to the wilderness of the Guyana area of Venezuela. The reading of national economic plans and their implementing directives is part and parcel of how market opportunities should be analyzed in the LDCs.

Market Goals

Using the analytical procedure outlined above, marketers are able to set goals for business institutions that can be realistically achieved. These range from an

---

[5] John P. Lewis, *Quiet Crisis in India* (Washington, D.C.: The Brookings Institution, 1962), p. 205.

[6] Same reference as footnote 5, p. 220.

[7] "The Role of Private Enterprise in Developing Indian Industry," *Foreign Trade,* Vol. 126 (October 1, 1966), pp. 11-12, at p. 12.

[8] Robert J. Shafer, *Mexico: Mutual Adjustment Planning,* National Planning Series, Vol. 4. (Syracuse, New York: Syracuse University Press, 1966). Also see Miguel S. Wionczek, "Incomplete Formal Planning: Mexico," in *Planning Economic Development,* Everett E. Hagen, ed. (Homewood, Ill.: Richard D. Irwin, Inc., 1963), pp. 150-182.

increase in sales volume, higher profitability, and greater return on investment to dominance of market position. Each goal is stated numerically as the result to be achieved at the end of the planning period under consideration. As long as these goals are predicated upon the reinvestment of earnings within the LDC, their achievement will lead to little resentment on the part of the local government. On the other hand, if these goals are predicated on the idea that earnings should be repatriated to the parent company on a long-term, continuing basis, then their achievement would be hindered and the company may open itself to a possible takeover by the local government.

There are no good rules of thumb about how much to reinvest and how much to repatriate. At the same time that the American government is insisting that U.S. firms overseas repatriate their profits as quickly as they can so that the American balance of payments position will be enhanced, serious study is being given in the LDCs to the notion that foreign businesses already have taken too much out of the economies of these countries. The petroleum and minerals extracting companies, which historically have paid only small amounts in taxes and have done little to increase the level of skills in the local work forces, have created a political environment in the LDCs that is highly suspicious of foreign direct investment. American marketers who insist on repatriation of profits because it will give them a payback period short enough to justify their higher assumed risks may find their markets taken over by German and Japanese marketers.

Local capital participation in joint venture arrangements plus Eurodollar financing can overcome some of these problems. However, such equity arrangements cannot overcome the basic unwillingness of American marketers to realize that the climate for their investments in the LDCs has changed. Consequently their goals concerning proper means for achieving market success in these countries must also change.

Market Organizations

India, Nigeria, and Mexico along with almost all LDCs have explicit policies encouraging business firms to employ only nationals in the local subsidiaries. Foreigners, whether they be former British civil servants turned commonwealth managers or American expatriate management, are restricted in number to less than 1% of the total number of people employed by the local subsidiary. That is, these governments would tolerate the president and perhaps another management officer not being a citizen, but beyond that the whole management structure and the entire work force have to be citizens of the country in which the subsidiary is located.

India, acting as if it already had a sufficient number of trained managers, would so delay the processing of work permits for foreigners that the foreign firm seeking entry into the Indian market would be driven in the end to utilizing local talent who were trained in a management environment that was based upon family and caste rather than on the basis of impersonal relations. It is only when a specific need for new technology is determined and no Indian can be found to provide this technology that the Indian government permits the local subsidiary to utilize foreigners in its organization. In these cases, too, the government encourages the "Indianization" of these positions as soon as Indians can be trained to carry them out.

Mexico's policy is similar, but it is not as strictly enforced. Many more management positions are held by foreigners, and their "Mexicanization" proceeds much more slowly. Where "Mexicanization" has been pushed some firms have organized Latin American divisions with one subsidiary being the Mexican subsidiary. Although Mexicans are now in marketing positions in the Mexican subsidiary, the foreigners have become the managers of the Latin American division and in one firm, the latter effectively manage both the division and the subsidiary. This change in form will last only until the Mexican government enforces its laws on the employment of foreigners within its national territory.

Certain firms in India, Mexico, and Nigeria have developed sophisticated employee training programs. In Nigeria for example, Shell-British Petroleum owns its own trade school and sends some of its graduates away for engineering degrees.[9] American firms now operating in West Africa found that they have to do the same thing for it is virtually impossible to get a sufficient number of Americans to live in that area of the world.

In most LDCs, the marketer is a scarce resource. Very few people in these types of countries know how to organize, administer, and risk resources for profit-making returns in highly fragmented markets. Few people can weld mass production to mass marketing for the overall improvement of a people's standard of living. When foreign marketers commit resources to an LDC, they commit themselves to training local people in the practice of marketing with the idea that local marketers will take over the marketing job in the not too distant future. Except for this requirement of local hiring whenever local talent is available, LDCs that are committed to the growth of a market economy rarely interfere in the internal management of private-sector enterprises.

Market Resources

There are several kinds of market resources needed by marketers for effective performance in the LDCs: foreign exchange; internal sources of supply; a transportation network; a wholesale-retail infrastructure; and internal sources for consumer credit.

Marketers who have planned to produce or at least assemble goods within an LDC using foreign raw materials or semi-finished goods will find that the availability of these foreign materials, whether they are coming from the parent corporation or from elsewhere, is *always* contingent upon the availability of foreign currency. The failure of the nation to sell all of their primary export commodities in the world market will reduce the quantity of foreign currency

[9] Alan Sokolski, *The Establishment of Manufacturing in Nigeria* (New York: Praeger Special Studies in International Economics and Development, Frederick A. Praeger, Publisher, 1965)), p. 75.

available for imports. Clear and precise choices as to which industry will receive scarce currency and which will not are often set forth in the development plan and supporting administrative documents. Marketers whose products are low on the priority list will be forced to adjust production runs and market commitments to lower levels until the foreign exchange situation eases. Marketers who rely on the importation of materials that could be made within the LDC will find that their permission to use foreign exchange for these items will not be forthcoming once their firms have sunk their investment dollar in fixed facilities.

In today's world, it is unreasonable for marketers to assume that governments of the LDCs will permit national markets to be supplied from foreign production sources. No marketer should include in his plans long-term dependence on foreign sources of supply. Within a year after Sears opened its Mexican retail operation, a severe currency crisis forced the Mexican government to forbid the importation of almost all goods from the United States. Up until that time, Sears had stocked its Mexican stores from United States sources of supply. Now it was forced to find local sources. The story of how Sears forced local manufacturers to produce quality items in standard qualities, sizes, and assortments, and how Sears established a distribution system to wholesale these locally manufactured items to its retail outlets is well known.[10] It has accomplished similar tasks in building up its own market resources in other countries of Latin America and is also carrying out these marketing activities in Spain.

Marketers who plan to produce goods in one region of an LDC and who want to market these goods throughout the national territory should carefully analyze the functional usefulness of existing transportation and distribution networks. Although they may exist on paper, their continued usefulness as market resources should not be accepted without question. There are numerous examples of how marketers built facilities on the assumption of being able to service the national territory, only to find after the plant was built that the critical market infrastructure worked occasionally or not at all. For example, slides and washouts close the dirt and gravel sections of the Pan American Highway and other highways in most Central American countries during the rainy season. Guerrillas in Guatemala have in the past prevented Kerns, whose canning facilities are located between Guatemala City and Puerto Barrios, from shipping their canned products to the capital for resale there or for wholesale distribution throughout Guatemala.[11] The forcing of trucks with foreign registry to unload their goods at the border of each Central American country and then reload them on trucks with domestic registry incurs higher costs for

[10] Richardson Wood and Virginia Keyser, *United States Business Performance Abroad: The Case Study of Sears, Roebuck de Mexico,* S.A. (Washington, D.C.: National Planning Association, May, 1953), pp. 3-45.

[11] Douglas F. Lamont, "Possible Alternative Goals that Can Be Achieved in the Short Run By the Business and Industry Committee of the Alabama-Guatemala Partners of the Alliance" (report submitted to the Alabama-Guatemala Partners of the Alliance, July 4, 1968).

these products.[12] Marketers who plan on using a "through" system of transportation and fail to judge correctly the kinds of market resources they have available to them may find their products spoiling in the short run and their plants operating at excess capacity levels in the long run. Such miscalculations breed losses rather than profits for marketers.

Consumer installment loans (or hire purchase agreements) are a function of the willingness of financial institutions to insure such installment payments. The availability of such loans assists mass production and mass distribution, and brings about rapid increases in the standard of living. Twenty years ago, Indians were able to make such agreements so that they could purchase durable goods. Today, a shortage of goods together with a lack of insured installment credit have eliminated this resource for marketers to use in raising India's standard of living.[13] In Nigeria, two West African trading companies, United African Company and John Holt, and several independent finance companies extended credit for such durable goods as automobiles, TV sets, refrigerators, and air conditioners.[14] Marketers depend upon such credit to support their own plans for market development, and its absence or potential diminution should be considered before risk capital is expended on an LDC

In the LDCs, market resources are generally not available in sufficient quantities for efficient and effective business performance. Their unavailability limits the size of final customer markets by impeding marketers from servicing these markets. Thus for marketers operating in the LDCs it becomes a question of what resources they can do without and still service a market of sufficient size for profit-making returns.

If marketers can generate sufficient volume and keep the price high enough to cover higher distributive margins, then the problem for marketers is which market infrastrucure activities are they willing to perform themselves in the short run, and which market infrastructure activities are they willing to develop by long-term marketing training of wholesale-retail distributors, warehousemen, and financial men.

Market Offerings

The real market in Nigeria is not the country's 40 million people but its many market segments fragmented by regional, cultural, and language differences. Before the war between Nigeria and Biafra, the surplus production of one area was rarely moved to other areas of the country. Market offerings had to be fashioned to service so many multiple cultural norms that the economies which could have been gained from mass production and mass distribution were lost and the Nigerian standard of living remained in its traditional setting. One of

[12] Thomas J. Greer, "The Central American Common Market: Political Setting and Transportation Infrastructure," *Southern Journal of Business,* Vol. 4 (April, 1969), pp. 261-268 at p. 265.

[13] S. Kesava Iyengar, *A Decade of Planned Economy: A Critical Examination of Indian Plans* (Mysore, India: The Indian Academy of Economics, 1961), pp. 218-219.

[14] Same reference as footnote 9, p. 142.

the results of the war has been to speed up the "Nigerianization" of the tribes and language groups supporting the Federal Nigerian Government. This had permitted marketers to provide more uniform market offerings in the food, clothing, shelter, and munitions that are being utilized by the troops and the supporting populace in the war against Biafra. When the war is over, there is no doubt that marketers will find that new social patterns have developed, and that completely new market offerings will have to be made to service a more integrated Nigerian market.

Market offerings in the LDCs are designed on the familiar bases of product, terms of sale, communication, and distribution strategies; only the cultural nuances and governmental requirements are different. For example, in terms of product strategies, the product line for Mexican made automobiles has been reduced from 25 models to 12 models.[15] GM, Ford, and Chrysler are allowed three models each by the Mexican government. The remainder of the production quota is taken up by Volkswagen, Datsun, and the new wholly owned Mexican company, Borgward. The government forced certain automobile manufacturers out of business, and forced others to cut down on the number of models produced or sold in Mexico. It is an attempt by a government to provide some economies of scale for domestic production and thereby lower the price to the final customer.

The market offering will be conditioned also by the supplies available for packaging purposes. Some LDCs lack adequate supplies of wood and paper products. Marketers of milk and soap powders have had to shift their package offerings to clear plastic containers. This has meant that they have had to devise new means for storing these items at retail locations and new ways of labeling the packages themselves.

Brand names, as well as the advertisements used in communicating about and promoting the market offering, must reflect new language and cultural norms, but there are dangers here for marketers. In Africa, when English or French language descriptions were given up in favor of local languages, many Africans refused to buy the products with the new labels for fear that they were getting inferior products. This problem is particularly acute for marketers in the food and bevarage industries. Carelessness in handling items that require high levels of sanitation is commonplace in the LDCs. Even Cola drinks, such as Coke, can be carriers of sugar bacteria that can make consumers ill. Tuberculin cows pass their disease on to the unsuspecting human when care is not taken to protect consumers. Those who have money will select products they know are safe. Brand names from the United States and Western Europe tell the illiterate but relatively affluent consumers in the LDCs that these products will not endanger their health. To meet the requirements of these consumers plus the new laws of the LDCs, marketers put their market information on packages in both the recognized western language and the locally required language.

How high should marketers set prices? It is the policy of governments in the LDCs to promote higher standards of living. One way to do this is to maintain

---

[15] Same reference as footnote 3, p. 277.

low retail prices on the basic necessities of life. Carnation was forced to sell its canned milk to the Mexican government's limited-line retail supermarkets (CONASUPO) at prices lower than it charged the privately owned middle class supermarkets.[16] Naturally, Carnation offset its CONASUPO losses with higher prices to the middle class supermarkets. The Mexican government was able to utilize the price offering of a firm to redistribute some of the wealth of the country. The Indian government, however, has been unable to do the same thing. Its traditional wholesalers are the dominant economic units in the commodities that make up the basic necessities of Indian life. No amount of persuasion has made these wholesalers change their habits of speculation on the prices of these commodities, and retail markets must continue to provide the consumer with low volume, high-priced necessities of life. Marketers will face continued pressure to price their products at some predetermined rate established by the government. It behooves them to know their costs, and to be willing to make their profits in market segments that are not under price control.

In summary, social behavior and impediments in inter-regional exchange are the givens for marketers in the LDCs. National market offerings are often a fruitless waste of resources; instead, market offerings carefully developed for local and regional markets will be both beneficial and profitable. Sales and advertising campaigns should be geared to local differences in taste and thought. Although the Esso tiger has been a phenomenal success as an advertising theme throughout the world, it is folly in many cases to import on a wholesale basis each and every piece of promotional material developed for the United States market. It is just as great a folly to import these campaigns from the capital city market to other areas within the LDC. Levels of literacy, economic sophistication, and local prejudices differ widely from one region to another in many of the LDCs. Thus, market offerings should be customized to fit into the local scene as well as possible. This means more than changing the language of the copy. It means putting additional clothes on female figures so as not to offend more conservative tastes. It means using dialect variations in so-called national languages rather than the phraseology considered proper in the capital city. Several authors have suggested that there is a place for standardized international advertising among the developed countries.[17] A case can be made for appealing to the market segment within the LDCs that relates more to international themes than national themes. Assuming this to be true, it would further strengthen the point that the tastes of the internationally oriented market segment within the capital city are not the tastes of the bulk of the national market within the LDC. And thus the folly of importing advertising themes from the capital city to the provinces is doubly compounded when this internationalized market segment is used as "the true national market consumer group." The care used by marketers in developing market offerings that match

[16] Same reference as footnote 3, pp. 275-276.

[17] John K. Ryans, Jr. and James H. Donnelly, Jr., "Standardized Global Advertising A Call As Yet Unanswered," *Journal of Marketing* Vol. 33 (April, 1969). See also Erik Elinder, "How International Can European Advertising Be?" *Journal of Marketing,* Vol. 29 (April, 1965), pp. 7-11.

real market segments will go a long way to insuring that international marketing is profitable.

Control Over Market Performance

There are two aspects to market control—who are the legal owners and how is the responsibility for the specific management functions divided up among the participating owners?

Each LDC has its own predilections as to how much equity foreigners should have in local subsidiaries. These run from 100% foreign ownership to some sort of joint venture arrangement in which the foreign firm can have either a majority or minority share in the local subsidiary. The Nigerians are willing to have the former; the Mexicans prefer the latter. Usually the Indian government prefers to have a foreign firm sell its production and marketing technology to an Indian firm. However, if this is not possible, the Indian government will permit a joint venture subsidiary to be established if the equity assets are "Indianized" through the sale of common stock as soon as possible.

The initial agreement for establishing a local subsidiary will outline which management functions will be controlled by the foreign parent and which areas will be controlled by the participating local businessman or governmental agency. The marketing area is usually reserved for the foreign parent until such time as there is a sufficient number of trained local marketers who know how to utilize the new marketing technology being brought into the country.

How can market performance be evaluated? It should not be judged on the same basis as performances are judged in other countries. Marketers must do two jobs in the LDCs rather than just one as in the parent company's country. First, they must translate parent demands for market performance into locally profitable market activities. As has been shown above, their analytical tools are cruder and less helpful in generating useful answers; their goals, organization, and resources must be in line with the conditions prevalent in the LDC; finally, their offerings must be adapted to such a variety of differences that many marketing concepts developed for a mass consumption of market are of little value in the LDCs. Second, they must alter local cultural habits to meet the performance standards set up by the parent company and other participating groups. Such local changes in work attitudes, shelf-space rotation, timeliness of advertising copy, and similar marketing activities are the hidden iceberg upon which many marketing performances of good marketers have floundered. These tradition-encrusted habits can only be changed over long periods of time. It is folly to set performance standards that do not take these things into consideration.

On-the-spot inspections by a team of technicians from the international headquarters rather than periodic written reports have worked well for a number of international firms in evaluating market performance. Where local subsidiaries have been left to work out problems by themselves, control has lapsed. A few local subsidiaries, such as Pan American Sulphur in Mexico or International Petroleum Company (IPC) in Peru, have failed to adapt themselves sufficiently to new local conditions. Pan American Sulphur was "Mexicanized" by the forced selling of its Mexican mineral assets to a group of Mexican businessmen who were backed by the National Financiera, the Mexican developmental bank.

IPC, Standard Oil of New Jersey's subsidiary in Peru, claimed ownership in fee simple of oil rights that it had been granted 50 years ago by a Peruvian government. Successive regimes, including the last democratically elected one, sought to convert this claim of ownership to sub-soil rights into a lease without any claim to ownership of the oil at all. Other American firms in Peru, such as Cerro, have sensed the desire of Peruvians to own and control their own natural resources, and have returned ownership rights to sub-soil minerals to the Peruvian government. (This put these companies in the correct position vis-a-vis the sub-soil minerals according to the traditional Roman-Hispanic law as to who owns what kinds of property in Civil Law countries; IPC's insistence on an ownership claim to its sub-soil petroleum holdings flew in the face of the common understanding of what is and what is not law in Peru. This was the same kind of refusal to recognize a different concept of law that led to the nationalization of Jersey Standard's assets in Mexico in 1937.) Instead of seeking an accommodation with the new military regime, IPC began destroying its geological documents and forcing all customers, even the Peruvian military, to pay for refined gasoline products in cash. Naturally, its assets were seized.[18] Perhaps if Jersey Standard had intervened in its subsidiary's continuing battle with successive Peruvian governments, it would still have refining and distribution capability in Peru. Clearly in today's world, parent companies that do not maintain proper control may have their assets expropriated or nationalized.

Future Market Prospects

A market audit, a firm's plan for establishing the validity of what it is presently doing and for deciding on the things it should be doing in the future, brings one back to a study of the conditions for economic development and the requirements of the development plan. Short-term changes in goals of the government can readily be adapted within the continuing market analysis. However, long-term shifts in both public goals and conditions of the market itself must be recognized as factors that will have a decisive impact upon the direction in which the businesses may pursue their own institutional goals. Thus, it behooves marketers to annually audit the market systems in which they operate, and to integrate into their plans for the future any and all changes that will significantly affect the profit-making potential of its local subsidiary. One example of what should be included in the audit would be an LDC's prospects for future integration within any of the emerging common markets. Marketers who failed to locate facilities in Guatemala or Salvador to service the emerging Central American Common Market have found for example that the choice locations were closed to them as this Common Market steadily progressed in

---

[18] "Peru Turns Tougher," *Business Week* (February 15, 1969), pp. 32-33.

creating a new market system. Those marketers who waited were consigned by the terms of the implementing treaty to locate in Honduras or Nicaragua. Their delay caused locational disadvantages in servicing the primary customer-market—that is, the zone running from Guatemala City west to Escuintla, Guatemala, and then turning south to and including the capital city of Salvador. Of course, their delay gave them small locational advantages over the original manufacturing facilities established in the Guatemalan capital city in servicing the San Jose, Costa Rica market. These trade-offs are not, however, equivalent, for the primary market in Central America remains in and around the Guatemalan-Salvadorian urban-rural agglomeration. This is the type of information that should be fed into the market audit so that marketers can plan ahead with greater care than they had in the past.

Marketing Adaptation: A Review

These seven business policies constitute a list of activities marketers need to perform to achieve business and public goals. Adaptations have been suggested using a particular national frame of reference. It would be a cardinal error to assume that because one LDC favored a particular form of adaptation others would favor the same or similar forms. Each country must be studied carefully. Its customs and prejudices need to be understood. Its internal differences must be known. When these things are accomplished, then and only then should marketers move to adapt their marketing technology to the local market.

Whatever adaptations are made should be those that fit together in a properly organized relationship. The business policies that come from those adaptations will form the basic pattern of marketing activity within a national market system. Unless marketers go into an LDC with the idea of totally adapting their marketing technology to local conditions they will fail. Unfortunately, in today's world a rash of marketing failures could turn an LDC away from a market economy to a centrally planned, state-oriented command economy.

This paper has suggested that marketers who do business in more than one country must make certain changes in their business activities. No two countries will react to the same stimuli. Moreover, no two environments will be the same. It is the job of marketers to find acceptable business policies that will produce profit-making returns for their firms and increased social welfare for their host countries.

VII MARKETING AND SOCIETY

Business firms justify their existence by serving the needs of society. Their reward for successful service is in the form of profits. Yet many argue that corporate objectives stated in terms of percentage returns on investment equip the firm with too narrow an outlook and an unfortunate readiness to ignore the broader impact of their decisions on their environment. Leslie Dawson presents this argument together with a plea to broaden the marketing concept in his article, "The Human Concept," which appeared in Part I.

The late Senator Robert Kennedy viewed the problem through the eyes of American youth:

> ... business as a whole has not sought the challenge of the nation's frontier. Of course, it may well be argued that the business of business is to make a profit, that to attempt more is to do less than its stockholders deserve. But does such an argument have relevance, ask the young, when a single company, like General Motors or AT&T, has annual profits greater than the gross national product of any one of seventy nations in the world?
>
> Even more distasteful to the young, as it has been to moralists for thousands of years, is the ethic that judges all things by their profit. They have seen high officers of the nation's largest corporations engage in conspiracies to fix prices, gathering in shabby secret meetings to steal pennies a month from each of millions of Americans. They have seen us send people to jail for the possession of marijuana, while refusing to limit the sale or advertising of cigarettes, which kill thousands of

405

Americans each year. They have seen us hesitate to impose the weakest of safety standards on automobiles, or require that a "respectable" store or lending company tell the simple truth about the interest rate it is charging on loans . . .

It is more than these abuses of the profit motive that they reject; often it is the very nature of materialism in our society, and what it has brought us . . . In short they think their elders have surrendered community values and personal excellence, in exchange for the tailfins and trinkets that Westbrook Pegler once called "a variety of dingbats for the immature."[1]

What are the social and ethical responsibilities of marketing executives? James M. Patterson searches for an answer in the first selection and proposes a method for developing guideposts for the business operation.

One of the most important constraints to the business operation is government. Government intervention in the form of laws and regulations can serve as a potent force in the efficient functioning of the market system. The impact of government on the marketing system is examined by E. T. Grether and Robert J. Holloway in the second selection.

The final selections deal with a household word—consumerism. The authors of the third selection define the term consumerism, evaluate its underlying causes, and stress the need for marketing involvement and new thinking about the deeper meaning of the marketing concept. Louis L. Stern argues for full disclosure of relevant decision information for the consumer in the final selection, entitled "Consumer Protection via Increased Information."

[1] Robert F. Kennedy, *To Seek a Newer World* (Garden City, N.Y.: Doubleday and Company, Inc., 1967), pp. 6-7.

Traditional ways of framing questions about the social and ethical responsibilities of marketing have on the whole been self-defeating. In fact, the discovery of workable answers to the question "What are the social responsibilities of marketing?" is quite unlikely. Is there a better way to proceed? **Yes.** *This article shows how marketing executives can develop some operational guides, even though not universal answers.*

What Are the Social and Ethical Responsibilities of Marketing Executives

James M. Patterson

There is no specific, concrete guide to responsible action for marketing executives, beyond a sort of "watered-down" commercial version of the Golden Rule.

Let us face the fact that the search for a general set of rules defining the social responsibilities of marketing is misguided in principle and doomed to fail.

Instead of asking, "What are the social responsibilities of marketing?", the question might better be, *"What workable guides are available to help a marketing executive to evaluate alternative courses of action in a specific concrete situation?"*

Responsible Actions

The really difficult problem of defining *responsible* marketing actions lies in

Reprinted by permission of the author and the publisher from the *Journal of Marketing,* published by the American Marketing Association, Vol. 30, No. 3 (July, 1966), pp. 12-15.

those everyday marketing activities that raise simple questions of *equity, fairness,* and *morality*–not just questions of legality. To quote from Howard Bowen's classic questions about the responsibilities of businessmen,

Should he conduct selling in ways that intrude on the privacy of people, for example, by door-to-door selling ...? Should he use methods involving ballyhoo, chances, prizes, hawking, and other tactics which are at least of doubtful good taste? Should he employ 'high pressure' tactics in persuading people to buy? Should he try to hasten the obsolescence of goods by bringing out an endless succession of new models and new styles? Should he appeal to and attempt to strengthen the motives of materialism, invidious consumption, and 'keeping up with the Joneses'?[1]

The marketing executive faces nagging questions about the propriety of attempting to *manipulate* customers, and in particular of the ethics of using emotional and symbolic appeals in various forms of persuasive communication. The list of problems might go on and on, but these examples serve to suggest the type of marketing actions in question.

For those who would act responsibly, the answers to such questions are not at all clear-cut, with the "good guys" lined up on one side and the "bad guys" on the other. How, then, is the marketing executive who actually wishes to behave responsibly to find his way through the labyrinth of ethical and moral issues?

Instead of trying to give general answers to questions that have not yet been asked, the objective should be for the harassed marketing executive to frame his problem in such a way that he can solve it for himself.

Abstract general rules offer little or no guidance to a marketing executive who is concerned about the quality of the tire he is forced to produce if he is to make a profit in the $12 price-line, or about the extent of headquarters intervention into the internal operations of his company's franchised dealers. What he needs is an approach, or way of thinking about these issues, which will help him to determine whether this particular decision with respect to product quality or that particular form of intervention is in some sense "wrong" or "unfair."

This search for the responsible course of action is not a problem unique to business and marketing. It is central to all areas of social thought and action. Consequently, the marketing executive might profitably borrow approaches and insights from other areas.

Three obviously relevant areas immediately come to mind: *ethics, law,* and *political theory*–ethics, because "right" conduct is a central concern; law, because it attempts to administer justice by means of specific case decisions; and political theory, because of its traditional concern with power and its regulation.

---

[1] Howard R. Bowen, *Social Responsibilities of the Businessman* (New York: Harper and Brothers, 1953), p. 215.

Ethics

As a branch of philosophy, ethics has been concerned for centuries with standards for decision-making and right conduct. Consequently, one would expect ethical writings to be an important source of guidance to the marketing executive in determining responsible courses of action.

Unfortunately, though, the connection between ethics and policy is not quite so clear-cut as one would wish. In fact, so long as ethics is looked to for answers, the decision-maker remains in the difficult position of having to apply abstract ethical principles to specific concrete situations which seldom if ever quite fit the general definition.

Take, for example, the moral commandment, "Thou shalt not steal." Is it stealing for a marketing executive to accept a gift from a supplier? The marketing executive is forced to resort to "common sense" to guide his decisions.

However, Wayne A. R. Leys, in an important book on ethics, argues that if policy-makers were to read philosophical ethics for critical or deliberative questions instead of conclusive answers, they would correct many sources of bad judgment.[2] He approaches ethics much as John Dewey did—not so much as a command to act in a certain way, but as a tool for analyzing a specific situation.[3] In other words, right and wrong should be determined by the total situation and not by the rule as such.

Here are some "deliberative questions," representative of those Leys derived from some of the different systems of philosophical ethics.

A. *Utilitarianism:*
   1. What are the probable consequences of alternative proposals?
   2. Which policy will result in the greatest possible happiness for the greatest number?

B. *Moral Idealism:*
   1. Is the practice right? Is it just? Honest?
   2. Does the policy put first things first?
   3. Can you will that the maxim of your action should become the universal law?
   4. Are you treating humanity as an end and not merely as a means?

C. *Instrumentalism:*
   1. What will relieve the conflicts and tensions of the situation?
   2. Does the proposed solution anticipate consequences in the larger environment as well as the immediate situation?

In effect, Leys would have us abandon the principles-approach in favor of the case-approach. This may not be bad advice. Perhaps if the marketing executive were to ask similar deliberative questions about a proposed policy, he too would

---

[2] Wayne A. R. Leys, *Ethics for Policy Decision* (Englewood Cliffs, New Jersey: Prentice Hall, Inc., 1952).

[3] John Dewey and Charles Tufts, *Ethics* (New York: Henry Holt and Co., 1932), p. 310.

find them of value in defining the responsible course of action. He might ask, for example, "Would it be desirable if *all* firms adopted this practice?"

Law

In his attempts to determine the responsible courses of action, the marketing executive should also consider law as a potential source of guidance.

In an important book, Edmond Cahn notes that judges, under the official guise of deciding technical legal issues, are frequently required to assess moral interest and to resolve problems of right and wrong.[4] Thus, he concludes that the great body of case law should be regarded as a rich repository of moral knowledge that is continually being reworked and refined.

One section of Cahn's book, dealing with what he calls the "Radius of Loyalty" is especially relevant to the marketing executive in his search for workable guides to responsible action:

The most valuable moral lesson the law can teach concerning loyalty (responsibility) is the lesson of relations . . . The duty always remains a function of the relation . . . By the same token, there can never arise in anyone's moral life an indefinite, unlimited duty of loyalty to any one creature or institution. Loyalty—however light or intense it may be—always has reference to a defined and specific relation . . .[5]

Those familiar with the distinction between the liability of a common carrier, an ordinary bailee, and a trustee will recognize this "relational" principle in action Perhaps this "lesson of relations" can also be applied to marketing.

Clearly a customer is related differently to a firm than is an employee, or a supplier, or even an audience-member who watches a sponsored television show. For that matter, even different customers are likely to have different relationships with a firm. If responsibility is in fact a function of a *specific relationship* involving a *specific kind of transaction,* then a more precise definition of the exact character of a customer-relationship might help to clear the air of nebulous admonitions to management to act responsibly.

Another approach for the marketing decision-maker was developed in an earlier book by Cahn.[6] In *The Sense of Injustice* he notes that over the years the frustrations attending the traditional search for abstract justice nearly led to its abandonment.[7] He further notes that were it not for the "sense of injustice"—that sympathetic reaction of outrage, horror, shock, resentment, and anger—society would be left entirely without empirical guidance in its search for a path to justice. He continues:

[4] Edmond Cahn, *The Moral Decision* (Bloomington, Indiana: Indiana University Press, 1955).

[5] Same reference as footnote 4, at pp. 151-152.

[6] Edmond Cahn, *The Sense of Injustice* (Bloomington, Indiana: Indiana University Press, 1949).

[7] Same reference as footnote 6, at p. 13.

Why do we speak of the "sense of injustice" rather than the "sense of justice"? Because "justice" has been so beclouded by natural law writings that it almost inevitably brings to mind some ideal relation or static condition or set of perceptual standards, while we are concerned with what is active, vital, and experiental in the reactions of human beings. Where justice is thought of in the customary manner as an ideal mode or condition, the human response will merely be contemplative, and contemplation bakes no loaves. But the response to a real or imagined instance of injustice is something quite different; it is alive with movement and warmth in the human organism.[8]

It follows that the responsible marketing action is the one that does not arouse the executive's "sense of injustice." Often when a time-worn trade practice is looked at in this light, one can see that it is not "fair," and this means that reform can be instituted. The change in the grading of items for export so that they now conform to domestic standards is a classic example of how an established practice is changed to reduce the "sense of injustice."

Political Theory

The third example comes from the area of political science.

Over the years political theorists have been concerned, among other things, with devising ways to subject potentially arbitrary power to the "Rule of Law," that is, to ensure that discretionary governmental power will be exercised responsibly.

Granting the differences in degree, this concern is quite similar to the concern of those who seek to ensure that discretionary market power will also be exercised responsibly. And it is demonstrable that *structural* limitations on potentially arbitrary power work better than *substantive* limitations.

Take, for example, the Anglo-American constitutional experience. Minimum reliance was placed on substantive limitations, that is, on generalized prescriptive commands of the "thou shalt not" variety, while maximum reliance was put on an intricate set of structural "checks and balances."

Of course there is a Bill of Rights; but much more important have been such structural limitations as the separation of certain key powers among the various branches of the federal government, the reservation of other powers to the several states, and the creation of a representative government which consciously reflects the variety and diversity of interests affected by governmental power. *In fact, the success of the Anglo-American experience is much more due to emphasis on structural rather than substantive limitations.*

The success of this structural approach argues strongly for its application in the realm of private power. Instead of attempting to specify elaborate codes of conduct, the wiser strategy would be to attempt to develop a set of structural limitations on private power, to ensure that it will be exercised responsibly, that is, in accordance with the legitimate purposes of society.

But this may not be as easy as it sounds. For example, the concept of

[8] Same reference as footnote 6, at page 13.

separation of powers may have no application in the private sphere. And of course, it is not at all clear what structural forms are appropriate for recognizing the legitimate interests of the various constituencies affected by the firm's marketing decisions—or for that matter, which constituencies ought even to be recognized.

Still, we are not entirely without structural precedent in the private sector. Several structural limitations have already been developed which give various constituent interests a "say" in the determination of those corporate policies which vitally affect their own interests. Collective bargaining, for example, structurally recognizes the interests of the employee constituency in corporate decisions relating to the terms and conditions of employment. Similarly, General Motors' dealer councils give structural recognition to the franchised dealer's interests in certain GM distribution policies.

But clearly the prime example of a structural limitation in the private sphere is *market competition.* Certainly competition is by far the most important and most pervasive structural limitation on the exercise of private market power.

And yet this is not an altogether effective limitation; and a certain amount of potentially arbitrary discretion remains. In fact, it is this element of freedom from competitive control that raises the whole problem of business responsibility in the first place.

Some Implications

If competition worked perfectly, by definition there would be no discretion in the marketplace, and therefore no need for the businessman to bother thinking about which course of action is the responsible one. However, an element of market power persists in all markets; and even the most vigorous enforcement of antitrust laws would be unlikely to increase the effectiveness of competition to the point where marketing decisions would be controlled in every detail.

Certainly attempts should be made to improve the performance of competition as a structural limitation on potentially arbitrary corporate discretion. In fact, effective competition is much to be preferred over substantive limitations in the form of government-imposed codes of conduct. The marketing executive ought to try to improve the effectiveness of *the structural limitations of competition,* simply to forestall potential impositions of *substantive limitations by government fiat!*

But even beyond improving market competition as a structural device for reflecting the interests of customers in the marketing decisions of the firm, and thereby making the decisions more "responsible," nonmarket structural arrangements are needed to reflect those interests the market fails to register.

For instance, customers' interests in the firm's marketing decisions might be partially recognized by the voluntary appointment of a representative "Customer Review Board," which would consider and react to most proposed marketing decisions. At minimum, this would provide the firm with a useful "sounding board" for testing proposed courses of action.

It might also be possible to select a representative sample from a firm's customer list, and then to use survey techniques to "tap" these customers' opinions as to contemplated marketing actions. This, too, would serve as a source of guidance in management's search for responsible marketing practice.

In neither case, however, would management be bound to abide by the opinions of the customer group. Still, if there were negative reactions from a representative group of customers, management would find this helpful.

The important point is that structural limitations on potentially arbitrary power have been so eminently successful in the public area that their application in the realm of private power deserves careful consideration.

This proposal for dealing with the problem of social and ethical responsibility in marketing has been a mere "prologue." The most important problems remain.

Clearly, the possibilities of developing new structural arrangements that will effectively recognize customers' legitimate interests in the marketing decisions of the firm have only begun to be explored. And of course, the actual workability of the ethical and political approaches in specific cases remains to be tested.

Suggestions are presented for research on the impact of governmental policies, programs, and regulations upon the functioning of the market system as a whole and upon specific subsystems. The authors point out that intervention by government at all levels is one of the two most significant environmental forces affecting marketing.

Impact of Government upon the Market System

E. T. Grether

Robert J. Holloway

The maintenance of a strong, widespread and varied private enterprise base in a society requires that the myriads of private choices and decisions mesh into and through an effective market system. In the United States, the highest judicial tribunals have insisted on the maintenance of the "rule of competition" through the market system by reiterating that the alternatives are direct governmental operation and regulation or private cartelization.

An acceptably effective general market system must have the capacities to:
1. Respond to the free choices of buyers at all levels.
2. Respond to general and specific *external* environment influences, forces, and conditions (that is, the system must be open ended).
3. Interact among the elements of the system *internally*, including particularly the adjustment of resources from lesser advantaged uses to products, services, or geographical areas of greater advantage.
4. "Regulate" in the sense of placing the participants in the marketing processes under strong compulsions for both (a) the efficient use of resources in production and in marketing and (b) the effective fulfillment of the wants and desires of the members of the society.

The market system as a whole and its specific subsystems are under the

Reprinted by permission of the author and the publisher from the *Journal of Marketing*, published by the American Marketing Association, Vol. 31, No. 2 (April, 1967), pp. 1-5.

continuing and increasing intervention of governmental policies and programs; that is, the market system, while "regulating," is also being "regulated." Most likely, the interventions by government at all levels (especially by the federal government) and the high rate of scientific and technological change are the two most significant external environmental forces affecting the market system. It is proposed, therefore, that both empirical and normative research studies be encouraged on the effects of governmental policies and programs on the functioning of the market system as a whole and on specific subsystems. Such studies should focus sharply upon the impacts of public policies and intervention upon the capacities of the market system as a whole to fulfill its basic functions of communication, coordination and organization, adjustment to strategic environmental forces and conditions, and internal interaction and regulation.

Obviously many thousands of helpful studies could be made with the general orientation and from its vantage points. Such studies, regardless of their number or whether they were essentially empirical or normative, would have accumulative value if focused as proposed. But since research resources are not infinite and there is high urgency for basic knowledge and wisdom to guide public policies, the following topical areas are highlighted:

1. Quantitative and qualitative analyses of the extent to which the economy is under the aegis of the competitive market system.
2. The influence of governmental policies and programs upon the leading classes of managerial decision making in marketing in the perspective of the requirements of an acceptable competitive general market system.
3. Special strategic topical issues in the context of current public policies affecting the functioning of the market system in the United States.

Empirical and Normative Studies

The traditional, classical models of the market system as a whole are derived from assumptions under which the market system and the economy are synonymous. There is a complete lack of quantitative measures of the extent to which the economy of the United States or other countries is, in fact, under the regulation of the market system. There are those who believe that even in the United States with its avowed policies in favor of regulation under the market system, the drift is inexorably away from the market system and hence away from a society with a private enterprise base. No systematic endeavors have been made to measure quantitatively or even to judge qualitatively the extent to which our economy is regulated by the market system. It is difficult to conceive of a study of greater potential significance for public policy than a careful quantitative and qualitative interpretive analysis of the extent to which the market system is operationally effective. A general or holistic approach, of course, would have to be considered only as tentative or preliminary. But it could have an enormous influence in guiding and stimulating research into special topics and areas and subsystems.

A possible approach would be through a breakdown of the components of the GNP in terms of the derivative relationship to or removal from the market system. A very difficult problem of appraisal arises in the areas of shared rule as between competition through the market system and governmental direct regulation It would be most helpful to have such areas highlighted with some indications of the quantitative nature of the sharing. Ideally, a general approach should be under the direction of a task force composed of persons with varied backgrounds and interests. Useful, preliminary studies, however, could be done under a single aegis by persons of broad background and experience. It is inconceivable, however, that definitive measures or judgments could be developed, since the bewildering labyrinths of governmental intervention now probably defy full charting and appraisal.

The Influence of Governmental Policies and Programs

The influence of governmental policies and programs is to be considered in the dual perspective of the requirements of effective private decision making and the requirements of an acceptable, competitive general market system. Under this approach some orderly trails would be blazed through a few of the labyrinths of public regulations from the point of view of business enterprises in making strategic decisions. Five broad areas of research are proposed.

Vertical Marketing Organization and Relationships (the Market Channels)

It is almost universally agreed that vertical organization and relations are uniquely the central area of the field or discipline of marketing. It is agreed also that it is a field of high and overlooked importance both in terms of private managerial decision making and of public policies affectig marketing. It has become increasingly evident that in modern complex industrial societies, competitive forces operate vertically as well as horizontally. But there is a great dearth of systematic knowledge and insight into the patterns and significance of vertical organization and relationships.

In the meantime, governmental policies and programs have intervened into this complex of relationships more or less haphazardly under antitrust enforcement, the Robinson-Patman Act, laws governing resale price maintenance ("fair trade"), special laws and actions affecting relationships between manufacturers and their dealers, actions affecting vertical integration and semi-integration, exclusive and selective dealer arrangements, franchising, and so on. But such legislative, judicial, or other interventions have not been investigated systematically in terms of the functioning of the market system. Thus, for example, regulation under the Robinson-Patman Act has never been examined in this framework and context. The Robinson-Patman cases and actions provide an almost ideal opportunity for research along these lines because of the focus upon primary, secondary and tertiary levels in the perspective of broad conflicting conflicts between types of enterprises. Yet the Act is couched and enforced in terms of a specific-commodity type of regulation of pricing almost guaranteed to avoid the most important issues. The effect of the Robinson-Patman Act is merely one example of fruitful areas awaiting research in terms of this approach. For example, there are the enormously important problems in numerous industries such as the automotive industries, involving not only the dealer structures and arrangements of manufacturers, but relations with suppliers. A very important area, of course, would be vertical integration upstream and downstream, in which there are great bodies of law, action, and judicial interpretation.

Geographical Marketing Organization
and Relationships

A primary test of the marketing system is its ability to support the geographical adjustment of market forces and conditions. This horizontal expression is the corollary of vertical organization and relationships. Involved here are governmental policies affecting sales territories, especially territorial confinement, laws and regulations affecting geographical pricing (as the basing point and other delivered price systems), interstate trade barriers (as through licensing and differential tax treatment), the favoritism of state and local governmental jurisdictions toward local industry, especially through subsidies, and other forms of differential treatment, and so on.

Product Policies, Including Innovation,
Diversification, Differentiation, and the
"Product Mix"

In many ways, the area of product decisions is the most important of all. Possibly, too it is the brightest spot of all in terms of the impacts of governmental policies and programs, except, perhaps, in a small number of industries under special legislation (as food and drug legislation). It would appear, however, that the enormous impacts of governmentally supported and encouraged research and development in relation to private efforts and programs, have fostered rapid technological advances and changes with respect to product innovation.

But there are conflicting interests and unsettled problems in connection with the patent system. And there are continuing problems in the endeavors to trademark, brand, package, and promote the *differentiated* products of particular enterprises. Antitrust implications and applications are becoming increasingly important in this area. Furthermore, product line diversification by the processes of acquisition are being questioned, increasingly, under antitrust. There is no doubt that the area of product policies in all of its expressions is basic and lends itself to a wide variety of research studies.

Promotion

Promotion is of the essence in marketing, and particularly in an environment of (1) rapid product development and (2) antitrust enforcement intended to optimize the rule of competition and to forbid cartelization. Hence, the character and impacts of the governmental policies and regulations affecting personal selling, advertising, trademarking, branding, packaging, labeling, the use of credit, etc., are basic. Research could be focused upon the impact of the enforcement of specific statutes (as food and drug legislation, or alcoholic beverages legislation), or as affecting functional areas (as advertising), or specific practices (as packaging, labeling, credit terms and practices). Important also would be the impact of public mores, standards and attitudes in general and upon specific regulations.

Research in this area could become a testing ground for relating the functioning of the market system broadly and specifically to ethical standards and precepts by reference to the host of common law or other more specific statutory and judicial constraints upon market behavior and practices. Research in this area could test product differentiation and brand promotion empirically in relation to the prevalent conceptualization under much of economical analysis derived from the theory of monopolistic competition and assumptions as to effects upon entry. It is likely that, in the main, in the United States, governmental regulations affecting promotion do not now inhibit managerial decision making and implementation in a strategic manner. One of the purposes of the research would be to check this generalization in general and in specific situations.

Pricing

Pricing is the "holy of holies" of both economic analysis and of antitrust enforcement in the United States. Consequently, there is a large literature of economic analysis and of public policy. From this standpoint, research needs are not as high as in other areas. What is needed, however, is empirical research into the exact nature of pricing and of its relationship to other aspects of decision-making and behavior in marketing. Many, perhaps most, economic analyses, make prices, pricing, and price structures and the price system the central aspects of the functioning of the market system and of the economy. Such emphasis, of course, is appropriate for the production and marketing of the great staple homogeneous products. This approach, however, is less appropriate for the modern, diversified business enterprise with rapid product innovation, which stresses product differentiation and promotion. Under these conditions, the totality of market offerings, practices, services, facilities, and relations affect market results—not merely the determination of the *basic prices* of specific products. Obviously pricing and the "price system" in the case of well-known homogeneous commodities has one set of connotations for the functioning of the market system, whereas a broader, more flexible conceptualization and analysis are required for firms in other situations. Research studies focused upon pricing in this latter context could be exceedingly illuminating in terms of the actual functioning of the market system in areas other than staple, homogeneous commodities.

Special, Strategic Topical Areas and Issues

The Definition of the Market and Industry
Under Various Types of Regulation

In many types of governmental regulation a basic aspect of regulation is the definition or determination of the "market" or "industry" or "product" or "line of commerce" or "area of effective competition," and so on. Such determinations have been and are being made unilaterally, statute by statute and in individual cases and situations. There has been no full endeavor to investigate such determinations for consistency and significance in relation to the impacts upon the regulation of the market system as a whole or upon specific subsystems. Thus, for example, under the Robinson-Patman Act the various provisions apply to commodities of "like grade and quality," and a physical characteristics test has been used for the most part instead of the economic test of market behavior.

All statutes governing specific industries require the delimitation of the areas of coverage—an increasingly difficult matter under our changing technologies and tendencies toward product and functional diversification. It would be exceedingly helpful to examine all governmental regulations involving such determinations (as tariff regulations, internal revenue definitions, the various antitrust statutes, Robinson-Patman, and the host of special statutes) in the dual contexts of consistency and significance in relation to the maintenance of a flexible, acceptable market system.

It is possible that the market system is being fragmented into segments by contradictory and arbitrary determinations and special regulations that run counter to the requirements of both effective, flexible adjustments and the inherent forces of modern technology which are tending increasingly to obliterate or break down traditional boundaries.

Character and Impacts of Governmental Subsidies
and of Subsidy-like Differential Treatment

Very likely, the most general, most insidious, and least understood of the various types of intrusions into the market system, as a whole and into specific subsystems, arise through governmental subsidies and subsidy-like differential treatment. The use of subsidies goes back deeply into American history, for the federal and state and local governments have engaged in a wide variety of such programs, intended often to expand local industry and to encourage foreign trade or to foster the provision of basic facilities. Thus, the railroads were the beneficiaries of land grants from 1850 to 1871 intended to encourage and speed railroad construction. Thus, too, the agricultural industries have received and still receive a wide variety of direct and indirect subsidies that have had and continue to have an enormous impact upon these industries. Currently, almost all major and minor sectors and segments of our economy are receiving or are under the impacts of various open or disguised forms of subsidies and differential, favored treatment. The worth of a congressman is often measured in terms of his ability to obtain federal assistance for his district. State and local governmental bodies are also deeply involved in similar programs. Thus many states and local governmental units try to influence the location of industry by tax exemptions and tax favoritism, financial assistance in building plants, tax exempt bonds, the provision of special facilities without cost or below cost, and so on.

The market system in general and specific subsystems are affected by a broad variety of impacts, influences, and interventions intended to serve special interests or areas. The number, character, and variety of such interventions are too great to allow simple generalizations. Subsidies and differential treatment might actually strengthen the market system. There is no guarantee or likelihood that this is so—in fact, to the contrary. There is a challenging opportunity here for special studies as well as for general analysis and interpretation. It is difficult to conceive of any other area so widely open for productive research.

Governmental Policies and Regulations
Affecting the Growth of Individual
Business Enterprises

In a society with a private enterprise base, it is of highest importance whether the total net effects of governmental policies and programs affect the growth of business enterprises favorably or adversely. All regulations intruding into the market system (such as subsidies and subsidy-like differential treatment) or affecting decision making in marketing by individual enterprises may affect their growth—one way or another. In general, there are strong positive endeavors to foster the growth of small business and to circumscribe or constrain the growth of large, powerful enterprises. Thus, there is the special Small Business Administration in the federal government dedicated to the interests of small business. Thus, too, the Supreme Court of the United States in recent decision, especially *Brown Shoe,* has made the preservation of viable small business a standard of action superior both to efficiency and the maintenance of competition in an abstract sense. Conversely, powerful well-established corporations find it increasingly difficult to grow by the simple processes of acquisition or merger.

The enforcement of the revised 1950 Section 7 of the Clayton Act is increasingly affecting the opportunities of growth by acquisition. Consequently, large enterprises are forced increasingly to plan growth through internal expansion—horizontally, vertically, functionally, and through conglomerate diversification. Possibly in the near future such avenues of internal growth may be under increasing questioning. Finally, the weight and specific character of taxes affect growth plans and opportunities.

Public Policies and Programs Affecting
Consumer-Buyer Decision Making and Behavior

The character and relative effectiveness of the free choices of consumer-buyers are the most basic factors in the functioning of the market system in general and throughout its myriad of subsystems. Hence it is of highest importance to investigate the impacts of the host of governmental regulations, facilities, aids, and interventions upon the quality and efficiency of consumer-buyer decision making. Of course, all forms of marketing regulations will have some influence upon consumers' choices by affecting the relative qualities, availabilities, and competitiveness of market supplies and offers. In addition, there are the specific laws and regulations governing weights and measures, packaging, labeling, deceit and misrepresentations, credit terms, and so on.

There is a common generalization that we are moving steadily away from the ancient doctrine of *caveat emptor* to an emerging *caveat venditor*. Regardless of the exact nature of our drift, there is no doubt that abundant basic research opportunities and needs exist in this general area both in general terms and in sharp focus upon specific industries (as foods, drugs, and alcoholic beverages).

In a sense, research studies in the general area of consumer-buyer behavior and decision making could be means of summing up the effects of the other areas of research.

What is consumerism, where did it come from, and where is it going? These are difficult questions at a time when the scope of consumerism is broadening rapidly. The authors emphasize market and societal problems that underlie the recent upsurge of interest in consumerism. Their analysis of casual factors provides the basis for projections of the future of consumerism.

A Guide to Consumerism

George S. Day

David Aaker

Consumerism has played an expanding role in the environment of business decision makers. Despite wishful thinking by some, the following analysis of consumerism is as relevant today as it was in 1964 when it was written:

1. As evidenced by consumer agitation at the local-state-federal levels, business has failed to meet the total needs and desires of today's consumers.
2. Into this business-created vacuum, government forces have quickly moved to answer this consumer need.
3. The areas of consumer interest are so diverse that they offer government agencies and legislators almost limitless reasons for additional regulation of business and commerce.
4. If business managers want to avoid such new government regulations (with the attendant possibilities of excessive and punitive legislation), they will have to take positive action to demonstrate that the business interest is in more general accord with the consumer's needs and wants.[1]

The ensuing six years has seen the passage of considerable consumerism legislation and a substantial broadening of the concept's scope. During this

Reprinted by permission of the publisher from the *Journal of Marketing*, published by the American Marketing Association, Vol. 34, No. 3 (July, 1970), pp. 12-19.

[1] Tom M. Hopkins, "New Battleground—Consumer Interest," *Harvard Business Review*, Vol. 42 (September-October, 1964), pp. 97-104.

period one constant factor has been a lack of agreement on the extent of the influence of consumerism or its long-range implications. Businessmen have suffered from a myopia that comes from perceiving consumerism primarily in terms of markets with which they are very familiar. Their emphasis on the peculiarities of these few markets often leads them to overlook similar problems in other contexts and, thus, to discount the seriousness of the overall problem they face. Legislators and members of the consumer movement are more responsive to the broad problems facing consumers, but their lack of understanding of specific market situations too often leads to inappropriate diagnoses and solutions. Fortunately the two basic perspectives are demonstrating a healthy convergence. The goal of this paper is to encourage this convergence by putting consumerism into a perspective that will facilitate understanding.

The Scope of Consumerism

The term *consumerism* appears to be uniquely associated with the past decade. Even in this short period it has undergone a number of changes in meaning. Vance Packard, one of the earliest adopters of the term, linked consumerism with strategies for persuading consumers to quickly expand their needs and wants by making them "voracious, compulsive (and wasteful)."[2] His usage clearly reflected the concerns of the fifties with planned obsolescence, declining quality, and poor service in saturated consumer goods markets. The term was not put to wider use until 1963 or 1964, when a variety of commentators identified it with the very visible concerns triggered indirectly by Rachel Carson, and directly by Ralph Nader's auto safety investigations and President Kennedy's efforts to establish the rights of consumers: to safety, to be informed, to choose, and to be heard.[3]

The most common understanding of consumerism is in reference to the *widening* range of activities of government, business, and independent organizations that are designed to protect individuals from practices (of both business and government) that infringe upon their rights as consumers. This view of consumerism emphasizes the direct relationship between the individual consumer and the business firm. Because it is an evolving concept, there is no accepted list of the various facets of this relationship. The following is representative:

1. *Protection against clear-cut abuses.* This encompasses outright fraud and deceit that are a part of the "dark side of the marketplace," [4] as well as the dangers to health and safety from *voluntary use of a product.* There is

[2] Vance Packard, *The Waste Makers* (New York: David McKay, 1960), p. 23.

[3] Rachel Carson, *Silent Spring* (Boston, Mass.: Houghton Mifflin Company, 1962); Ralph Nader, *Unsafe At Any Speed* (New York: Pocket Books, 1966); and "Consumer Advisory Council, First Report," Executive Office of the President (Washington, D.C.: U.S. Government Printing Office, October, 1963)

[4] Senator Warren Magnuson and Jean Carper, *The Dark Side of the Marketplace* (Englewood Cliffs: Prentice-Hall, 1968).

substantial agreement in principle between business and consumer spokesmen that such abuses must be prevented, but there is often a wide divergence of opinion on the extent of the problem. As a result the government has taken the initiative in this area, usually after the divulgence of a sensational abuse. This has been the case with much of the legislation dealing with drug, tire, auto, and pipe line safety, and meat and fish inspection. Even so, this is the least controversial and oldest aspect of consumerism.

2. *Provision of adequate information.* The concern here is with the economic interests of the consumer. The question is whether the right to information goes beyond the right not to be deceived, to include the provision of performance information that will ensure a wise purchase. Much of the controversy and confusion over consumerism revolves around this basic issue.[5] The two polar positions identified by Bauer and Greynor are the business view that the buyer should be guided by his judgment of the manufacturer's reputation and the quality of the brand, versus the view of the consumer spokesmen that information should be provided by impartial sources and reveal performance characteristics.[6]

3. *The protection of consumers against themselves and other consumers.* Some of the thrust behind consumerism comes from the growing acceptance of the position that paternalism is a legitimate policy. Thus, the National Traffic and Motor Vehicle Safety Act of 1966 is not concerned with the possibility that the buyer has an expressed but unsatisfied need for safety, and emphasizes instead that carelessness may have undesirable consequences for innocent participants.[7] There is a sound basis in economic theory for such intervention whenever the action of a buyer serves only his own best interest and fails to take into account the effects on others. However, this principle is being extended to situations of "implied consumer interest" where the individual is deemed unable to even identify his own best interest (e.g., the mandatory installation of seat belts and the provision for a "cooling off" period after a door-to-door sale). This is a strong justification for the protection of inexperienced, poorly educated, and generally disadvantaged consumers. More controversial by far is the extension of this notion to all consumers on the grounds that manipulated preferences may be disregarded when the consumer is not acting in his best interest.[8]

The above three facets of consumerism suggest the current thrust of the movement. Yet, it would be naive to portray consumerism as a static entity. It has had a dynamic past and continues to evolve and change at an increasingly rapid rate. For example, the emphasis of the consumer movement of the thirties and later was on dangerous and unhealthy products and "dishonest or

[5] Freedom of Information in the Market Place (Columbus, Mo.: F.O.I. Center, 1967).

[6] Raymond A. Bauer and Stephen A. Greyser, "The Dialogue That Never Happens," *Harvard Business Review*, Vol. 45 (November-December, 1967), p. 2.

[7] Robert L. Birmingham, "The Consumer As King: The Economics of Precarious Sovereignty." *Case Western Reserve Law Journal*, Vol. 20 (May, 1969).

[8] Same reference as footnote 7, p. 374.

questionable practices which are believed to hamper the consumer in making wise decisions ... and obtaining useful information.[9] The emphasis today is clearly much broader.

There is a high probability that the scope of consumerism will eventually subsume, or be subsumed by two other areas of social concern; distortions and inequities in the economic environment and the declining quality of the physical environment. The forecast of a greater identity between these social problems and consumerism rests on the fact that they are associated with many of the same basic causes, have common spokesmen, and seem to be moving in the same direction in many respects. Yohalem has indicated that the ultimate challenge of consumerism to industry is "toward ending hunger and malnutrition ... toward alleviating pollution of the air, water and soil ... toward educating and training the disadvantaged ... toward solving these and other problems of a society rather than strictly of an industrial nature."[10]

Concern over the *economic environment* dates back to the end of the last century. The long-run manifestation of this concern has been antitrust law and enforcement, which has swung back and forth between protecting competition and protecting competitors. Despite various ambiguities in antitrust interpretation, this has been a major effort to ensure consumers' "right to choose" by increasing the number of competitors. Some regard it is "the fundamental consumer edifice on which all other measures are bottomed."[11] Judging from the recent intensification of concern over the economic role of advertising and promotion (insofar as they increase price and raise barriers to entry to new markets), reciprocity, restrictive distributive arrangements, conglomerate mergers, and related topics, it appears that antitrust issues will be a continuing impetus to consumerism. In a period of rapid inflation it is not surprising that advertising and promotion costs have come under additional scrutiny for their role in contributing to high prices, particularly food prices. This promises to be a durable issue, considering a task force of the White House conference on food, nutrition, and health has recommended lower food prices, by reducing promotion not related to nutritional or other food values, as a major item in a national nutrition policy.[12]

More recently, consumerism has become identified with the widespread concern with the quality of the *physical environment*. The problems of air, water, and noise pollution have become increasingly salient as the tolerance of the public for these abuses has decreased. In effect a "critical mass" of explosive

[9] Fred E. Clark and Carrie P. Clark, *Principles of Marketing* (New York: The Macmillan Company 1942), p. 406.

[10] Aaron S. Yohalem, "Consumerism's Ultimate Challenge: Is Business Equal to the Task?" address before the American Management Association, New York, November 10, 1969.

[11] Statement of Leslie Dix (on behalf of the Special Committee on Consumer Interests), Federal Trade Commission, *National Consumer Protection Hearings* (Washington: U.S. Government Printing Office, November, 1968), p. 16.

[12] "Food Ads to Get Wide Ranging Scrutiny at White House Session," *Advertising Age*, Vol. 41 (December 1, 1969), p. 1.

concern has suddenly been created. The consumer movement has rapidly rearranged its priorities to become a part of this critical mass. This shift is not surprising in view of the desire to broaden consumerism to include problems arising from indirect influences on the consumer interest. It also follows naturally from the long standing concern with built-in obsolescence and poor quality and repairability, for these problems contribute to pollution in a "disposable" society.

As the consumer movement joins with conservationists and interest legislators there is a growing likelihood of government action. The argument for such intervention has been well stated by Andrew Shonfield:

Increasingly the realization is forced upon us that the market, which purports to be the reflection of the way in which people spontaneously value their individual wants and efforts, is a poor guide to the best means of satisfying the real wishes of consumers. That is because market prices generally fail to measure either social costs or social benefits. In our civilization these grow constantly more important. Simply because some amenity—let it be a pleasant view or an uncongested road or a reasonably quiet environment—is not paid for directly by those who enjoy it, there is no measure of the cost of the disinvestment which occurs when a profitable economic activity destroys what already exists. Unless the State actively intervenes, and on an increasing scale, to compel private enterprise to adapt its investment decisions to considerations such as these, the process of economic growth may positively impede the attainment of things that people most deeply want.[13]

The result may well be increased controls on producer-controlled emittants and, perhaps, "quality standards . . . or other regulatory devices in the interest of upgrading product quality and repairability.[14]

The Underlying Causes of Consumerism

Additional insights come from a consideration of the factors underlying the recent upsurge of interest in consumerism. It appears that increasingly discontented and aroused consumers have combined with a growing number of formal and informal institutions capable of focusing discontent, to create enough pressure to overcome the advantage of the traditionally more effective lobbies representing the producer's interests. Since a particular government action means much more to the individual producer (who will be totally affected), than to the individual consumer (who divides his concern among many items), this clearly involved a significant effort.

The Discontented Consumer

The discontented consumer is not part of a homogeneous group with easily

[13] Andrew Shonfield, *Modern Capitalism: The Changing Balance of Public and Private Power* (New York: Oxford University Press, 1965), p. 227.

[14] Stanley E. Cohen, "Pollution Threat May Do More for Consumers Than Laws, Regulations," *Advertising Age*, Vol. 41 (March 2, 1970), p. 72.

described complaints. The fact is great variation exists among consumers in the extent of their discontent and there is a wide variety of underlying causes. Nonetheless, it is possible to distinguish specific sources of discontent that are traceable to the marketing environment from other more pervasive concerns with the nature of society.

Problems in the Marketplace. To some observers the leading problem is imperfections in the state of information in consumer markets.[15] They believe consumers would be adequately cared for by competition *if* they could learn quickly about available brands and their prices and characteristics. However, as products and ingredients proliferate, each consumer is less and less able to make useful price and quality comparisons. This inability leads to "increasing shopper confusion, consequent irritation and consequent resentment."[16] The problem is more severe for products which are purchased infrequently, exhibit a rapid rate of technological change, and whose performance characteristics are not readily apparent. Hence, increasing pressure is applied for tire standards, unit prices, truth-in-lending, truth-in-funds, information about the design-life of durable goods, and so on. The truth-in-packaging bill is another manifestation of this problem, for it aims to help the consumer cope with the volume of information available relative to grocery and drug products. Since advertising has not been notable as a source of adequate, or even accurate information that could alleviate the problem, it has been under continuing attack.[17] To the extent that retailing is becoming more and more impersonal, the whole situation may become worse. Thus,

> . . . as a result of the character of contemporary retail establishments, the vastly increased number of consumer products, and the misleading, deceptive and generally uninformative aspects of advertising and packaging, the consumer simply lacks the information necessary to enable him to buy wisely.[18]

This is not an unusually intemperate charge; nor is it denied by the finding that 53% of a sample of adults disagreed with the statement that, "In general, advertisements present a true picture of the product advertised." This response measures both a concern over genuine deception and differences in people's tolerance for fantasy.[19] Nonetheless the potential for dissatisfaction is large.

The proliferation and improvement of products, resulting from attempts to better satisfy specific needs and/or reduce direct competition, has also had other

[15] Richard H. Holton, "Government-Consumer Interest: The University Point of View," in *Changing Marketing Systems*, Reed Moyer, ed. (Chicago, Ill.: American Marketing Association, Winter, 1967), pp. 15-17.

[16] E. B. Weiss, "Line Profusion in Consumerism," *Advertising Age,* Vol. 39 (April 1, 1968), p. 72.

[17] Louis L. Stern, "Consumer Information Via Increased Information," *Journal of Marketing,* Vol. 31 (April, 1967), pp. 48-52.

[18] Richard J. Barber, "Government and the Consumer," *Michigan Law Review*, Vol. 64 (May, 1966), p. 1226.

[19] Raymond A. Bauer and Stephen A. Greyser, *Advertising in America: The Consumer View* (Boston: Graduate School of Business Administration, Harvard, 1968), p. 345.

consequences. As one appliance executive noted, ". . . the public is staging a revolt of rising expectancy. Customers today expect products to perform satisfactorily, to provide dependable functional performance and to be safe. This threshold of acceptable performance is steadily rising. . ."[20] Unfortunately the complexity and malfunction potential of many products has also been rising.[21] The result is an uncomfortable level of dissatisfaction with quality, compounded by inadequate service facilities.[22] This situation is not confined to hard goods, for one result of rapidly rising sales is overburdened retail and manufacturing facilities, which leads to deteriorating quality and service for almost all mass-merchandised goods.[23]

These problems are occurring at a time when consumers are generally less willing to give industry the benefit of the doubt—an understandable reaction to the well-publicized shortcomings of the drug, auto, and appliance manufacturers. Even without these problems, more skepticism is to be expected from consumers who have found that their assumptions about the adequacy of laws covering reasonable aspects of health, safety, and truthfulness are wrong. Recent disclosures involving such vital issues as meat inspection and auto and drug safety have hurt both government and industry by contributing to an atmosphere of distrust. According to Stanley Cohen, the meat inspection battle was particularly important here, "because for the first time the public had a clear cut demonstration of the jurisdictional gap (between state and federal governments) that limits the effectiveness of virtually all consumer protection legislation."[24]

Problems in the Social Fabric. The present imperfections in the marketplace would probably not have generated nearly the same depth of concern in earlier periods. The difference is several changes deep in society that have served as catalysts to magnify the seriousness of these imperfections.

The first catalyst has been the new visibility of the low-income consumer. These consumers suffer the most from fraud, excessive prices, exorbitant credit charges, or poor quality merchandise and service. Unfortunately, solutions oriented toward improving the amount and quality of product information have little relevance to low-income buyers who lack most of the characteristics of the prototype middle-income consumer.[25]

- Low income consumers are often unaware of the benefits of comparative shopping.

[20] Robert C. Wells, quoted in James Bishop and Henry W. Hubbard, *Let The Seller Beware* (Washington: The National Press, 1969), p. 14.

[21] "Rattles, Pings, Dents, Leaks, Creaks—and Costs," *Newsweek*, Vol. 45 (November 25, 1968), p. 93.

[22] See, Federal Trade Commission, "Staff Report on Automobile Warranties" (Washington: no date), and "Report of the Task Force on Appliance Warranties and Service" (Washington: January, 1969).

[23] "Consumers Upset Experts," *New York Times* (April 13, 1969), F. 17.

[24] Stanley E. Cohen, "Business Should Prepare for Wider Probe of Consumer Protection Laws," *Advertising Age,* Vol. 39 (January 8, 1968), p. 59.

[25] Lewis Schnapper, "Consumer Legislation and the Poor," *The Yale Law Journal*, Vol. 76 (1967).

- They lack the education and knowledge necessary to choose the best buy, even if it were available. Because of their low income they have fewer opportunities to learn through experience.
- They often lack the freedom to go outside their local community to engage in comparative shopping.
- They lack even a superficial appreciation of their rights and liabilities in post-sale legal conflicts.
- Nothing in their experience has reinforced the benefits of seeking better value for their money; consequently, the low-income buyer lacks the motivation to make improvements in his situation.

Thus, the low-income consumer environment is a perfect breeding ground for exploitation and fraud. The extent of the distortion in the ghetto marketplace has only recently been widely comprehended and related to the overall failure of society to help the disadvantaged.[26]

The second catalyst is best described as a basic dissatisfaction with the impersonalization of society in general, and the market system in particular. Evidence for this point of view is not difficult to find, particularly among young people. A survey of college student opinion found 65% of the sample in strong or partial agreement with the statement that "American society is characterized by injustice, insensitivity, lack of candor, and inhumanity."[27] Similar levels of disenchantment were reported among parents and nonstudents of the same age. The need seems to be felt for social organizations that are responsive—and perhaps the impression of responsiveness is as important as the specific responses that are made.

There is little doubt that large American corporations are not regarded as responsive by their customers. According to Weiss, both manufacturers and retailers are "turning a deaf ear," while increasingly sophisticated consumers are demanding more personal relationships and security in their purchases.[28] This situation stems from a series of changes in the marketing environment—the rise of self-service and discounting (in part because of the difficulty of obtaining good sales employees), the high cost of trained service personnel, and the intervention of the computer into the relationship with consequent rigidifying of customer policies and practices. The prospects for improvement are dim, because the benefits of good service and prompt personal attention to complaints are difficult to quantify and consequently are given low priority when investment decisions are made. As more consumers are seeing the government as being more sympathetic, if not more helpful, the prospect for arbitration procedures to settle complaints is increased.

The most disturbing feature of the catalyzing effects of the recently visible low-income consumer, the growing dissatisfaction with the impersonalization of society, and concern over the quality of the physical environment is their

[26] David Caplovitz, *The Poor Pay More* (New York: The Free Press, 1963).

[27] Jeremy Main, "A Special Report on Youth," *Fortune*, Vol. 79 (June, 1969), pp. 73-74.

[28] E. B. Weiss, "The Corporate Deaf Ear," *Business Horizons*, Vol. XI (December, 1968), pp. 5-15.

intractability. These problems are almost impervious to piecemeal attempts at correction. In view of the small likelihood of large-scale changes in social priorities or social structures, these problems will be a part of the environment for the foreseeable future.

The final and most enduring catalyst is the consequence of an increasingly better educated consumer. The Chamber of Commerce recently noted that the consumer of the present and future "expects more information about the products and service he buys. He places greater emphasis on product performance, quality and safety. He is more aware of his 'rights' as a consumer and is more responsive than ever before to political initiatives to protect these rights."[29]

The Activist Consumer

The discontented consumer found many more effective ways to express feelings and press for change during the 1960s than ever before. The development of means of translating discontent into effective pressure distinguishes recent consumer efforts from those of the 1910 and 1935 eras.

The consumer has been more ably represented by advocates such as Ralph Nader, Senator Warren Magnuson, and a number of journalists who pursue similar interests. These men are able to identify and publicize problems, and to follow up with workable programs for improvement. In a real sense, they are self-elected legal counsels to a typically unrepresented constituency. Many consumer problems would have remained smoldering but unfocused discontents without their attention. New product researchers have frequently found consumers do not seem to know what is bothering them or realize that others are similarly troubled until the extent of the problem is publicized or an alternative is provided.

The institutional framework has also been expanded and strengthened in recent years. Traditional bodies, such as Consumers Union and Consumers Research, Inc., have now received support from permanent bodies in the government such as the Consumer Advisory Council and the office of the Special Assistant to the President for Consumer Affairs. These agencies have been specifically developed to avoid the problems of excessive identification with regulated industries which plague some of the older regulated bodies.

This decade has also seen greater willingness on the part of consumers to take direct action. Consider the protest of housewives in Denver over the cost of trading stamps and games. While this was probably due to general dissatisfaction over the effects of inflation on food prices, it did represent an important precedent. More sobering is the extreme form of protest documented by the National Commission on Civil Disorders. "Much of the violence in recent civil disorders has been directed at stores and other commercial establishments in

[29] Report of Council on Trends and Perspective on, "Business and the Consumer—A Program for the Seventies" (Washington, D.C.: Chamber of Commerce of the United States, 1969).

disadvantaged Negro areas. In some cases, rioters focused on stores operated by white merchants who, they apparently believed, had been charging exorbitant prices or selling inferior goods. Not all the violence against these stores can be attributed to 'revenge' for such practices. Yet, it is clear that many residents of disadvantaged Negro neighborhoods believe they suffer constant abuses by local merchants."[30]

The Changing Legal and Political Scene

Pressures for change have been directed at a legal and political structure that is much more willing to take action than before:

1. Overall, there is more acceptance of government involvement in issues of consumer protection. Also, the federal government has been more prepared to take action because the state and local governments have generally defaulted their early legal responsibility in this area.[31]

2. A combination of factors has contributed to the expanded role of the federal government. Congress is no longer so dominated by the rural constituencies who appear less interested in these matters; consumer legislation is relatively cheap and appears to generate goodwill among voters; and various tests of the influence of business lobbyists have shown that their power is not as great as originally feared.[32] In fact, many observers feel that industry may have been its own worst enemy by often opposing all consumer legislation without admitting any room for improvement or providing constructive alternatives.[33] Worse, they may have demonstrated that industry self-regulation is not workable.[34]

3. The consequence is a Congress that is responsive to the economic interests of consumers. A significant proportion of the enacted or pending legislation is a result of Congressional initiative and is directed toward ensuring that consumers have adequate and accurate shopping information. This is very different from earlier legislation which was enacted because a tragedy dramatized the need to protect health and safety.[35]

4. A large number of legal reforms have been slowly instituted which attempt to correct the imbalance of power held by the manufacturers; e.g., the expansion

[30] "Exploitation of Disadvantaged Consumes by Retail Merchants," *Report of the National Commission on Civil Disorders* (New York: Bantam Books, 1968), pp. 274-277.

[31] Ralph Nader, "The Great American Gyp," *New York Review of Books*, Vol. 9 (November 21, 1968), p. 28.

[32] Stanley E. Cohen, "'Giant Killers' Upset Notions That Business 'Clout' Runs Government," *Advertising Age*, Vol. 40 (July 14, 1969), p. 73.

[33] Jeremy Main, "Industry Still has Something to Learn About Congress," *Fortune*, Vol. 77 (February, 1967), pp. 128-130.

[34] Harper W. Boyd, Jr., and Henry J. Claycamp, "Industrial Self-Regulation and the Consumer Interest," *Michigan Law Review*, Vol. 64 (May, 1966), pp. 1239-1254.

[35] Philip A. Hart, "Can Federal Legislation Affecting Consumers' Economic Interests Be Enacted?" *Michigan Law Review*, Vo. 64 (May, 1966), pp. 1255-1268.

of the implied warranty, and the elimination of privity of contract.[36] Of special interest are current efforts to give the individual consumer more leverage by making the practice of consumer law profitable for attorneys. The mechanism being promoted is the consumer class action which permits suits by one or a few consumers on behalf of all consumers similarly abused.[37] This will make fraud cases, where individual claims are smaller than legal costs, much more attractive to investigate and litigate.

The Future of Consumerism

One of the main conclusions from past efforts to forecast social phenomena is that naive extrapolations are likely to be wrong. A better approach in this situation is to utilize the interpretation that consumerism is, at least partially, a reflection of many social problems that are certain to persist, and perhaps be magnified in the future. This diagnosis rules out the possibility that consumerism activity will decline significantly in the future; the unanswered questions concern the rate of increase in this activity and the areas of greatest sensitivity.

One index of activity, the amount of federal consumer legislation pending, should slow its rate of increase. Only a limited number of consumer bills can be considered at a time; over 400 such bills were pending in Congressional committees at the end of 1969.[38] Also more attention will have to be given to implementing and improving existing legislation, rather than writing new legislation. For example, there is evidence that the truth-in-lending bill will not achieve its original goals; partly because of lack of understanding of the problem and partly because of inadequacies and confusion in the enacted legislation.[39] Similarly, it is dismaying that after two years of experience with the truth-in-packaging bill it is being referred to as "one of the best non-laws in the book."[40] In this particular situation the problem seems to lie with the interest and ability of the various regulatory agencies to implement the law. This is not an isolated example of enforcement failures. The Food and Drug Administration (FDA) recently estimated that fewer than two-thirds of all food processors have complied with standards to prevent some forms of food contamination. One

[36] David L. Rados, "Product Liability: Tougher Ground Rules," *Harvard Business Review*, Vol. 47 (July-August, 1969), pp. 144-152.

[37] David Sanford, "Giving the Consumer Class," *The New Republic*, Vol. 40 (July 26, 1969), p. 15. Partial support for this concept was given by President Nixon in his "Buyer's Bill of Rights" proposal of October 30, 1969.

[38] See, "Nixon shops for consumer protection," *Business Week* (November 1, 1969), p. 32.

[39] "A Foggy First Week for the Lending Law," *Business Week* (July 5, 1969), p. 13. This result was accurately forecasted by Homer Kripke, "Gesture and Reality in Consumer Credit Reform," *New York University Law Review*, Vo. 44 (March, 1969), pp. 1-52.

[40] Stanley E. Cohen, "Packaging Law Is on Books, But Ills It Aimed to Cure Are Still Troublesome," *Advertising Age*, Vol. 40 (September 1, 1969), p. 10.

result has been an increased pressure for a powerful central consumer agency[41] to implement, modify and coordinate the 269 consumer programs that are presently administered by 33 different federal agencies.[42]

The very nature of the contemporary marketplace will probably continue to inhibit basic changes in business operations. Weiss points out some manufacturers and retailers will always equate responsibility with legal behavior.[43] These tendencies are reinforced by the competitive structure of many markets where success depends on an ability to appeal directly to the "marginal float." One view of this group is that they constitute a minority who are "fickle ... particularly susceptible to innovation that may not be relevant, and to attention getters such as sexy TV jokes or giveaway games.[44] While research support is lacking, this widely held view helps explain some of the behavior consumerists complain about.

There are signs that concerned parties are making efforts to rise above emotion to rationally identify and realistically attack the problems. Two major, if embryonic, research efforts are under way which aim at providing decision makers in business and government with empirically based knowledge to supplement the intuition on which they now too often solely rely. The first is the Consumer Research Institute sponsored by the Grocery Manufacturers Association, and the second is an effort by the Marketing Science Institute.[45] Although both research organizations have close ties with business, neither was established to justify or defend vested interests. Their objectives are to promote basic, academic research that will be respected by all parties. The MSI group specifically proposes to obtain participation at the research-design phase of each project of those who would potentially disagree about policy. Although the government now has no comparable effort, it is reasonable to expect movement in this direction. Cohen has suggested that the FTC should establish a Bureau of Behavioral Studies "whose function would be to gather and analyze data on consumer buying behavior relevant to the regulations of advertising in the consumer interest."[46]

An early study, which might be regarded as a prototype to the CRI and MSI

[41] Same reference as footnote 18, and Louis M. Kohlmeier, Jr., "The Regulatory Agencies: What Should Be Done?" *Washington Monthly*, Vol. 1 (August, 1969), pp. 42-59.

[42] "Wide Gaps Exist in Consumer Food Safety," *Congressional Quarterly* (November, 1969).

[43] E. B. Weiss, "Marketeers Fiddle While Consumers Burn," *Harvard Business Review*, Vol. 46 (July-August, 1968), pp. 45-53.

[44] See Stanley E. Cohen, "Consumer Interests Drift in Vacuum as Business Pursues Marginal Float," *Advertising Age*, Vol. 40 (March 24, 1969), p. 112.

[45] "Business Responds to Consumerism," *Business Week* (September 6, 1969), p. 98, and Robert Moran, "Consumerism and Marketing," *Marketing Science Institute Preliminary Statement* (May, 1969).

[46] Dorothy Cohen, "The Federal Trade Commission and the Regulation of Advertising in the Consumer Interest," *Journal of Marketing*, Vol. 33 (January, 1969), pp. 40-44.

efforts, experimentally examined the relationship between deceptive packaging (with respect to content weight) and brand preference.[47] It demonstrated that experimentation can provide useful information to policy makers.

These research approaches and the forces behind them should not only generate influential information, but should also help stimulate some basic changes in orientation. We can expect to see, for example, the simplistic "economic man" model of consumer behavior enriched.[48] The last decade has seen great progress made in the study of consumer behavior. This progress should contribute directly to a deeper analysis of consumerism issues. Hopefully, the dissemination of relevant knowledge will help eliminate present semantic problems.[49] Such a development must accompany rational discourse.

Business managers, whether progressive or defensive, can be expected to develop new, flexible approaches toward insuring that the rights of the consumer will be protected. Even though the motives may be mixed, there is no reason why effective programs cannot be developed.

[47] James C. Naylor, "Deceptive Packaging: Are Deceivers Being Deceived?" *Journal of Applied Psychology*, Vol. 6 (December, 1962), pp. 393-398.

[48] David M. Gardner, "The Package, Legislation, and the Shopper," *Business Horizons*, Vol. 2 (October, 1968), pp. 53-58.

[49] Same reference as footnote 6.

Will "truth-in packaging" lead to "truth-in-advertising"? Will "full disclosure" blossom without legislative nourishment? Are demands for consumer protection a political sham? The author discusses the trend of present consumer-protection efforts and takes a controversial positon.

Consumer Protection via Increased Information

Louis L. Stern

What about consumer protection?

The great concern of businessmen about recent demands for consumer protection is indicated by the establishment of: (1) a consumer-information service by the National Association of Manufacturers, known as Techniques in Product Selection (TIPS); and (2) a program of cooperation between the Association of Better Business Bureaus and federal departments and agencies that affect consumer-business relationships.

Although the NAM and ABBB programs may be public-relations efforts to mollify demands for consumer protection, nevertheless their creation reflects businessmen's concern that, "Unless business moves to organize some communication apparatus, it will soon be confronted with a benevolent, bureaucratic structure that will take over such functions."[1]

Nor is such concern unfounded. Consider recent proposals to establish an Office or Department of Consumers, and for the federal government to engage in "Consumer Union" types of product-evaluation and reporting. Is it madness to speculate that the precedents set by the Drug Amendments of 1962 (1962) and

Reprinted by permission of the author and the publisher from the *Journal of Marketing*, published by the American Marketing Association, Vol. 31, No. 2 (April, 1967), pp. 48-52.

[1] "GF's Cleaves Calls for Food Industry Consumer Information Unit," *Advertising Age,* Vol. 36 (April 19, 1965), p. 16.

the "fair labeling and packaging" bill might lead to proposals for a "fair advertising" law?

Probably no other Congress ever faced as many consumer-protection proposals as the 89th. Even the U.S. Supreme Court showed an interest in consumer protection, as evidenced by its handling of the Rapid Shave case.[2]

Other signs of increasing government interest in consumer protection include:

1. Completion by Congress, the Food and Drug Administration, the National Commission on Food Marketing, and the Consumer Advisory Council of voluminous reports relating to consumer protection.
2. Establishment of a special division within the U.S. Department of Agriculture to handle the Department's labeling programs.
3. Establishment by the Office of Economic Opportunity of an experimental program of consumer education.
4. Within the Federal Trade Commission, setting up of a new office of federal-state cooperation; new studies of consumer-goods marketing practices; and new trade-regulation guides and rules pertaining to the marketing of consumer goods.

But perhaps the best indication of the great amount of government interest in consumer protection is the statement of Charles Sweeny, Chief of the FTC's Bureau of Deceptive Practices: "The present Commission is more deeply determined to combat consumer deception than any Commission I have known in my 30 years of service."[3]

Why is there so much interest in consumer protection?

One reason is that rising incomes and cornucopia of new products has multiplied the number, value, and variety of consumers' market transactions. Therefore, there are far more opportunities for consumer deception than ever before. Furthermore, the mounting variety of consumer products is increasing the competitiveness of our economic system. In turn, this may be leading to a deterioration of business ethics, thus giving rise to added interest in consumer protection.

Yet it is not at all clear that deception in the marketplace has, in fact, increased. What is clear is that the history of the United States is a record of accumulated social and technological efforts to protect the individual from adversity of every sort. The drive for consumer protection may be viewed as simply a continuation of those efforts.

The Need for Product Information

Do consumers have a right to be informed, as distinct from a right not be deceived?

Our economic system is based on the belief that free and intelligent decisions in the marketplace, rather than by government fiat, will produce the most

---

[2] Colgate Palmolive Co. v. FTC, 85 S. Ct. 1035.

[3] "Druggist May Be Liable for Brand Copy in His Ads," *Advertising Age* Vol. 36 (June 7, 1965), pp. 1 and 135, at p. 1.

efficient allocation of resources toward the achievement of private and social goals. To exercise free and intelligent choices in the marketplace, consumers must have access to terms of sale and product information.

However, it is likely that the loss of personal relationships in the marketplace has reduced both the availability and the reliability of product information.

A second factor contributing to the problem is the rising level of technology. New materials, new operating principles, new functions, new designs, and new packaging have increased the difficulty of choosing one product or brand over another. The growing number of synthetic textiles and textile mixtures with varying prices and performance characteristics amply illustrates this situation.

Because of their usually greater complexity, durable products may reflect more advances in technology than nondurable products. Hence, the problem of adequacy and comprehension of product-performance information may be compounded in the case of durable goods. Furthermore, consumers are less capable of personally evaluating durable products because the long life and varied conditions under which these products are used cloud post-purchase brand comparisons. To make matters even more difficult, the reports of such organizations as *Consumers Union* are quickly rendered obsolete by model changes or model number changes.

A third factor contributing to the problem of adequacy of product information is the language of advertising. From Martineau to Weir, many advertisers and copy writers have preached the sermon of *image.*

In the words of Pierre Martineau, "It is generally insufficient to convince a person on intellectual grounds. His feelings must be involved. And this we achieve by affective or esthetic suggestion and imagery, by the meanings behind the words and pictures."[4]

Consider also the "heretical" words of William D. Tyler, *Advertising Age* columnist: "Most advertising down the years has done little more than say sweet nothings about a product ... It has contained the least information, the fewest facts, of almost anything ever written. We have relied mainly on adjectives, on charm, on manner of presentation, coupled with unspecific, unsupported claims of superiority."[5]

The question is how greater disclosure of product and terms-of-sale information can be achieved. The difficulties of attempting to provide greater information to consumers are substantial. The problem of communicating technical information to a non-technical audience, the time and space limitations of the vehicle of communication, and the cost of the time and space used must all be taken into account.

On the other hand, there is the question of *methods.* Will the methods of information be voluntary or compulsory? Will they involve standards, labeling requirements, consumer-advisory services, consumer-education programs, or some combination of these?

[4] Pierre Martineau, *Motivation in Advertising* (New York: McGraw-Hill Book Co., 1957), p. 187.

[5] William D. Tyler, "Is Competitive Comparison Really Bad in Advertising? Reform With Care," *Advertising Age,* Vol. 37 (March 14, 1966), pp. 61-61, at p. 61.

Voluntary Disclosure

Private industry has made great strides in attempting to provide information to consumers and to forestall government activity. Consider the following:
1. Formation over the years of codes of ethics by various associations in the packaging field.
2. Adoption by the 50th National Conference on Weights and Measures (June, 1965) of a standard for conspicuous labeling, as an amendment to the Model State Regulation Pertaining to Packages. (The new standard defines officially and nationally for the first time what constitutes a "clear and conspicuous" statement of net contents on package labels.)
3. Adoption by the American Standards Association, the National Bureau of Standards, and many other groups of standards for the size, shape, or performance ratings (such as BTU output) of innumerable products and containers.

Government Intervention

Of course, government regulations are sometimes unduly rigid, and create legal hazards for even the conscientious corporate citizen. (For example, the present standard of identity for butter was formulated at the turn of the century and does not permit the addition of emulsifiers or preservatives to butter, an unconscionable shackle to the butter industry's competition with margarine. Neither does it provide for the addition of vitamins to butter or the continuous-process method of manufacturing butter, both of which are common today.) Nevertheless, even more regulations probably are in prospect.

Terms of Sale

Aside from regulations pertaining to safety or gross misrepresentation, the greatest need for consumer protection is in regard to clarity of terms of sale. The least restrictive measure would require merely a statement of net contents on the package. However, mere knowledge of the weight or quantity of a product is an inadequate basis for intelligent choice; and if the statement of net contents is inconspicuous or the shopper unobservant, not even that much information will be known.

A further level of protection would be to provide for standardization of weights and quantites in which a consumer product may be distributed for retail sale. State laws already provide for standard package sizes for a few staple food products such as bread, butter, margarine, milk, cream, and flour.

Standardization of weights and quantites would provide informational gains to consumers. It would enable many shoppers to compare the price of equivalent amounts of alternative brands. In contrast, indications of price per ounce carried out to several decimal places would be no real improvement, and actually might distract consumers from making price comparisons of total amounts.

Standardization of weights and quantities would also call attention to price increases, which are otherwise hidden from some consumers in the form of a reduction in quantity.

It would be desirable, therefore, to establish standard weights or quantities in which selected consumer goods might be distributed. Provision for variations from these standards in multiples of 25% of the standard amounts would probably satisfy most consumer preferences for size of unit of purchase.

Establishment of standard weights and quantities might reduce the number of opportunities for using one size and style of container for packaging a variety of products as soup, cracker, and cereal companies now do. Considerable expense would also be involved in adjusting packaging machinery to the new weight or quantity standards. Nevertheless, the long-run advantages to consumers probably would exceed these disadvantages.

A still higher level of restriction, to regulate container sizes and shapes, is not only unnecessary but contrary to consumers' interests. It would severely inhibit package innovation. However, the International Organization for Standardization, whose standards may acquire the effect of law in over 50 member nations, has launched a program to develop retail package size standards that would affect *all* consumer products. Its program could, within a few years, force U.S. manufacturers to adopt similar standards for export purposes.

Standards and Grade-labeling

Compulsory standards of minimum quality or performance can be a useful form of consumer protection where health or safety is involved. Minimum standards can also serve to prevent consumers from being sold grossly inferior products.

Product standards usually impose minimum product requirements. On the other hand, grade-labeling involves an attempt to communicate in one or more symbols the relative quality of a product as influenced by a variety of characteristics.

Because grade-labeling requires a high degree of agreement as to what constitutes the best combination of product characteristics, its utility is limited to simple products having few attributes. Yet these products tend to be those which consumers are most capable of evaluating themselves. And even for these products, the whirlwind pace of product and package innovation occurring today would present an enormous grade-labeling task.

Furthermore, the effects of grade-labeling upon product research and innovation must also be considered. Grade-labeling would reduce product differentiation and thereby tend to promote price competition. As a result, smaller marketing margins would yield less research-and-development revenues.

Consumer Advisory Services

As proposed by Donald Turner, Chief of the U.S. Justice Department's Antitrust Division, another means of communicating more information to consumers would be for the federal government to evaluate products and publish its evaluations, or to subsidize organizations such as *Consumers Union.*[6] Such

[6] "Anti-Trust Chief Urges Alternative to Advertising," *Advertising Age*, Vol. 37 (June 6, 1966), pp. 1 and 147-148, at p. 147.

publications as *Consumers Bulletin* or *Consumer Reports* provide a source of clear and continuing product information; and their evaluations can be both capsulized and detailed.

On the other hand, their value is limited by their remoteness from the point of purchase. A more serious disadvantage, were they to achieve widespread consumer influence, would be the power they would come to possess over the economic fate of individual companies. If the majority of consumers followed their brand recommendations, producers of lower-rated brands would be strongly induced to imitate the preferred brand as closely as possible.

Accordingly, product differentiation might be expected to decrease, and this would be to consumers' disadvantage. Simultaneously, a loss of product differentiation might lead to a reduction in the number of producers, another undesirable effect.

Full Disclosure

"Full Disclosure" has a variety of implications. Most commonly, it is assumed to imply disclosure of the dangerous nature of a product. Such laws as the Flammable Fabrics Act (1953), the Hazardous Substances Labeling Act (1960), the Drug Amendments of 1962 (1962), and the Cigarette Labeling Act (1965) already impose this level of meaning.

A second level of meaning would compel disclosure of component ingredients, net contents, and other terms-of-sale information, such as interest and related charges. Laws such as the Food, Drug and Cosmetics Act (1938), the Wool Products Labeling Act (1939), the Fur Products Labeling Act (1951), the Textile Fiber Products Identification Act (1958), and the Automobile Information Disclosure Act (1958) are intended to provide legislative mandate for this type of disclosure. Disclosure of component ingredients is primarily useful in relation to determining the healthfulness, safety, value, or performance of a product. Over and above this, compulsion of such disclosure might be interpreted as protection for and responsiveness to the existence of individual preferences for certain products.

The next higher level of disclosure is the revelation of a product's performance characteristics. To some extent this level of disclosure is implemented voluntarily by manufacturers of above-average quality products who employ rational selling appeals. Horsepower ratings, BTU ratings, and lumber ratings are familiar voluntary disclosures by manufacturers and distributors of performance characteristics. But unfortunately, many voluntary performance descriptions are meaningless or unreliable and sometimes refer to inputs rather than outputs.

Most manufacturers prefer to avoid direct performance statements in favor of evocative expressions or episodes. This is especially likely to be the case where no substantial differences in performance exist among rival brands, because for these products disclosure of meaningful performance information would tend to reduce the apparent differentiation among brands.

The Drug Amendments of 1962 (1962), although passed in the wake of the thalidomide scare and applying to a narrow and emotionally-charged area of consumption, provide a legislative precedent for regulatory agency concern with product performance *even where health and safety are not involved*. Witness the FDA's attempt to require vitamins to be labeled with the statement: ". . . Except for persons with special medical needs, there is no scientific basis for recommending routine use of dietary supplements." A likely outcome of regulations pertaining to *nonperformance* would be regulations pertaining to *degrees* of performance.

As to the question of consumers' abilities to understand performance information, this problem will diminish over time in response to rising levels of education, the enormous capacity of consumers to learn informally, the effectiveness of media in informing consumers, and, most importantly, the challenge to learn presented by the availability of such information.

A still higher level of disclosure pertains to potentially derogatory information unrelated to health, safety, terms of sale, or performance of a product—illustrated by the FTC requirement of disclosure, where applicable, of the foreign origin of a product or component part. Conceivably, the FTC requirement could be extended to include disclosure, where applicable, of ratings by such groups as *Consumers Union*, production by companies not subscribing to voluntary codes of advertising practice, or production by nonunionized labor, etc.

The U.S. Supreme Court decision pertaining to disclosure of use of television mockups falls within this category of compulsory disclosure.[7] The Court took the extreme position that not only misrepresentations, but also deceptive presentations of valid claims, even if necessary to compensate for the technical deficiencies of communications media, are illegal.

Note especially that the FTC may be capable of expanding its disclosure requirements without the aid of new legislation. FTC Commissioner Everette MacIntyre has been quite explicit on this matter.[8]

Furthermore, the position taken by the Commission is this: "The question . . . is not whether the Commission may declare substantive standards and principles, for it plainly may and must. The question is whether the Commission may . . . promulgate them only in the course of adjudication."[9]

In the Commission's opinion, it is also free to promulgate them in formal rule-making proceedings.

The issue is whether consumers have expectations of receiving some standard of product performance, say, average for the industry's product. If they do, then failure to disclose the fact that a particular brand is below the standard of expectation would appear to be deceptive. If, in addition, the performance factor in question is material to the consumer's purchase decision, its nondisclosure violates the FTC Act.

[7] Same reference as footnote 2.

[8] *The Packaging-Labeling Controls Bill* (Washington, D.C.: Chamber of Commerce of the United States, 1965), p. 14.

[9] Same reference as footnote 8, at p. 18.

The principle that nondisclosure of material information constitutes a misrepresentation is well established in law.[10] Moreover, the U.S. Supreme Court made abundantly clear in the Rapid Shave case that reviewing courts should ordinarily accept the Commission's judgment as to what constitutes deception.[11] ". . . When the Commission finds deception it is also authorized, within the bounds of reason, to infer that the deception will constitute a material factor in a purchaser's decision to buy."[12] Accordingly, the opportunity for the FTC to widen its requirements for full disclosure is clear.

The selection of what additional disclosures should be required is admittedly a difficult administrative decision, particularly so the more complex the product involved.

Nevertheless, a reasonable compromise could be reached whereby certain information would have to be provided with the product, and whereby other, more extensive, information would have to be made readily available on request. Nothing in this proposal would prevent a manufacturer from extolling additional characteristics of his product. Nor does this proposal imply that compulsory disclosures should be included in advertising or in promotion.

In short, this proposal would improve the functioning of the marketplace by increasing the amount of information therein. It would enable consumers to choose products rationally *if* they wished to do so.

In Conclusion

The consumer-protection movement is definitely in the ascendancy. The issue is not whether consumers will be better protected, but what form the protection will take.

Better and more reliable product and terms-of-sale information on package labels is perhaps the most economical and least restrictive type of consumer protection. Moreover, *full disclosure* might help to dissuade current demands for additional restrictions on advertising.

[10] P. Lorilard Co. v. FTC, 186 F2d 52; Raladam Co. v. FTC, 283 U.S. 643. But see also Alberty v. FTC, 182 F2d 36, Certiorari denied, 340 U.S. 818.

[11] Same reference as footnote 2, at p. 1043.

[12] Same reference as footnote 2, at p. 1046.

NAME INDEX

Aaker, David, 422-434
Abbott, Lawrence, 347
Abelson, Robert P., 170
Ackoff, Russell L., 142, 143
Adler, Lee, 108, 204
Alderson, Wroe, 29, 164, 194, 250, 298, 333
Alexander, Ralph S., 191, 213-223, 254, 255, 333
Allen, Myron S., 188
Amory, Robert, 296
Arnold, John, 176, 188
Asch, Solomon E., 54

Bach, George Leland, 306
Backman, Jules, 192, 306-316
Bain, Joe S., 307
Baker, Stephen, 238
Barber, Bernard, 70
Barber, Richard J., 427
Barnett, H. G., 59
Barnett, Norman L., 126, 128
Barton, Samuel G., 171
Barzun, Jacques, 11, 25-26
Bass, Frank M., 164
Bauer, Raymond A., 62, 424, 427
Bayton, James A., 264
Beida, 82
Bell, Martin L., 108
Bell, William E., 60, 62
Bendix, Reinhard, 70
Bensman, Joseph, 67, 68
Bentham, Jeremy, 44
Bergel, Egon Ernest, 72
Bernstein, Alex, 170
Birmingham, Robert L., 424
Bishop, F. P., 293
Blank, David M., 313
Boas, 52
Boone, Louis E., 41, 58-65, 76-80
Bonno, John A., 76-80
Borden, Neil H., 293, 309
Bowen, Howard, 408
Boyd, Harper, 124, 126, 431
Breyer, Ralph, 237, 240, 242, 243
Brien, Richard H., 82, 105-113
Brody, Robert P., 125, 126
Brown, Arthur A., 142
Brown, C. G., 248
Brown, Milton, 251

Brown, R. D., 236, 240
Brown, Robert G., 279
Buchanan, James M., 343
Buck, N. S. 339,
Bucklin, Louis P., 192, 260-269
Buzzell, Robert D., 146, 164, 199

Cahn, Edmond, 410-411
Caldwell, John J., 133
Caplovitz, David, 67, 68, 70, 76, 429
Carman, James, M., 124
Carmone, Frank J., 127, 129
Carper, Jean, 423
Carson, Rachel, 423
Caves, Richard, 307
Chamberlin, 114, 334, 335
Chase, Stuart, 308
Clark, Carrie P., 425
Clark, Donald F., 142, 143
Clark, Fred E., 425
Claycamp, Henry J., 431
Cohen, Dorothy, 433
Cohen, Joel, 123
Cohen, Stanley, H., 426, 428, 431, 432, 433
Coleman, J., 59
Coleman, Richard P., 67, 68
Converse, Paul D., 332, 335, 339
Copeland, Melvin T., 56, 192, 260, 261, 262
Copernicus, Nicolaus, 3, 4, 50
Corlun, Arnold, 250, 256, 257
Cox, Donald F., 109, 134, 135
Cox, Eli P., 251
Cox, Reavis, 192, 194, 231-241, 242, 333
Craig, David, 251
Crawford, Robert P., 188
Cross, James S., 255
Crutchfield, R. S., 295
Cunningham, Ross M., 255
Cunningham, Scott M., 255

Darling, John R., 391
Darwin, Charles, 50
Davis, Kenneth, 251
Dawson, Leslie M., 2, 28-40
Day, George S., 422-434
Dean, Joel, 335
De Florio, 329
Dewey, John, 176, 409
Dichter, Ernest, 51, 367-377

SUBJECT INDEX